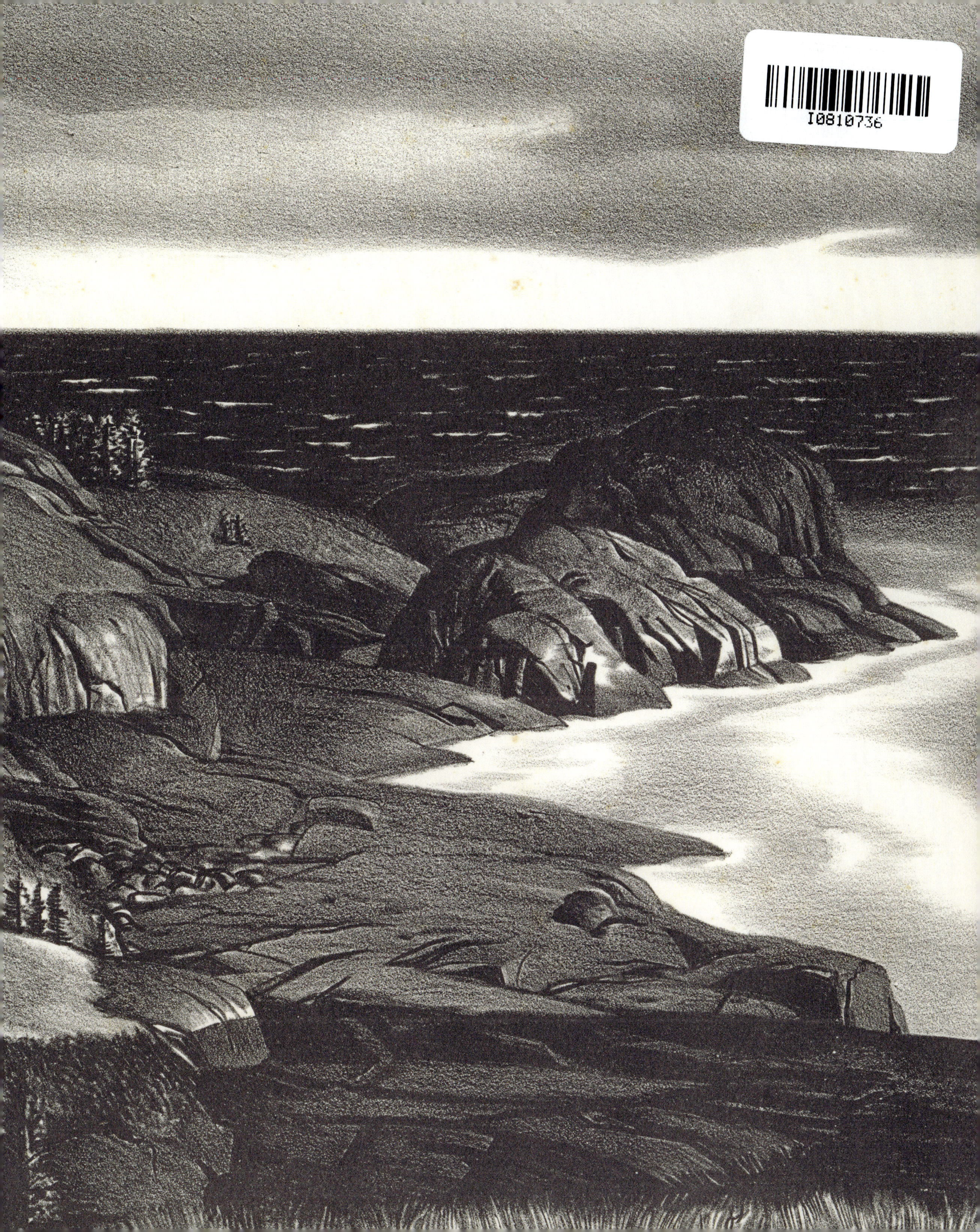

Art, Ecology, and the Resilience of a Maine Island

The Monhegan Wildlands

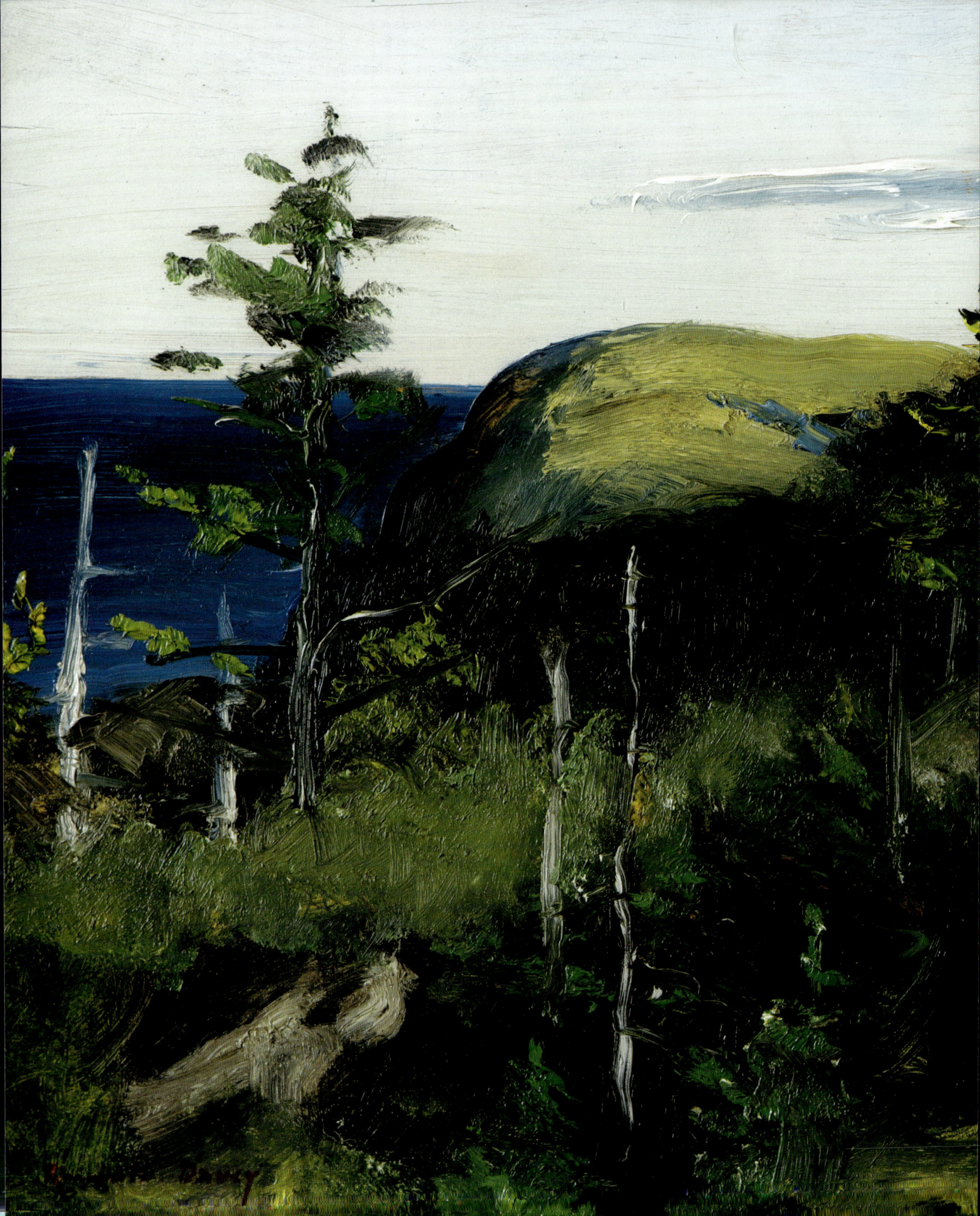

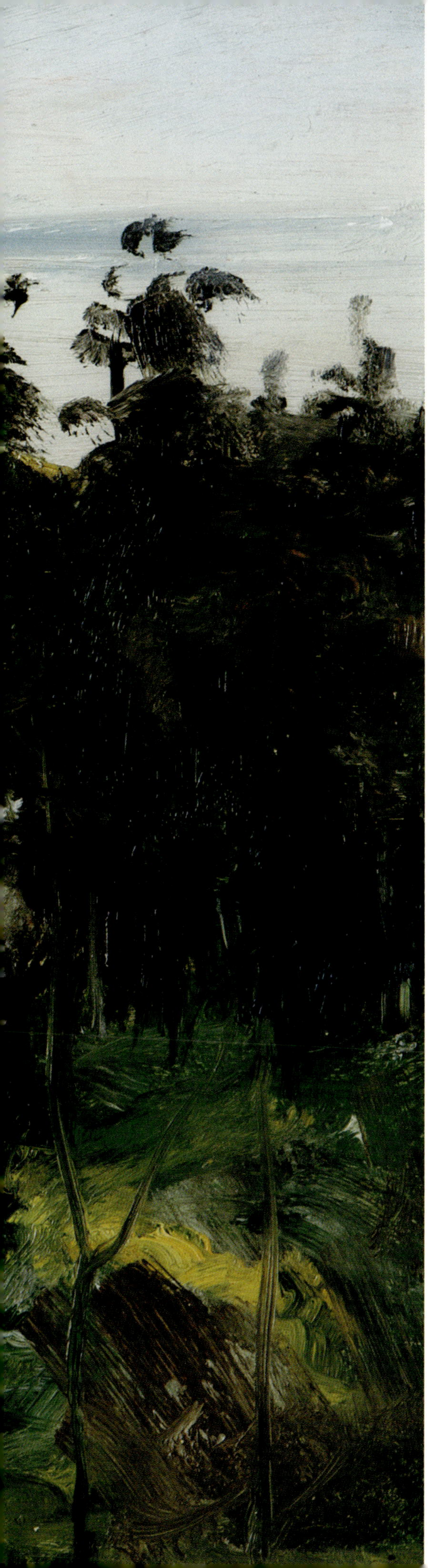

Art, Ecology, and the Resilience of a Maine Island

The Monhegan Wildlands

Barry A. Logan
Samuel S. Butcher Professor in the Natural Sciences, Bowdoin College

Jennifer Pye
Director, Monhegan Museum of Art & History

Frank H. Goodyear III
Co-Director, Bowdoin College Museum of Art

Rizzoli Electa

Contents

Foreword

David Foster, Director Emeritus, Harvard Forest, Harvard University

To preserve for posterity the natural wild beauty, biotic communities, and desirable natural, artificial, and historic features of the so-called "wild-lands" portions of Monhegan Island, Maine, and its environs.
—Certificate of Organization of Monhegan Associates, Inc., State of Maine, 1954[1]

Wildlands are tracts of any size and current condition, permanently protected from development, in which management is explicitly intended to allow natural processes to prevail with "free will" and minimal human interference.
—David Foster et al., *Wildlands in New England: Past, Present, and Future*, 2023[2]

Wilderness recognizes our way of relating to the land and the earth. The wilderness idea that humans are part of a larger "community of life" (and should act like it) has been known to my people for millennia. . . . We understand if we take care of the land, the land will take care of us. We are interconnected to the land, water, and animals.
—Bernadette Demientieff, "A Gwich'in Perspective," 2021[3]

Cathedral Woods Trail. Photograph courtesy of Monhegan Associates, Inc.

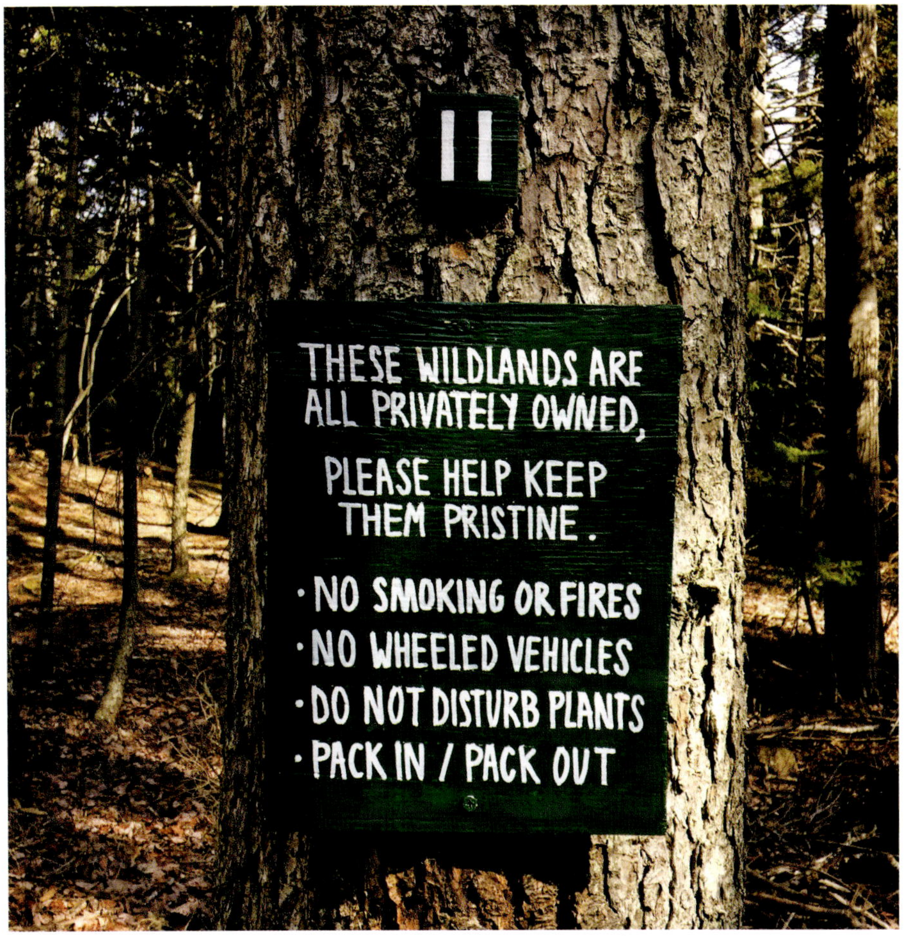

In 2005, I gathered colleagues at the Harvard Forest to discuss whether our science supported the establishment of new wilderness areas and reserves in New England, areas we called "Wildlands" that are designated for natural processes to operate freely without any active management. The question arose because the region has a lengthy Indigenous and colonial history, the former living with the land and the latter advancing exploitative deforestation for agriculture and intensive logging of remaining forests. Given this long cultural history, did it make sense to allow nature to recover and rewild?

One strong argument for wild areas was the region's recent ecological history. Since the mid-nineteenth century, when deforestation peaked and Henry David Thoreau lamented that the snapping turtle is "the heaviest animal found wild in this township," many farmers had abandoned their fields for lands out west or jobs in local factories.[4] Miraculously, trees that had reclaimed the fallow ground and vibrant forest ecosystems began flourishing regionally outside of northern Maine, where intensive industrial forestry has continued. Today, New England is the most heavily forested region in the United States, and wildlife species absent from Thoreau's Concord are now thriving—bear, deer, moose, beaver, bobcat, coyote, turkey, and many others. This natural rewilding confirms the resilience of nature left alone. And this regional history garnered our support for Wildland conservation and lent promise that the region will again support long absent old-growth forests.

That decision and the clear value of the majestic natural and cultural landscape of New England led us to advance an ambitious conservation initiative—Wildlands, Woodlands, Farmlands, and Communities—that proposes to address the crises in climate change, biodiversity loss, and human well-being by conserving up to 80 percent of New England in an integrated mosaic of sustainably managed forests and farms, wild areas, and thoughtfully developed communities. We argued that at least 10 percent of the region should be Wildlands—small urban parks, suburban reserves, and expansive tracts of forest, lakes, and streams that receive minimal management and rival the three million wild acres in New York's Adirondack Park.

One problem immediately frustrated this proposal. No inventory existed of the public and private Wildlands of this or any region of the United States. Federal wilderness areas are readily identified and tallied, but there is no comprehensive record of the wild areas owned by state agencies or the region's three-hundred-plus private conservation organizations.

It took fifteen years to secure the funding to develop that inventory for New England and to examine the region's eighteen thousand conserved areas to identify the few that are forever wild. After three years of additional research, our study reached an ambivalent conclusion: 423 Wildlands representing a significant conservation achievement comprise a meager 3.3 percent of New England. Although far from the goal of 10 percent, the diversity of these wild areas is captivating, ranging from sizable tracts in Baxter State Park and the White and Green Mountains to large state parks, private reserves, and pockets of wild forest in every state. More than 125 organizations and municipal, state, and federal agencies contribute to this accomplishment. Initiated quietly with Thoreau's pronouncement "that in Wildness is the preservation of the world,"[5] Wildland conservation is now widely embraced and the fastest growing form of land protection in New England.

Quite inadvertently, it was this study that took me to Monhegan Island. In late summer 2020, as we drove up the coast to explore prospective Wildlands in northern Maine, my wife suggested a detour to the island, which we knew only for its reputation of roadless quiet, a small community, and a long history of art. Anxious to get on with the study that motivated our trip, I relented to a day visit on what emerged as a gorgeous morning. Arriving at the island, we departed the ferry, wound our way up past houses toward the forested eastern side of the island, entered an old dark wood, and spied a hand-painted sign: "These Wildlands are all privately owned. Please help keep them pristine. No smoking or fires. No wheeled vehicles. Do not disturb plants. Pack in / Pack out."

I was astonished. Quite serendipitously, the detour from our mission had brought us to the edge of a magnificent wild forest that was unknown to our study. Although our subsequent research led us to countless properties across New England, the images of that sign, the wonderfully wild woods, and Monhegan's rugged shoreline stuck with me. Each appeared, in text and photographs, in our final report. That visit also led me to undertake considerable study of the history of these Wildlands and the people who have safeguarded them. Though the insights that emerged from these investigations and conversations are unique to Monhegan, they are emblematic of the motivations behind Wildland conservation globally.

Monhegan's Wildlands are the product of nature, history, and the vision of a singular individual—Ted Edison, youngest child of inventor Thomas Edison, who began his acquisitions in 1929 and formed the Monhegan Associates, Inc. (MAI), which stewards them today. The group's persistence is testament to the power of individuals, neighbors, and communities to secure a nourishing environment for nature and people alike.

The island's history parallels that of the New England region, as well as many parts of the globe: an Indigenous homeland for millennia abruptly degraded by colonial settlement and resource extraction followed by a gradual reduction in extensive use. From this tumultuous history, an opportunity emerged to redefine human relationships with nature based on respect for the inherent values it possesses. Today, Monhegan's older woods support a mosaic of ancient trees scraggly with lichens and patches of blowdown timber. Younger woods on abandoned sheep pasture entertain a dynamic interplay of forest succession, competition among native and non-native species, and legacies of past land use.

If left unconstrained and allowed to grow, the future of Monhegan's Wildlands, like all Wildlands, will be increasingly wild and forever unpredictable. That is the beauty, mystery, and challenge of Wildland conservation. To leave nature alone unleashes strong natural forces, invites great uncertainty, and generates novel conditions impossible for humans to conceive of or achieve. But granting that freedom confronts the hubris of humans seeking to "help" nature in ways that accommodate their own sensibilities and needs. This challenge was articulated by one resolute guardian of Monhegan's Wildlands in the minutes of a Monhegan Associates meeting in which he argued for minimal management of invasive species. Lifetime resident Richard Farrell, a fourth-generation islander actively involved in MAI for over five decades, whose mother was among the organization's incorporators, noted that while the island may celebrate Ted Edison's vision in words and social events, "It was obvious we were not preserving primeval woodland. . . . And yet, this man, precise in his language, used the term 'wild-lands.' I believe it was a description of how he expected Monhegan Associates to exercise stewardship of the land. He, and the other founders of Monhegan Associates, expected us—as far as practicable— to let nature take its course and to re-establish a natural, wild area."[6]

Monhegan is a place that couples the isolation and beauty of a remote and rocky island, a long light-handed history of native and colonial settlement, and an unfolding legacy of artistic exploration with an unrivaled commitment to the preservation of community and land. It is these qualities and the deft work of the authors in forging a highly integrated volume from diverse voices that makes this such a valuable and enjoyable contribution. It conveys the many dimensions of the island by drawing from ecology, art, history, and personal reflection to share stories, scenes, and experiences from a captivating island community where more than 75 percent of the enveloping landscape is forever wild. It illuminates a unique place while offering insights into New England and the globe. Beyond Monhegan, the region and world are challenged to conserve a network of equally wild and free places. On island, this volume provides a solid grounding for the responsibility that Monhegan carries forward into its own future.

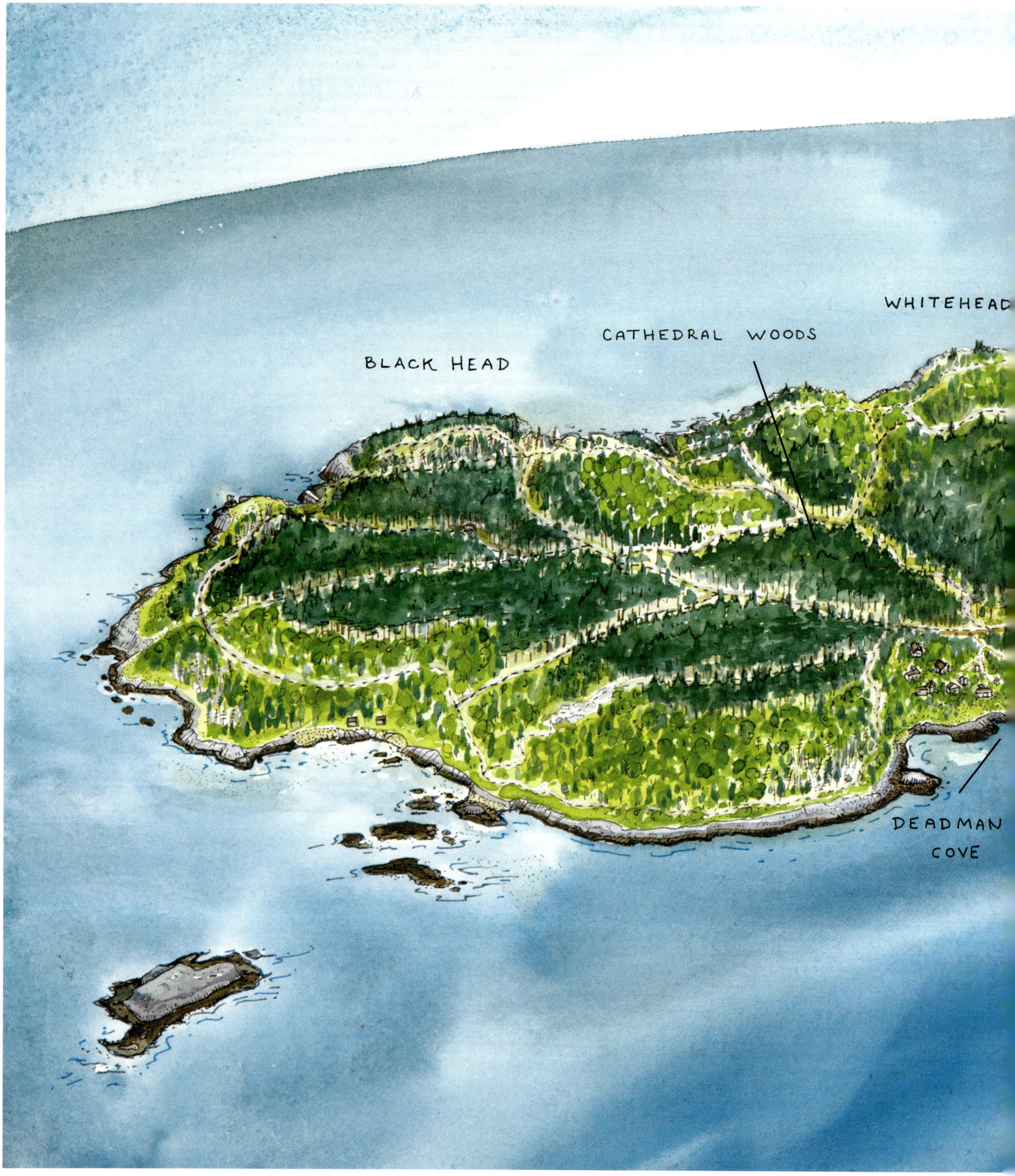

Molly Holmberg Brown (born 1978), *Ecological Bird's-Eye View of Monhegan*, 2023. Watercolor and ink on paper, 12 x 21 inches. Courtesy of the artist

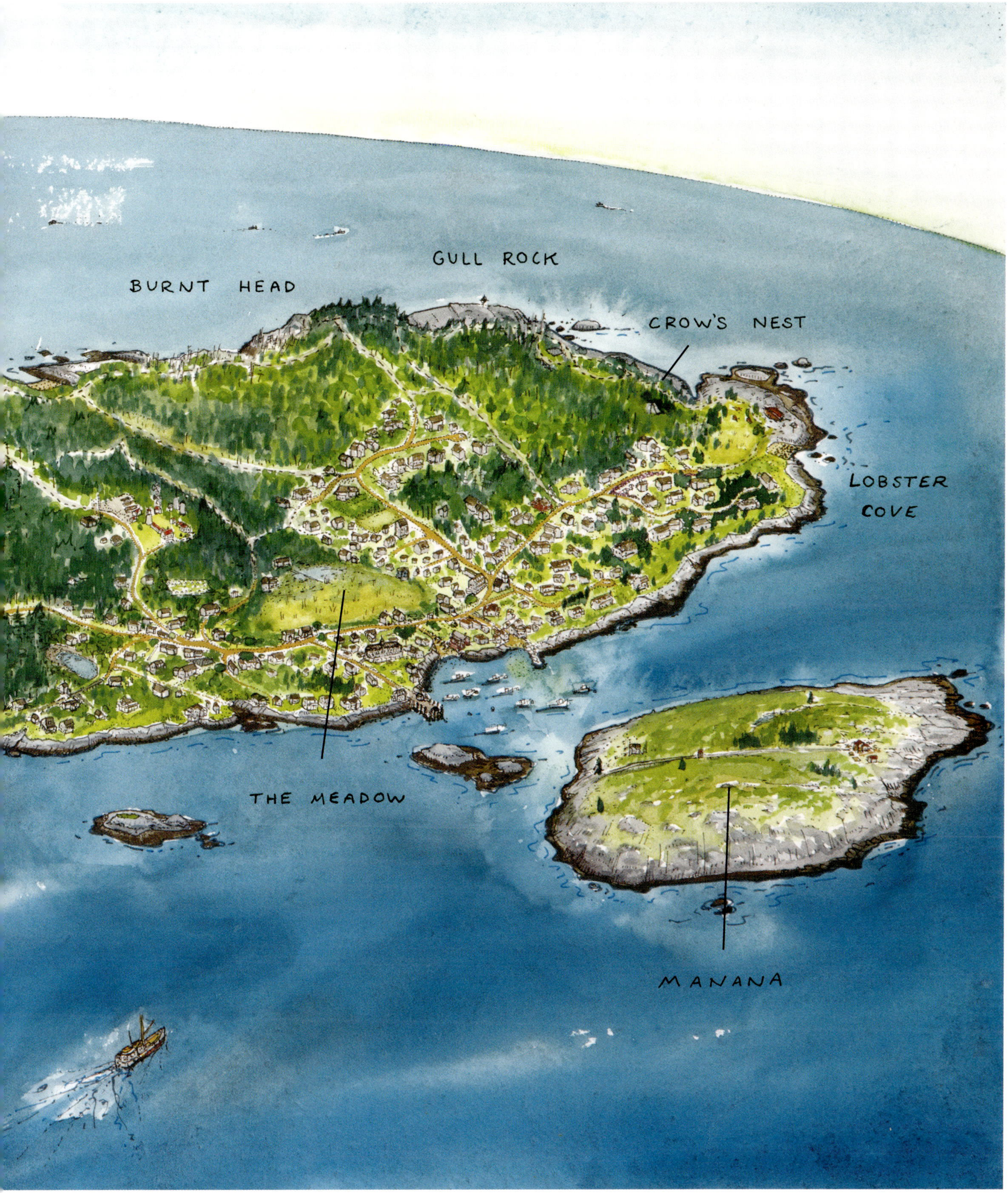
GULL ROCK
BURNT HEAD
CROW'S NEST
LOBSTER COVE
THE MEADOW
MANANA

Introduction

Monhegan Island sits ten nautical miles from the mainland, the outermost island of Muscongus Bay, along Midcoast Maine. The name "Monhegan" is an Indigenous place-name that derives from the Maliseet or Mi'kmaq term for "out-to-sea island." An alternate spelling first appeared on a European map in 1646. Just shy of a square mile in area (approximately 550 acres), its long axis is roughly two times its narrow axis. The neighboring small island of Manana shelters Monhegan Harbor, around which the village is located.

Five dozen people, give or take, claim Monhegan as their year-round home. That number swells severalfold with summer residents. Day-trippers and visitors staying in hotels and guesthouses bring bustle and a source of income. In summer, you can travel by ferry to Monhegan from three mainland ports several times daily. Outside of the summer season, two ferries weekly connect the island to Port Clyde—that is, unless weather leads to ferry cancellations. Monhegan has no paved roads. The island generates its own electricity with a diesel-driven generation plant. A bog known as the "Meadow," nestled in the village, serves as the sole municipal water source. Island schoolchildren gather through eighth grade to learn in a one-room schoolhouse, whereupon they head to the mainland to complete their education.

On clear days, you can see the mainland from Monhegan. Yet part of the island's appeal is its remove from the wider world. Even in summer, when visitors crowd the village's main road and are encountered on the walking trails that crisscross the island, you still get the feeling that you are situated on a large rock far out at sea. This sense of being apart underlies the romance of Monhegan and helps explain its attraction to those who have ventured to its shores. Since the permanent settlement was established in the 1780s, islanders have cultivated a spirit of independence and self-reliance.

Fishing first drew ancestors of the Wabanaki to Monhegan several thousand years ago. Situated amid historically bountiful fisheries in the Gulf of Maine, the island served this community as a fishing encampment from which they pursued swordfish and other catch. Monhegan remains an active fishing

Warner Taylor (1880–1958), *Blackhead Seascape,* 1930s. Gelatin silver print, 10⅞ x 14 inches. Monhegan Museum of Art & History. Gift of Lucia Taylor Miller

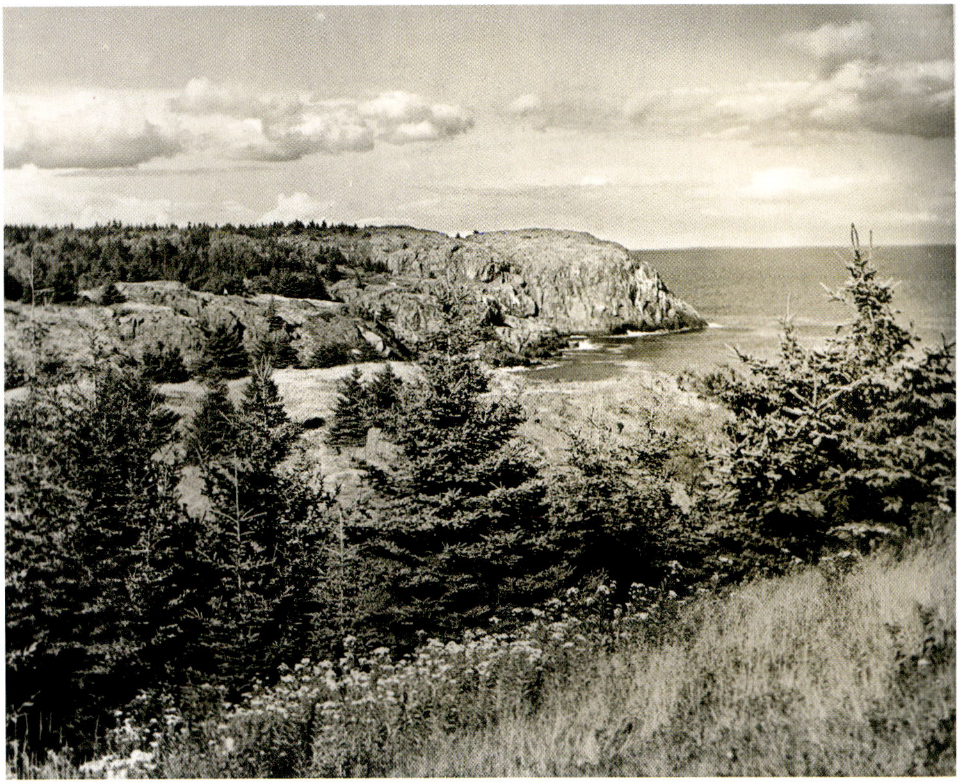

community, though today mainly for lobsters and, for those, only between the months of October and June. In summer, islanders work an assortment of other jobs, many in support of the tourist trade, with some pursuing remote work made possible by satellite connections to the mainland. Over the past two centuries an increasing number of vacationers—as well as artists, writers, and other creative types—have discovered the island, often returning year after year for inspiration and respite. On Monhegan, it is easy to feel that you are far away from the modern world. Artists have reinforced this perception, choosing to foreground the island's wild beauty and remoteness. Authors and historians have done the same.

While you might imagine the island to be a unique outlier, in many ways the history of Monhegan resembles that of other island communities in Maine. As traditional fishing grounds for Maine's Indigenous people, offshore islands also provided convenient outposts and centers of trade for seafaring European explorers and settlers in the early seventeenth century. Monhegan has played an important part in a dynamic trading network with towns throughout Midcoast Maine and well beyond. Led today by an elected three-person board of assessors and organized as Monhegan Plantation, a form of governance unique to Maine that resides between "unincorporated area" and "town," it has nonetheless held long political and cultural allegiances—and its share of rivalries—with those on the coast and throughout the region.

Monhegan's ecology shares features with forested landscapes encompassing much of northern New England and Maritime Canada. The island sits in an ecoregion known as the New England-Acadian-Wabanaki forest type or

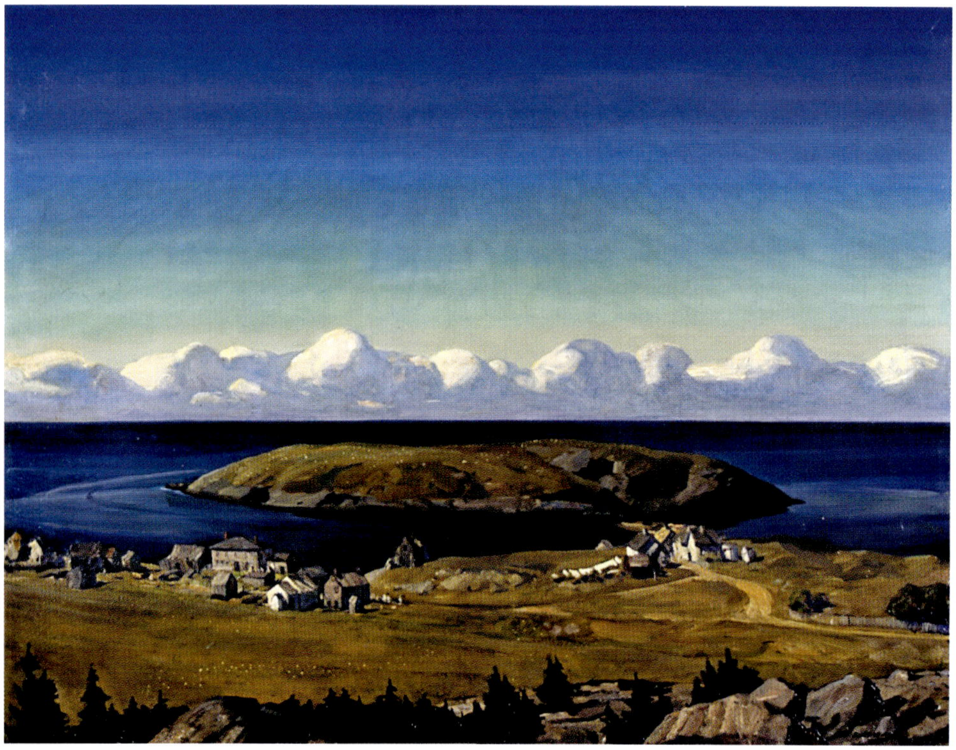

Rockwell Kent (1882–1971),
Island Village, Coast of Maine, 1909.
Oil on canvas, 42⅛ x 55¹⁵⁄₁₆ inches.
The State Hermitage Museum,
St. Petersburg, Russia

as some combination of those three monikers. Forests of this region vary but generally possess a character reflective of their boundary position between deciduous forests to their south and evergreen coniferous forests to their north, lending to their richness. Today, red spruce and balsam firs dominate Monhegan's interior old-growth Cathedral Woods, as they have for recorded history. This resemblance to spruce-fir forests farther north has led some to refer to coastal forests, including those on Monhegan, as boreal.

Monhegan stands out for its dedication to land conservation. Fully three-quarters of the island—almost all of the land outside of the village, an area known as the Wildlands—is reserved for nature and managed by the island's land trust, the Monhegan Associates, Inc. From its origins in the middle of the twentieth century, this organization has drawn its leadership from within the island community. Many islanders, year-round and seasonal residents alike, express their passion and appreciation for the Wildlands by volunteering with the Associates. These community members, drawn from an array of professions and personal histories, come together to grapple with the many complexities of responsibly stewarding this natural wonderland.

Those venturing into the Monhegan Wildlands commune with features of arresting beauty. Waves crash against the tallest cliffs along the Maine coast. The incessant calls of nesting gulls remind us that we, not they, are the visitors to this place. Seals fish in the coves and haul themselves up on the rocks to rest, watching hikers as intently as those hikers watch them. In contrast to the raucous shoreline, the stillness of Cathedral Woods conjures a solemnity that evokes this forest's name. Forest outside of Cathedral Woods is younger, having reclaimed pasture abandoned near the turn of the twentieth century. This so-called secondary forest diverges in character from the ancient forest of Cathedral Woods. Indeed, emerging from Cathedral Woods to enter the more youthful secondary forest feels like a passage, as though you have walked through a doorway.

Clues revealing its dynamic history mark the present-day appearance of the secondary forest. Evidence of intense use as sheep pasture in the nineteenth century can be found today in bedrock exposed by erosion and spreading mats of unpalatable juniper. Deer, first introduced in the mid-twentieth century, then removed four and a half decades later, long suppressed broad-leafed trees. Those birches, aspens, mountain ash, and maple are now released and claiming their place in the canopy. Age-old natural processes, such as interactions between native spruce trees and parasitic mistletoe, were knocked out of equilibrium by two centuries of human disturbance, with outsize effects upon Wildlands ecology.

For well over a century, artists and photographers have observed and depicted this changing landscape and the enduring Cathedral Woods. Scientists, too, have documented change, and stasis, on Monhegan, drawing upon the methodologies of forest and historical ecology to describe what came before and to elucidate mechanisms shaping the trajectories of forest succession. The extraordinary natural resilience displayed by the Monhegan Wildlands is only possible thanks to conservation-minded islanders, perhaps no one more so than Ted Edison. Rightly regarded as the architect of the Monhegan Associates, Edison dedicated decades to land acquisition and stewardship of the organization and the Wildlands it holds. The broad arc of events on Monhegan—the formation and abandonment of pastureland, forest recovery, and the critical importance of land conservation—are mirrored elsewhere along the Maine coast and in the greater New England region. The story of the Monhegan Wildlands, however, is uniquely well told by artists, ecologists, historians, and community members alike.

This catalogue opens with Rockwell Kent's arrival on Monhegan in 1905. A singular artistic talent, Kent was formed by his experiences on Monhegan and contributed greatly to the establishment of the island's ongoing artistic tradition. Kent was present for the closure of the era of vast island pasture. He participated in the expansion of the seasonal community and the greater orientation of the village toward tourism. Kent's arrival marked critical ecological, creative, and social points of inflection for Monhegan. Thus, although Kent was not the first artist to depict Monhegan, his arrival serves as a fitting beginning. Ensuing chapters reach back in time and then forward to the present and beyond, to relate a history of the Monhegan Wildlands through an ecological lens and through the paintings, photographs, maps, and other works representing this incomparable landscape.

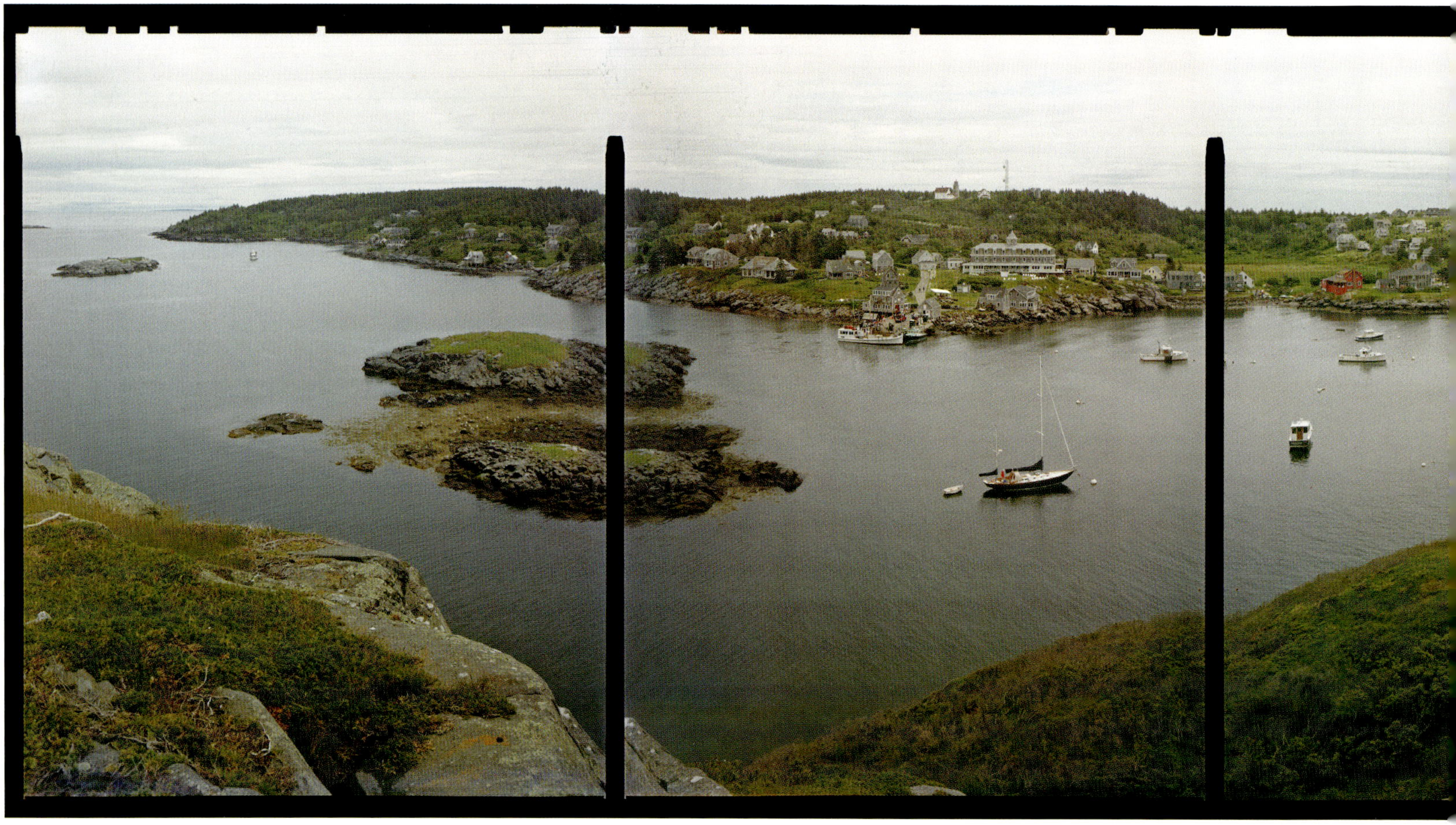

Accra Shepp (born 1962),
Monhegan from Manana,
2023. Archival pigment ink
print. Courtesy of the artist

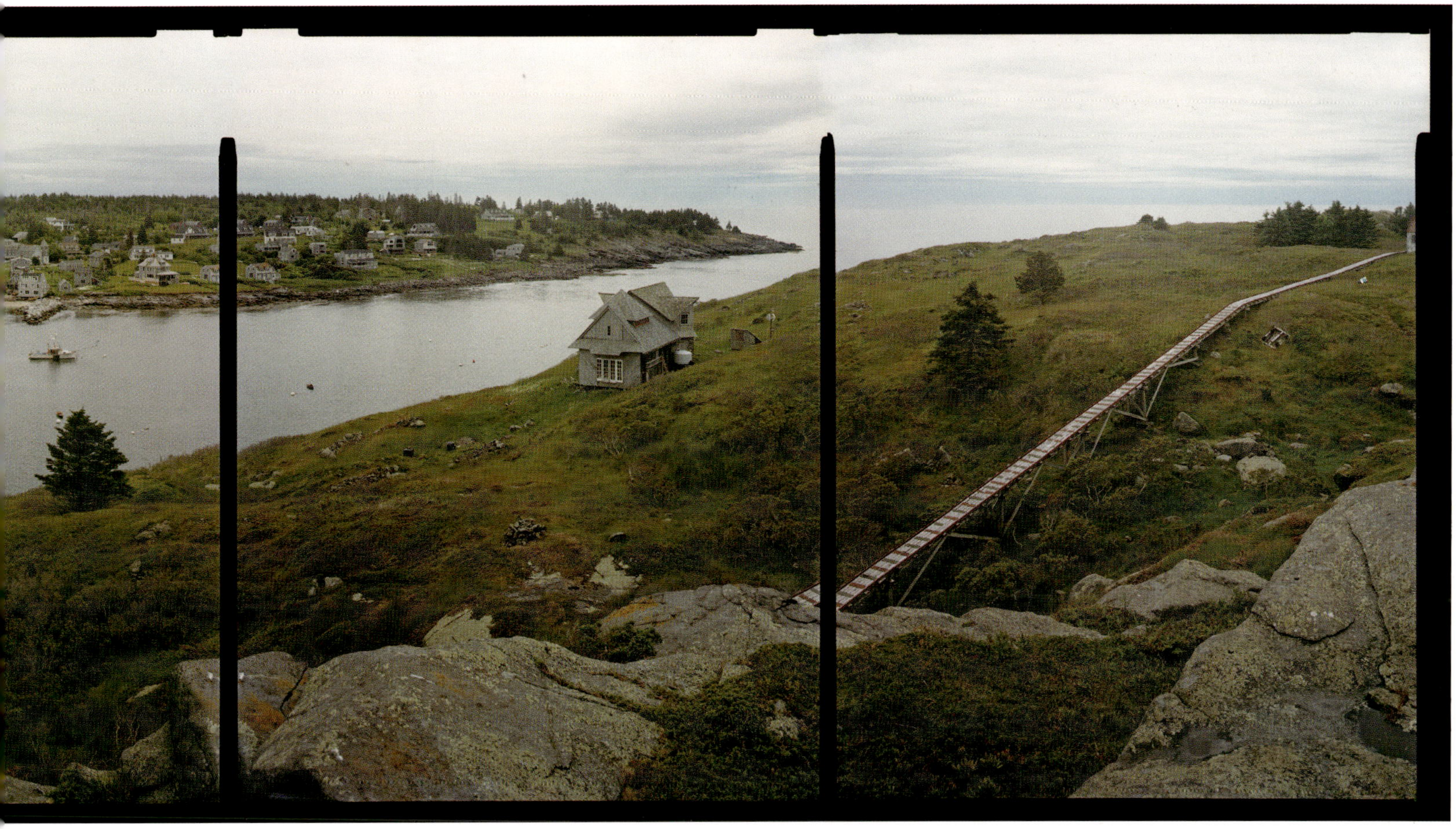

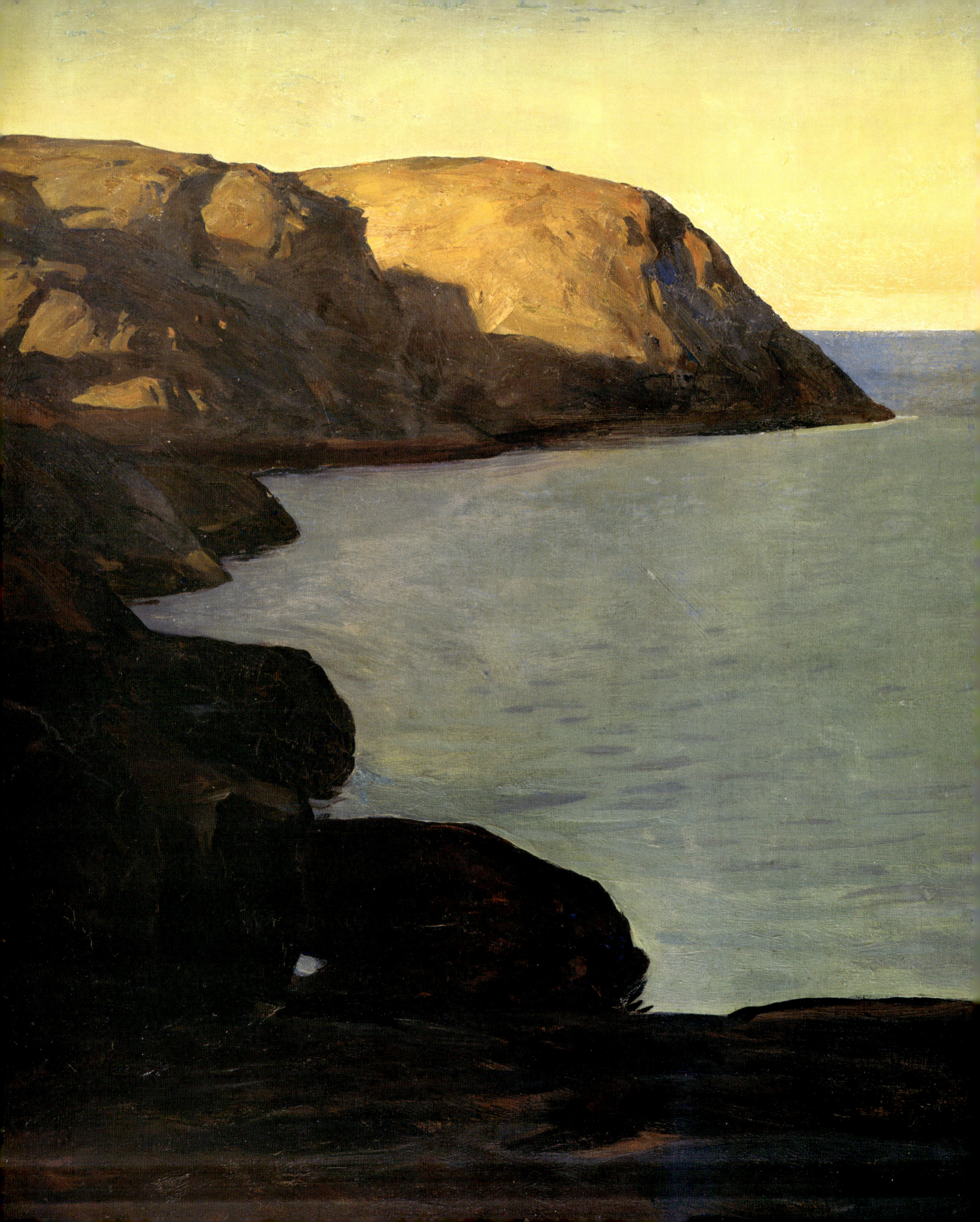

Chapter 1

Forest Recovery and Monhegan's Emergence as a Tourist Destination and Artist Colony, 1897 to 1928

On a June morning in 1905, artist Rockwell Kent boarded the *Effort* in Boothbay Harbor, bound for Monhegan Island. Upon his arrival, Kent, by his telling, and like so many before and after, hurriedly deposited his belongings at his guesthouse and charged out to explore. From the village at the southwestern end, he followed the eastern contour of the island northward, encountering Burnt Head, then Whitehead, a magisterial cliff rising more than 160 feet above the surf. Its twin, Black Head, greeted him next. He continued to wind counterclockwise around Monhegan, crossing Green Point, and ultimately reaching the upper shore of Deadman's Cove, across which the settlement resumed. What did Kent encounter? "Green grass and dandelions at [his] feet" atop Whitehead. On Green Point, "grassy slopes, . . . thickly starred with the blossoms of strawberries to be." In marked contrast, a "dark spruce forest" dominated the island interior, known then, as now, as Cathedral Woods.[1]

Born and raised in the suburbs of New York City and educated at Columbia University, Kent sought a place where he might be closer to nature and where he might live and paint uninterrupted by the frenetic pace of the crowded city. On Monhegan, he found both. However, Kent

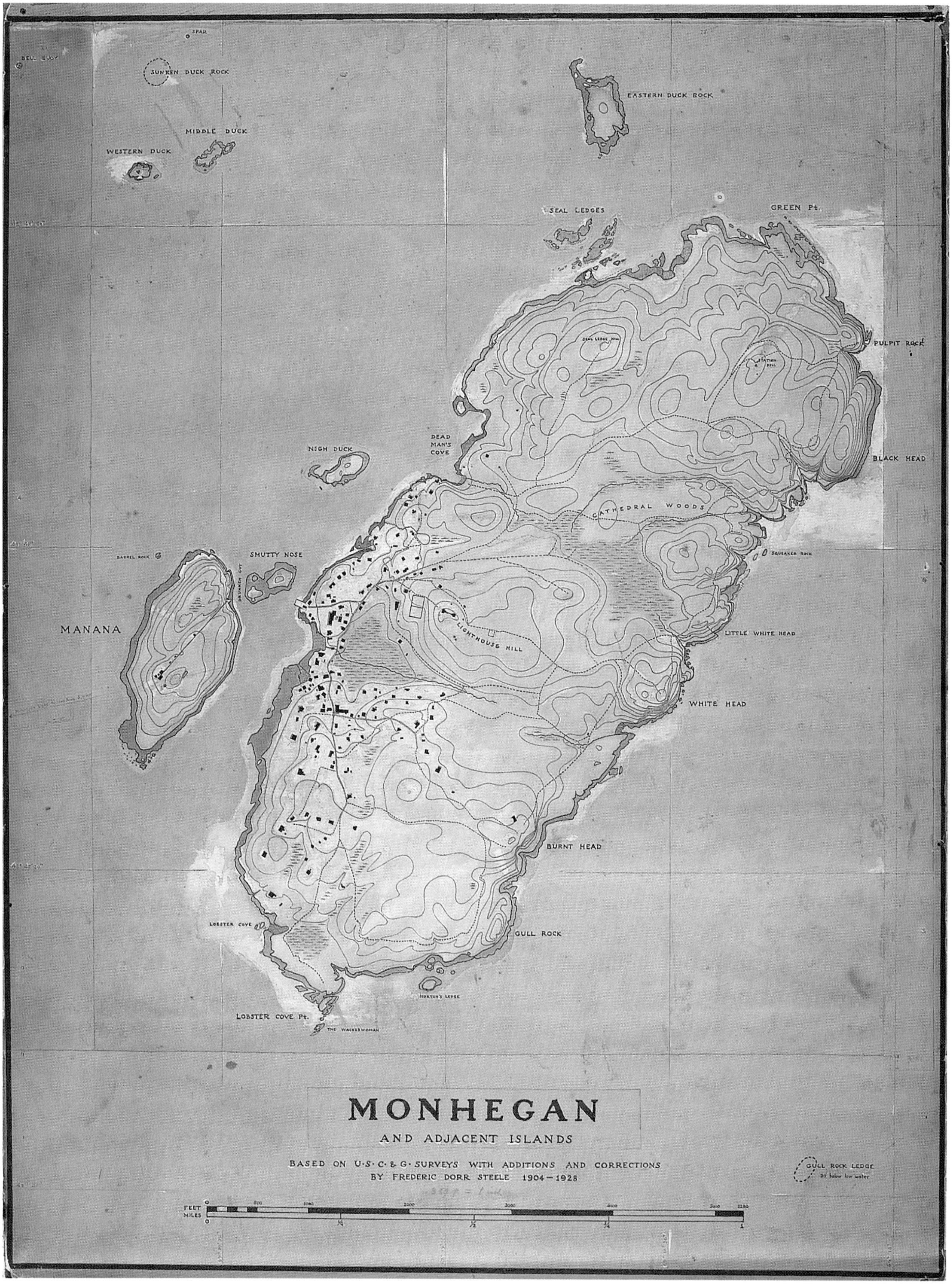
SPAR
BELL BUOY
SUNKEN DUCK ROCK
EASTERN DUCK ROCK
MIDDLE DUCK
WESTERN DUCK
SEAL LEDGES
GREEN Pt.
SEAL LEDGE HILL
PULPIT ROCK
DEAD MAN'S COVE
NIGH DUCK
BLACK HEAD
CATHEDRAL WOODS
BARREL ROCK
SMUTTY NOSE
SQUEAKER ROCK
MANANA
LIGHTHOUSE HILL
LITTLE WHITE HEAD
WHITE HEAD
BURNT HEAD
LOBSTER COVE
GULL ROCK
NORTON'S LEDGE
LOBSTER COVE Pt.
THE WASHERWOMAN
MONHEGAN
AND ADJACENT ISLANDS
BASED ON U·S·C·&·G· SURVEYS WITH ADDITIONS AND CORRECTIONS
BY FREDERIC DORR STEELE 1904–1928
GULL ROCK LEDGE
3' below low water
FEET
MILES

Right: Frederic Dorr Steele (1873–1944), *A Daring Insurgent Named Kent*, August 1910. Watercolor and ink on paper, 21 x 15⅜ inches. Collection of Edward L. Deci

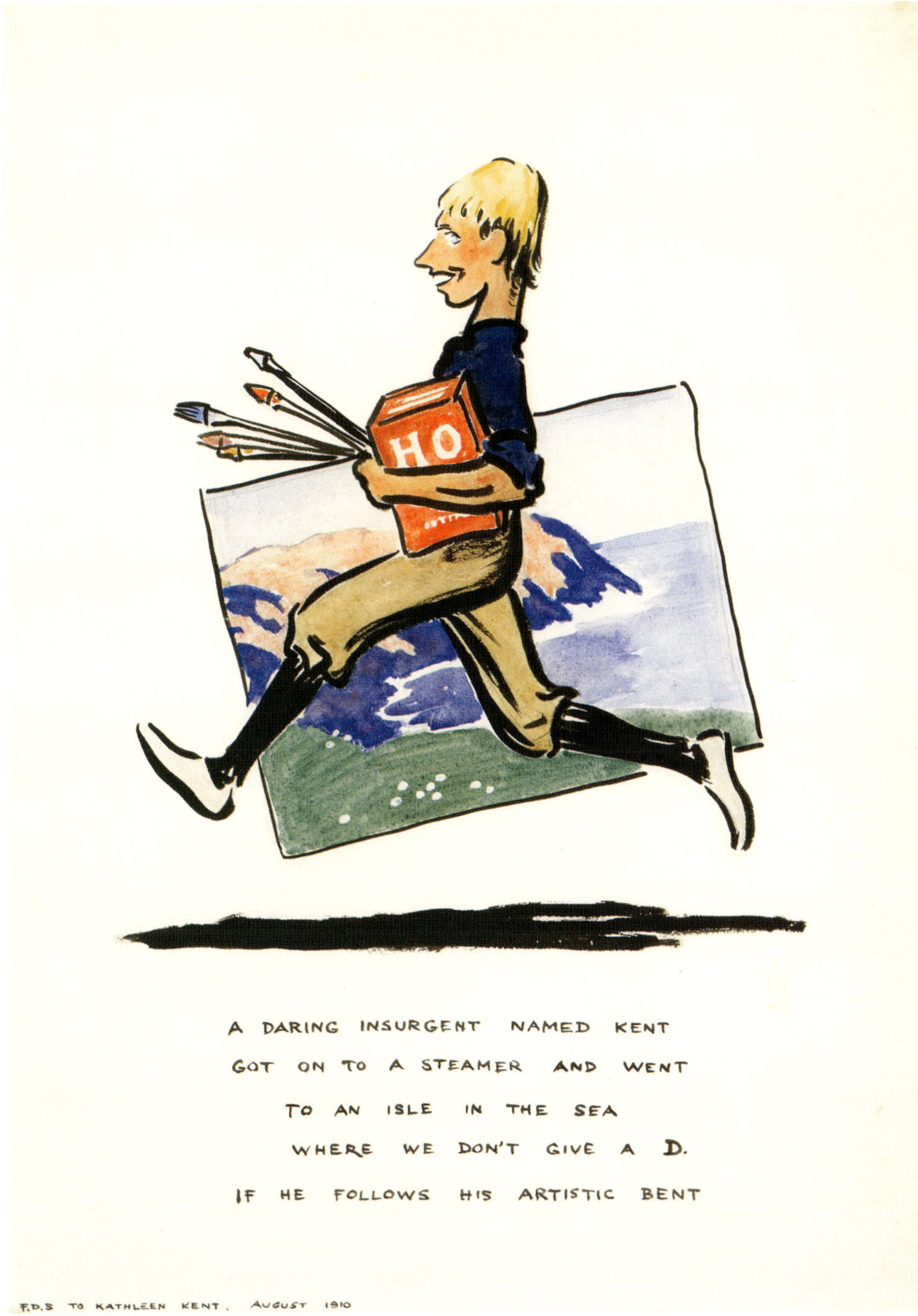

leaves unmentioned—perhaps he did not fully appreciate—that the island that so exalted him was, in fact, in the earliest stages of recovery from its greatest human disturbance. Over the previous century, broad swaths of the perimeter and headland forest had been removed to create pasture for livestock, chiefly sheep. The number of free-roaming sheep had dwindled to close to zero as the nineteenth century came to a close.[2] The grassy, open ground Kent strode across and reveled in on his first day was a legacy of livestock farming.

On Monhegan, as elsewhere in New England, abandoned pastureland returned to forest without assistance. The landscapes of the region exhibit remarkable resilience in this regard. Much of the Monhegan Wildlands has

Opposite: Frederic Dorr Steele (1873–1944), *Monhegan and Adjacent Islands,* 1928. Ink and gouache on paper, 32 x 24 inches. Monhegan Museum of Art & History. Gift of Anne Steele Marsh

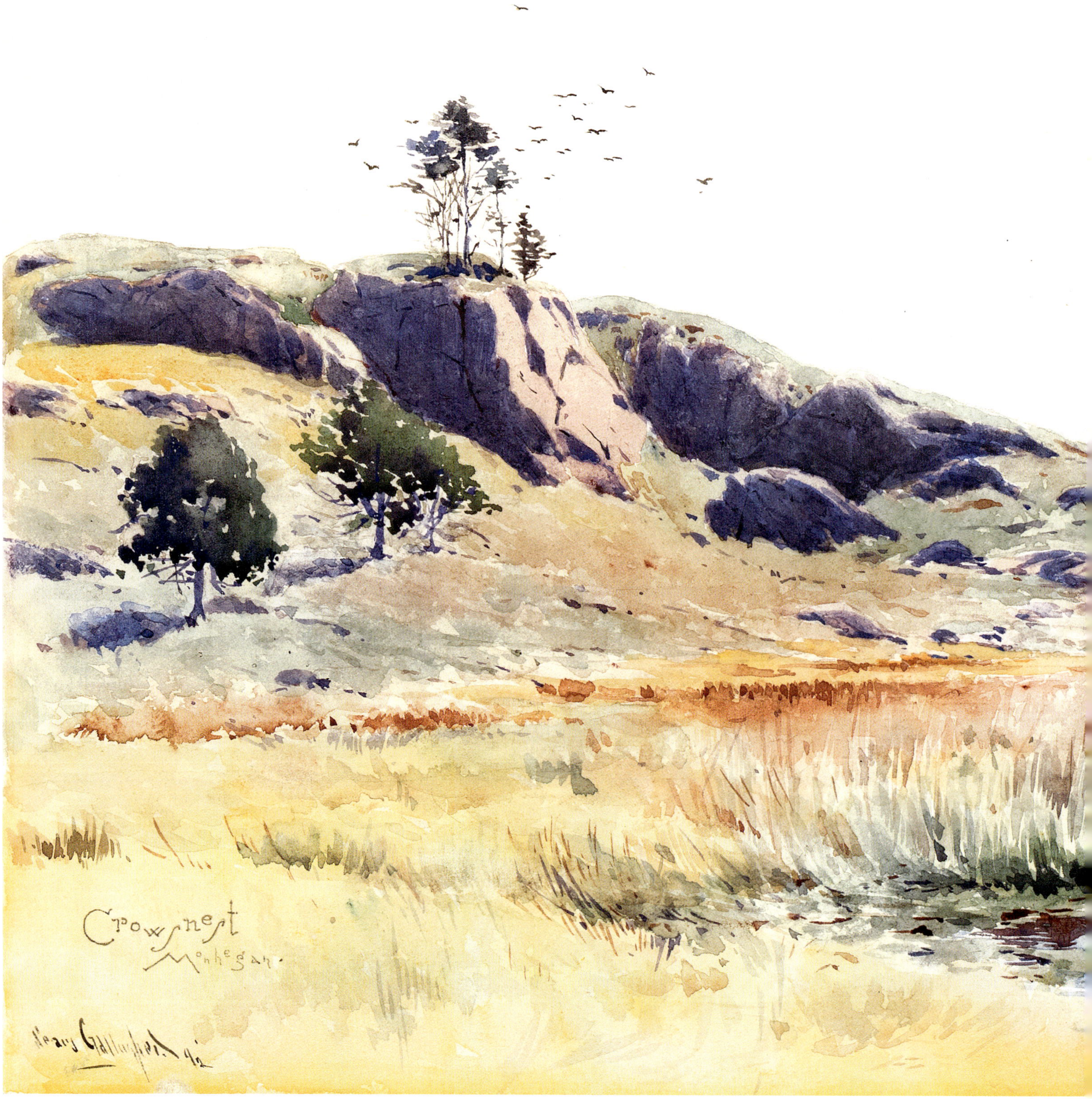

Sears Gallagher (1869–1955), *Crowsnest, Monhegan*, 1892. Watercolor on paper, 9½ x 13¼ inches. Monhegan Museum of Art & History. Gift of Remak Ramsay

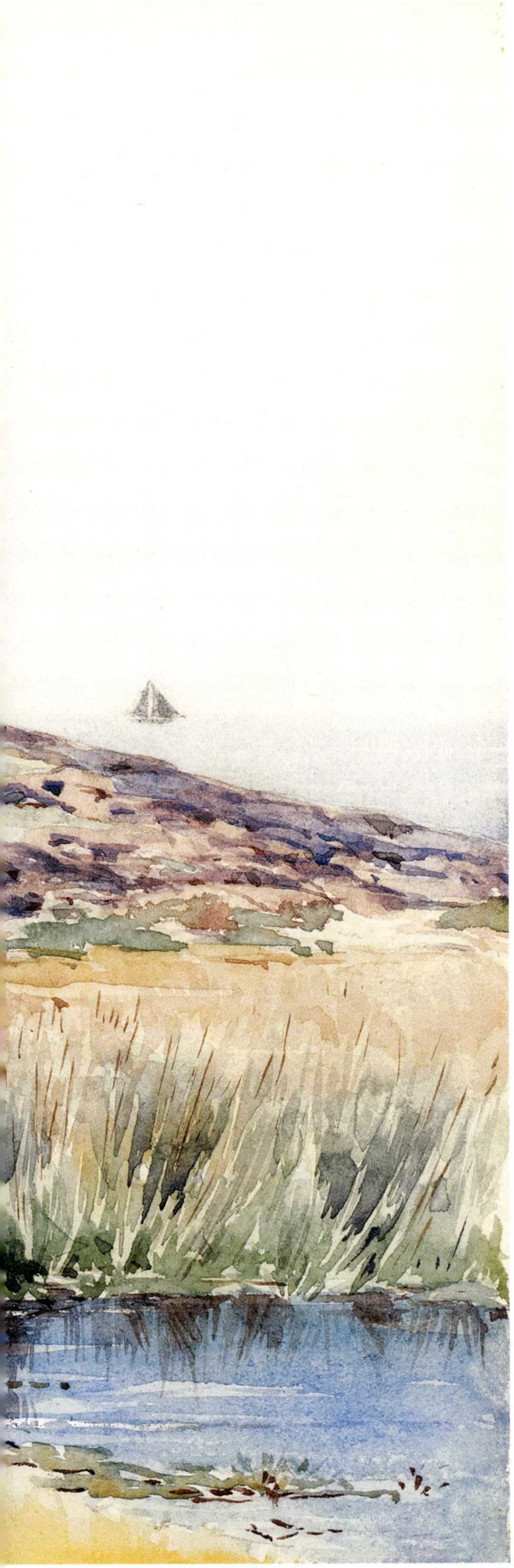

been in a state of dynamic recovery since the removal of sheep. Kent painted on Monhegan during the first two decades of the twentieth century and returned to paint there again in the 1940s and 1950s. He witnessed tremendous change to the Wildlands, and a review of landscape paintings by him and others over a half century suggests the extent of this transformation. The headlands on the island's eastern side, for example, were largely barren of trees and shrubs at the beginning of the century. Fifty years later, as Kent's painting *Young Spruces, Maine Coast* (see p. 140) reveals, a new forest was beginning to emerge. After more than a century without grazing livestock, today that forest again grows to the edge of the rocky coastline or nearly so, all around the island.

One can stand where Kent and the many renowned artists of Monhegan's past stood; however, one's view will not be theirs. Old pasture has yielded to shrubs and trees. Over the years since trees reappeared, the composition of this forest community has undergone profound further change. Dynamic change persists. The Wildlands will not appear in coming decades as they do today. Kent, as a first-time visitor in 1905, would not have immediately recognized these changes, nor understood how past human decisions had altered the island landscape. Yet he was a close and reliable observer of the natural world, a characteristic of his artistic practice introduced and championed by New York artist William Merritt Chase, who was one of Kent's early teachers. Chase advised, "Go before nature, use your eyes, and then paint what you see."[3] Kent, in time, gathered more wisdom and insight from later instructors, among them Abbott Handerson Thayer, who was himself a distinguished naturalist, and Robert Henri. It was Henri who, having first painted on Monhegan in 1903, urged Kent to visit the island. As Kent later recalled, Henri exclaimed: "You know, Kent, there's a place in Maine where I think you'd like to paint. It's a small island quite a way out to sea: Monhegan Island."[4]

In venturing there, Kent joined a wave of modern American artists who found the island a notable destination. During the previous decade, a handful of artists with connections to Boston had discovered Monhegan and painted there, including Sears Gallagher, Eric Hudson, Maud Briggs Knowlton, Mary King Longfellow, and Samuel Peter Rolt Triscott. A few built homes and became either seasonal or full-time residents. While each had their own artistic voice, their work shared a commitment to the colorful plein air painting then popular in Boston artistic circles. Almost all gravitated to the dramatic coastline and the village, subjects that inspire artists to this day. In addition, this group also found the shade of Cathedral Woods an attractive place to paint. Triscott's watercolor *In the Woods, Monhegan*, one of the earliest paintings to represent this thickly wooded ground, depicts ancient forest largely undisturbed by livestock grazing. Obscuring the horizon line, Triscott surrounds his viewers with trees and rocks, transporting them to the middle of this wild place.

The turn toward realism and authenticity among modernist painters was paralleled in the literary arts. Writers such as Jack London and Willa Cather, adherents of literary naturalism, focused attention on the environment and foregrounded the grittiness of American life. At the same time, Irish poet and Nobel Prize laureate William Butler Yeats exhorted the younger Irish writer J. M. Synge to "give up Paris, you will never create anything by reading Racine. . . . Go to the Aran Islands. Live there as if you were one of the people themselves; express

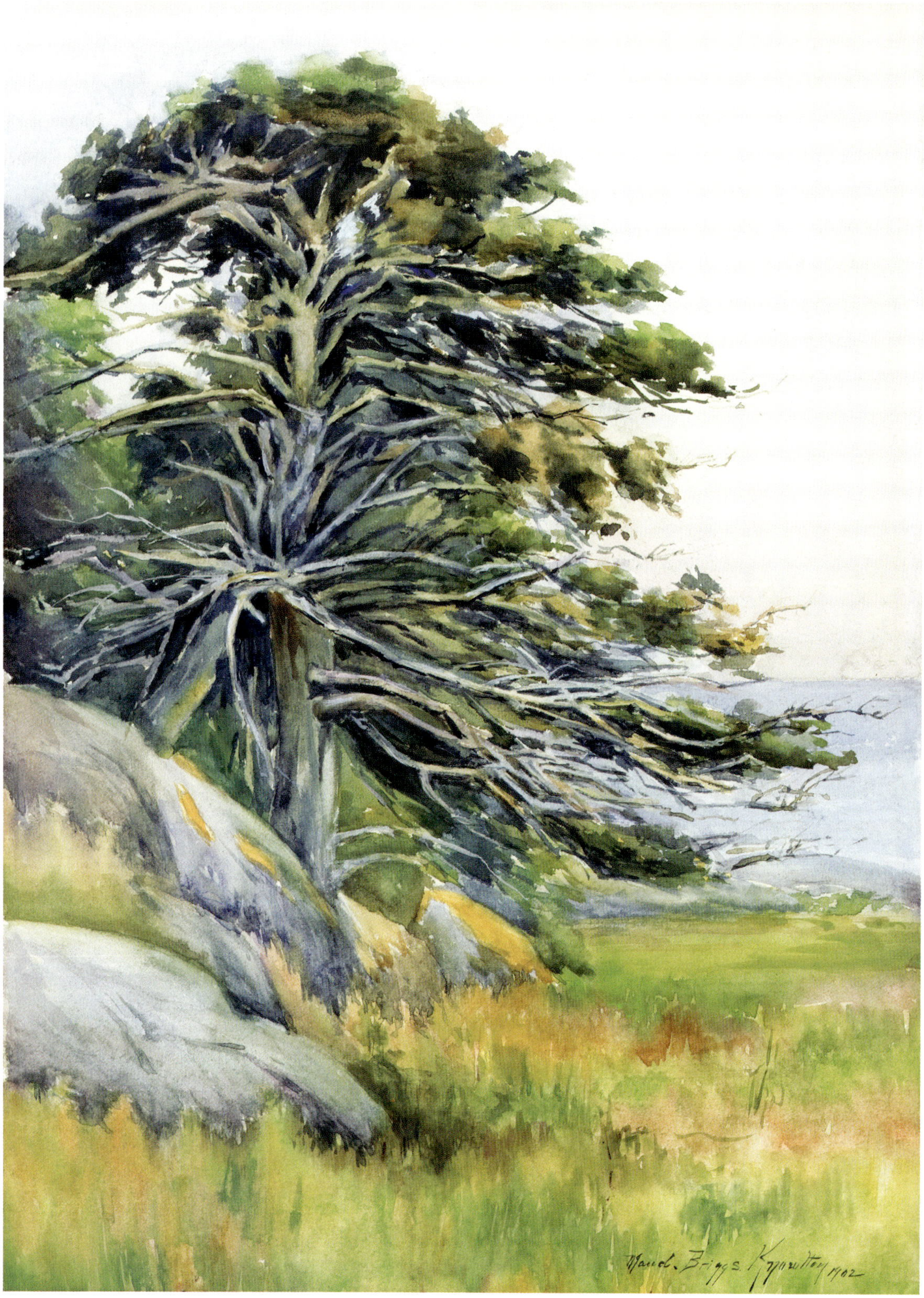

Maud Briggs Knowlton (1870–1956), *Spruce Tree,* 1902. Watercolor on paper, 15 x 10¾ inches. Collection of Edward L. Deci

Mary King Longfellow (1852–1945), Untitled, ca. 1900. Watercolor on paper, 14 x 21 inches. Monhegan Museum of Art & History. Gift of Earle G. Shettleworth, Jr., in honor of Linda L. Bean

a life that never found expression."[5] Synge, like Kent, followed suit, living off western Ireland among the Aran Islanders at the mouth of Galway Bay and publishing *The Aran Islands,* a seminal work of twentieth-century Irish literature, in 1907.

The arrival on Monhegan of Boston artists coincided with the beginning of a seasonal tourism trade. Described in 1898 in *New England Magazine* as "the Mecca of the summer pilgrimage of a constantly increasing number of unspoiled and cultured people," the island began to gain a reputation during this period for being a popular summer destination.[6] Tourists had visited earlier in the nineteenth century, but the new century saw new accommodations—such as the Island Inn, which opened to guests in 1907—and new infrastructure meant to cater to this trade. In 1908, a new wharf was built that could more easily handle boats carrying seasonal passengers as well as residents with building supplies and larger bulk cargoes. In that same year, heirs of the Starling family—one of the first year-round families to settle on Monhegan in the late

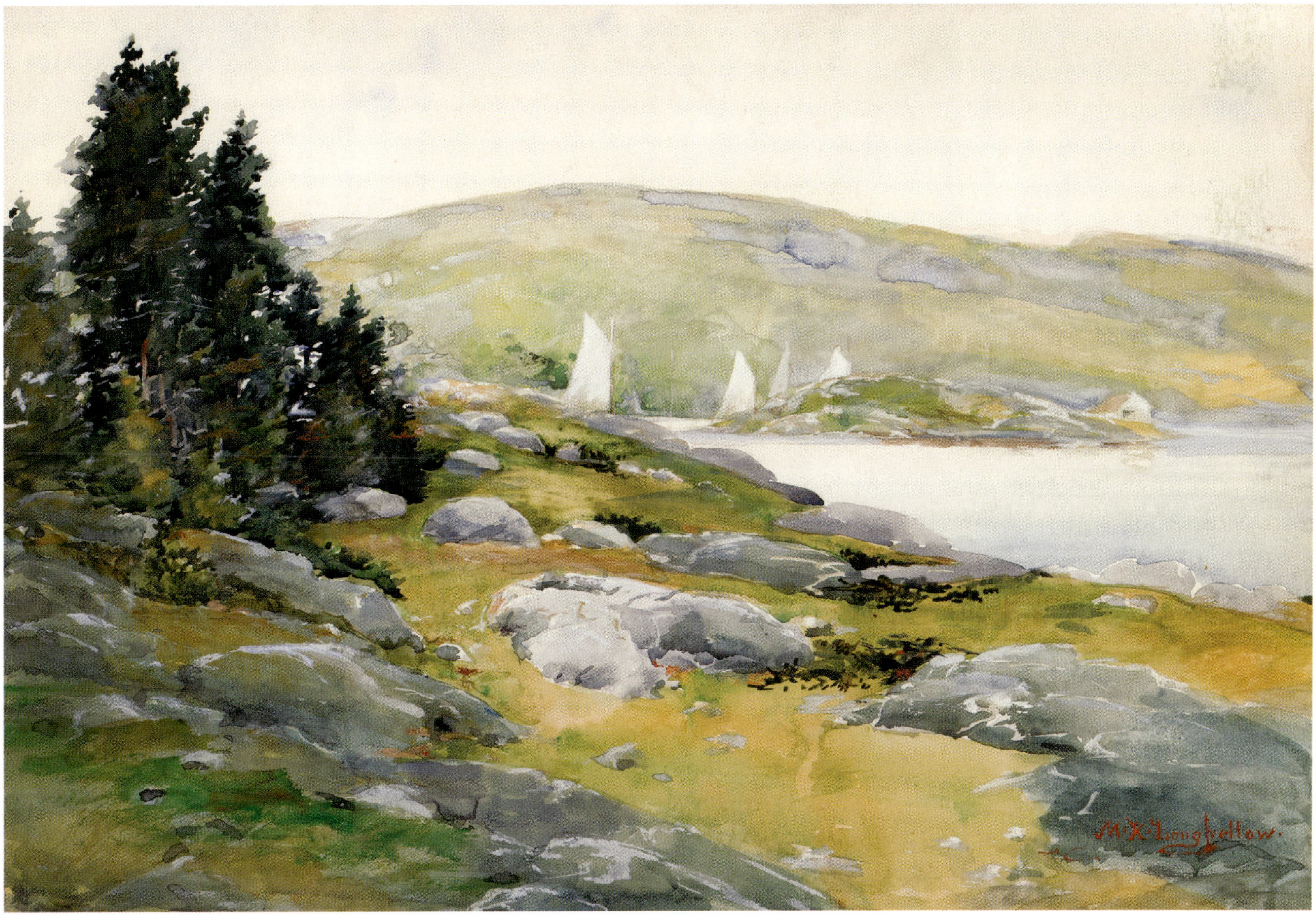

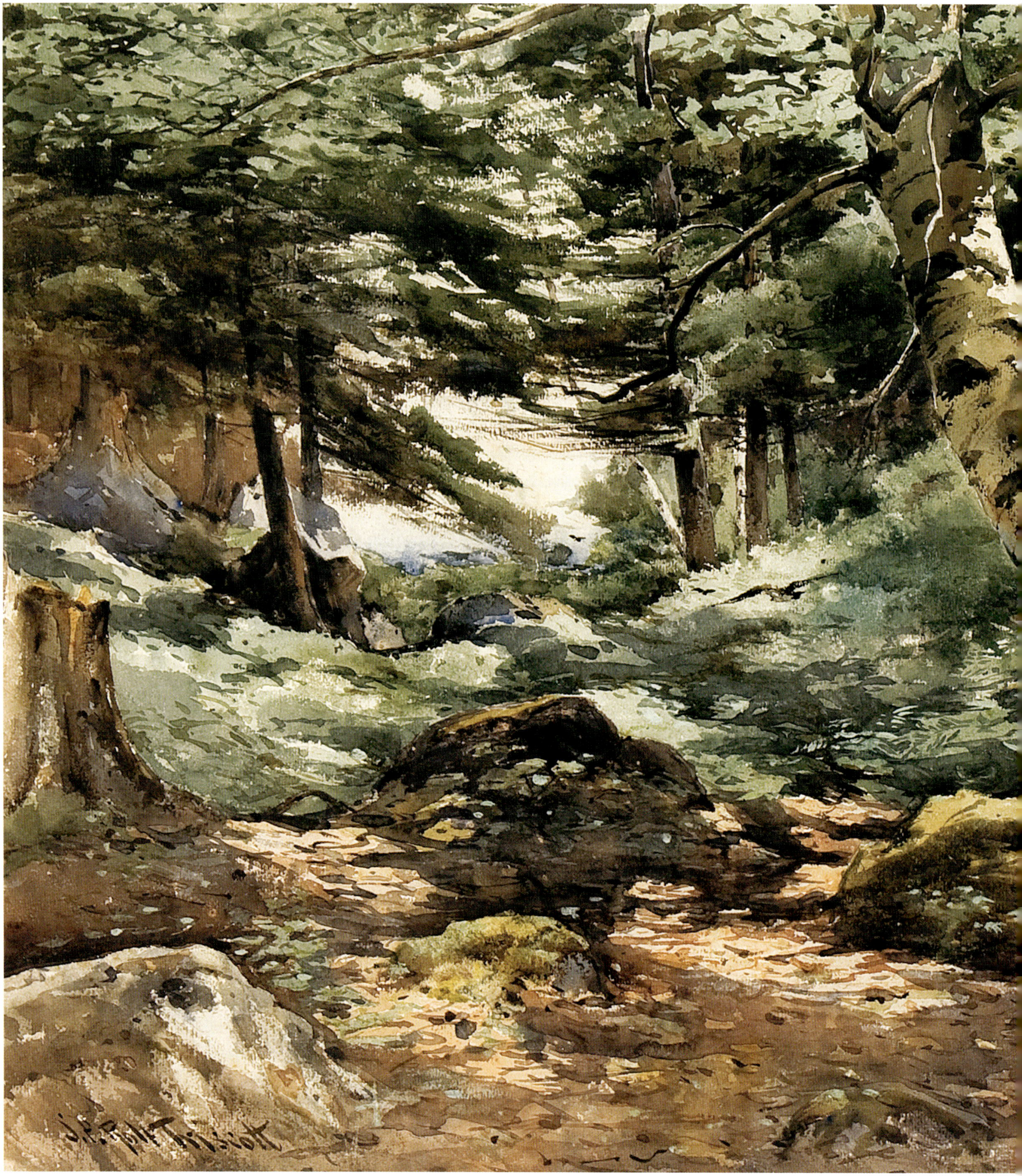

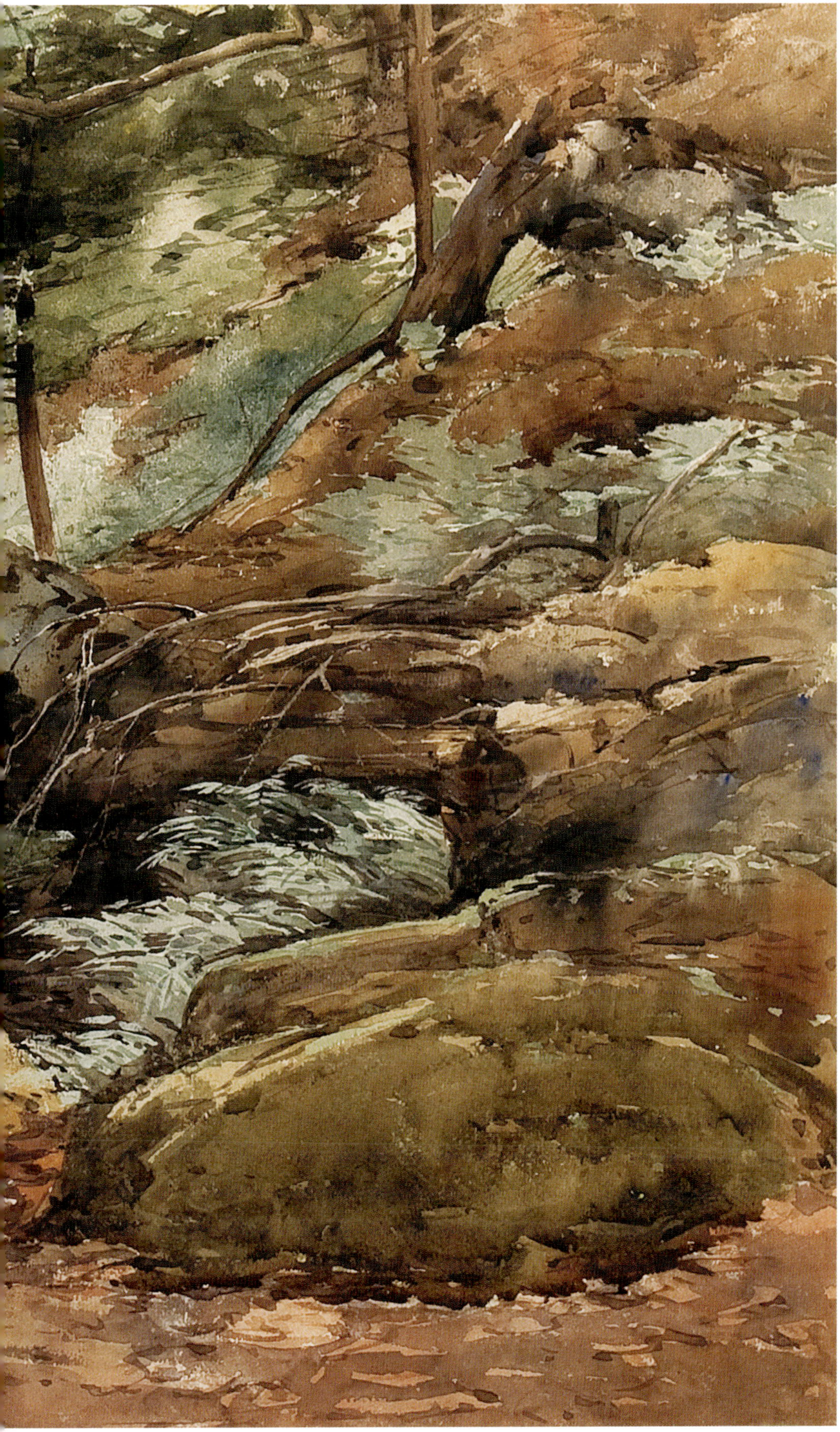

Samuel Peter Rolt Triscott (1846–1925),
In the Woods, Monhegan, ca. 1900.
Watercolor on paper, 17 x 24¼ inches.
Monhegan Museum of Art & History.
Gift of Remak Ramsay

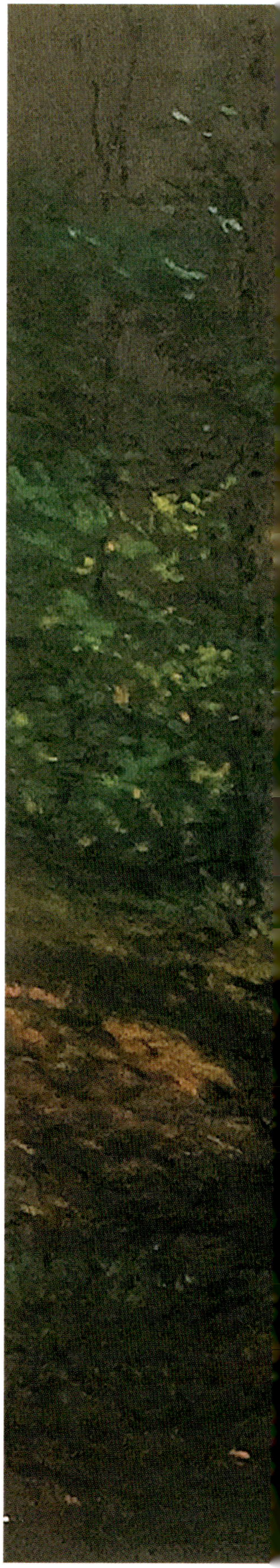

William Partridge Burpee (1846–1940),
Monhegan Spruce Forest, ca. 1904.
Pastel on paper, 14 x 11¼ inches.
Monhegan Museum of Art & History.
Gift of Remak Ramsay

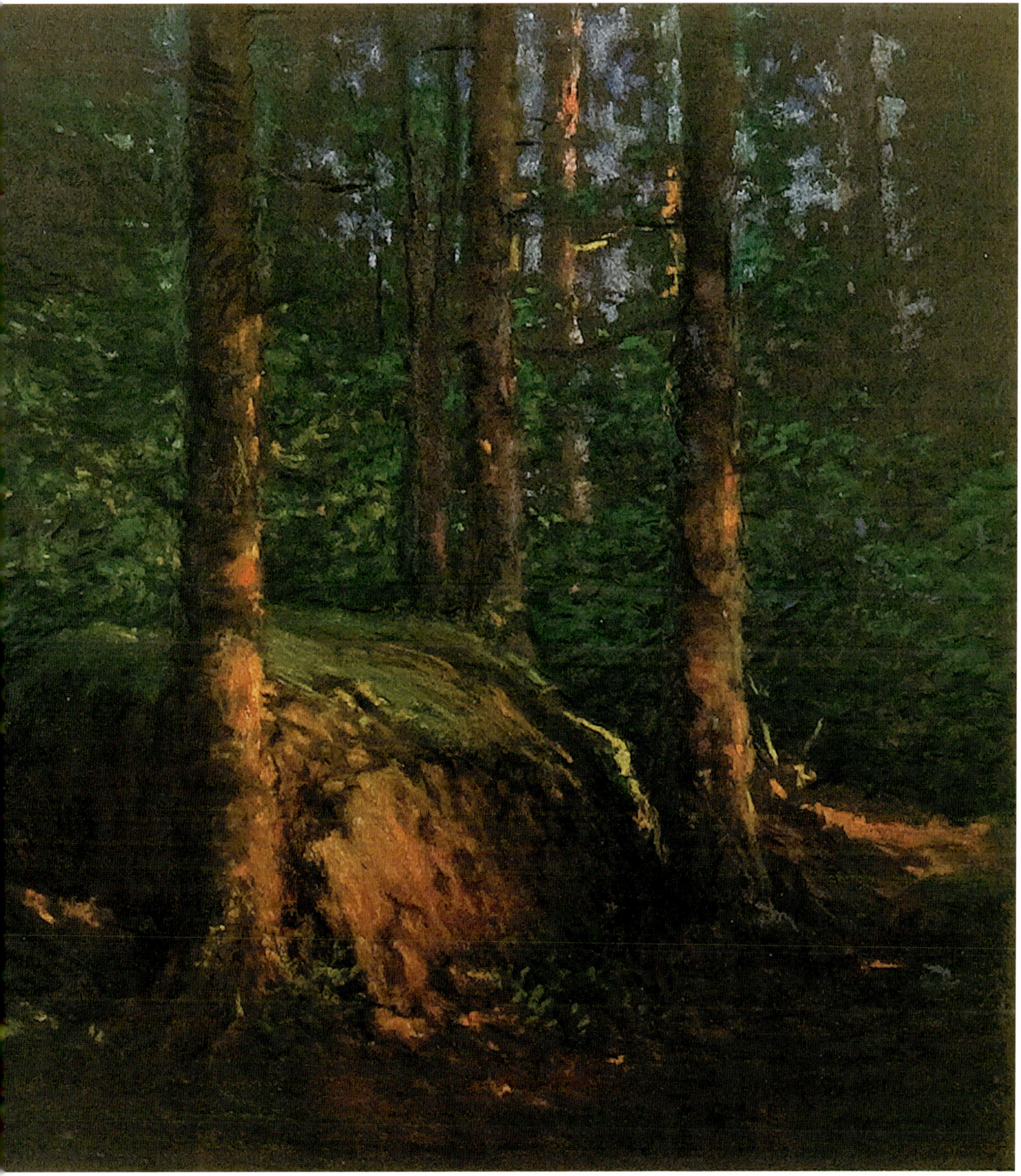

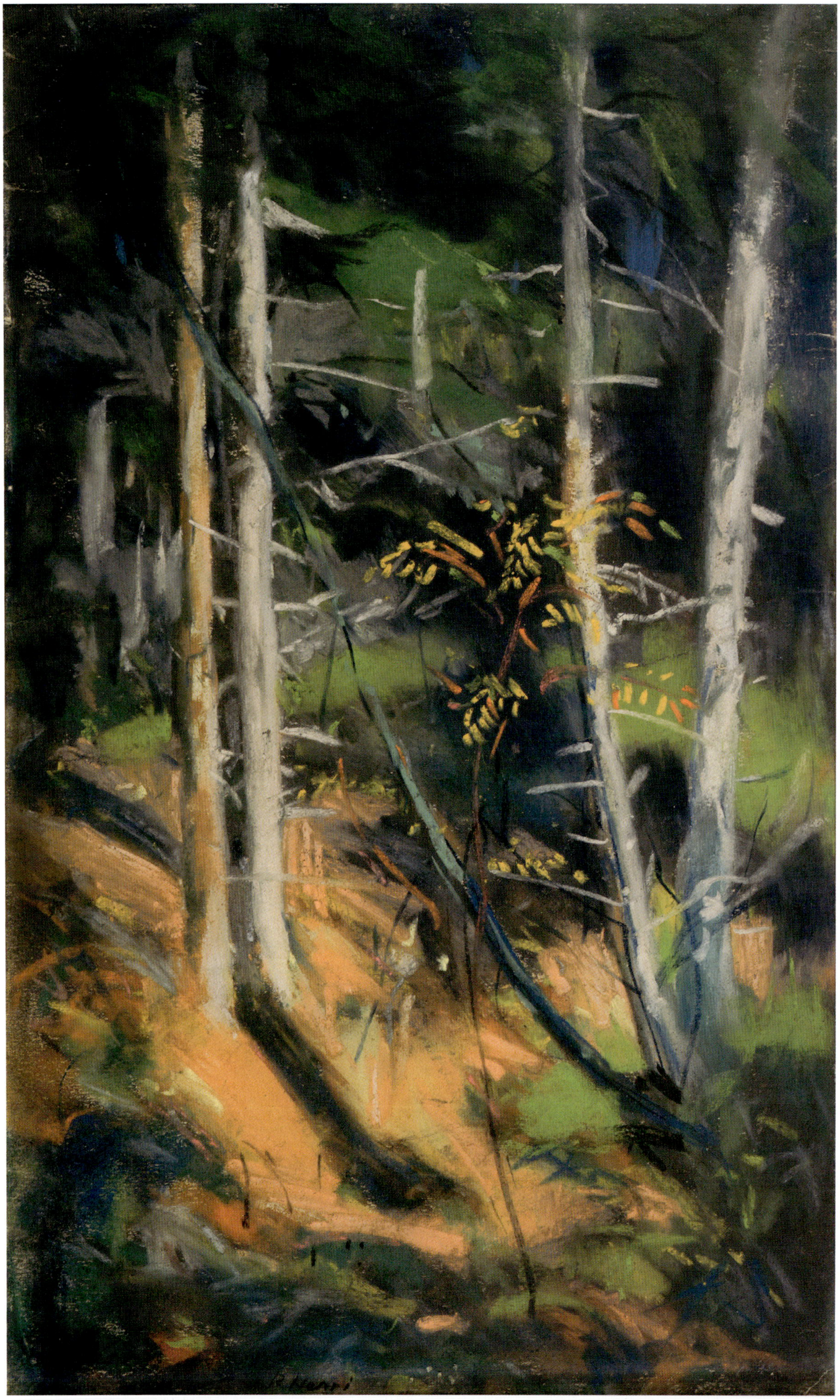

Robert Henri (1865–1929), *Cathedral Woods, Monhegan Island*, 1918. Pastel on paper, 20 x 12 inches. Collection of Stephen S. Fuller and Susan D. Bateson

Attributed to Oliver Patterson Watts (1865–1953), Cathedral Woods, ca. 1920. Gelatin silver print, 6⅞ x 8$^{13}/_{16}$ inches. Monhegan Museum of Art & History. Gift of William McCartin

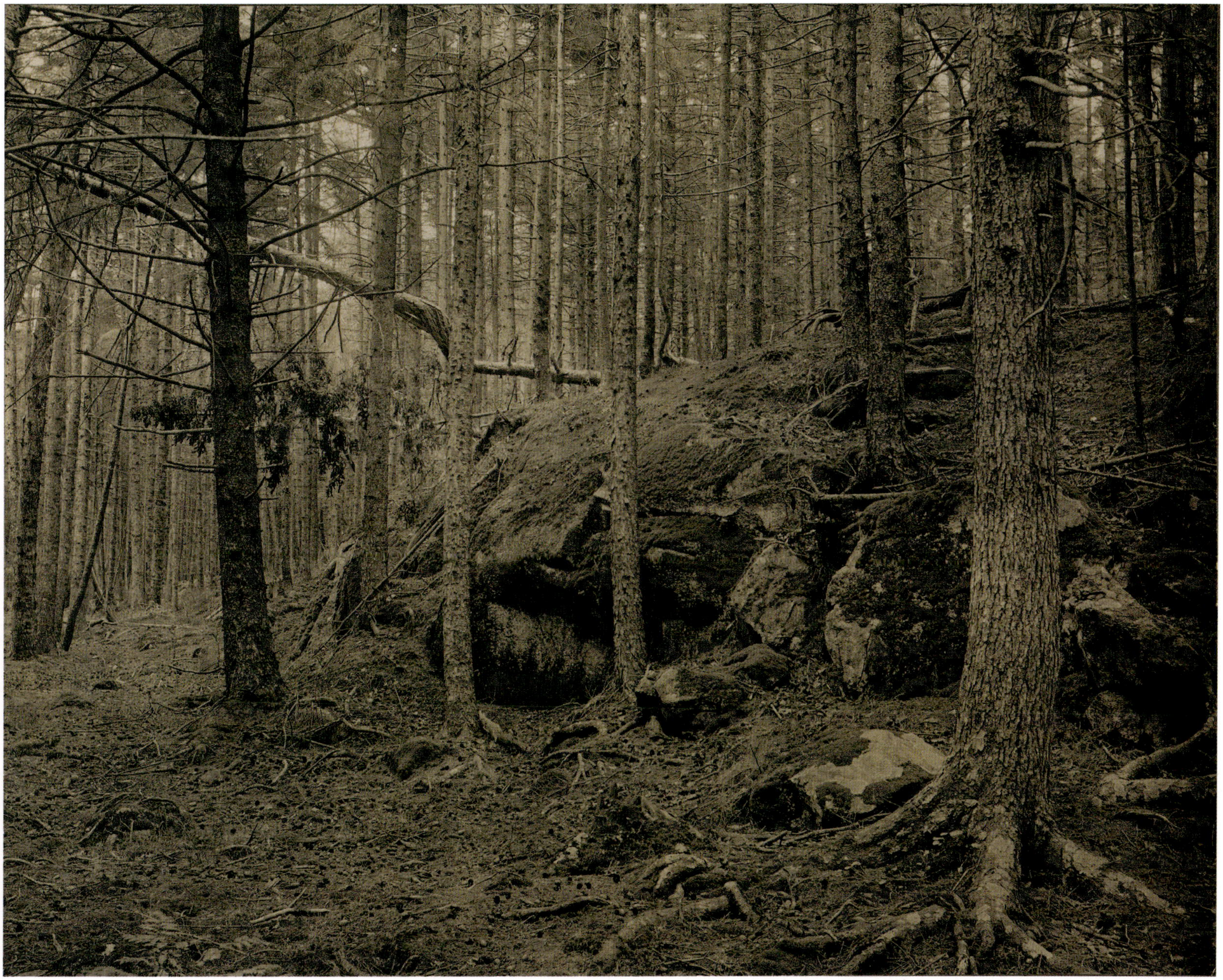

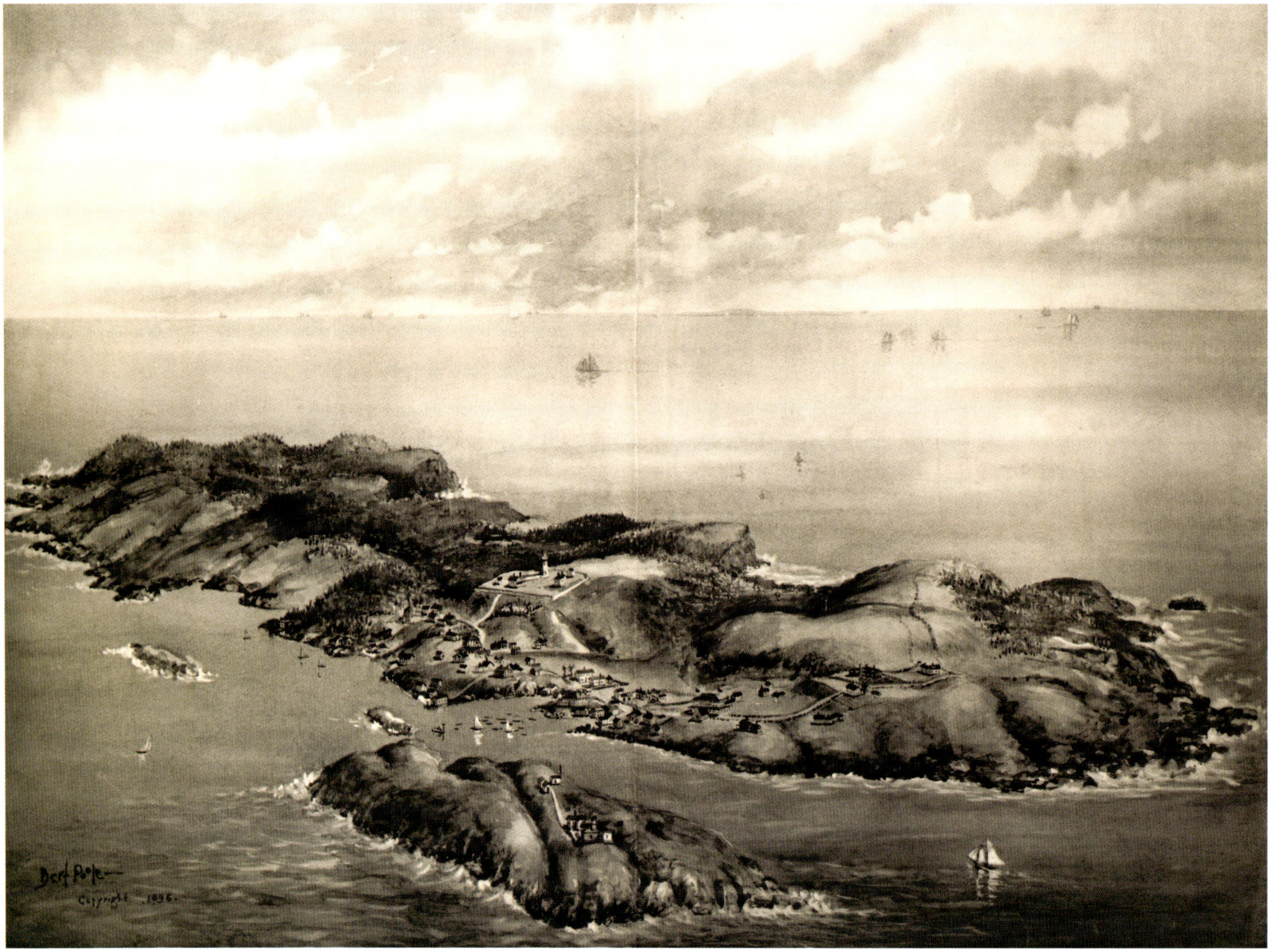

Bert Poole (1853–1939), *Monhegan, Me*, ca. 1896. Lithograph, 15¾ x 22¹⁄₁₆ inches. Library of Congress, Geography and Map Division

eighteenth century—established the Monhegan Land Company to sell lots to new home builders. Shortly thereafter, the number of seasonal nonresidents began to exceed the number of full-time residents.

It was then that the first wave of young artists from New York City discovered Monhegan. Robert Henri led the way, taking up summer residence in 1903. Henri trekked throughout the island and painted colorful land- and seascapes until literally running out of artistic supplies. Before departing, however, he purchased land on Horn's Hill, expecting to make Monhegan an annual destination in future years. Though he did not make it back until 1911, he encouraged others from the artistic circles he frequented. In addition to his student Rockwell Kent, painters from New York over the next two decades included George Bellows, Randall Davey, Edward Hopper, and Leon Kroll. Whereas the Boston painters tended to adhere to traditional landscape conventions, the New Yorkers—inspired by European modernism—found Monhegan to be a place where they might experiment with color, mark-making, and composition. Their canvases are characterized by bold, expressionistic brushwork and uncommon cropping decisions.

Like earlier artists, they often gravitated to the coast, creating dramatic landscapes of the headlands. These views document how barren this land along the coast had become because of livestock grazing, and they offer rich evidence of the island's ecology at this moment in time. Historic maps, too, provide great insight. A 1922 map in the possession of the Monhegan Museum of Art & History shows extensive pasture along much of the island perimeter as well as atop the headlands (see p. 44). Contrasting this map to a US Coast and Geodetic Survey map created in 1873 (see p. 80) reveals that pastureland expansion over the intervening fifty-year period involved felling forests on the headlands; pasture elsewhere was already extant. Artworks created on the headlands and described above help narrow the time frame further. Headland forests there must have been converted to pasture before or during the first few years of the twentieth century. As will be explored in chapter 3, this aligns well with the expansion and eventual late nineteenth-century decline in island livestock grazing.

With a critical mass of artists now residing on the island, Monhegan began to gain a reputation as an artists' haven. Other places in Maine—including Mount Desert Island, Georgetown, and Ogunquit—also drew artists during this period, though few attracted so many to such a small and remote community. Adding to the island's artistic reputation, Kent and fellow artist Julius Golz

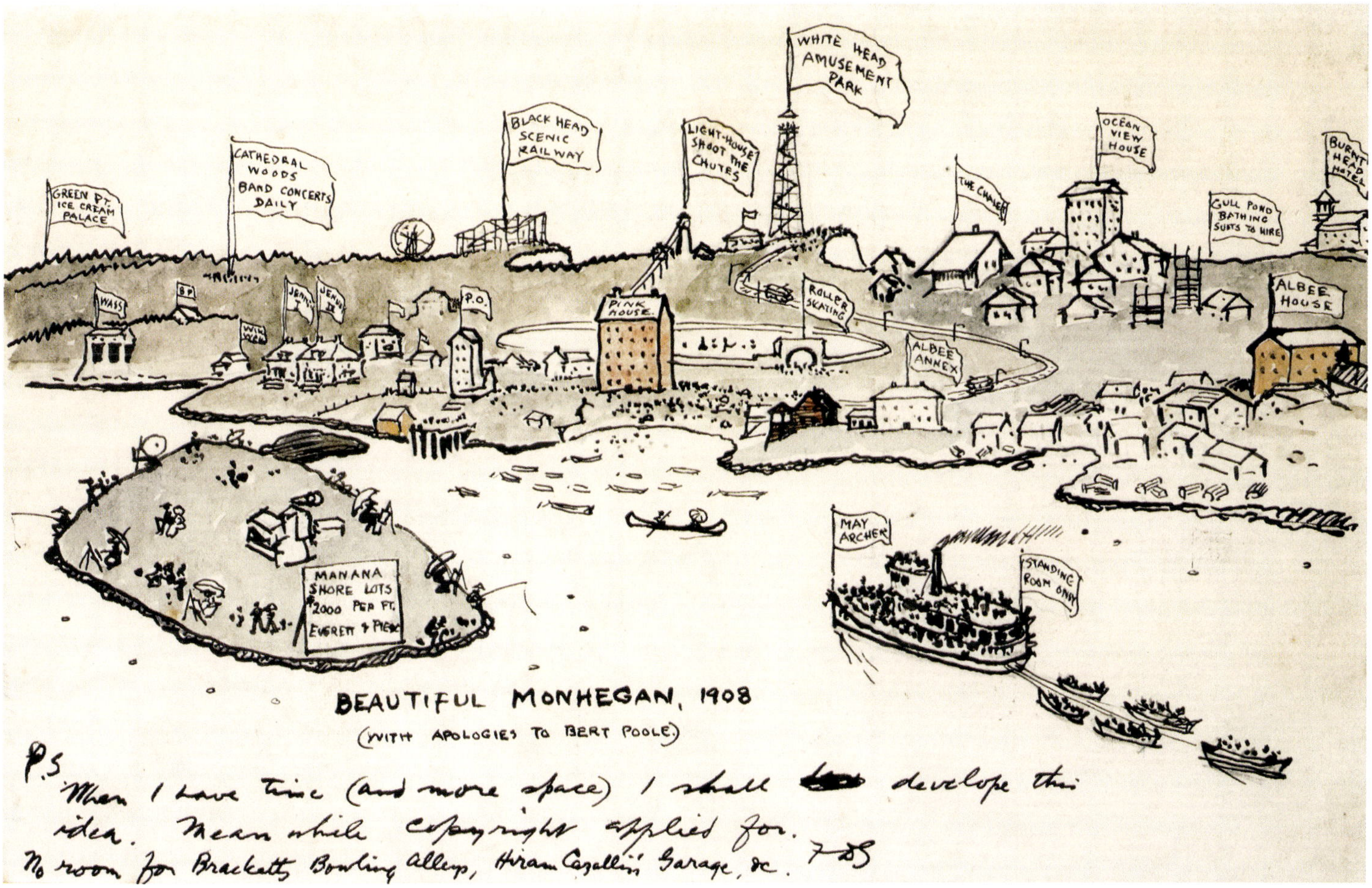

Frederic Dorr Steele (1873–1944), *Beautiful Monhegan,* 1908. Watercolor and ink on paper, 4⅞ x 7⅞ inches. Collection of Glenn and Carol Burdick

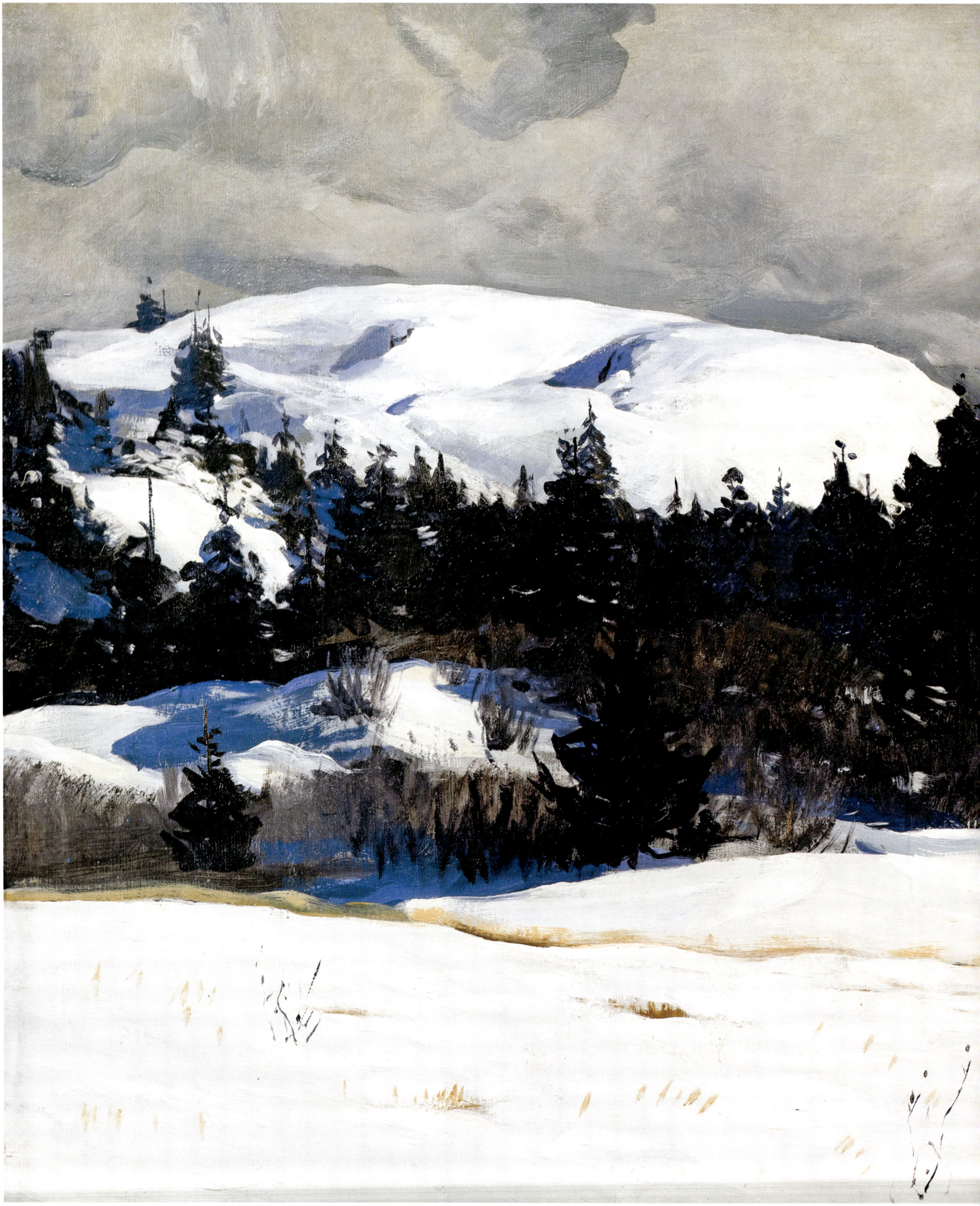

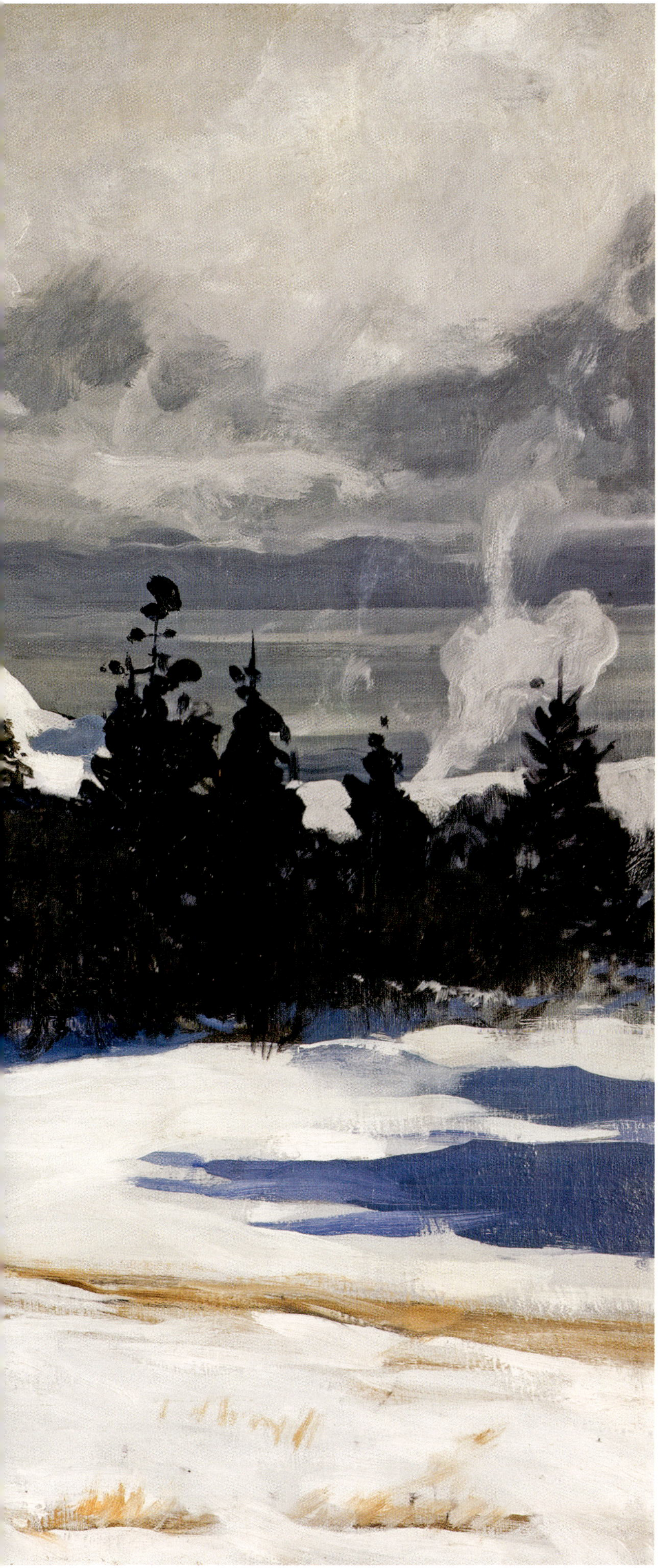

Rockwell Kent (1882–1971), *Maine Coast*, ca. 1907. Oil on canvas, 28⅛ x 38 inches. Collection of the Farnsworth Art Museum, Rockland, Maine. Bequest of Mrs. Elizabeth B. Noyce, 1997.3.25

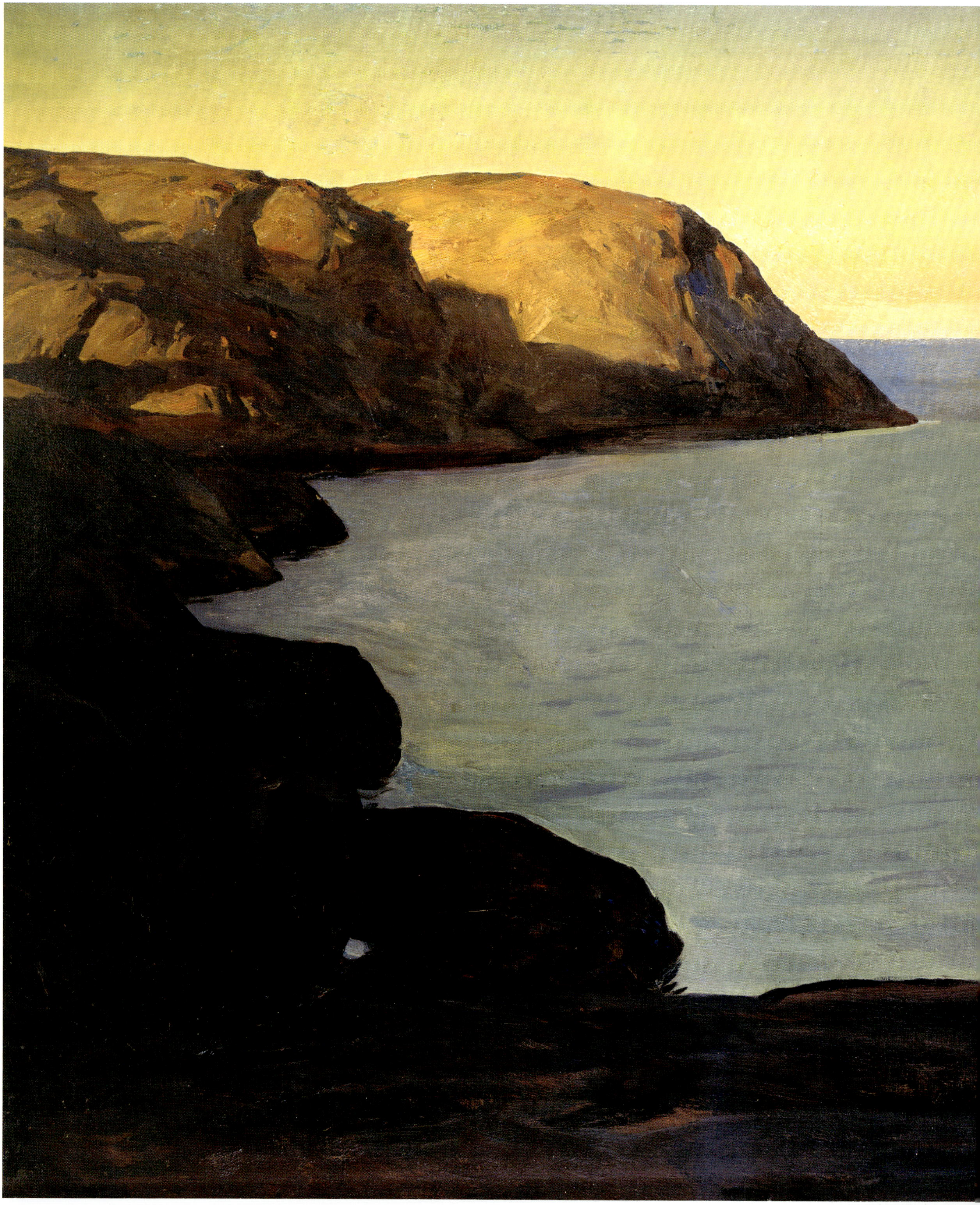

Rockwell Kent (1882–1971),
Monhegan Headlands, 1905.
Oil on canvas, 33 x 43½ inches.
Collection of Jamie Wyeth

George Bellows (1882–1925), *Ocean Headland, Black Head, Monhegan*, 1911. Oil on panel, 11½ x 15½ inches. Collection of Stephen S. Fuller and Susan D. Bateson

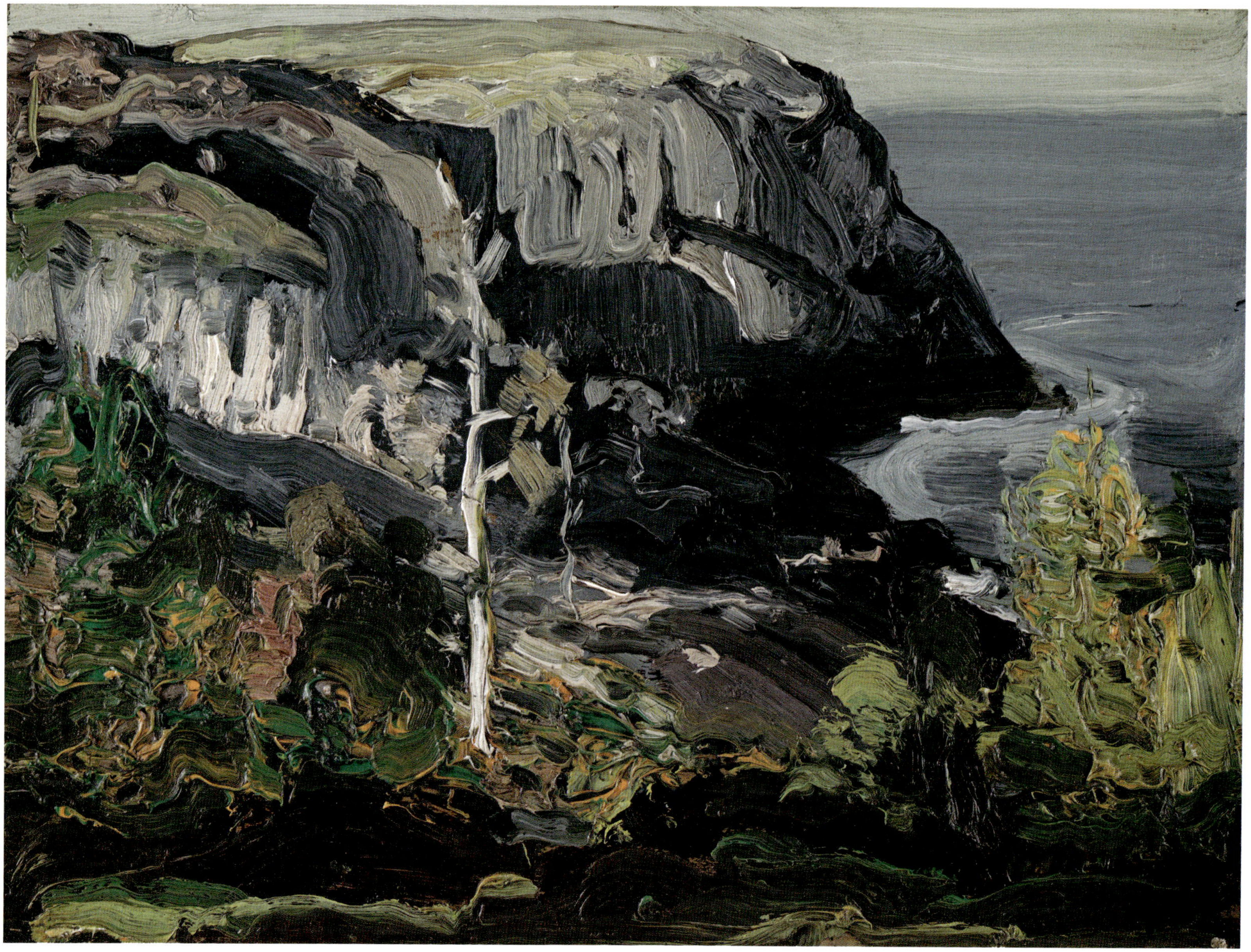

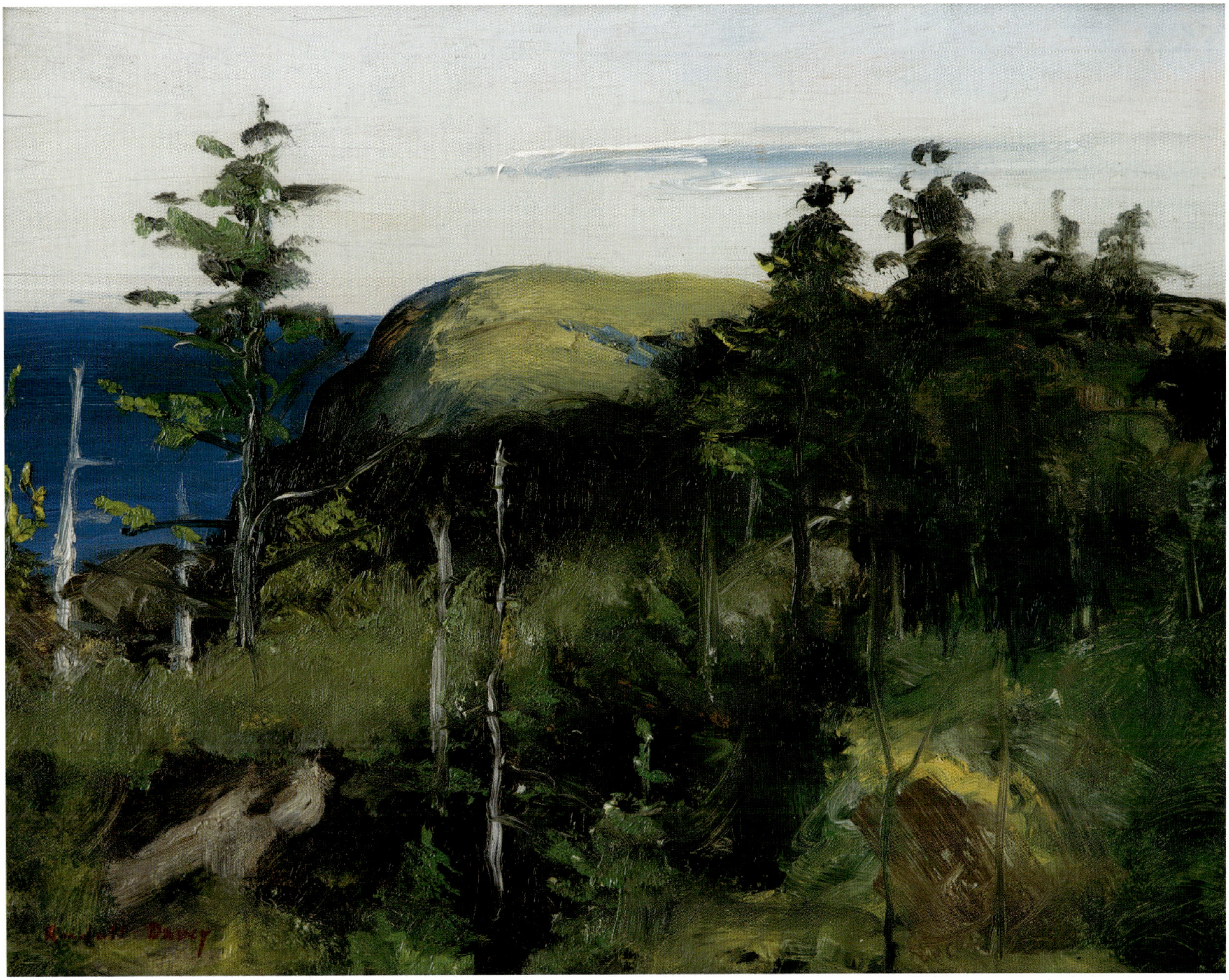

Randall Davey (1887–1964),
Headland and Sea, 1914. Oil
on board, 15 x 19½ inches.
Collection of Stephen S. Fuller
and Susan D. Bateson

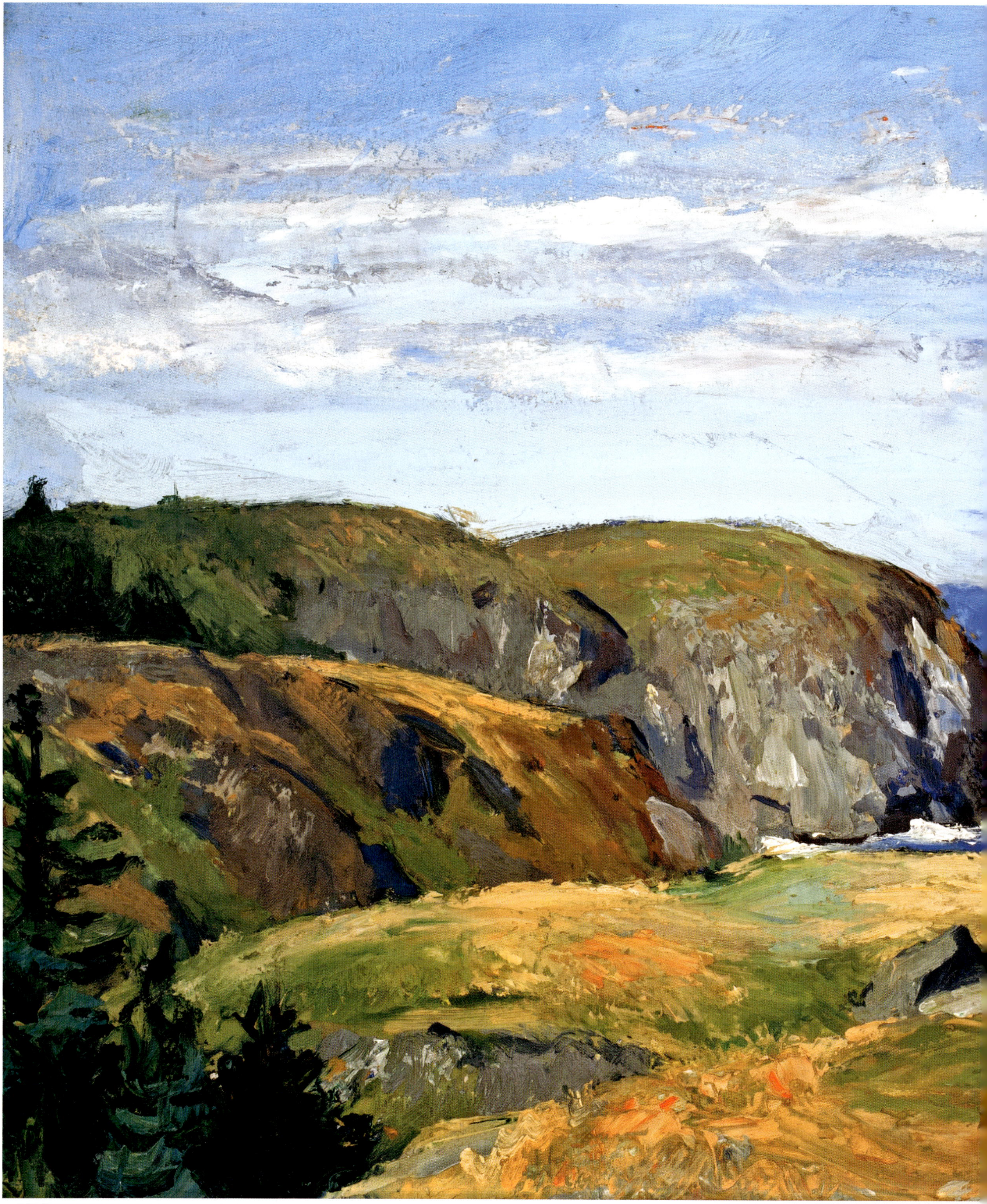

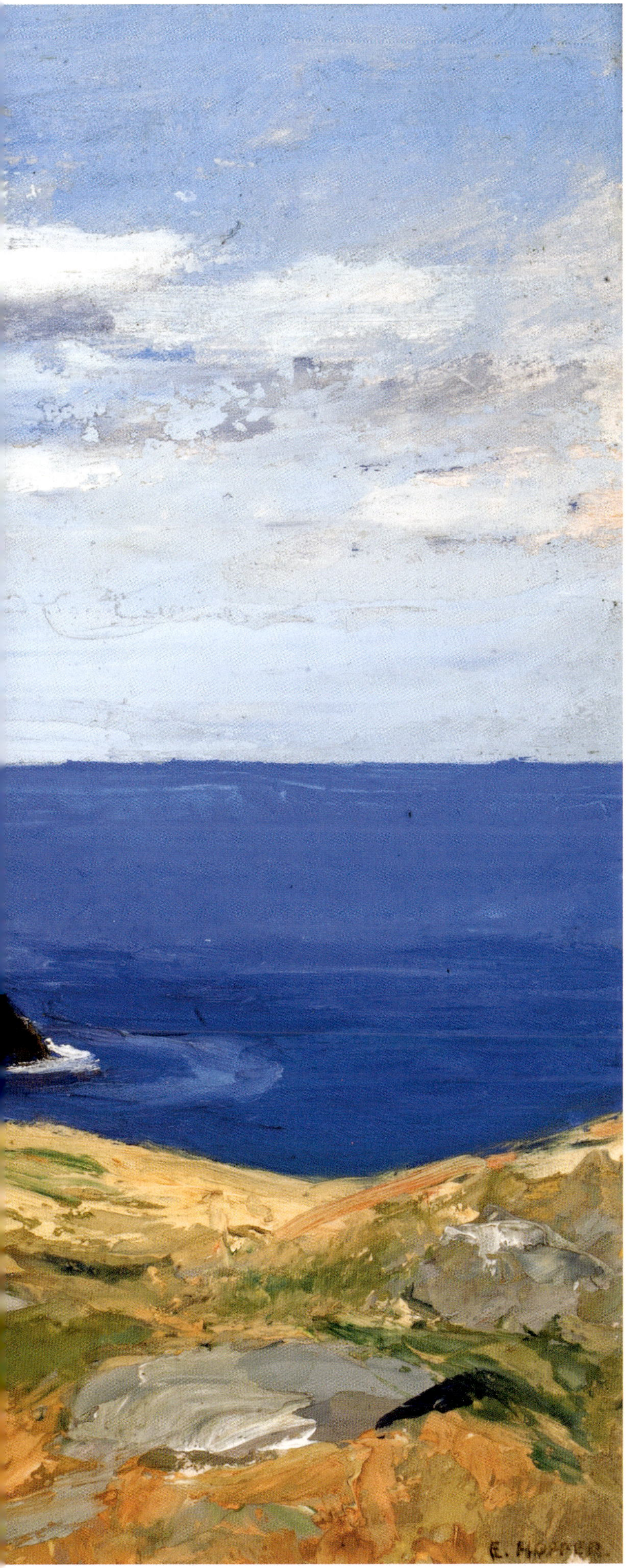

Edward Hopper (1882–1967),
Black Head, Monhegan, ca. 1918.
Oil on panel, 11½ x 16 inches.
New Britain Museum of American Art. Gift of Olga H. Knoepke

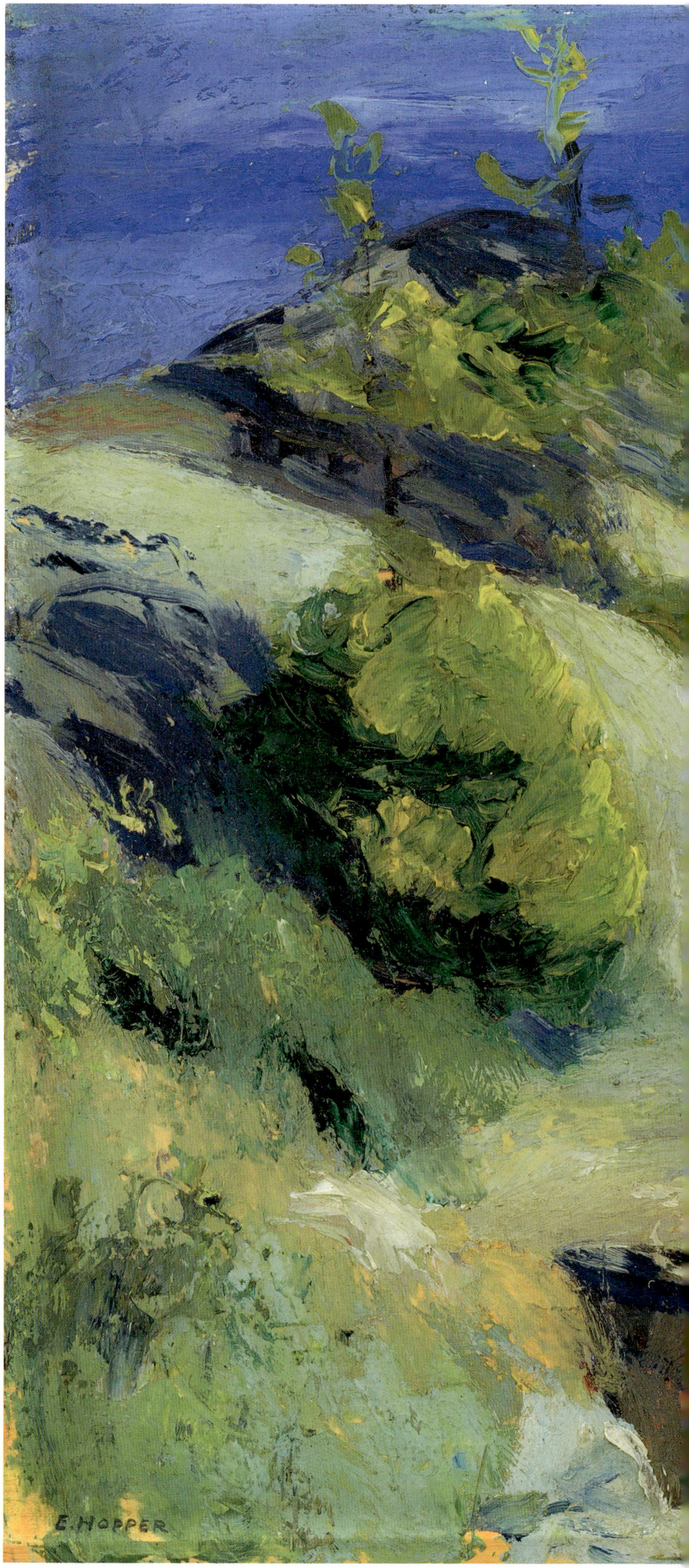

Edward Hopper (1882–1967),
Monhegan Landscape, ca. 1916–19.
Oil on panel, 12 x 17 inches. Collection
of the Herbert F. Johnson Museum
of Art, Cornell University. Gift of
Herbert Gussman, Class of 1933

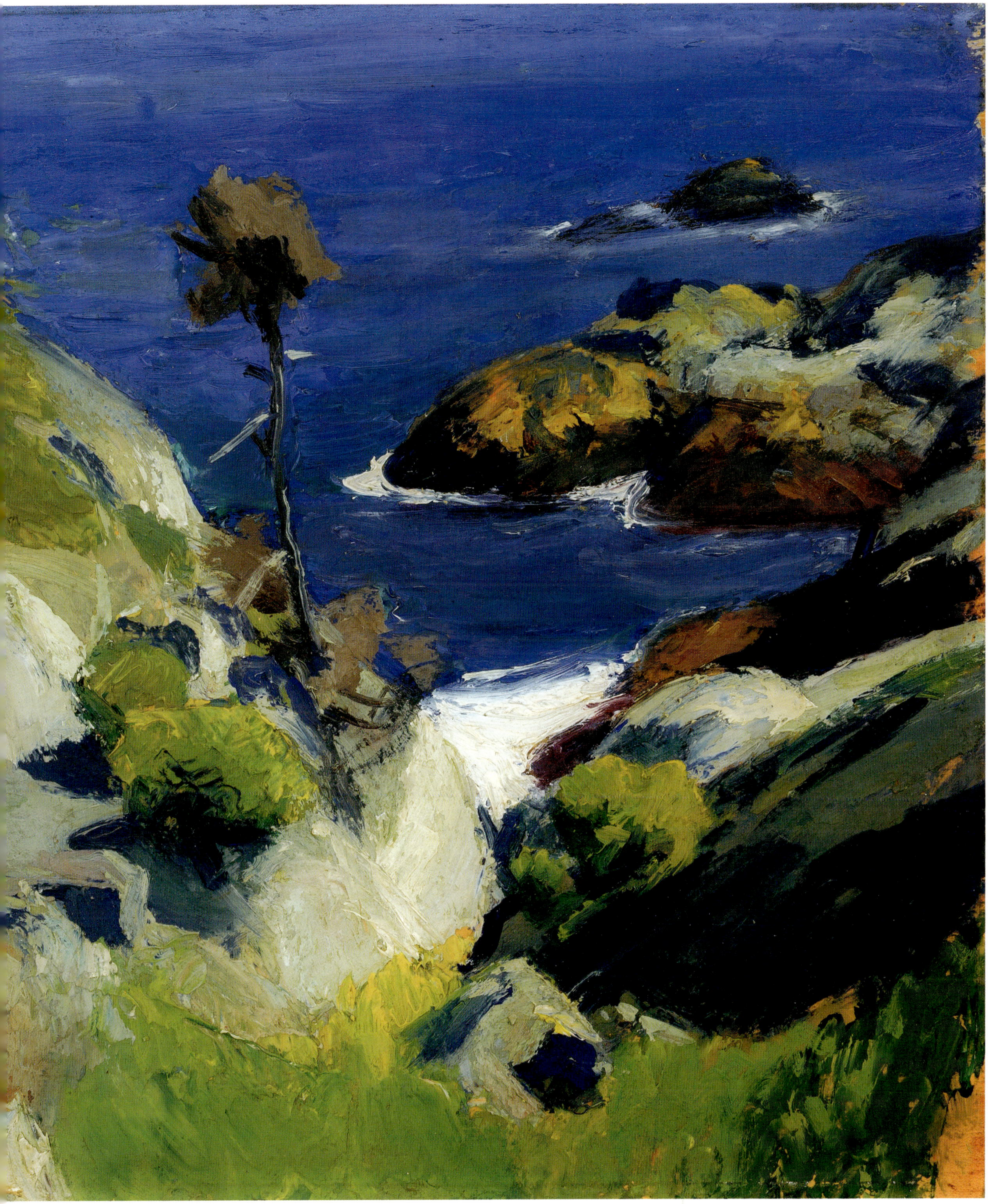

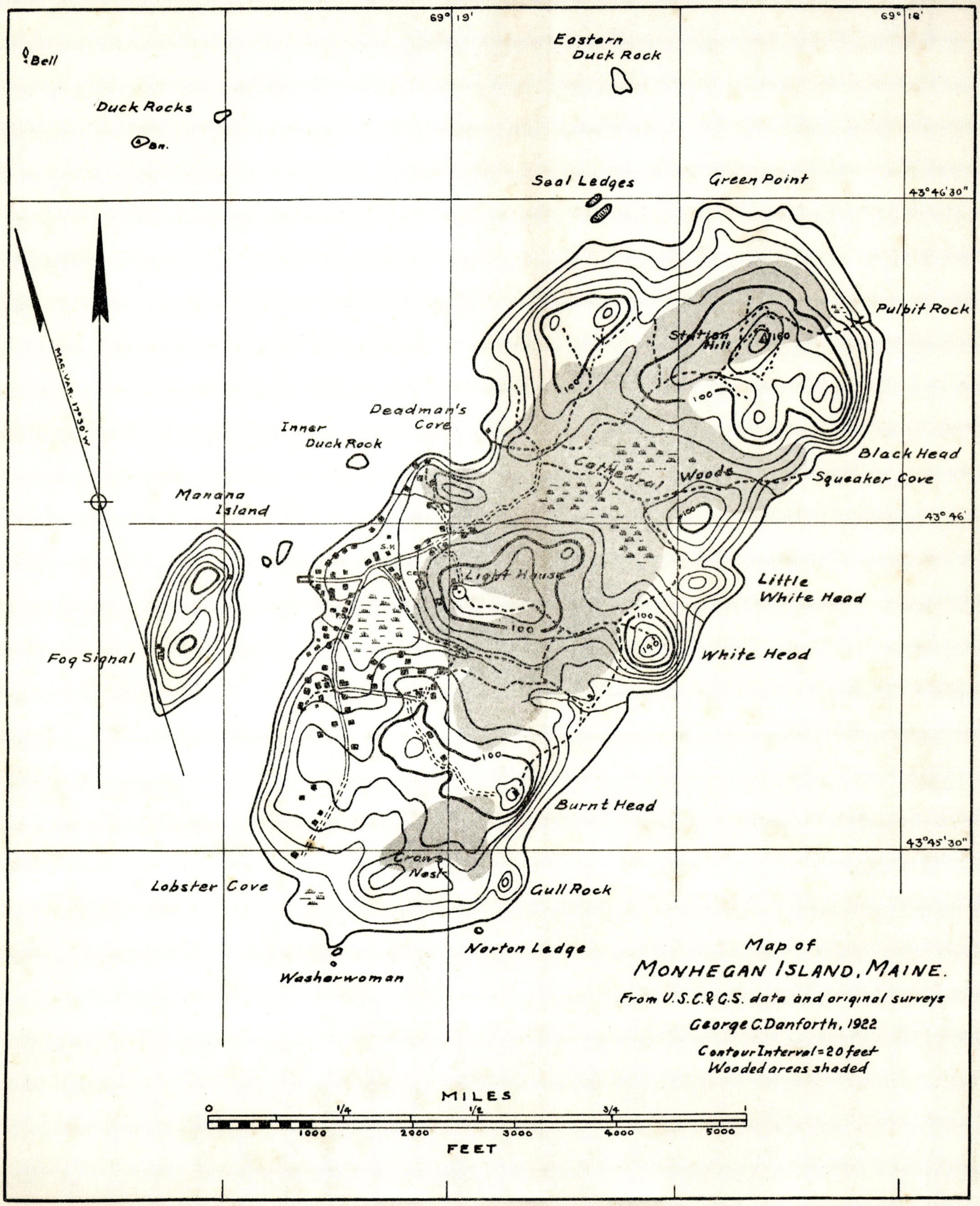
69° 19'
69° 18'
Bell
Eastern
Duck Rock
Duck Rocks
Bn.
Seal Ledges
Green Point
43° 46' 30"
MAG. VAR. 17° 30' W
Pulpit Rock
Station Hill
100
Deadman's Cove
Inner
Duck Rock
Black Head
Cathedral Woods
Squeaker Cove
Manana Island
43° 46'
S.H.
Light House
Little
White Head
100
140
White Head
Fog Signal
Burnt Head
43° 45' 30"
Crows Nest
Lobster Cove
Gull Rock
Norton Ledge
Washerwoman
Map of
MONHEGAN ISLAND, MAINE.
From U.S.C.&G.S. data and original surveys
George C. Danforth, 1922
Contour Interval = 20 feet
Wooded areas shaded
MILES
0
1/4
1/2
3/4
1
1000
2000
3000
4000
5000
FEET

established a summer art school on Monhegan in 1910. Though it attracted a good number of students, the school only lasted one season. Nevertheless, when an on-island art exhibition was proposed on the occasion of the three hundredth anniversary of Captain John Smith's 1614 visit to Monhegan, eighteen artists contributed works to a show that elicited reviews in newspapers as far away as Boston.[7] This and other exhibitions demonstrated that the island had become a notable artistic colony.

Painters were not the only artists to venture to Monhegan. Photographers too found the island an alluring subject. At the turn of the twentieth century, individuals such as Edward Knowlton, Eric Hudson, and Edward Robinson all made accomplished photographs on Monhegan. Samuel Peter Rolt Triscott also made photographs and, at times, painted directly on his prints. These photographers sought out the same destinations as the painters and sold their resulting images to visitors and others. Photographs dating to the 1890s offer explicit evidence of free-roaming sheep. One Triscott photograph captures bleached stumps at the feet of sheep, clear evidence that pastureland formation was an active intervention.

As the early decades of the twentieth century passed, abandoned pasture on Monhegan came to be overtaken by white spruce, the conifer that would dominate the island's secondary forests through the remainder of the century. White spruce exhibits an extraordinarily broad range. Stretching from Newfoundland to the Alaskan interior, it forms much of the North American Arctic tree line. This largely boreal tree is an important part of the flora of the Adirondacks, skirts across the northern regions of Vermont and New Hampshire, and extends to the Maine coast, largely dropping out of the flora as one moves south from the mouth of the lower Kennebec River near Bath, Maine. White

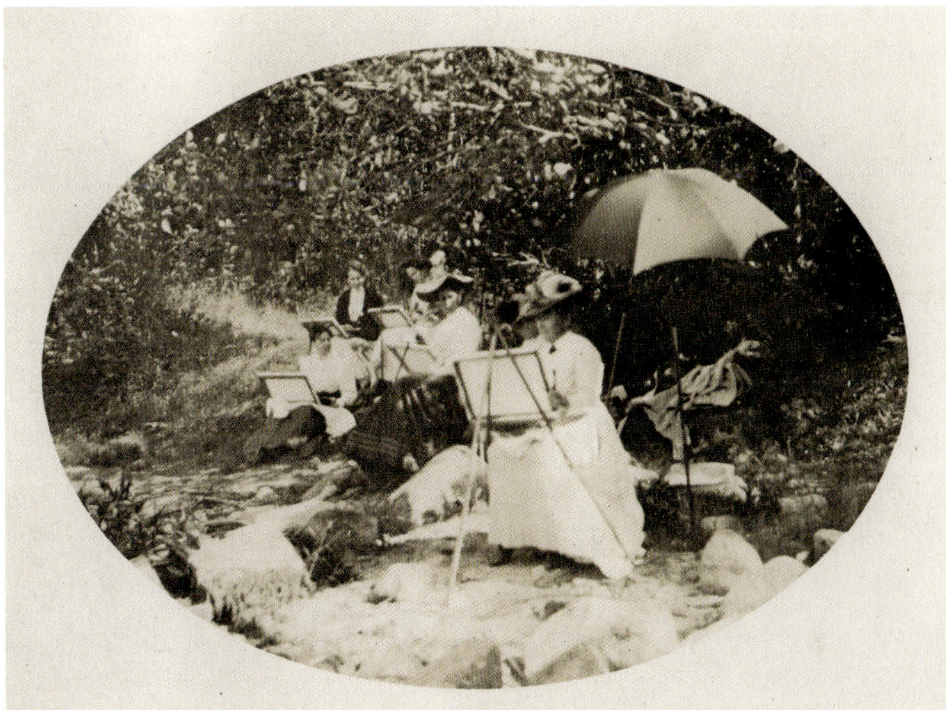

Opposite: George C. Danforth (1881–1946), *Map of Monhegan Island, Maine*, 1922. Monhegan Museum of Art & History. Gift of Julie Hudson. In this map, forest cover is indicated by shading.

Right: Edward Knowlton (1860–1957), Artists on Monhegan, ca. 1900. Gelatin silver print, 3⅜ x 5⅜ inches. Monhegan Museum of Art & History. Gift of Leo and Berniece Meissner

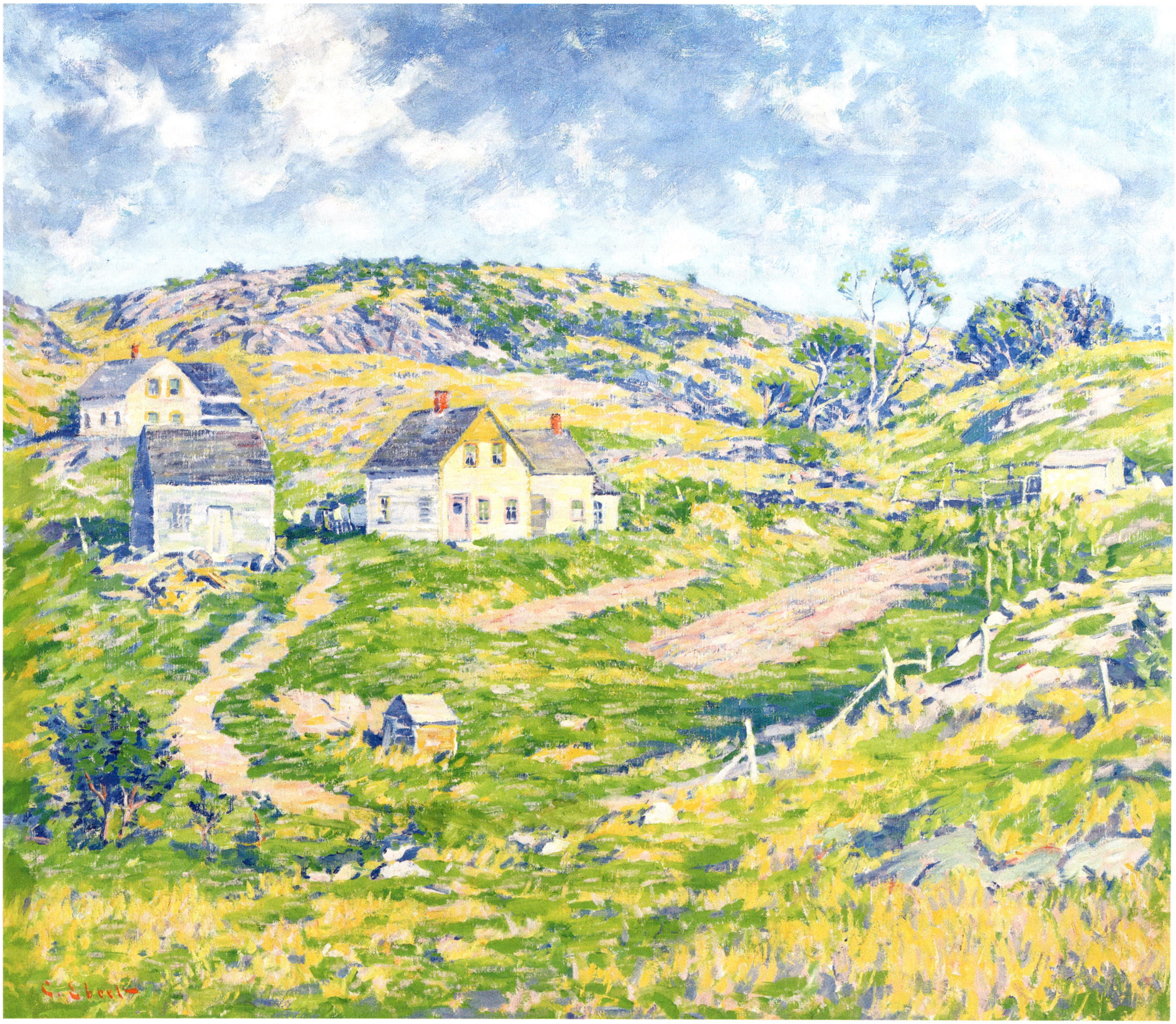

Charles Ebert (1873–1959),
Grammy Richards' House, ca. 1914.
Oil on canvas, 30 x 36 inches.
Monhegan Museum of Art &
History. Gift of Elisabeth R. Ebert

Samuel Peter Rolt Triscott (1846–1925), Sheep on Monhegan, ca. 1895. Maine Historic Preservation Commission

spruce possess broad habitat tolerance, as befits a species with such a large range. Its wind-dispersed seeds germinate into seedlings that prefer direct sunshine and can tolerate dry, less fertile soils offering little rooting depth.[8] These are the very qualities one might expect in once heavily grazed, now abandoned pasture on a rocky island in the Gulf of Maine. Prior to pastureland formation by deforestation, white spruce was probably a less prominent member of the forest community, settling for gaps and edges. Pastureland formation and subsequent abandonment provided white spruce the opportunity to greatly increase its footprint on Monhegan, with consequences that will be explored later. An equivalent phenomenon has played out across central and southern New England, where white pine, bearing many of the features of white spruce, but not its cold tolerance, has come to dominate abandoned farmland.

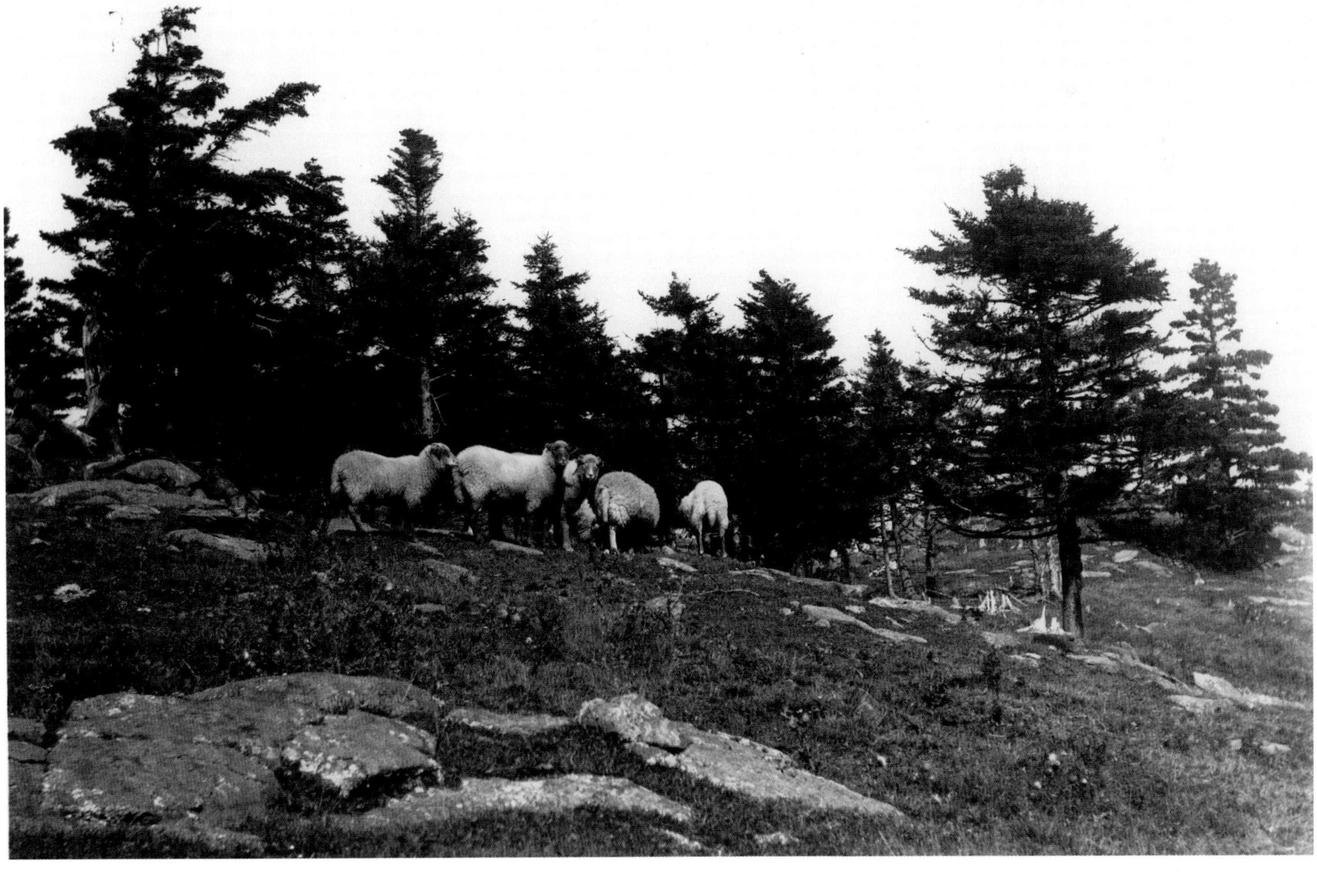

Bertrand Wentworth (1868–1955), *The Last Tree*, ca. 1915. Gelatin silver print, 11½ x 13⅜ inches. Monhegan Museum of Art & History. Gift of Clark H. Gleason

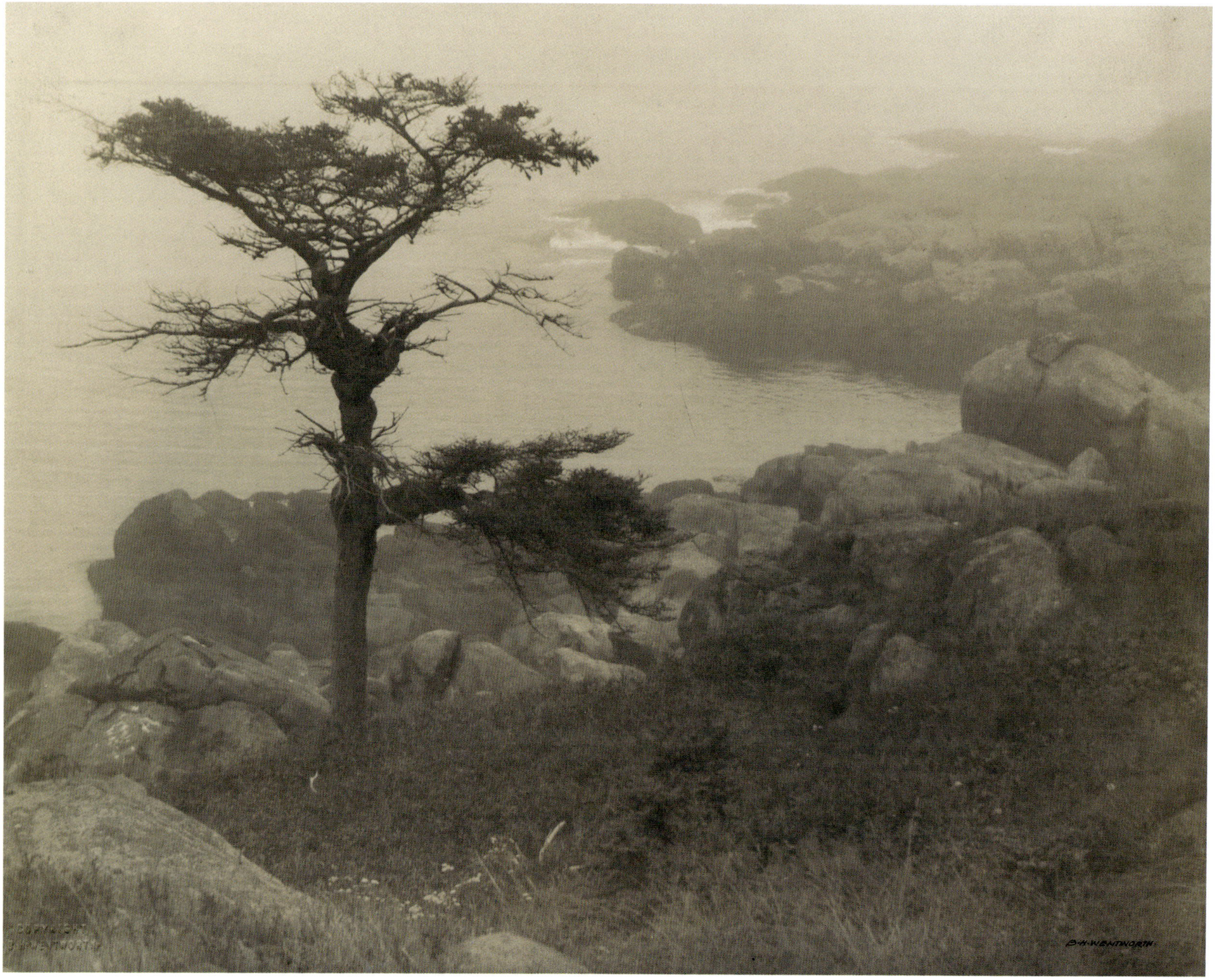

Edward Knowlton (1860–1964), *White Head from Burnt Head*, 1897. Gelatin silver print, 8¾ x 11⅛ inches. Monhegan Museum of Art & History. Gift of Leo and Berniece Meissner

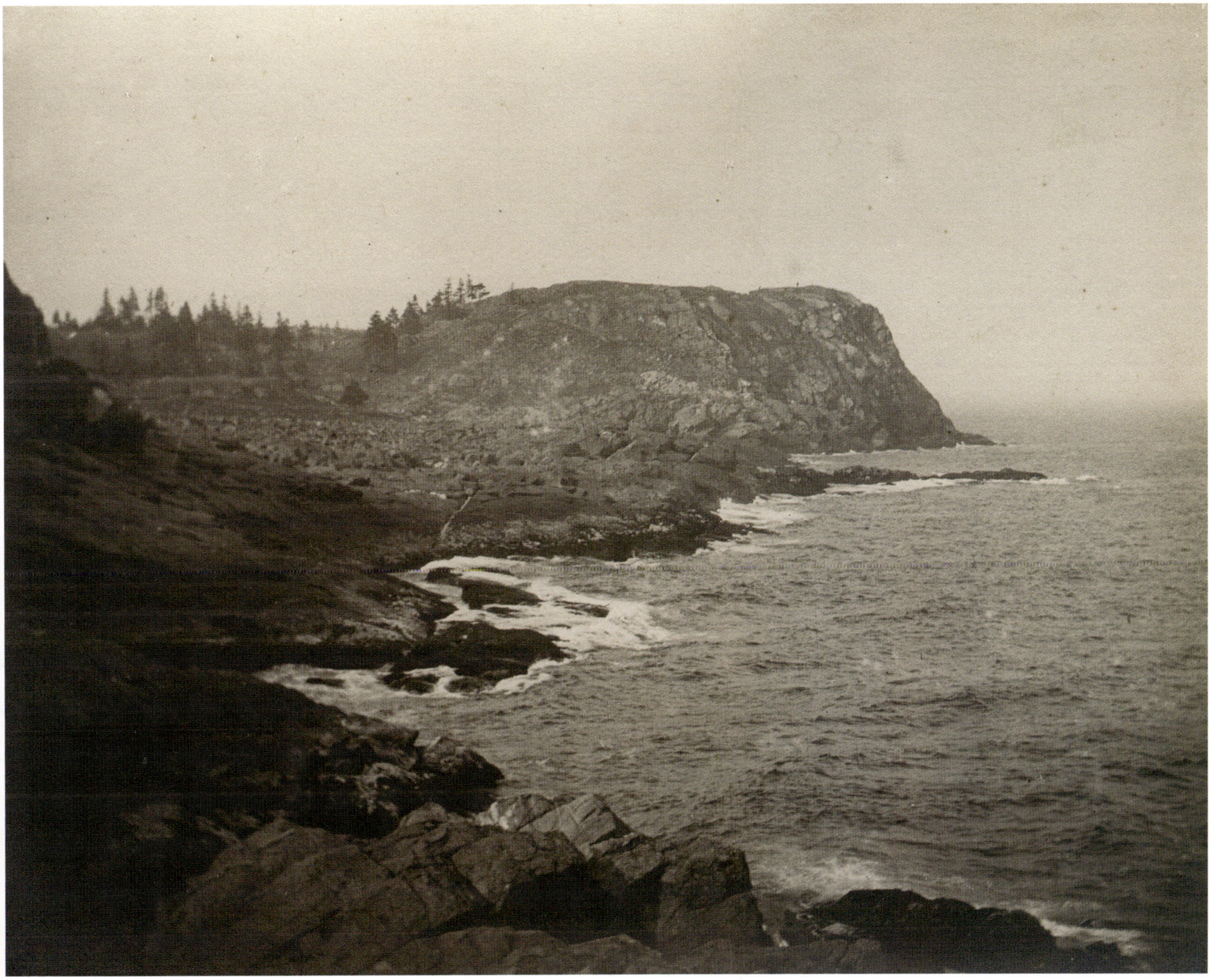

Monhegan's Forest Health

William Livingston, Director of the School of Forest Resources, University of Maine at Orono

Cathedral Woods. Say that to those who know the forests of Monhegan Island, and many will picture a quiet, majestic scene of tall red spruce filtering the sun's rays down to a forest floor of ferns, mosses, and young trees. The feeling is timeless, and there is a sense that the setting will exist forever. Expand the perspective to view the island, and you will see a mosaic of buildings, wetlands, and woods with trees of multiple species and different sizes, some of which are dying. This is a dynamic landscape that begins to reveal the true nature of Monhegan's forests.

I first came to Monhegan in 2000 in response to a request to investigate why so many spruce trees had died on the island during the previous ten years. What killed the trees was simple to see: a fascinating plant parasite that grows inside the twigs, creating "witches' brooms" of branches that draw energy from the rest of the tree. Like a cancerous tumor, the dwarf mistletoe infection becomes severe enough to be fatal. However, understanding why the trees died, why the dwarf mistletoe could kill trees on one part of the island but not in Cathedral Woods, was not such an easy question to answer.

To find the answer, one needed to consider not only the whole island perspective but also the island through time. By looking at old pictures of Monhegan, by viewing old maps drawn by residents, clues could be assembled to clarify the dynamics of its landscape. Maps and pictures created near the turn of the twentieth century show open fields for sheep, while those created in later decades do not. White spruce began to grow on the abandoned fields but were widely spaced because few other tree species could survive the competition with the grasses for water. The eastern dwarf mistletoe, which can also be found on red spruce in Cathedral Woods, followed the white spruce. While the red spruce can tolerate and outgrow the plant parasite, the white spruce, which is a more vulnerable host, offered abundant healthy branches for infection. The parasite could easily shoot its seed from one tree to the next, and thus over several decades, the witches' brooms continued to develop. Eventually, the white spruce trees began to die and were either removed or left to decay in the old fields.

This story was a revelation for me. A tree health problem was clearly related to changes in the landscape over time due to human use. Normally, native trees, pests, and pathogens do not interact to cause mortality of mature forests. You can see the natural interactions, that is, the interactions that evolved over time, in Monhegan's Cathedral Woods. There, white spruce remain on forest margins of the island shores, and red spruce dominate the interior, shaded forest. Dwarf mistletoe could survive in the red spruce forest without being fatal to the trees and yet probably killed scattered white spruce along the forest margins.

Historic forest clearing for agriculture and grazing left fields dominated by grasses. When these fields were abandoned, the new interactions among grass, white spruce, and dwarf mistletoe resulted in the unprecedented die-off of the spruce.

After disturbances, landscapes will continue through a succession of species that are adapted to the changing conditions. In the old fields of Monhegan, for example, trees continued to regenerate, and the initial stands of white spruce created conditions (less grass, more shade) favorable to other tree species—such as red spruce, balsam fir, mountain ash, and aspen—enabling them, in turn, to regenerate. This more diverse, dense forest will reduce the incidence of dwarf mistletoe and future tree mortality.

Unfortunately, forest disturbance can favor the development of invasive, non-native woody plants. In addition, past populations of deer on the island would graze on native vegetation but leave the less palatable invasive plants. On Monhegan, for example, Japanese barberry, a non-native plant, has colonized many parts of the island because the deer did not eat it. The removal of the island's deer population by 1999, combined with active attempts at eradication, reduced the threat of invasive species.

The residents of Monhegan value the forests but also want to protect human-built structures from potential forest fires. On the island, there is active discussion about whether intervention, such as removing invasive plants and fire hazards, is necessary. As in the past, human actions will impact the future of Monhegan's forest dynamics. If no future interventions are made, Cathedral Woods will continue to develop as an old-growth red spruce forest. The cool, moist maritime environment is ideal for red spruce and should buffer the forest from the potential stress of higher temperatures and drought associated with climate change that will affect the red spruce forests of inland Maine. The forests on the old fields will slowly go through succession and become more like Cathedral Woods. The risk of dwarf mistletoe mortality will be restricted to scattered white spruce at the forest margins, and increased fire risk due to dwarf mistletoe infections will not return. Nonetheless, other dangers exist. A storm could cause a massive blowdown of trees, and the spruce bark beetle will become more of a threat to spruce as the trees increase in size and age. Such disturbances could increase fire risk and the need to choose between removing dead trees or letting them lie. If the invasive Japanese barberry is left unchecked, it will slowly replace the native understory species in some locations. What Monhegan's forests will look like in the future, how they will inspire future artists, will continue to be influenced by natural dynamics and human stewardship.

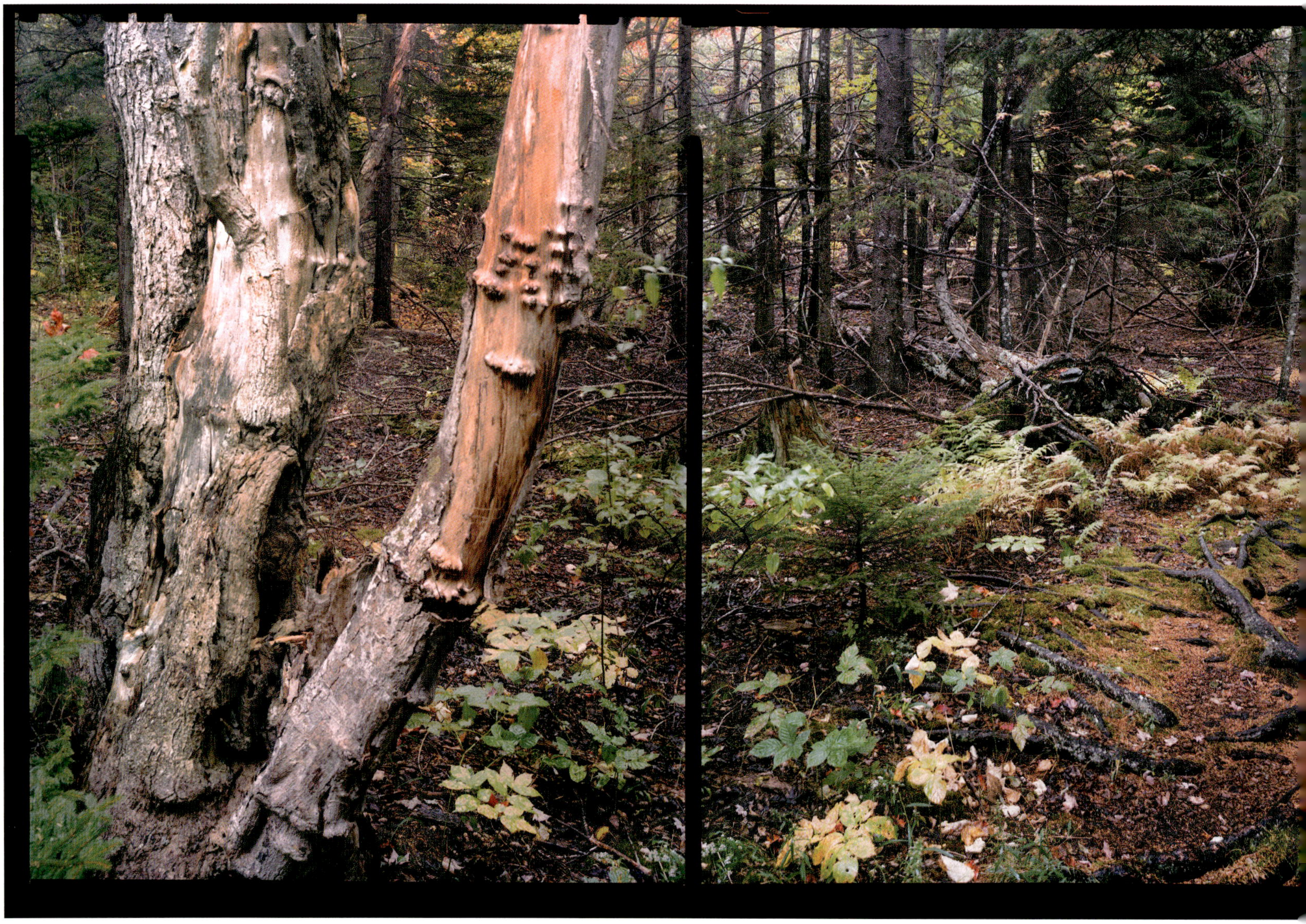

Accra Shepp (born 1962),
Knotty Tree, Maple Trail,
2022. Archival pigment ink
print. Courtesy of the artist

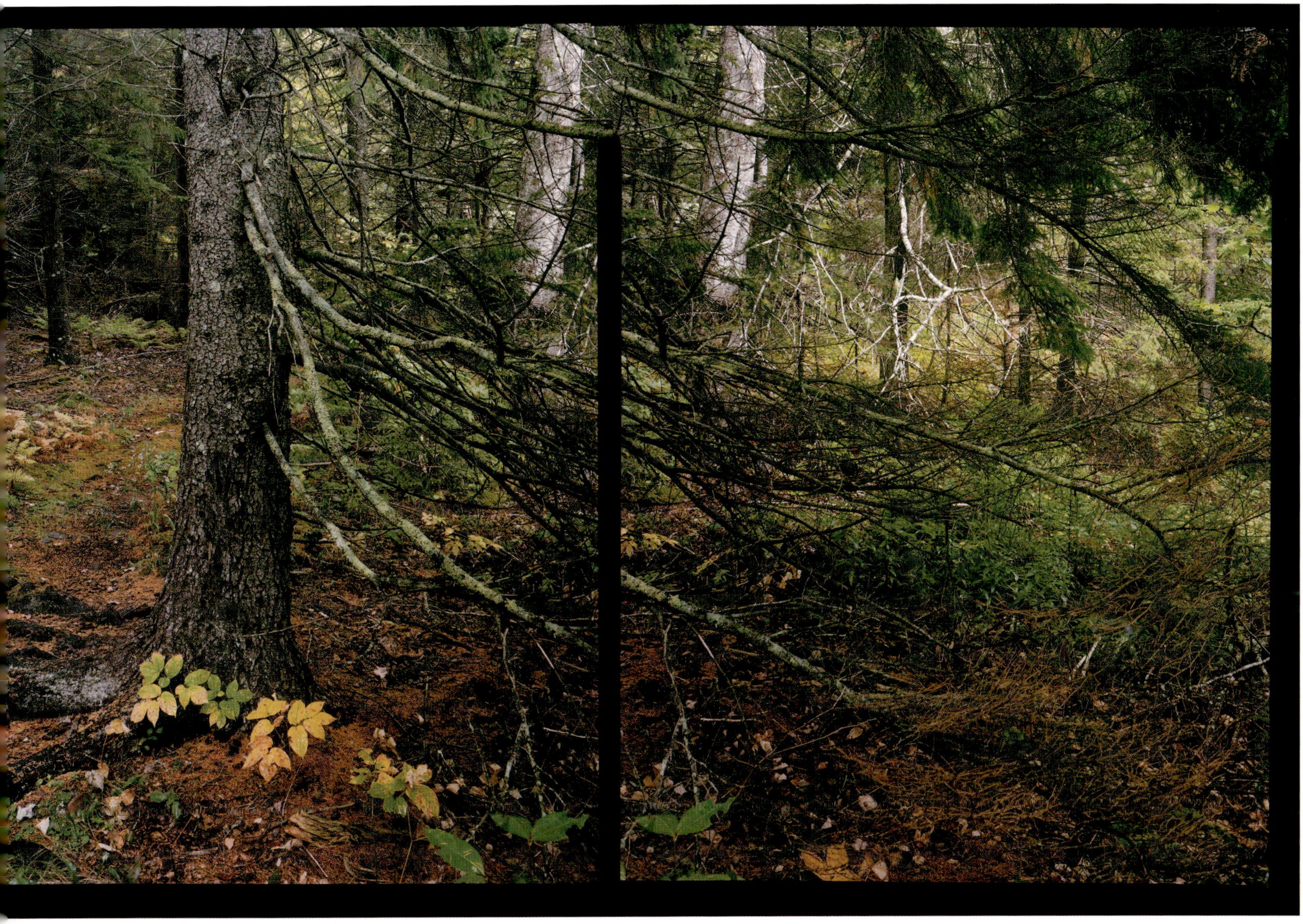

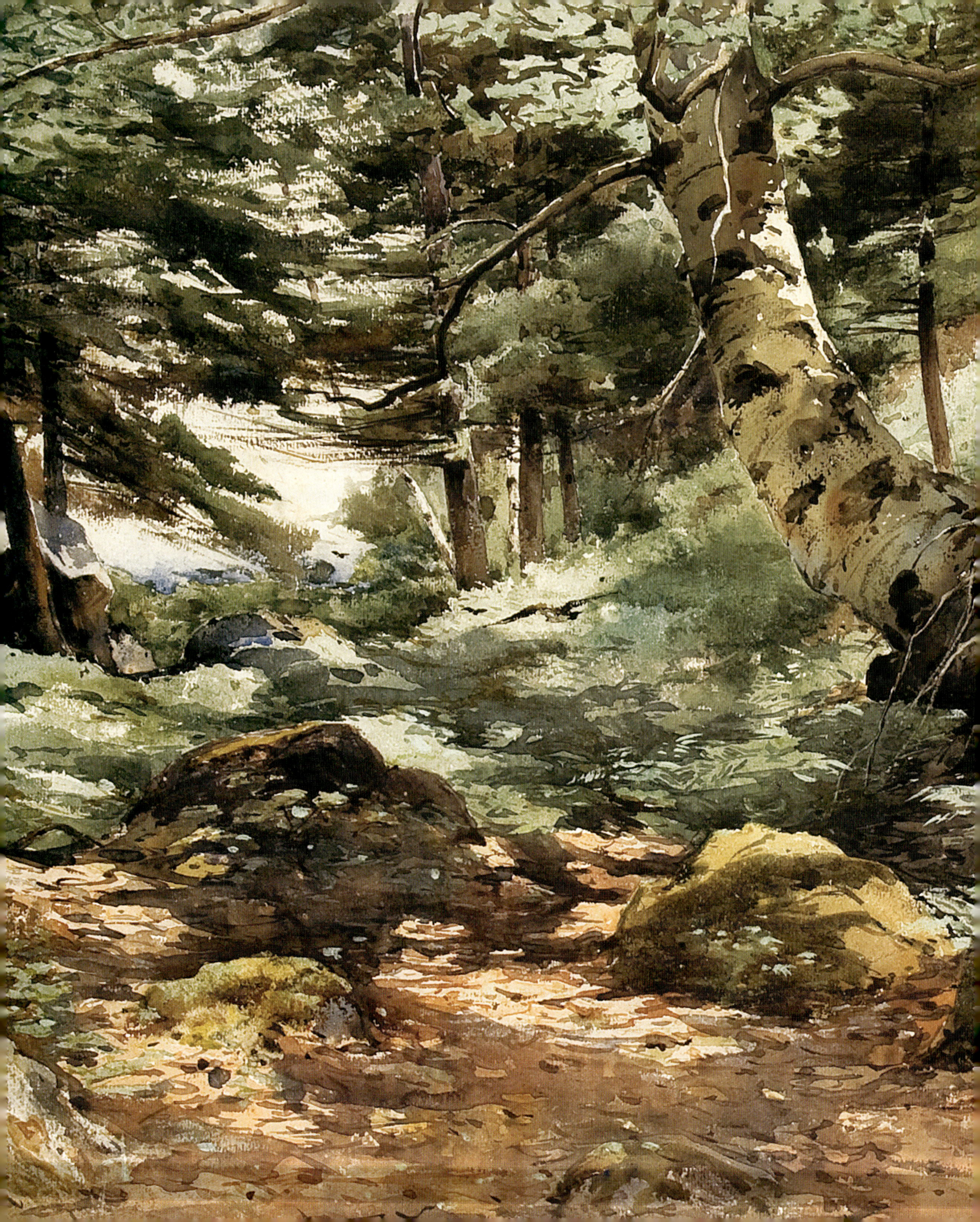

Chapter 2

Retreat of the Ice Sheet to Ongoing Year-Round Settlement of Monhegan and Maine Statehood, circa 20,000 Years before the Present to 1820

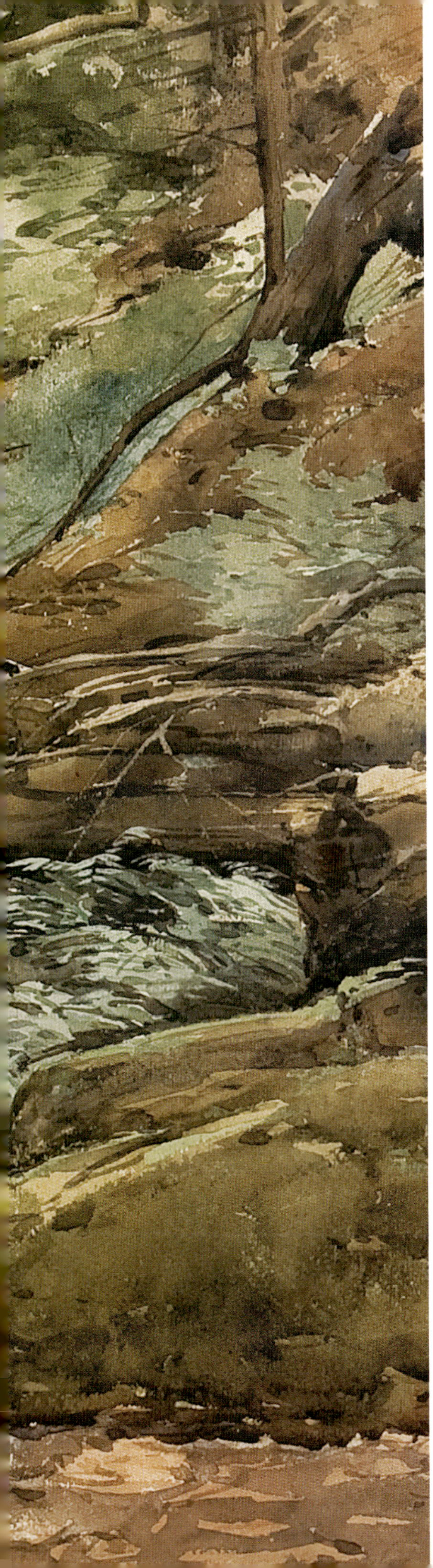

The timeless appearance of Monhegan, a whaleback island far out to sea, with its soaring headlands and Cathedral Woods, belies its dynamic deep history. Twenty thousand years ago, the landmass known today as Monhegan may have been a part of the mainland, although this would have been hard to discern, as ice more than a mile thick—the Laurentide ice sheet—capped the region. That ice formed when changes in the tilt of the earth's axis reduced sunlight exposure near the poles. The earth was further ushered into this ice age by shifts in the boundaries and positions of continents, driven by plate tectonics, which weakened the currents that might otherwise have delivered warm tropical waters to the poles. As snow fell at northerly latitudes through millennia and was pressed into accumulating ice, its sheer weight led a glacial front to exude southward, reaching as far as Martha's Vineyard and New York's Long Island and scouring vegetation, soil, and surface material in its path.

In time, the ever-changing tilt of the earth's axis once again favored warmer and longer summers, which broke the grip of this most recent ice age. Ice melt outpaced accumulation and glaciers began their retreat. Monhegan emerged from the ice sometime between seventeen thousand

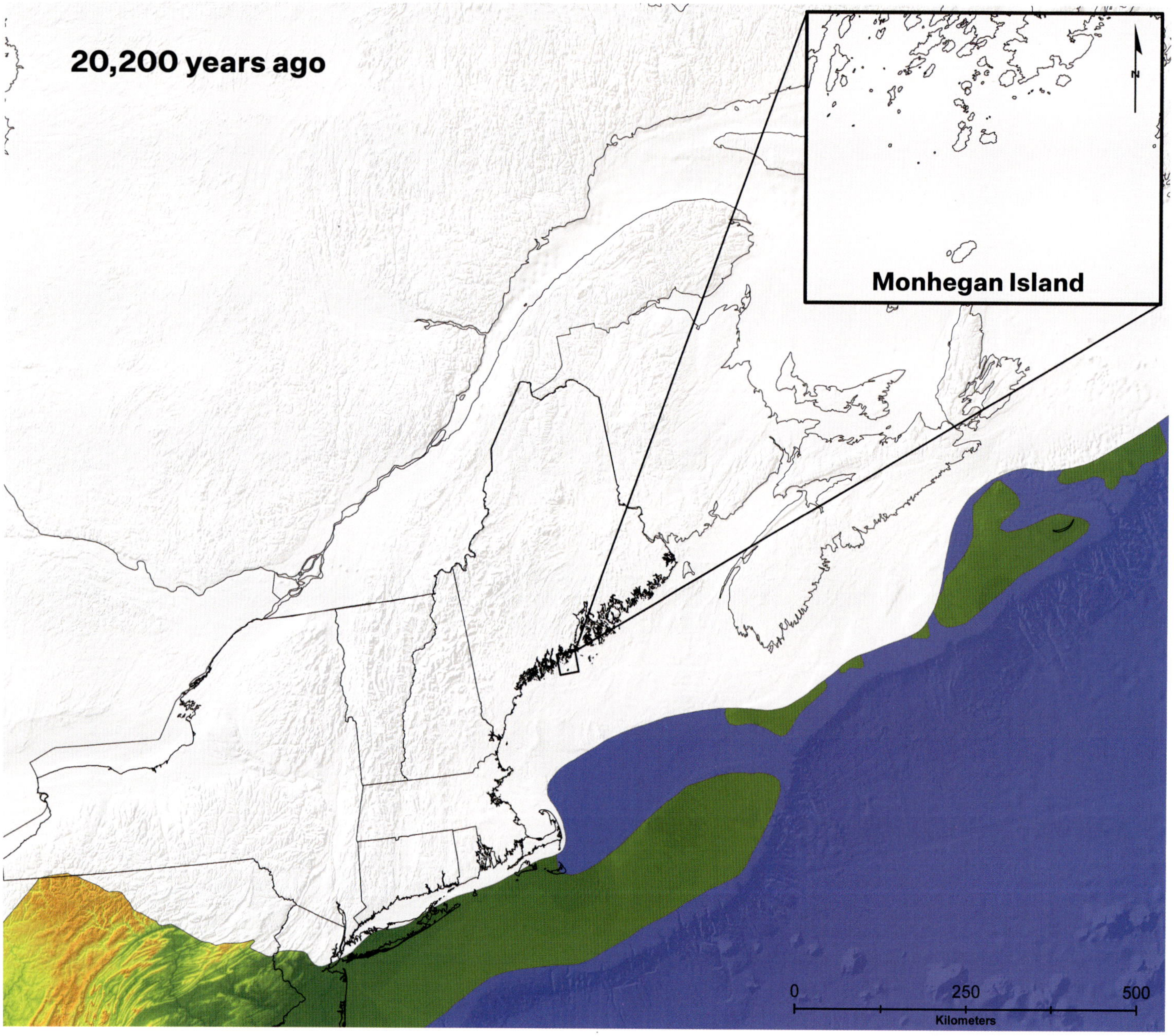

and thirteen thousand years ago. Competing forces dictated whether Monhegan and the broader region were above or below sea level at any given historical moment. Melting ice resulted in sea-level rise, favoring inundation. “Crustal rebound” operated in opposition. During the peak of the ice age, the mass of ice had compressed the earth’s crust, just as a heavy weight might crush a foam pad. When glacial retreat lifted that weight, the earth’s crust rebounded.[1]

At some point not long—geologically speaking—after Monhegan emerged from the surrounding sea, the present-day forests of the Wildlands got their start. What did those early forests look like? This is a natural question to pose in any conservation effort. To answer it, ecologists turn to clues left behind in

Susan Winchell-Sweeney, New York State Museum, "20,200 Years Ago," 2019. Adapted from map created for "Early Human Settlement of Northeastern America," by Jonathan C. Lothrop, Darrin L. Lowry, Arthur E. Speiss, and Christopher J. Ellis, in *PaleoAmerica* 2, no. 3 (2016). This map shows the greatest extent of the Laurentide ice sheet.

the form of pollen grains. These tiny, almost microscopic grains contain cells akin to sperm. When transferred from one plant to another, pollen allows plants to perform sexual reproduction despite being immovably rooted in the ground. Many plant species produce pollen copiously, lofting it in the wind in hopes that some grains will reach their target. Most, of course, will not. On Monhegan, some pollen blows into the Meadow, the island's most prominent body of fresh water, where it sinks, contributing to the accumulation of sediment. Pollen grains are remarkably resistant to decay, remaining intact for millennia, as layer upon layer of sediment accumulates with time. Moreover, the pollen grains of a given plant species can be distinguished from pollen of other species. By examining sediment, and then isolating, identifying, and censusing the pollen, one can reconstruct the history of the plant community on the surrounding land.

In the 1970s, Lisa Gay Bostwick, at the time a researcher at the University of Maine at Orono, did precisely this on Monhegan, extracting a forty-two-foot-long plug of sediment from the Meadow. She then employed carbon-14 dating to determine the age of the sediment layers, and used microscopy and botanical expertise to decipher the story preserved within. She discovered that the deep history of Monhegan's forests is one of dynamism not stasis. Spruce trees, which dominated the first postglacial forests on Monhegan, bear a striking resemblance to the trees in today's Cathedral Woods. Pines then established dominance as cold and moist conditions gave way to cool, drier conditions. Hemlocks, birches, and oaks established themselves during a relatively warm and wet period approximately eight thousand to five thousand years ago. An ensuing warm and drier period witnessed increasing dominance by birches. That is curious, as birches are not especially suited to such conditions. Bostwick suggests that a quirk of these pollen studies may explain the prevalence of birches in the record over this period. Those warm, dry conditions may have lowered the water levels of the Meadow, transforming it into a swamp dominated by shrubby birches. Cooler, moist conditions, and the spruce that favor them, returned within the most recent two millennia.[2]

On Monhegan, prevailing climate conditions during this twelve-millennia period largely mirror those of the broader New England region, although Monhegan's climate was also influenced by local maritime conditions and the formation and collapse of ocean currents.[3] This oceanic dynamism was driven by forces including alterations in the size and shape of the Gulf of Maine that were controlled by changes in sea level, which influenced access to warm southerly waters and dictated the strength of the tides. Grasses appear as major contributors to Bostwick's pollen record about four hundred years ago, just when the human historical record suggests that the creation of pasture on Monhegan began in earnest.

Mirjami Tolonen of the University of Helsinki picked up this line of inquiry in the 1980s, examining the uppermost forty inches of accumulated peat in the Meadow for evidence of human land use and transformation over the past four centuries. Barley and corn pollen appear in peat layers laid down in the seventeenth century, along with charred particles generally associated with land clearance employing burning.[4] This discovery is consistent with historical evidence that the earliest settlers of European descent cultivated crops on Monhegan. An increase in grass pollen through the eighteenth century reveals

Reconstructing Monhegan's Ancient Forests: The Pollen Record

Pollen is typically carried by wind between trees but most misses its target. Some pollen grains land in water and sink to the bottom, where they persist in the sediment. Pollen grain appearance can be used to determine the source tree identity.

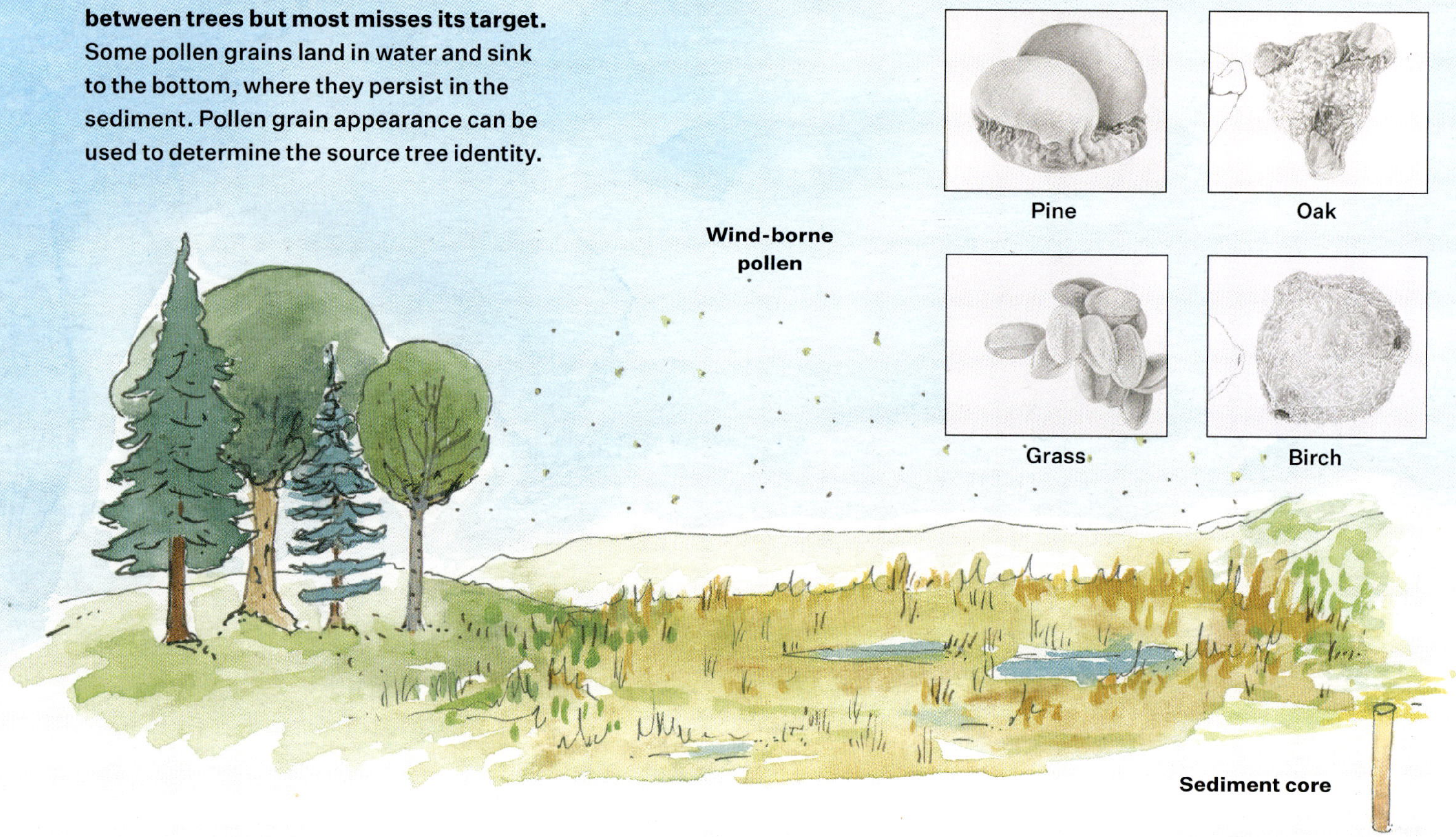

Monhegan's primary source of freshwater holds 12,000 years of island forest history.
The Meadow at the center of the village is a peat bog with thick sediment. This ancient wetland has collected pollen since the last ice age. Examining sediment layers can paint a picture of past Monhegan forest composition.

Surface: current time

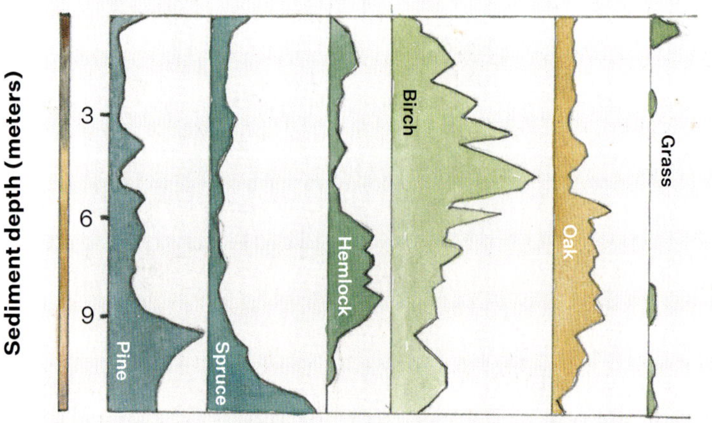

Bedrock: 12,000 years ago

Thickness conveys pollen contribution of each tree type to the sediment at each depth

An ever-changing forest is revealed.
Over time, forest composition shifted from spruce to pine dominance, which gave way to oaks, hemlocks, and birches, eventually returning to spruce and firs.

These changes were influenced by a shifting regional climate and local effects driven by the formation and collapse of currents in the Gulf of Maine.

Grass pollen appears in large numbers only in recent centuries with settlement and pasture formation.

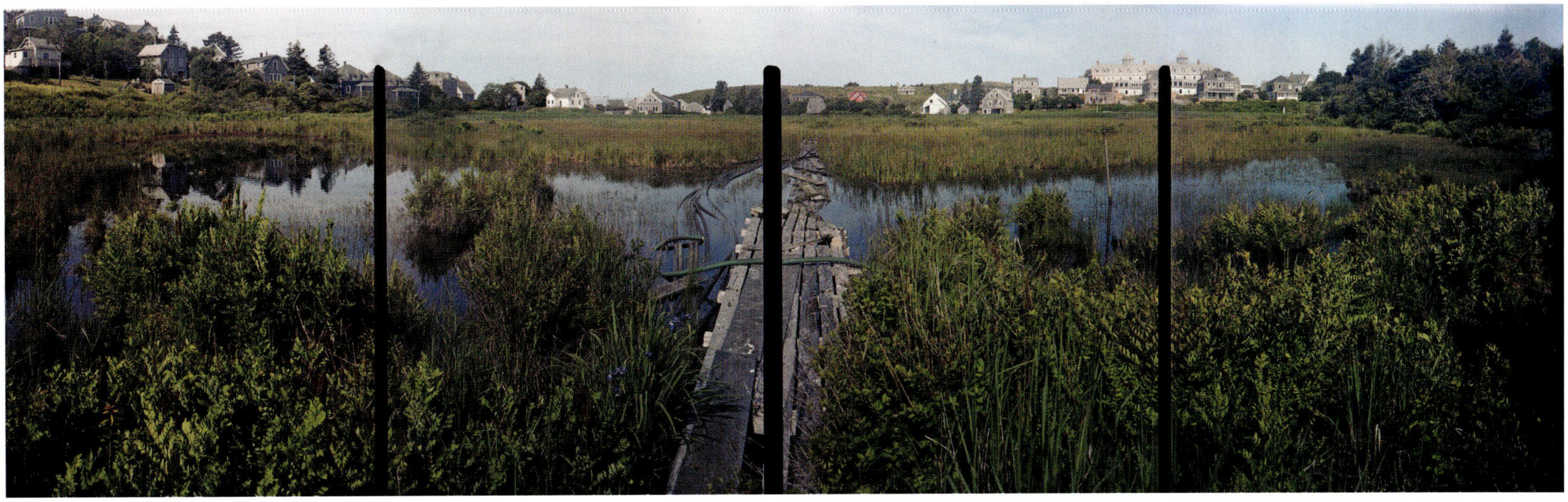

Accra Shepp (born 1962),
The Meadow, 2023.
Archival pigment ink print.
Courtesy of the artist

the expansion of pastoral activity, as does an increase in mineral matter washing into the Meadow, which resulted from erosion, a common consequence of deforestation. Intensively grazed pastures served as havens for familiar introduced weed species such as ragweed and dandelion. The pollen of juniper, an unpalatable evergreen shrub that favors the bare patches created by heavy grazing, also appears in the record at this time. To this day, junipers remain a feature of the plant community in once-grazed secondary forests of the island. At the beginning of the twentieth century, evidence of forest recovery appears with a decline in so-called ruderal plants (that is, those plants inhabiting disturbed ground). Taken together, the pollen and associated records show that no lasting forest archetype was ever found on Monhegan. Instead, change prevailed, as it does today, although the pace of change over the past few centuries far exceeds that of the deeper past.

The ancestors of today's Wabanaki nations have lived on this region's lands for more than thirteen thousand years. Humans arrived approximately one thousand years after the ice sheet's retreat and eventually created communities all along the Gulf of Maine shoreline. Because of sea-level rise, the oldest coastal sites today are about five thousand years old; most are younger than 3,500 years. Over the past century, in the course of their work, fishers, especially scallop draggers, have pulled up stone tools that indicate encampments at locations that are now underwater.[5] Tools have also been discovered on Monhegan. Archaeological evidence suggests that humans established seasonal camps on the island. As Penobscot historian and University of Maine professor John Bear Mitchell explores in the essay that accompanies this chapter, Monhegan was historically used as a base for swordfish and mackerel fishing. Though these coastal communities might have subsisted on other more easily obtained maritime food sources, they ventured offshore in canoes to pursue larger and more elusive fish.

As one of the largest islands in the Gulf of Maine, Monhegan was no stranger to Indigenous peoples, or to the earliest European sailors who crossed the Atlantic. Indeed, with a hill that rises 160 feet above the high-tide line and prominent headlands on its east side, the island was highly visible. A protected harbor made it especially attractive, as did its ready supply of freshwater and timber. Located in the center of what was then one of the most bountiful fishing grounds on the East Coast of North America, the island was known to many during the early years of European travel and exploration in the North Atlantic. The Norse and Irish fished in the region at least a thousand years ago, and it is probable that some might have harbored and resupplied on the island.[6]

While Christopher Columbus's four trips across the Atlantic between 1492 and 1504 did not bring him into the Gulf of Maine, many of the European explorers who followed shortly thereafter did venture into the region. A map drawn by Castilian navigator Juan de la Cosa in 1500 depicts an unnamed island where Monhegan is located. Over the next century, during a period characterized by intense international rivalries and war among several European nations, Monhegan became more widely known. In 1524, Florentine sailor Giovanni da Verrazzano gave the island its first non-native name: Anne, after a French princess, the daughter of the duc d'Albret and his wife, the queen of Navarre. As Spain, France, and England, among others, vied for land in North America and initiated colonial enterprises, Monhegan was increasingly considered a desirable island in a much larger territory.

The Wabanaki likely continued to utilize Monhegan as a seasonal fishing station during this period, though they were eventually displaced by European newcomers. By the beginning of the seventeenth century, European explorers saw the island, as well as the larger region, as a target for possession and a place where they might establish a permanent settlement. With the defeat of the Spanish Armada in 1588, British and French maritime activities increased in the North Atlantic. Various expeditions explored the coast, and several either sailed by or stopped at Monhegan. In 1605, two such adventurers recorded their visits, and each gave the island a new name. British explorer George Weymouth named it Saint George in honor of his nation's patron saint. Later in the same year, his French rival Samuel de Champlain sailed through Muscongus Bay and named the island La Nef, thinking it resembled a great ship.

James Rosier, a member of Weymouth's party aboard the ship *Archangel*, left the first detailed written record of the island, a place he believed the "most fortunate euer yet discouered." Rosier's account provides a description of the ship's arrival and the island's forested lands:

> About twelve a clocke that day, we came to an anker on the North side of this Iland, about a league from the shore. About two a clocke our Captaine with twelue men rowed in his ship boat to the shore, where we made no long stay, but laded our boat with dry wood of olde trees upon the shoreside and returned to our ship, where we rode that night. This Iland is woody, grouen with Firre, Birch, Oke, and Beech, as farre as we saw along the shore; and so likely to be within. On the verge grow Gooseberries, Strawberries, Wild pease, and Wild rose bushes. The water issued forth down the Rocky cliffs in many places: and much fowl of divers kinds breed upon the shores and rocks.[7]

This description suggests that, at this time, Monhegan was home to a mature forest composed of a mix of broad-leafed deciduous trees and conifers.

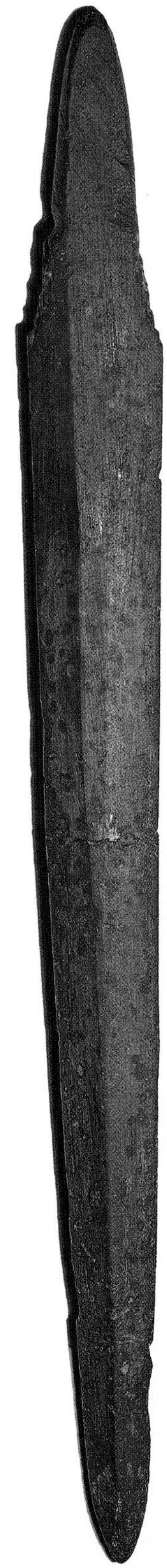

Ground slate bayonet, archaic period. Monhegan Museum of Art & History. Ron Stanley Collection, gift of Mary Stanley

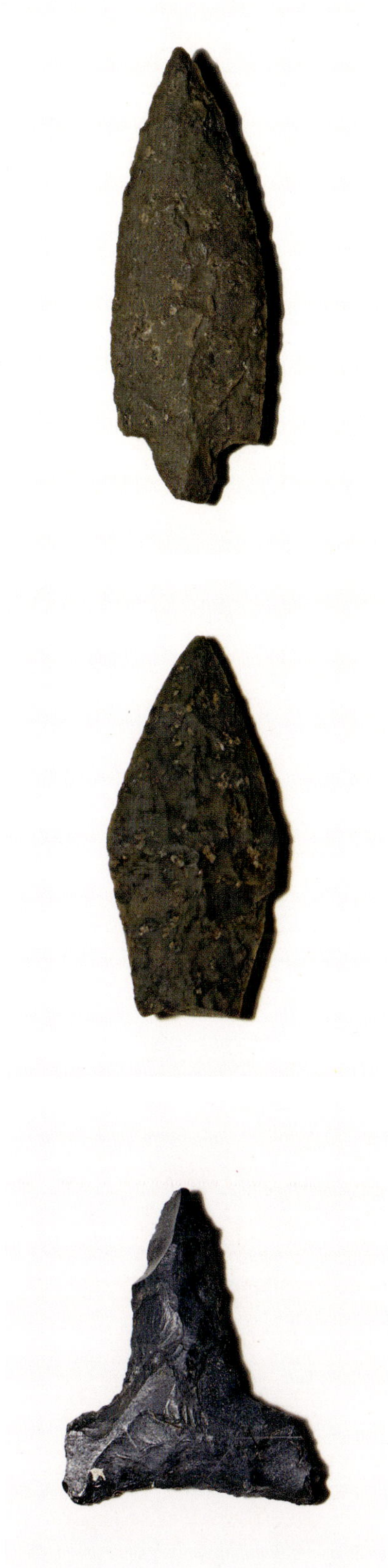

Top to bottom: Retracting stem point, ceramic period; retracting stem point, archaic period; and flaked drill. Monhegan Museum of Art & History. Ron Stanley Collection, gift of Mary Stanley

No large mammals were known to exist on the island. The forest grew largely undisturbed, apart from the occasional ship that landed to resupply. What was disturbed during this period, however, were the relations between these visitors and the Indigenous nations of the region. When Weymouth returned to England, he left with five Wabanaki men aboard, having forcibly abducted them from their homes. Though the men were later able to return, this and other interactions led to an increasing pattern of discord and conflict that continued largely unresolved for centuries thereafter.

English and French settlements also began to appear in the region. A year prior to Weymouth's visit to Monhegan, French explorer Pierre Du Gua, sieur de Monts, entered the Bay of Fundy and established a short-lived colony on Saint Croix Island. In 1607, the same year that English settlers from the Virginia Company of London settled in Jamestown, George Popham and Raleigh Gilbert led a party of 120 English settlers to the mouth of the Kennebec River, only a short distance from Monhegan, where they attempted to establish a permanent community. Though the men constructed the first English-built ship in North America during their time there, various challenges, including Wabanaki resistance, forced Popham and Gilbert to abandon this settlement the following year.

Also, during this period, English explorer Captain John Smith landed on Monhegan in 1614 with two ships and forty men. Smith had played an important role in the establishment of Jamestown seven years earlier, though he left the community after several years. In 1614, he resumed his explorations in a region he later named New England. During this summer, he spent ten weeks on the island, which he named Barty, after the English family on whose estate he had been born. As before, he did not stay long, though his followers founded a fishing station that lasted a decade or two. In 1616, desirous of promoting settlement in North America, Smith authored a book-length description of New England in which he wrote effusively about the available abundant natural resources. About the region where Monhegan resided, he explained that "this Coast is all Mountainous and Iles of huge Rocks, but ouergrowen with all sorts of excellent good woodes for building houses, boats, barks or shippes; with an incredible abundance of most sorts of fish, much fowle, and sundry sorts of good fruites for mans vse." Later he explored in greater detail the variety of trees: "Oke is the chiefe wood; of which there is great difference in regard of the soyle where it growth. Firre, pyne, walnut, chesnut, birch, ash, elme, cypresse, ceder, mulberrie, plumtree, hazell, saxefrage, and many other sorts."[8] Like Rosier before him, Smith witnessed a rich and diverse forest ecology.

After the Smith expedition's extended stay on Monhegan during the spring and summer of 1614, the island attracted numerous English fishing vessels. In 1622, Abraham Jennings, a wealthy merchant and fisherman who helped establish the English colony of Plymouth in Massachusetts, became the first individual to hold a land grant for the island. He did not settle there, though during the first year of the Plymouth colony, when food was scarce, residents from Monhegan assisted by sending supplies to their compatriots to the south. The fishing station closed in 1626 when Jennings sold the island for £50 to two English merchants, Abraham Aldworth and his nephew Gyles Elbridge, who were then amassing a sizable private landholding centered in Pemaquid on the mainland. Over the next century and a half, Monhegan's ownership changed

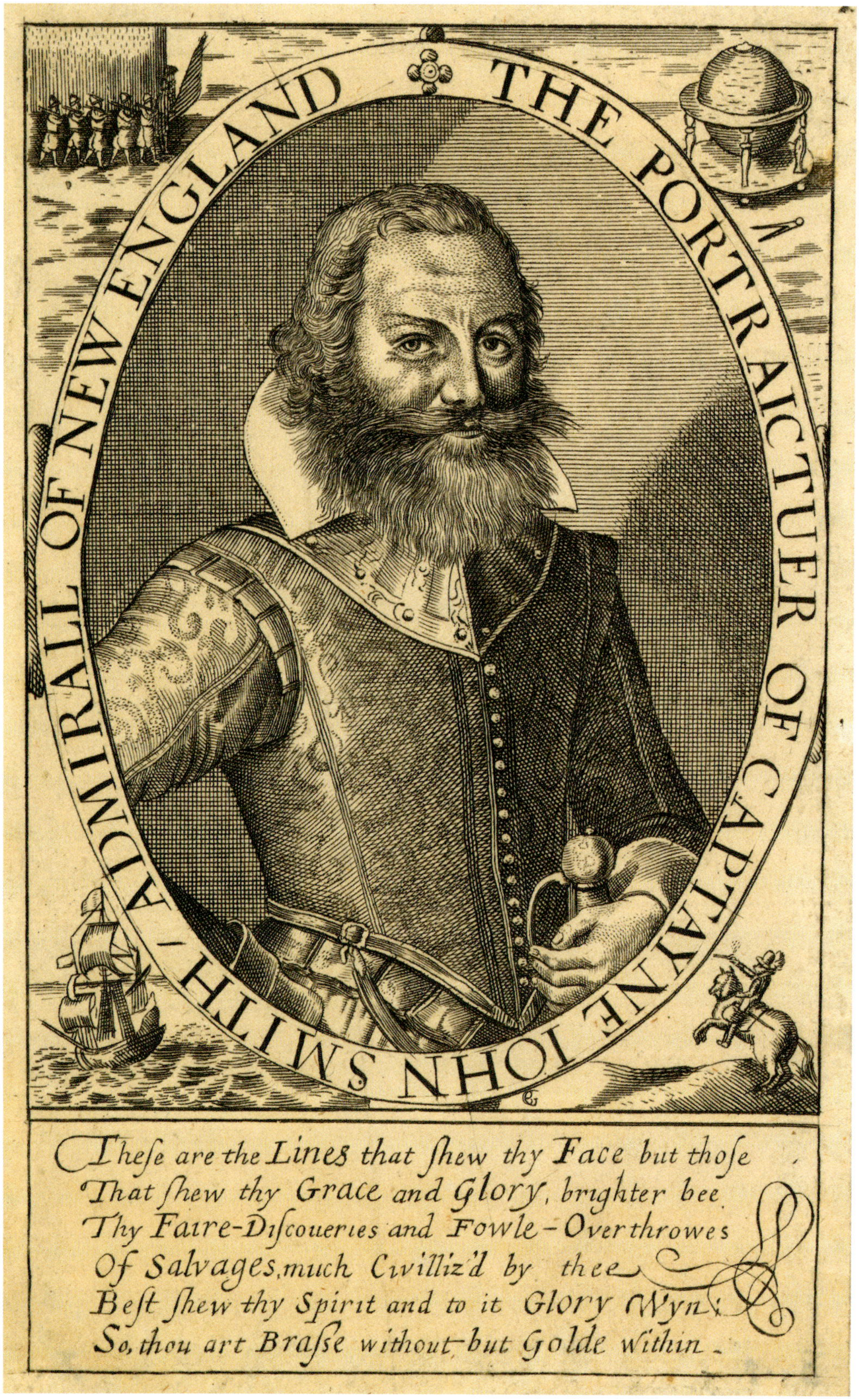

Unidentified artist, possibly after Simon de Passe (ca. 1595–1647), *John Smith*, ca. 1617. Engraving, 5⅞ x 3⅝ inches, National Portrait Gallery, Smithsonian Institution

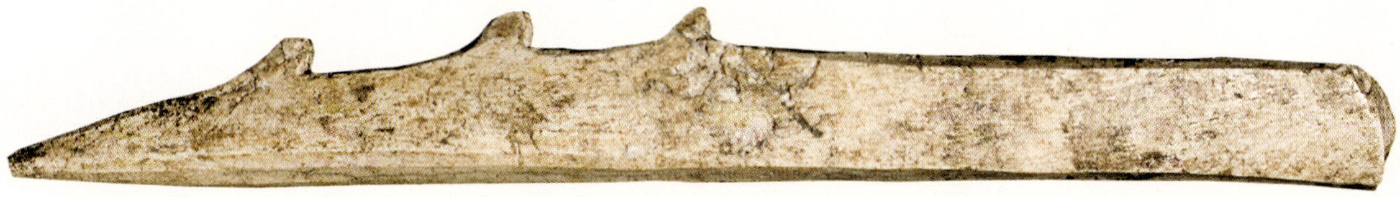

Bone harpoon, ceramic period. Monhegan Museum of Art & History. Ron Stanley Collection, gift of Mary Stanley

hands among various English land speculators six times. None were especially interested in establishing a permanent settlement.

Throughout the seventeenth century and in the first two-thirds of the eighteenth, the French vied with the English for control of the lands along the Gulf of Maine coast. They were often allied in this contest with the Wabanaki, who rued the presence of both European powers, though tended to prefer the French over the English. Beginning in 1634, the French claimed all land east of Pemaquid; later in the century, they drew their boundary line farther west at the Kennebec River. Until the signing of the Treaty of Paris in 1763, when France surrendered its authority in the region, towns on the mainland were the site of on-again, off-again conflict. Despite the proximity of the Wabanaki and French, fighting did not extend to Monhegan, though on repeat occasions, English settlers at Pemaquid chose to flee to the island for safety. This extended conflict limited Monhegan's growth, and for long stretches of time, few if any people lived there year-round. Given the lucrative market for haddock and cod, however, fishing in the Gulf of Maine remained robust, and Monhegan continued throughout this period to be an important seasonal fishing station.

After 1763, with peace at hand, settlement and trade accelerated throughout New England. Yet, France's defeat exposed a long-concealed rivalry between England and the American colonies, as well as growing friction between the Massachusetts Bay Colony and the Province of Maine, which was first established in 1622. During the latter half of the eighteenth century, Maine's population was smaller than that of its neighbors to the south and less closely aligned to a specific church. Though Maine became one of three districts of Massachusetts in 1778, its political voice and economic concerns during moments of crisis were little respected by those in Boston. In peaceful times, the region was largely ignored. Such divisions eventually led to the decision by Maine residents to separate from Massachusetts, and in 1820, Maine statehood was made official.

On Monhegan, the era of the current settlement began during the same period as the American Revolution. In 1777, Henry Trefethren, the son of Welsh immigrants and a cabinetmaker from Kittery, purchased the island for £300. Shortly thereafter, three of his children—Sarah, Mary, and Henry Jr.—began to build their lives there. They constructed houses, married and had children, and cultivated the land. Though gardens had been built in the past, the new

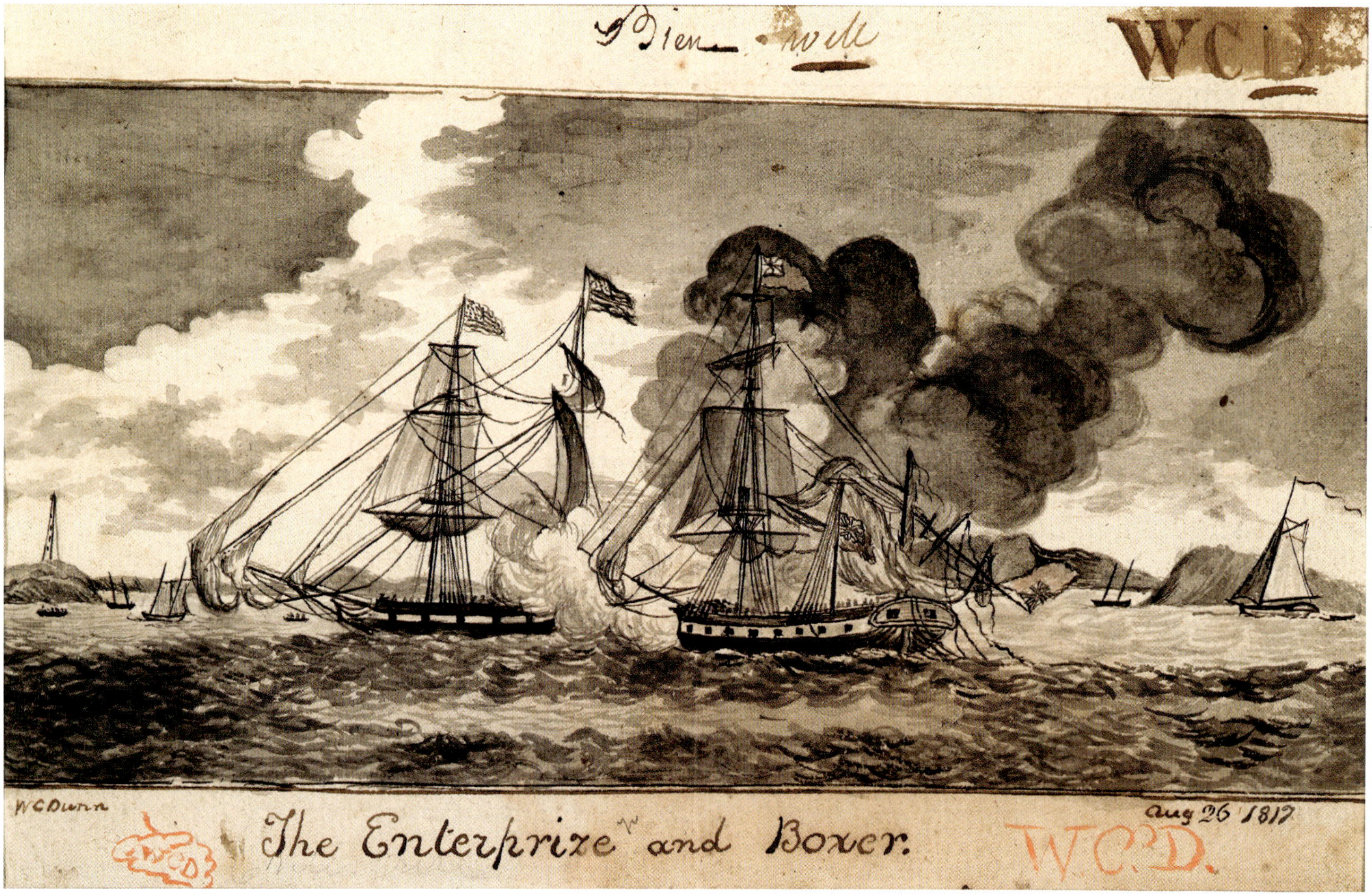

Above: W. C. Dunn, *The Enterprise and Boxer*, 1817. Pen-and-ink on paper, 8 x 10 inches (framed). Naval History and Heritage Command

Opposite: Robert Dudley (1574–1649), *Carta Seconda Generale del' America*, 1646. Etching, 9 x 8¼ inches. Osher Map Library, University of Southern Maine. Osher Collection (OS-1646-2). Monhegan, by an old spelling, is the only named island off the Maine coast.

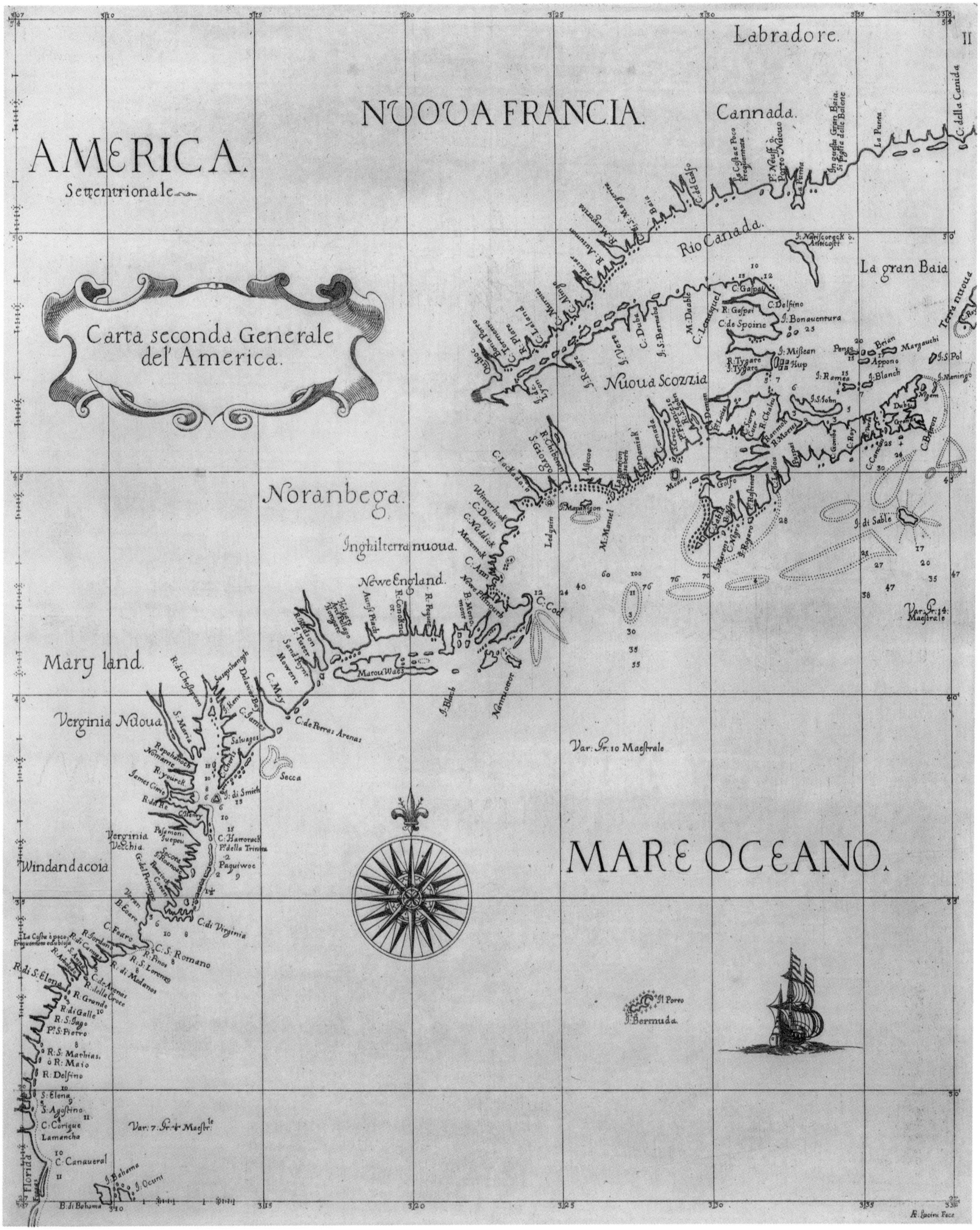
Labradore.
NUOUA FRANCIA.
AMERICA.
Settentrionale
Cannada.
Carta seconda Generale del' America.
Rio Canada.
La gran Baia
Nuoua Scozzia
Noranbega.
Inghilterra nuoua.
Newe England.
Mary land.
Verginia Nuoua
Verginia Vecchia
Windandacoia
Var: Gr. 10 Maestrale
MARE OCEANO.
I. Bermuda.
C: Cod
C: di Virginia
C: Canaueral
Florida
I. di Sable
Matou Wacs
Var: 7. Gr. Maestr.
B: di Bahama
I. Bahama
I. Ocuni
Secca
C. Breton
Terra nuoua
R. Lucini Fece

residents transformed large parcels into plots for growing foodstuffs and for tending livestock. When Trefethren died in 1807, his offspring split the island into five parcels, each to be owned separately. From this point forward, no single individual would own Monhegan in its entirety.

Though American independence had been won, foreign challenges continued, especially in the Atlantic. Like many of the preceding conflicts in North America, the War of 1812 between the Americans and the English was decided in several theaters, including the Gulf of Maine. On September 5, 1813, the two nations fought a naval battle in the waters between Seguin Island and Monhegan. Just a day before, Samuel Blyth, captain of the HMS *Boxer*, stopped on Monhegan and allowed his ship's surgeon and three other men to remain ashore to attend the injured son of Mary (Trefethren) and Josiah Starling—an indication perhaps of the good relations that the current generation of islanders maintained with others. The four Englishmen and the island residents watched from atop a high hill as the USS *Enterprise*, under the command of William Burrows, fought a pitched battle against the *Boxer*. Both captains died in the exchange of cannon fire, though ultimately, the *Enterprise* prevailed. This victory was much celebrated locally and nationally and helped affirm American control over New England waters.

An ink sketch of the battle drawn four years later shows the two ships exchanging cannon fire. At the left edge of the drawing, the Seguin Island Light Station, originally built in 1795, appears. At the right edge, an island with high cliffs rises out of Muscongus Bay. The artist W. C. Dunn provides few details about this landmass, though one might surmise it represents Monhegan. If so, the drawing is the first non-cartographic depiction of the island. Over the next century, Monhegan would become a well-known haven for artists from near and far. Their images shaped the wider public's understanding of this place. Today they also help reveal dramatic changes in the ecological history of the island.

Joseph F. W. Des Barres (1721–1824), *Coast of Maine—From Spurwink River to Moose Point, or, from Musketo Island to Cape Elizabeth, including Kennebec River*, 1777. Engraving, 41 x 29 inches. Osher Map Library and Smith Center for Cartographic Education, University of Southern Maine. Osher Collection (OS-1777-5)

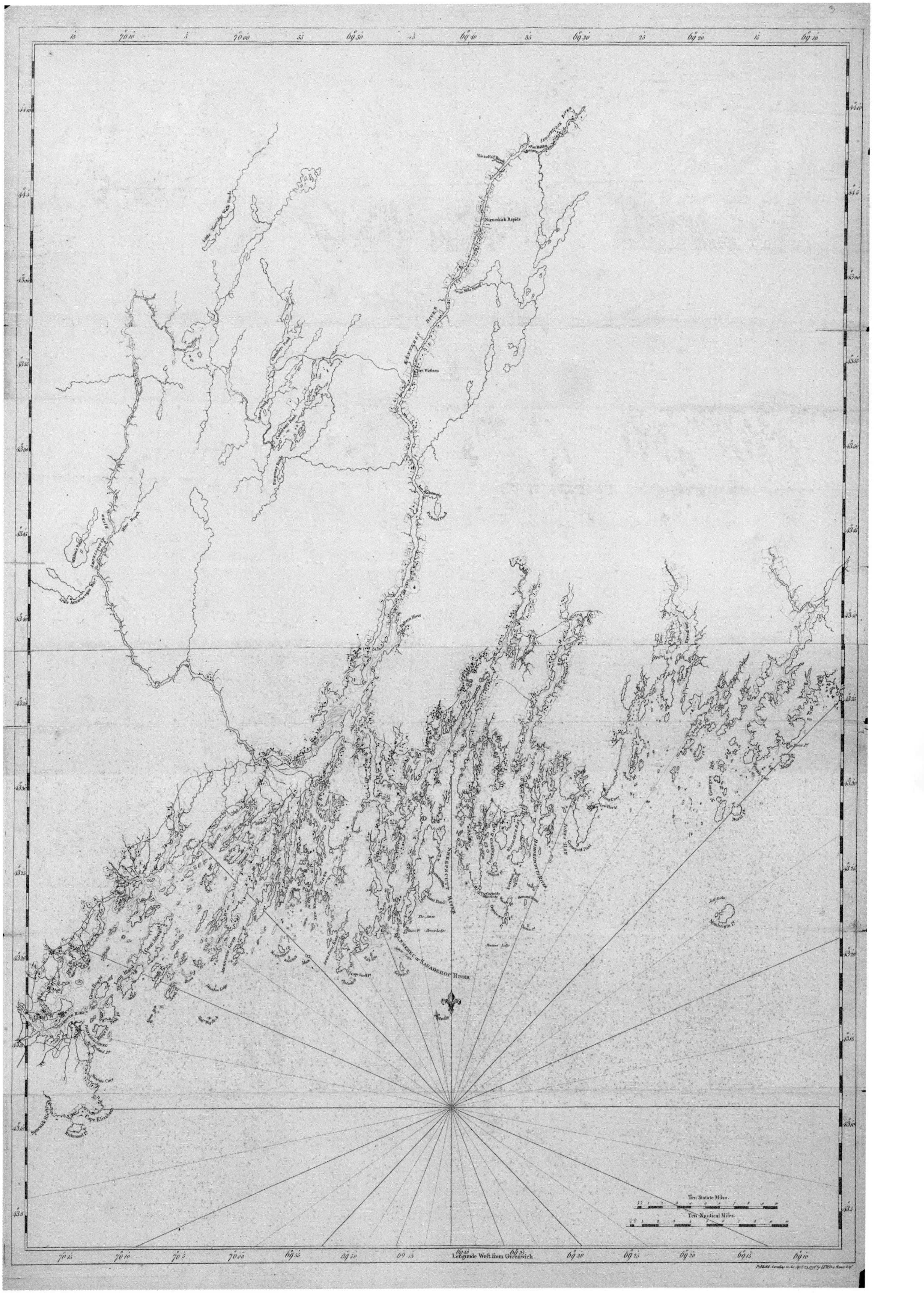

Nigumkick Rapids
Sebasticook River
Kennebeck River
Sheepscutt River
Damariscotta River
Kennebec or Sagadehoc River
Long Island
Great Hog Id.
Falmouth Harb.
Portland Sound
Cape Elizabeth
Richmond I.
Ten Statute Miles.
Ten Nautical Miles.
Longitude West from Greenwich.

Wabanaki Homelands—A Tribal Fisherman's Tale

John Bear Mitchell (Penobscot), Lecturer of Wabanaki Studies and Multicultural Studies, University of Maine at Orono

It's spring and with the temperature changing from freezing to warm, we know it's time to begin preparing for next winter. As a hunter-gatherer people, we must work every day preparing food for storage in anticipation of the upcoming cold weather. Yes, when wintertime ends and spring arrives, we begin our process of restocking our food supplies for the forthcoming winter. Some of us hunt on the land; however, we open spring by hunting on the ocean. It is fishing season and our place to fish is far off the coast in the deep ocean water. We are going to travel by canoe down the Penobscot River and Bay to Muscongus Bay and settle for a few weeks on the island of Monhegan—"out to sea and on its own," off the shoreline of Pemaquid Point. This island offers us instant access to the deep water on its east side. We are going there to hunt for the great fish we respect as a powerful and nurturing source of food: *pihcossekonat*, the swordfish, "the one with the long fin."

The canoe is our source of transportation. Birch bark is its skin, the outermost layer of the large basketlike container that will bring us to our necessary fishing place. A thin layer of white pliable bark is holding together a puzzle of craftsmanship. The canoe is the necessary tool for us, the Wabanaki hunter-gatherers, and in this instance, it carries both fishermen and fisherwomen. A single sheet of birch bark, cedar for the ribs and lining, black ash for the gunnels and seats, and split, wrapped spruce root bind and hold the pieces together tightly. To make it truly waterproof, a sticky tar-like substance made from mixing the right amount of sand, animal fat, and pine or spruce pitch is melted together over fire and smeared in the seams. When it dries, it hardens and keeps the canoe dry on the inside.

The weather has to be just right before we can paddle to Monhegan. For safe travel, the wind, tide, and weather must be precise. We are at the mercy of Mother Nature. If we are not respectful and cautious, we will quickly learn of her merciless power.

The tide is our only barrier to travel. We must respect its powerful force. Glooscap, "the one who tells the truth," created the tide, and we are taught to honor its power. I often tell this story to teach about the power of the tide and the respect we need to keep in mind about its force.

Glooscap lived on the top of a mountain near the ocean. He could see everything from his mountaintop home. In the bay, there lived a family of beavers. They did as they knew and that was to build dams. With great interest, Glooscap watched them build many dams. However, one day, they built a great dam in the ocean and blocked the open ocean from the Bay of Fundy. Glooscap became very angry with this because now the ocean was rising to his doorstep. He knew he had to destroy this dam immediately. Glooscap then reached over and pulled off the top of a nearby mountain and threw it at the dam, thus breaking it and releasing the water that was backed up in the Bay of Fundy, allowing it to pour back into the open ocean. Glooscap's house was no longer in jeopardy of being flooded. The force of the dam breaking made a great momentum, and it so agitated the waters, it caused the tide to surge twice a day as it still continues to do to this very day.

We begin traveling south from the freshwater of the Penobscot River to its mouth on Penobscot Bay. Our destination is Monhegan Island. Though it can be seen for many miles on approach, it is far away. Alone in the open ocean, Monhegan is an essential place for us to hunt swordfish. In its shallow waters on the west side of the island, Monhegan also offers us a place to drop weighted nets to entrap schools of mackerel. These fish will be processed, smoked, and stored. They will be used at a much later time, when we need sustenance most.

After four days of travel, we arrive at Pemaquid Point, which "is situated and rests at the end." This is our safest place to cross the open ocean, and it is the shortest distance to Monhegan. This area is our safest entry point, where there are fewer of the ocean's currents and less wind, as well as fewer pods of harbor porpoise to disrupt our travel. We set up our temporary camp and get some food and rest. Tomorrow, we will embark on our last day of travel and set up our camp on Monhegan.

Morning comes quickly. We pack our canoe for the ten-mile journey. After high tide, we head out. The ocean is gentle, and we venture out into the open bay with our end goal clearly in our sight the entire way. On our approach, the island of Manana, the "little island," seems to grow larger. We make our way around the north side of it and enter the calm waters that are cradled between it and Monhegan. We are not alone. Several other Wabanaki fishermen and fisherwomen have already set up; their summer homes are completely constructed. The sweet smell of woodsmoke permeates the air.

I construct our summer lodge near the freshwater pond. This source of clean drinking water is an absolute necessity for living on salt water. It's time to get started on building my aboveground lodge. It is dome-shaped so that it will withstand any wind or sudden storms. I gather twelve small beech trees because beech is a flexible hardwood. Each tree is approximately twelve feet tall and no more than six inches in circumference. Stabbing them into the ground and bending them inward, over my hip toward the opposite pole, I finish by lashing them together with my basswood bark rope. My lodge is ten feet wide and thirty feet in circumference and gives us plenty of room to live and work when the weather requires us to utilize that space. Once the framework is done, I cover my lodge with mats made from the island's shoreline grasses. This layer is four inches thick, and the outer layer of the lodge is wrapped in any bark that is plentiful on the island. Here, I use birch bark where it is available. I finish the construction by strapping a few miscellaneous tree branches over the bark to keep it from blowing off.

Now I rest. It has been a long trip. Tomorrow, I will gather with the other fishermen and fisherwomen, and we will begin our plan to hunt for swordfish. It will be a tremendous amount of work, but for the sake of survival, it is not optional. I look forward to this hunt and all the new memories I will make.

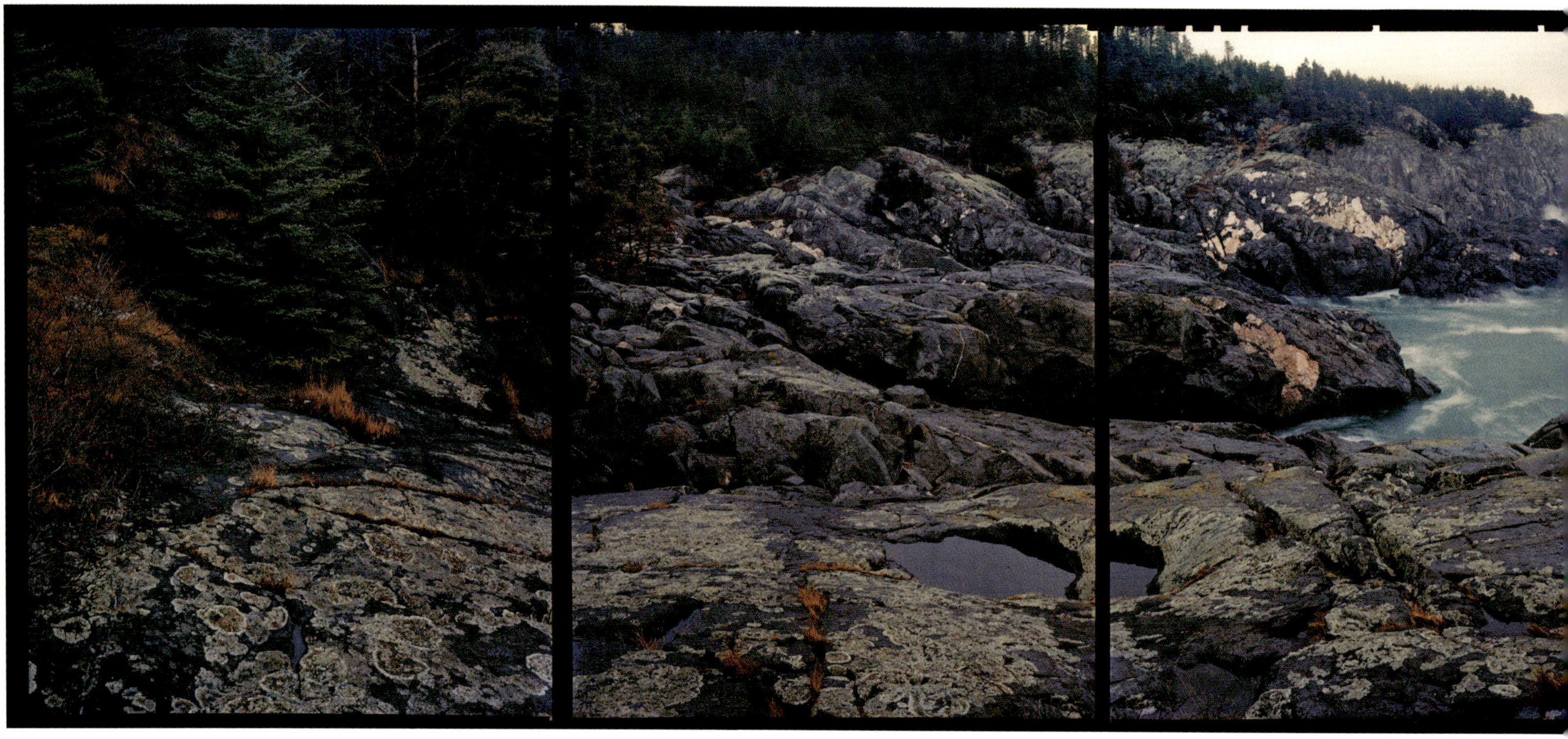

Accra Shepp (born 1962),
White Head from Burnt Head,
2022. Archival pigment ink
print. Courtesy of the artist

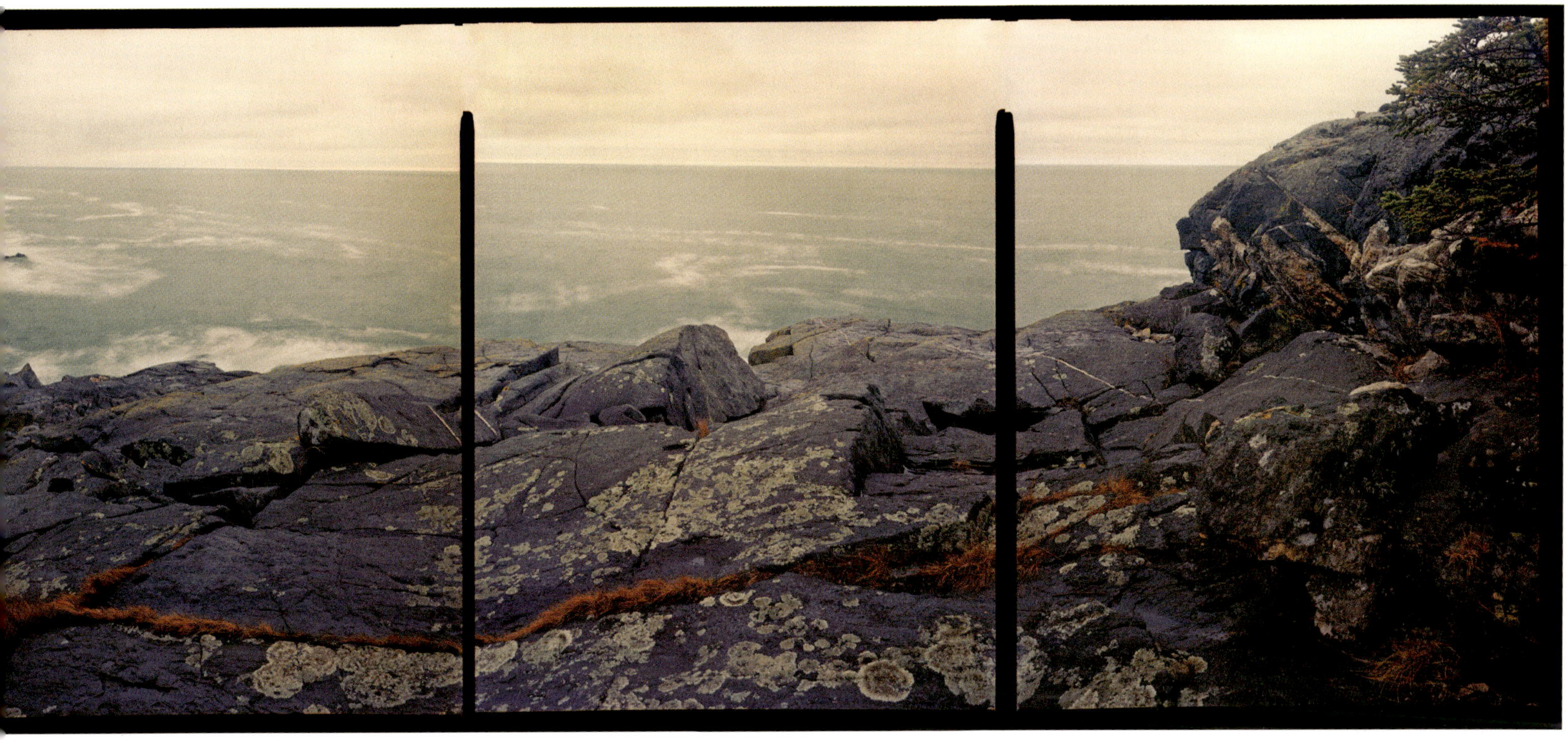

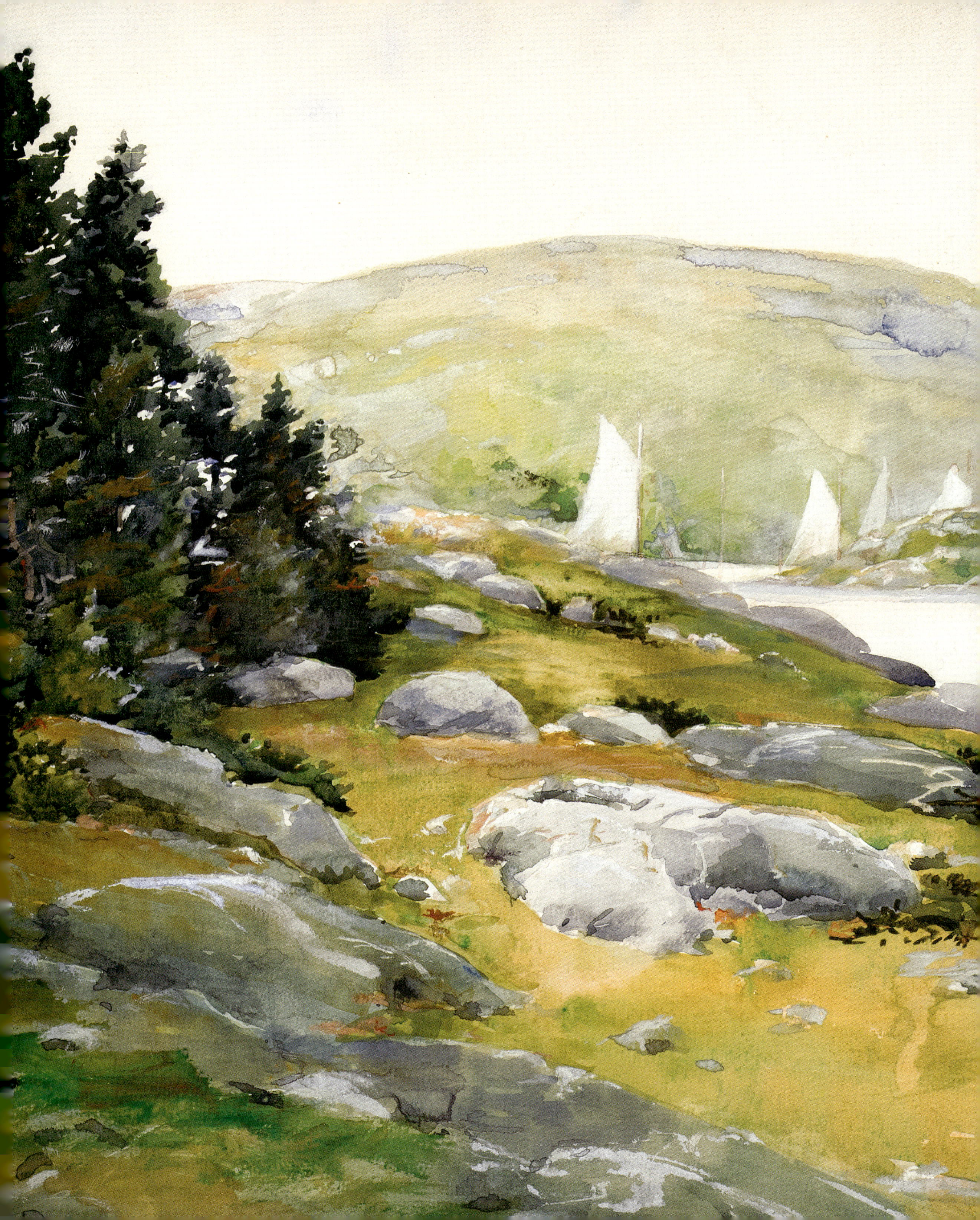

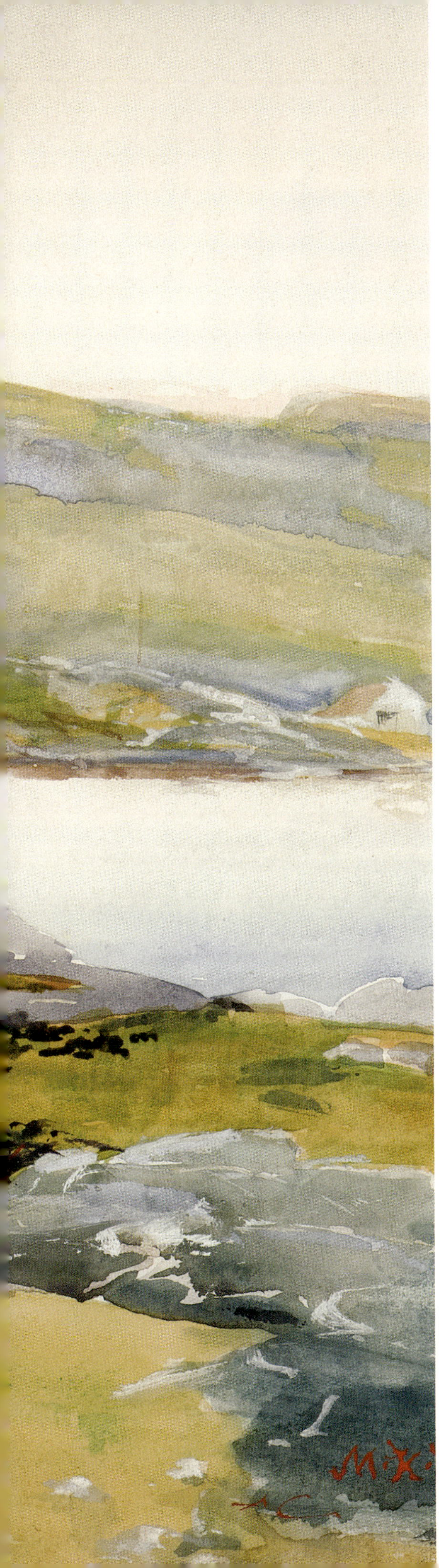

Chapter 3

Year-Round Settlement to the Arrival of Rusticators and the Removal of Sheep, 1821 to 1896

William D. Williamson, the second governor of Maine and later one of its first historians, singled out Monhegan in 1832 as "without exception, the most famous [island] on the seaboard of this State. It was the land aimed at and first mentioned by the original voyagers and fishermen about these waters."[1] In his day, it was no longer only a notable landmark and seasonal fishing station, but also a permanent year-round community. Williamson's published description of Monhegan provides the earliest account of the settlement that grew up in the early nineteenth century:

> The number of people on the Island is between 75 and 100, who inhabit 12 or 14 dwellinghouses, and are the owners of the soil, industrious, moral and well-informed. They have a schoolhouse where their children are educated, and religious meetings are attended. Fishing and agriculture are the employments of the men; they own several vessels; and while the more able bodied are engaged in the former business at home, and in the codfishery on the Grand Banks, the old men and boys cultivate the land, raising good crops, keeping cows, swine, and sheep.

> The Island, though within the county of Lincoln, belongs to no town. It is a democratic community: It has no officers of any kind, not even a Justice of the Peace. The people's affairs are governed and guided by themselves, conformably to certain prudential rules and usages which they have mutually established. They have paid one United States' direct tax, otherwise they are strangers to taxation, except what they pay towards the support of their school.[2]

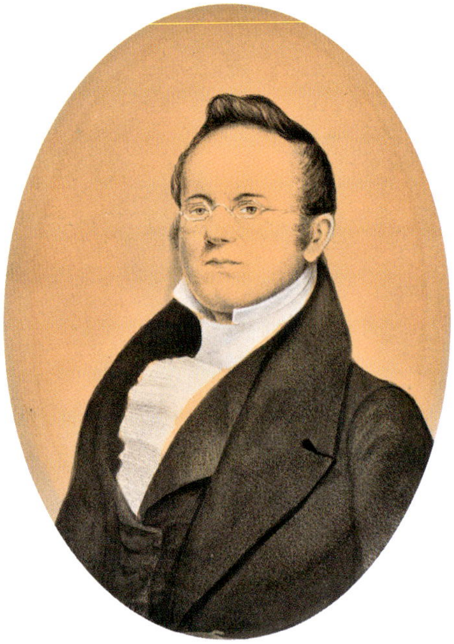

Unidentified artist, *William D. Williamson*, ca. 1821. Ink and gouache on paper. Maine State Archives, 29-207232-F001-I059

Williamson's account presents Monhegan as a veritable peaceable kingdom, where humankind lived in harmony with nature, independent from most others. Based in Bangor, then one of the nation's leading lumber towns, the former governor was a prominent advocate for Maine statehood and its economic growth. For him, Monhegan exemplified the hardy self-sufficiency that characterized life in the new state and suggested to would-be settlers an attractive alternative to a crowded urban existence.

In many respects, Williamson captured well the island's vitality during this period before the American Civil War. Under the stewardship of the Trefethren family—at least initially—the foundation of a self-supporting community was being laid. Of note, much construction took place then. Homes and other structures were built, a schoolhouse was completed, and in 1824, the first lighthouse was finished on top of what would become known as "Lighthouse Hill." After weather damage, a new granite structure was commissioned in 1850; a bronze fog bell was added on Manana in 1855 to further aid ship traffic. Though some wood for these buildings was sourced on the island, most was imported from the mainland as Monhegan never operated its own sawmill.

As in the past, the livelihoods of the island's residents were built primarily on fishing. Boats departed year-round from Monhegan to fish the rich waters directly offshore as well as to venture farther down east to the Grand Banks. Cod and haddock dominated during the early nineteenth century, though by mid-century, the era of dragging or purse seining for mackerel had started as traditional fish stocks began to decline. Fishermen cleaned, dried, and stored their catch in shoreline buildings on Fish Beach before selling to fish merchants from Portland and elsewhere. It was not until the 1870s that lobstering began—today the dominant fishery on Monhegan.

While Williamson mentions the agricultural industry and the presence of livestock on the island, he does not explain that farming and husbandry—unlike fishing—were largely new. Although beasts of burden were a necessity as were milking cows, like much of New England, Monhegan embraced sheep farming through the middle and late nineteenth century. Various factors explain the commitment of land to sheep. A primary catalyst was the introduction to North America of the merino variety. Merino sheep produce fine, soft, high-quality wool and display uncommon hardiness in the face of harsh conditions. First developed in Spain several centuries earlier, the merino breed was closely guarded and confined to the Iberian Peninsula. Death faced any Spaniard found to have exported a merino sheep. Napoleon's conquest altered this calculus, however, as sheepherders feared that his armies might eradicate the breed in an act of war. To counter this possibility, merino sheep were released to the courts of several European kingdoms. From there, they spread across the globe.

Edward Robinson (1865–1929),
Deadman's Cove, ca. 1895.
Modern print from glass plate
negative. Maine Historic
Preservation Commission

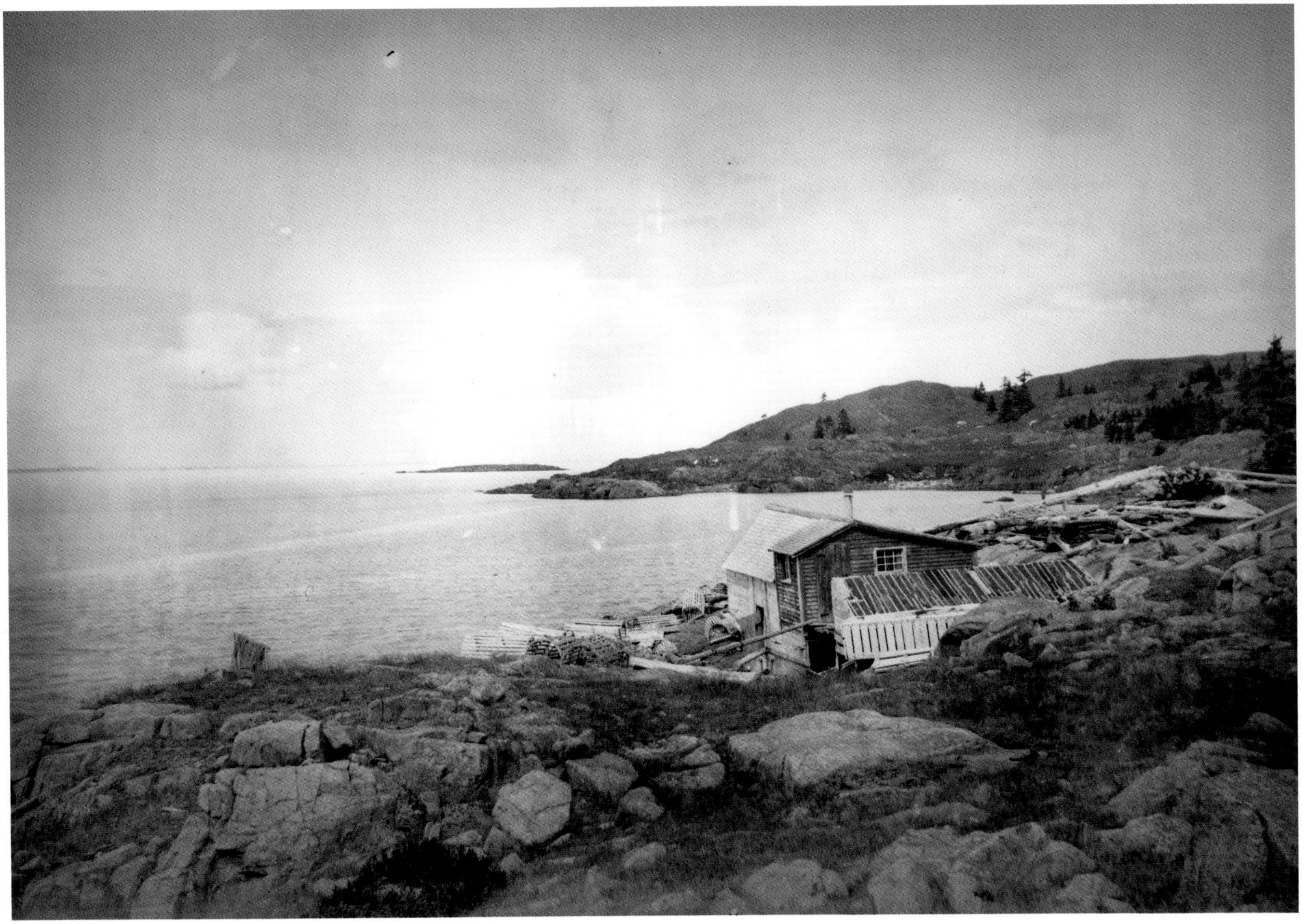

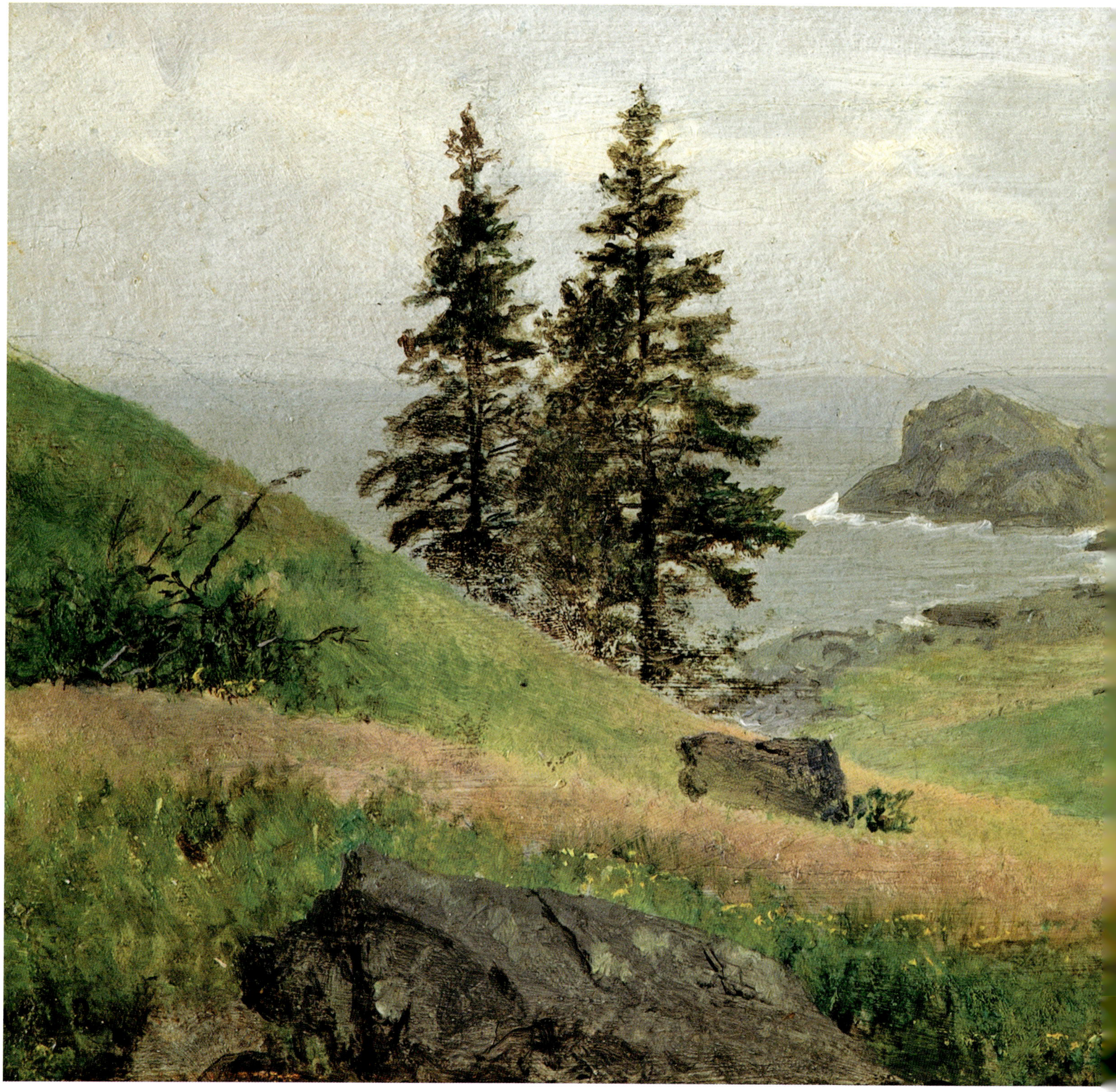

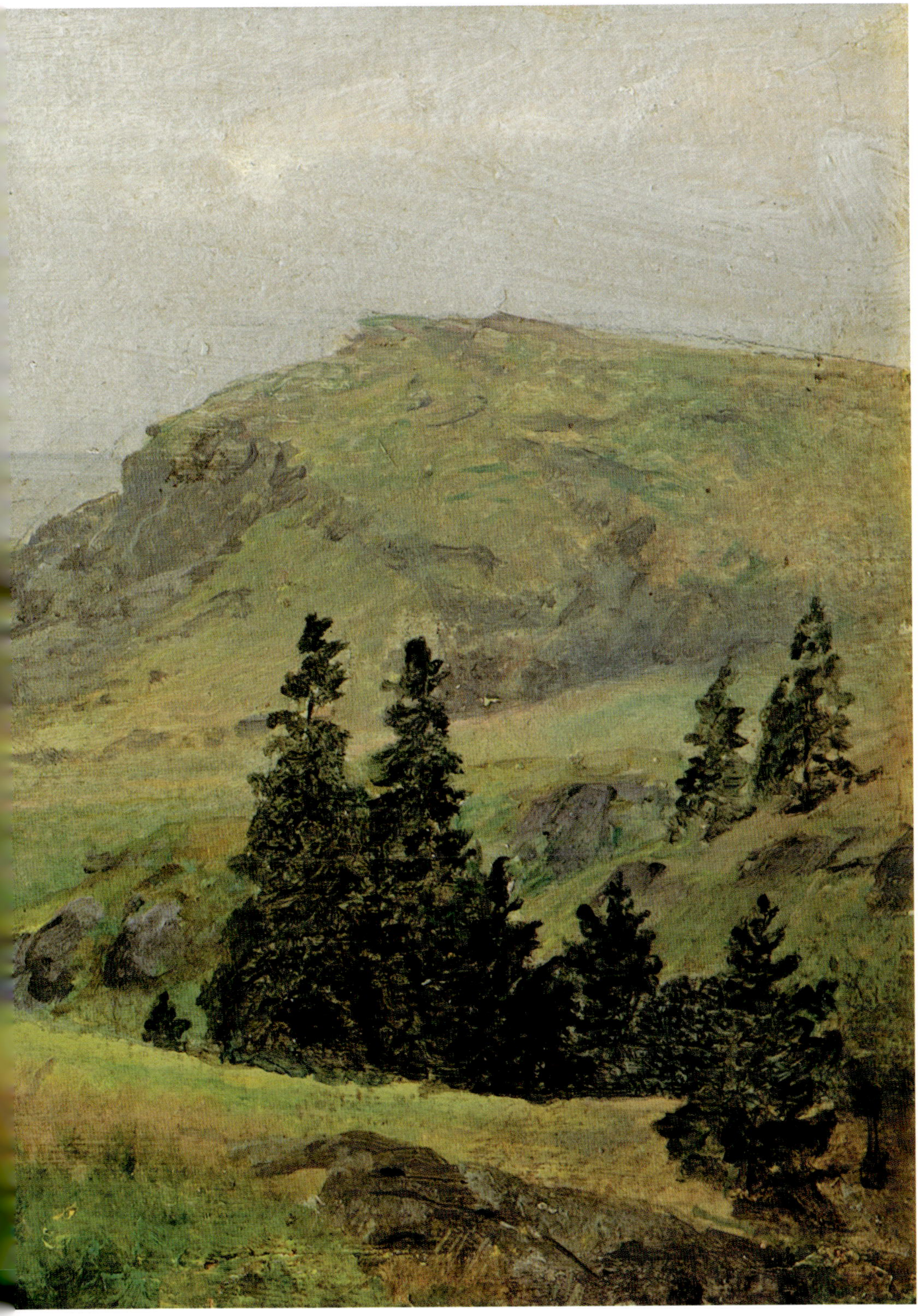

William Trost Richards (1833–1905), *Pine Trees, Monhegan Island, Maine*, ca. 1902. Oil on panel, 16 x 23½ inches. Collection of Stephen S. Fuller and Susan D. Bateson

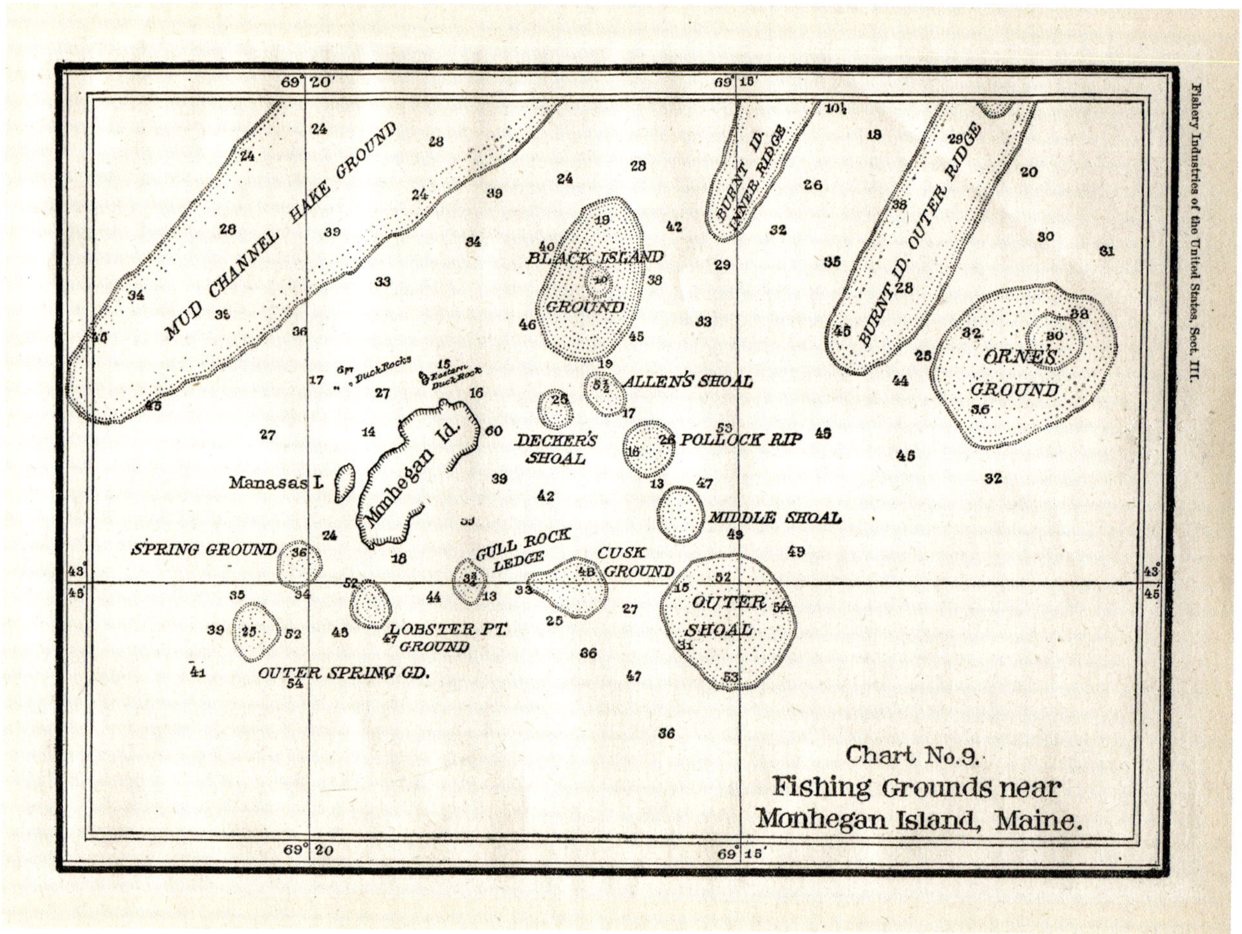

Unidentified artist, *Fishing Grounds near Monhegan Island, Maine,* 1887. Monhegan Museum of Art & History. Gift of Harry T. Bone

Sheep are especially well suited to islands, which, of course, confine the animals, obviating the need for fencing. They can be raised there without fear of predation. Also, in comparison to cattle, sheep require very little water. If forage is lush and ewes are not raising lambs, sheep can extract the water they need from vegetation alone. In winter, they can remain hydrated by eating snow. Although these features allow for low-effort sheep pasturing on islands such as Monhegan, one sizable commitment required to raise sheep involves the creation of pasture. In the nineteenth century, the Monhegan landscape was transformed accordingly as islanders undertook the conversion of forest. Cartographic evidence indicates that perimeter forests were felled comprising as much as half of what would become the Monhegan Wildlands. An especially informative map drawn in 1873 by the US Coast and Geodetic Survey distinguishes forested from cleared land. The portion of the island in forest then neatly circumscribes the eventual Cathedral Woods.

As Maine State Historian Earle G. Shettleworth, Jr., explores in the essay that accompanies this chapter, Monhegan began to witness the arrival of other outsiders to its shores in the mid-nineteenth century—in this case, artists and recreational travelers. Landscape painting enjoyed a particular vogue in the United States during this period, and artists and other wilderness adventurers traveled widely in search of new subjects and experiences. In Maine,

Samuel Peter Rolt Triscott (1846–1925), The Meadow, ca. 1895. Modern print from glass plate negative. Maine Historic Preservation Commission

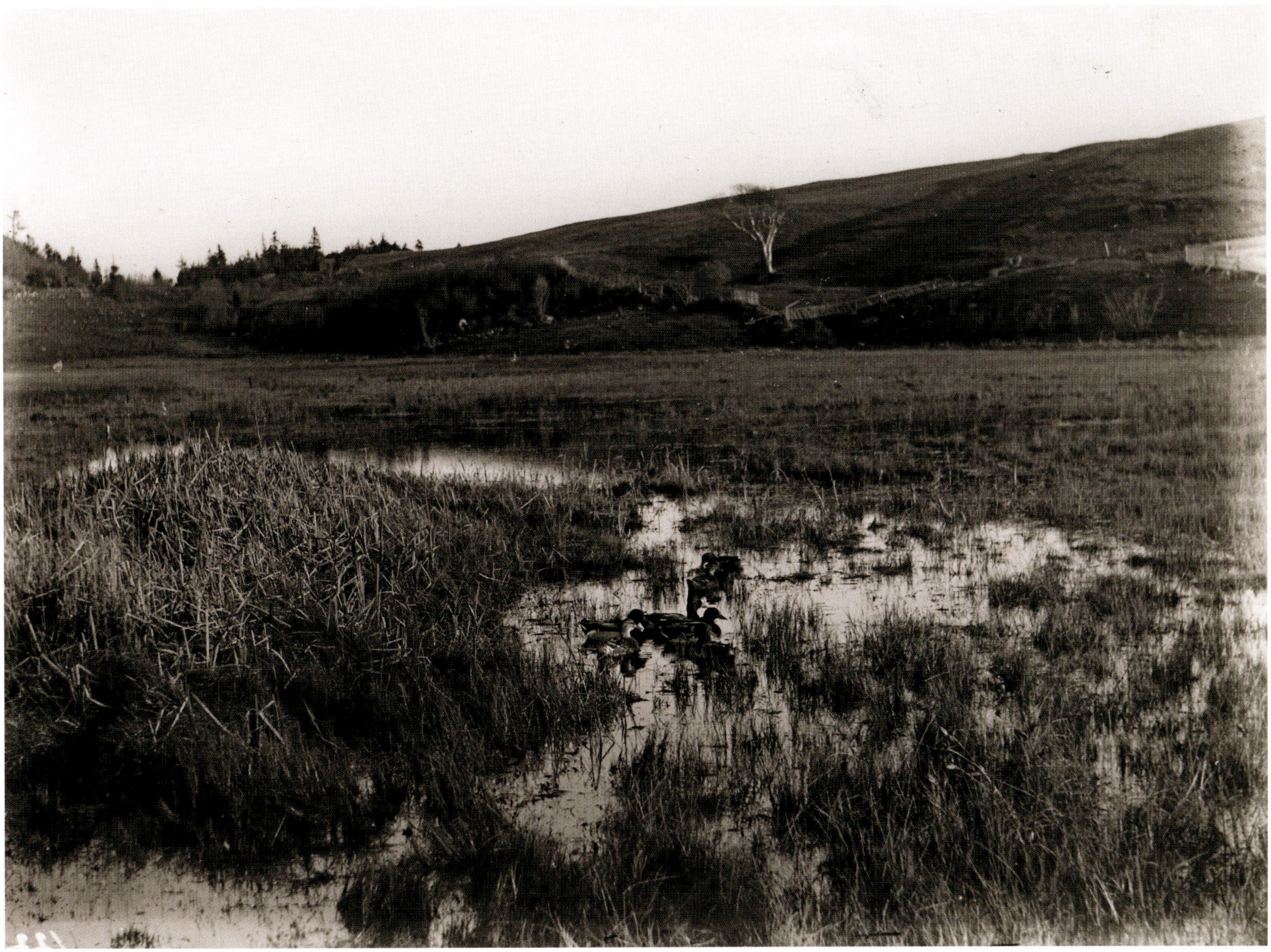

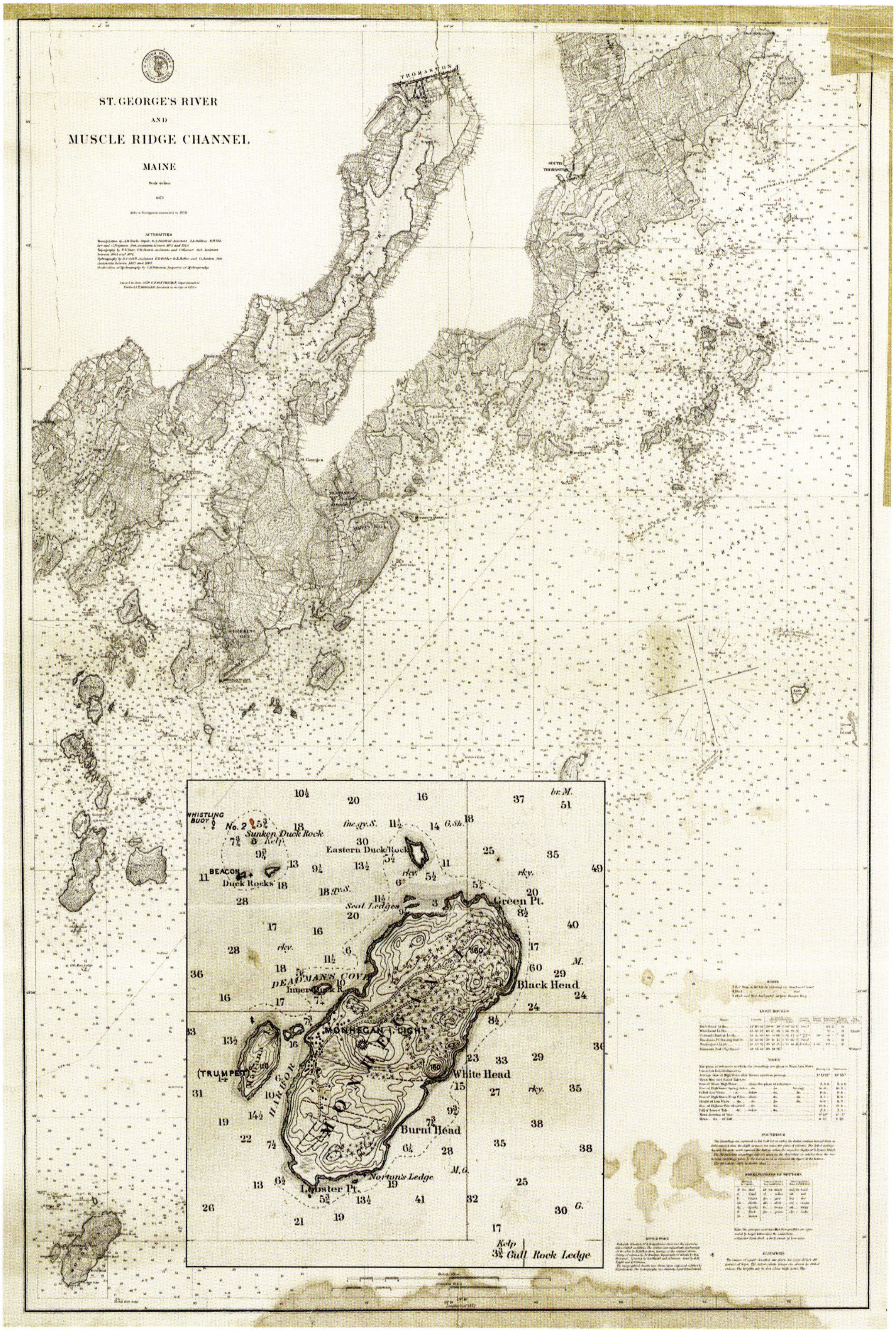
ST. GEORGE'S RIVER
AND
MUSCLE RIDGE CHANNEL
MAINE
WHISTLING BUOY
No. 2
Sunken Duck Rock
Eastern Duck Rock
BEACON
Duck Rocks
Seal Ledges
Green Pt.
DEADMAN'S COVE
Black Head
MONHEGAN LIGHT
(TRUMPET)
White Head
Burnt Head
Norton's Ledge
Lobster Pt.
Gull Rock Ledge

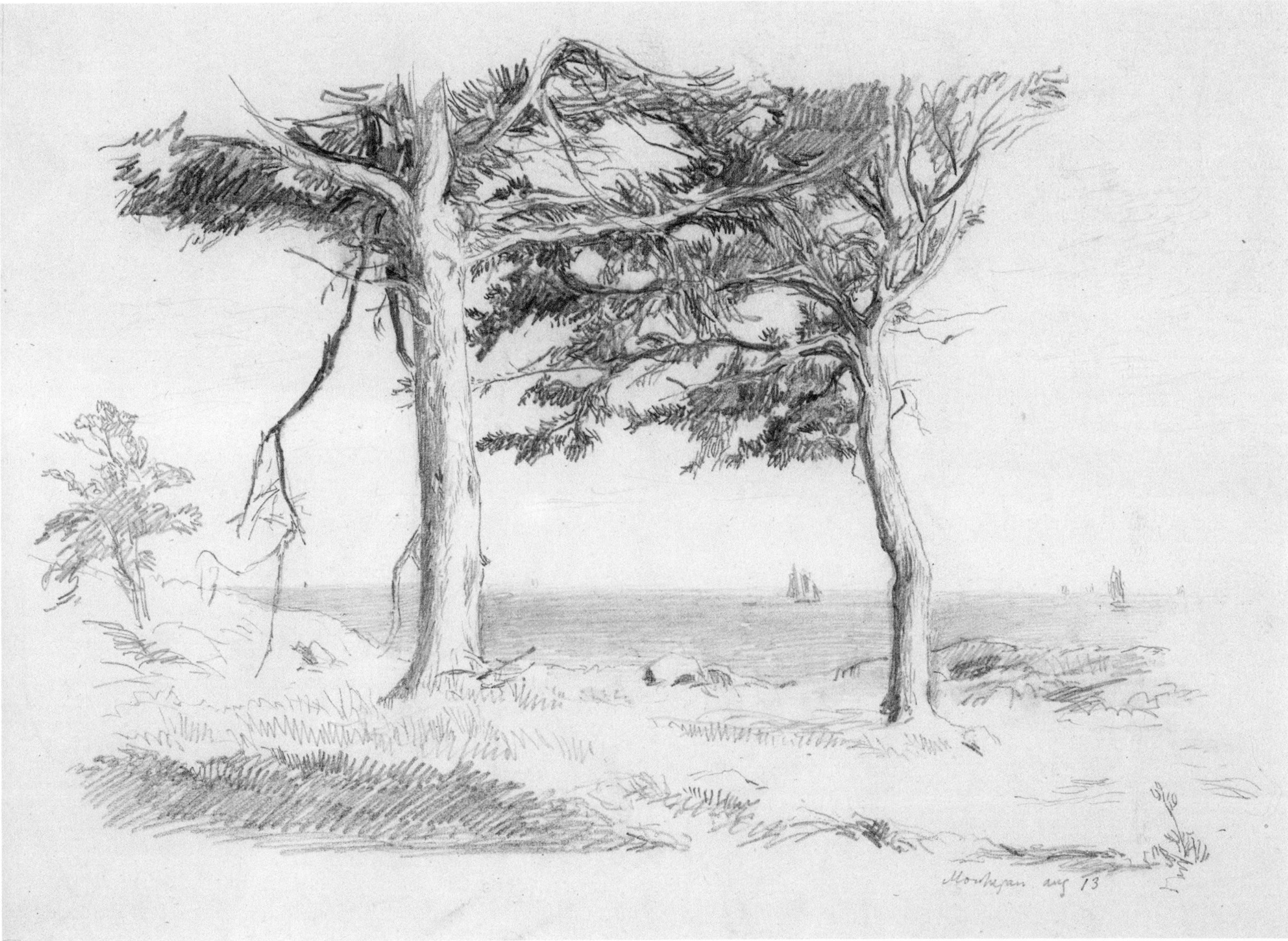

Opposite: US Coast and Geodetic Survey, *St. George's River and Muscle River Channel—Maine*, 1873. Engraving, 42 x 30 inches. Penobscot Marine Museum, Jasper Sargent Chart Collection (LB2007.2.1944). Forest was largely confined to the northwest region of Monhegan in 1873, as is evident in the enlarged inset.

Above: John Henry Hill (1839–1922), *Monhegan Trees,* 1857. Graphite on paper, $5\frac{11}{16}$ x $8\frac{1}{8}$ inches. Monhegan Museum of Art & History. Gift of Edward L. Deci

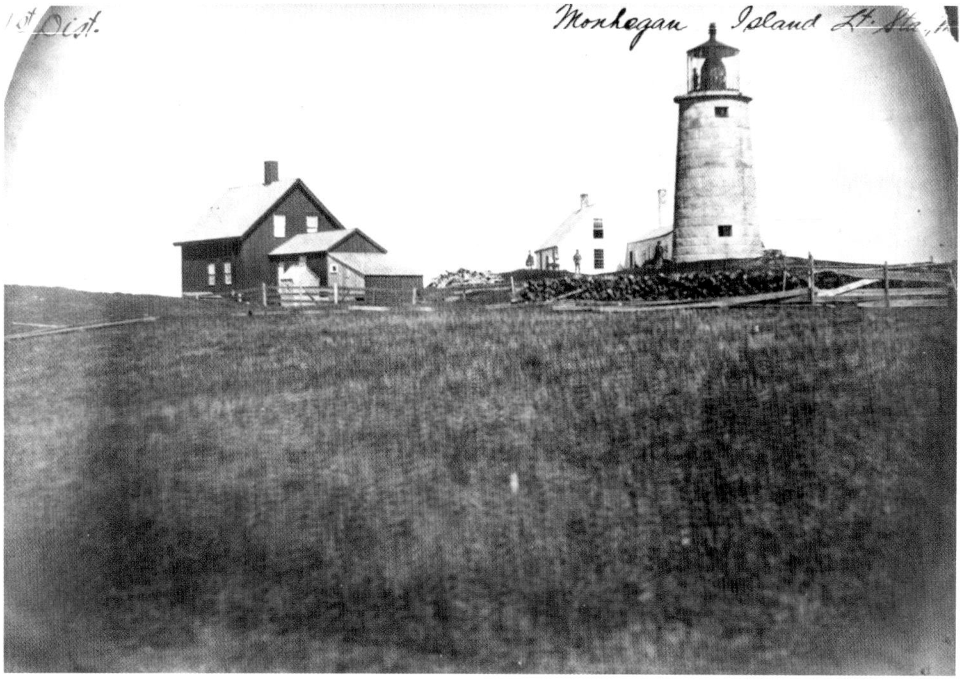

William McLaughlin,
Monhegan Island Light Station,
1859. National Archives

destinations such as Mount Katahdin and Mount Desert Island had been discovered by non-native travelers during the first half of the nineteenth century. There, they marveled at the beauty of unspoiled nature and reveled in the perception that they were the "first" to encounter such places. Their paintings, prints, and published travel accounts spurred a new era of tourism in Maine and beyond.

In 1857, eighteen-year-old John Henry Hill, son of an artist from West Nyack, New York, became the first landscape painter to arrive on Monhegan with the purpose of completing a series of plein air sketches. He was likely not there long as only one drawing is known to exist. It depicts two spruce trees in the foreground amid a grassy plain with the sea in the background. Although Hill chose not to show any sheep in this scene, the drawing reveals the type of pasture that would have supported sheep farming and that had become common, especially on the southern half of the island. The diversity of vegetation that had historically characterized this land is altogether missing. Six years later, in 1863, Hill became one of the founding members of the Society for the Advancement of Truth in Art, a group of American artists influenced by the English author John Ruskin and devoted to rendering with precision the natural world. While modest in size, this early drawing suggests this commitment.

Other painters soon followed. In 1858, Aaron Draper Shattuck, also based in New York, and Harrison Bird Brown, from Portland, stopped on Monhegan during a trip aboard a US Lighthouse Service ship that was inspecting lighthouses along the Maine coast. Again, few resulting works are known to exist today. What does survive from this trip provides evidence of an island that was in the process of being deforested to support other priorities. For example, Shattuck's *On the Maine Coast* (1858) presents the rocky Monhegan coastline without a single tree. Whereas trees and other vegetation had once grown to the

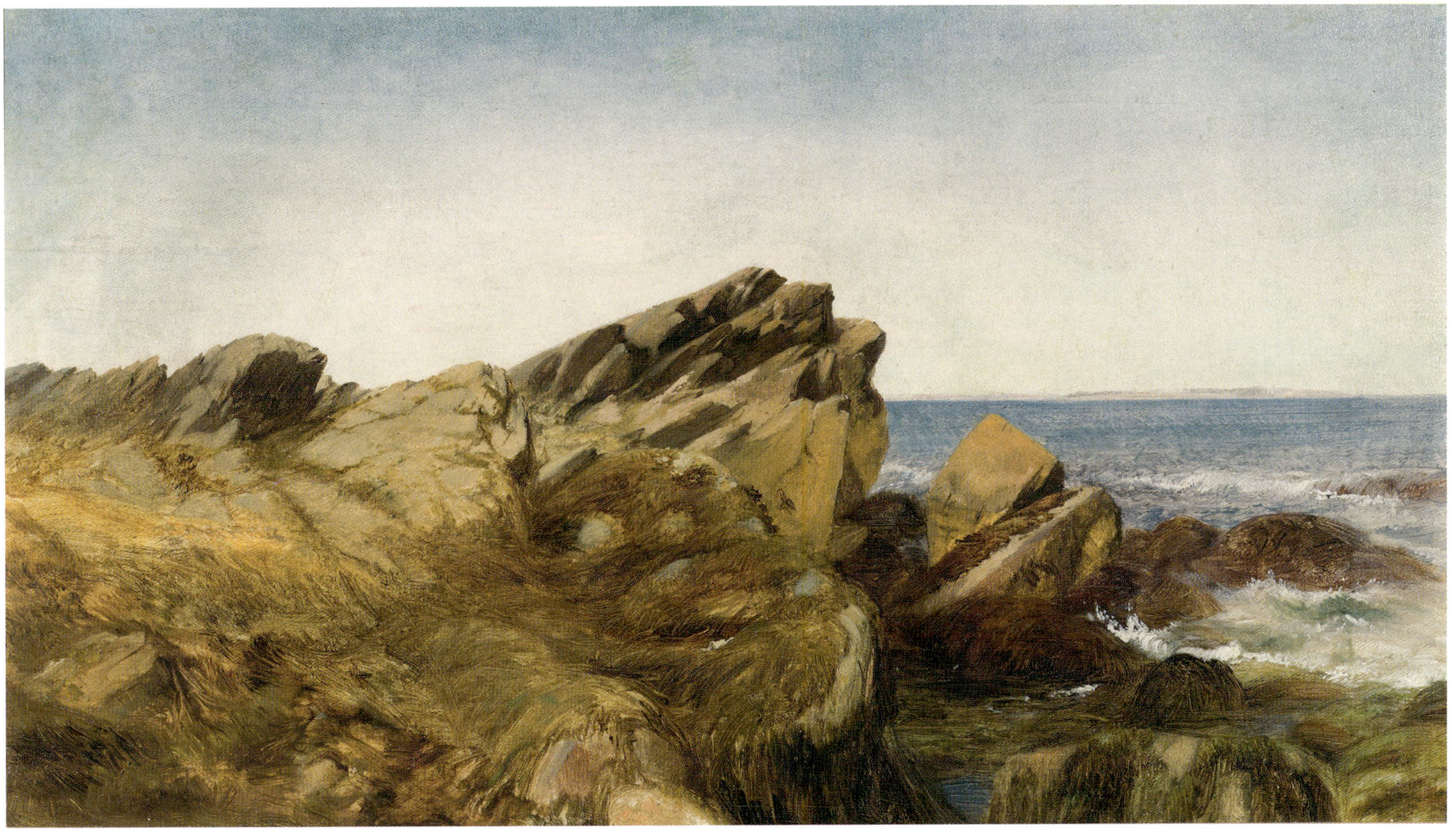

Aaron Draper Shattuck (1832–1928), *On the Maine Coast*, 1858. Oil on canvas, 11 x 19 inches. Monhegan Museum of Art & History. Gift of Robert and Virginia Snow

edges of the shoreline, such was no longer the case, at least as recorded in this painting. In a letter to his soon-to-be wife, Marian Colman, Shattuck observed: "Monhegan Island has some wonderful things about it, lots of beautiful coves and grand cliffs rising high out of the sea. The surf was dashing terribly on the Eastern shore, throwing its spray like rain upon the rocks."[3] For Shattuck and generations of Monhegan artists after him, the dramatic surf as seen from the island's eastern headlands was an especially popular subject. Of less interest during this period was the island's forested interior.

Three related photographs from a decade or so later—some of the earliest created on the island—provide more concrete evidence of how residents were actively engaged in building a community and, in the process, transforming the lands on Monhegan. It is not known who created this set of photographs or for what purpose. Taken near the village and from Manana, they reveal the island's demographic and economic growth. No longer a seasonal fishing station, Monhegan had become an industrious settlement. Homes and other structures are visible alongside the boat-filled harbor. Stone walls mark property lines and control the grazing of cattle and other livestock.

Visiting Monhegan in 1880, Connecticut-born journalist and novelist William Henry Bishop observed the island during a period when the sheep population had reached its highest recorded mark, approximately three hundred animals. Tramping across the island, Bishop noted that "there were plenty of sheep, but little agriculture, no roads, nor use for any except to haul a little wood from the other end of the island in winter. In this service cows as well as a few

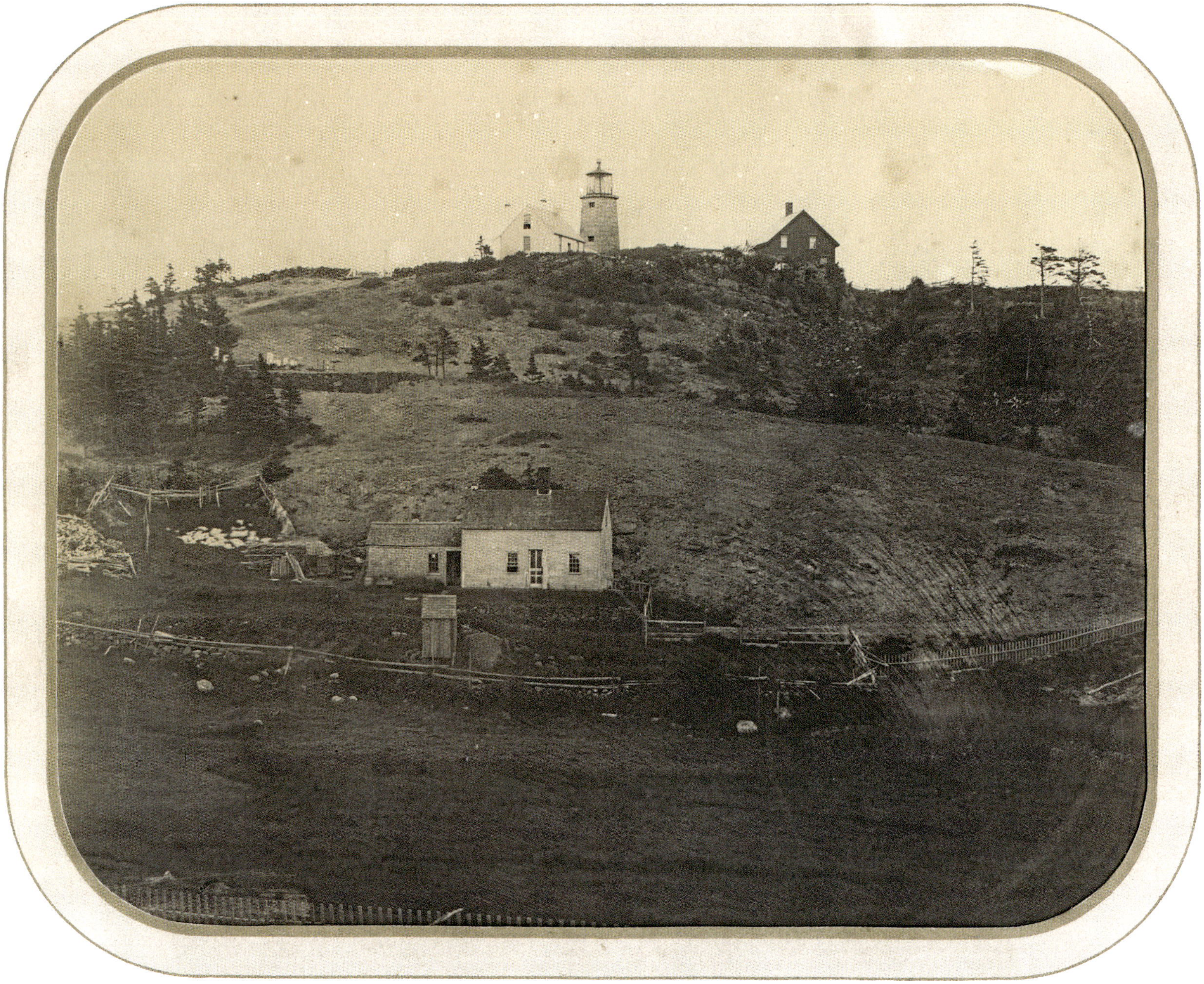

Unidentified photographer, Richard Davis House and Lighthouse Hill, Monhegan, ca. 1870. Albumen silver print, 8⅝ x 10½ inches. Monhegan Museum of Art & History. Gift of Lisa Brackett

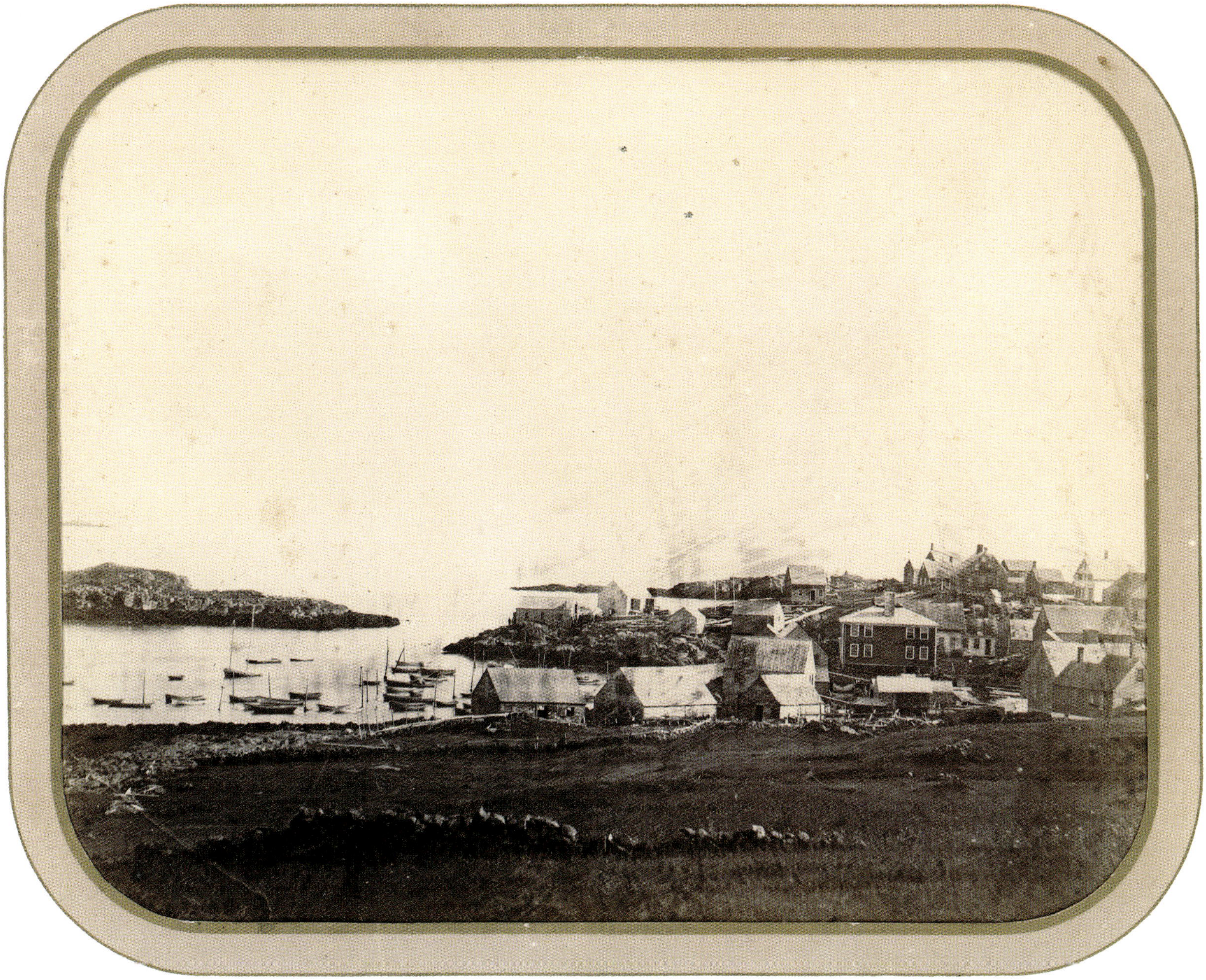

Unidentified photographer, Monhegan Village, ca. 1870. Albumen silver print, 8¾ x 10⅜ inches. Monhegan Museum of Art & History. Gift of Lisa Brackett

Unidentified photographer, Monhegan Village from Manana, ca. 1870. Albumen silver print, 8¾ x 11 inches. Monhegan Museum of Art & History. Gift of Lisa Brackett

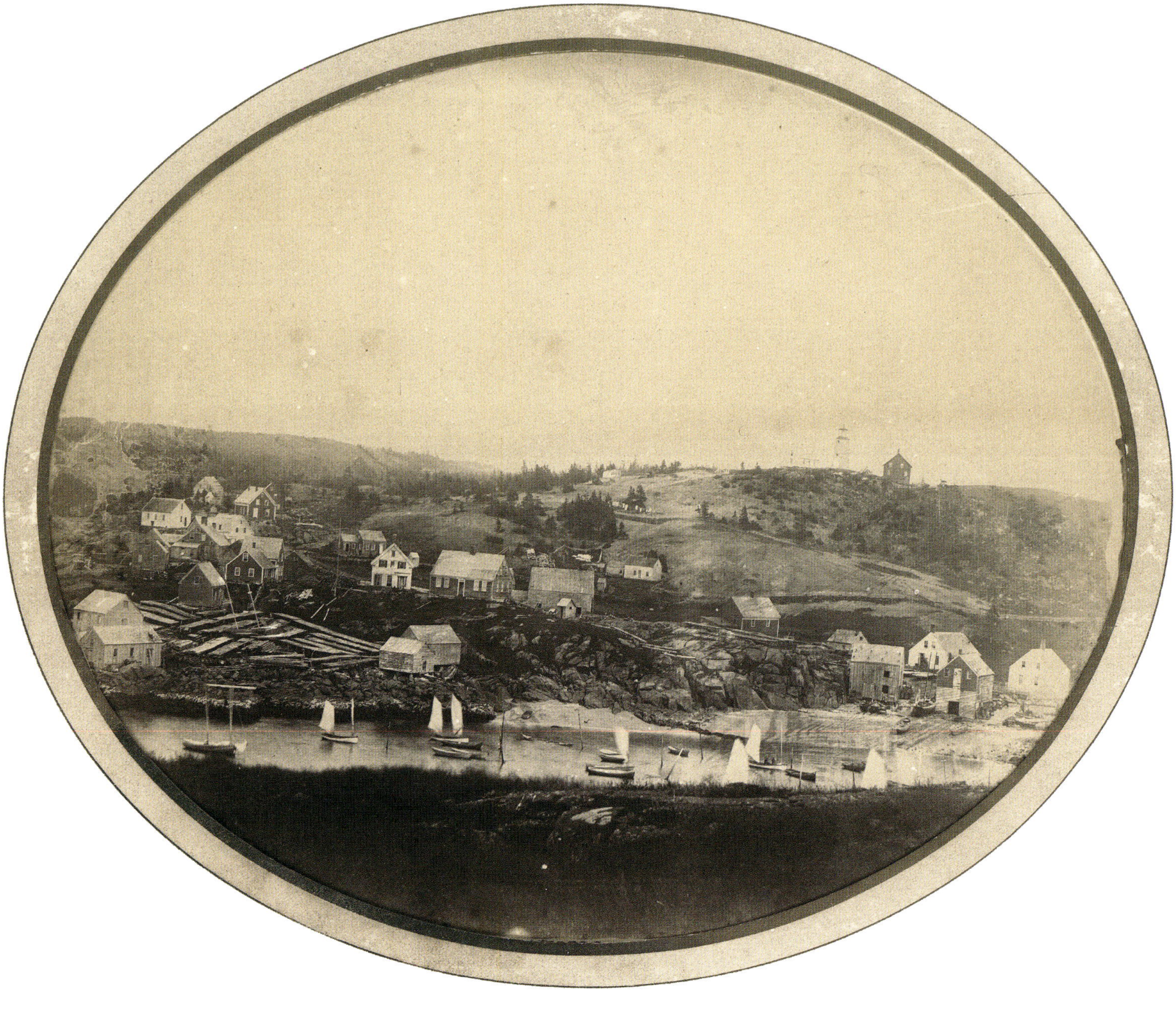

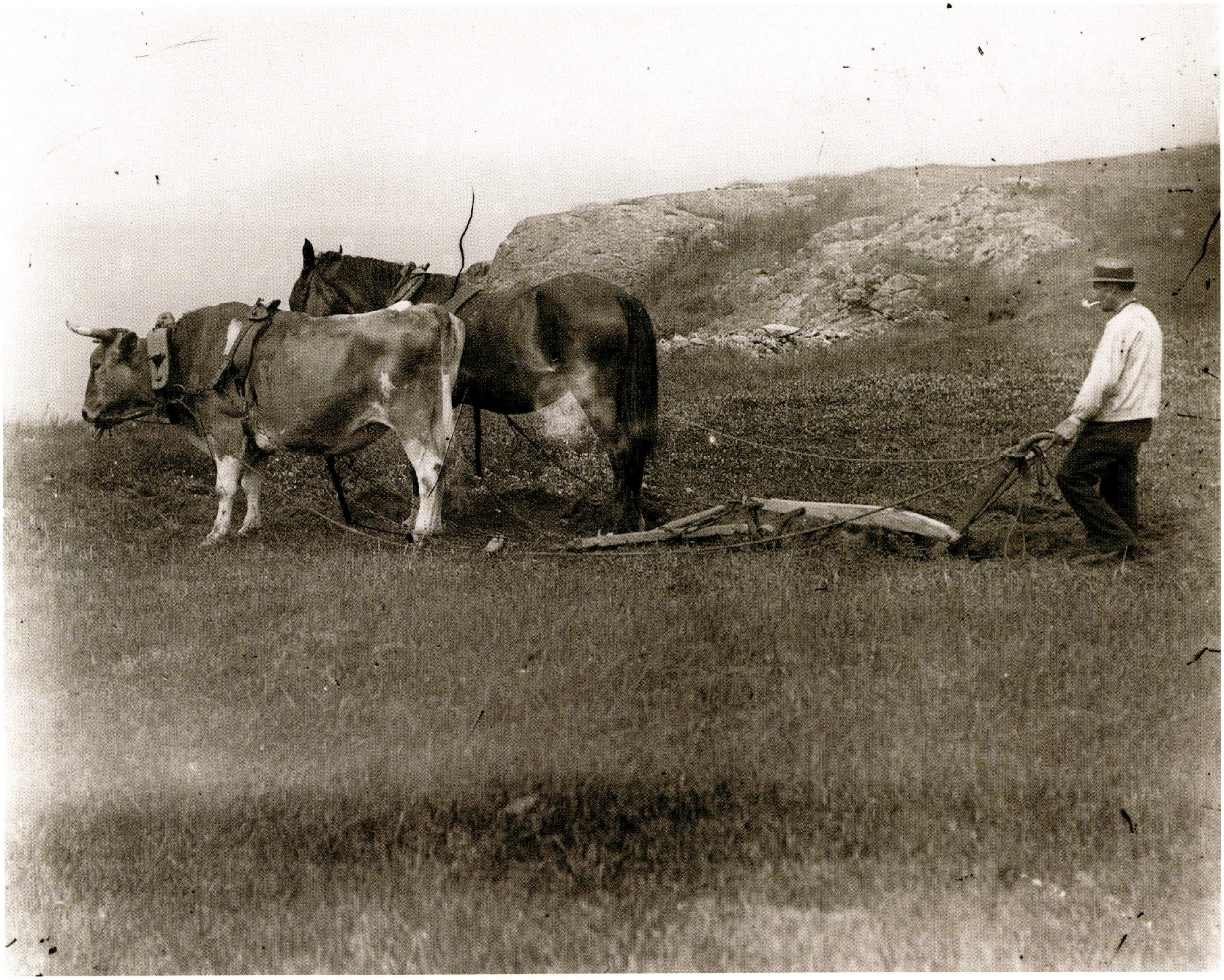

Eric Hudson (1862–1932), Ox and horse plowing a field, ca. 1898. Modern print from glass plate negative. Maine Historic Preservation Commission

oxen were put under the yoke."[4] Tax documents serve as another useful record of the rise and eventual fall of sheep on Monhegan. The number of sheep listed among the assets of islanders and nonresidents peaked in the 1885 assessment at 295. A mere eight cows and oxen are listed.[5]

Bishop also ventured into the forest interior and provided one of the earliest written accounts of this section of the island: "Though but a mile long, the centre and eastern end of the island had still the most virgin and savage air. Gorges containing the whitened bones of ancient cedar-trees and wet morasses barred the way. The low, thick, resinous groves, too, were impenetrable, except for some dark burrows like lairs where the sheep had gone through. Long gray moss, like the drift of some deluge, hung from the branches of the spruces; but the carpet was of an overluxuriant, vivid kind, more suggestive—though starred with scarlet bunch-berries—of death and decay even than the graveyard on the slope."[6] Bishop did not then refer to this section as Cathedral Woods, though an unidentified person had assigned it that name by the century's end. Evoking the grandeur and sanctity of a building designed for worship, the name Cathedral Woods began appearing on maps as early as 1904.

During the last quarter of the nineteenth century, tourism became its own industry on Monhegan. While recreational travelers had ventured there in earlier years, islanders began to board visitors in their homes and, not long thereafter, to establish inns to cater to the increased demand. They also advertised travel opportunities in newspapers on the mainland. These efforts were buttressed by an increasing number of artistic images as well as published stories about the island. In 1875, acclaimed journalist and travel writer Samuel Adams Drake authored an account of his travels along the New England coast in which he described Monhegan as "the most famous island you can find on the New England map" and predicted that it "must one day become a resort as famous as the Isles of Shoals."[7]

By the 1890s, summer visitors on Monhegan began to outnumber island residents. Many were artists who came to paint and draw at sites across the island. The eastern headlands and the village harbor led in popularity, though visitors took advantage of a rich network of trails to trek throughout the island. Most stayed at newly established boardinghouses or inns. Some began to purchase land and build their own seasonal homes. English watercolorist Samuel Peter Rolt Triscott, having first visited Monhegan in the summer of 1892, was among the first artists to purchase a home. Initially it was a summer retreat, but he decided to move to the island and live there year-round beginning in 1902. Many artists have followed his example since then.[8]

While fishing remained the principal occupation of residents, the tourism industry began to precipitate changes—small at first, though more significant in later years—in the traditional patterns of island life. An increasing number of residents moved into jobs to meet the demands of their off-island visitors. Although many of these positions were seasonal, they altered established habits and work routines. The introduction of tourism led to an important new source of revenue for islanders. Yet, as most visitors worked in different professions and did not share similar life experiences or expectations as their hosts, their presence was a mixed blessing to many. A *Boston Daily Globe* profile of the island in 1894 suggests that off-island visitors were met with consternation

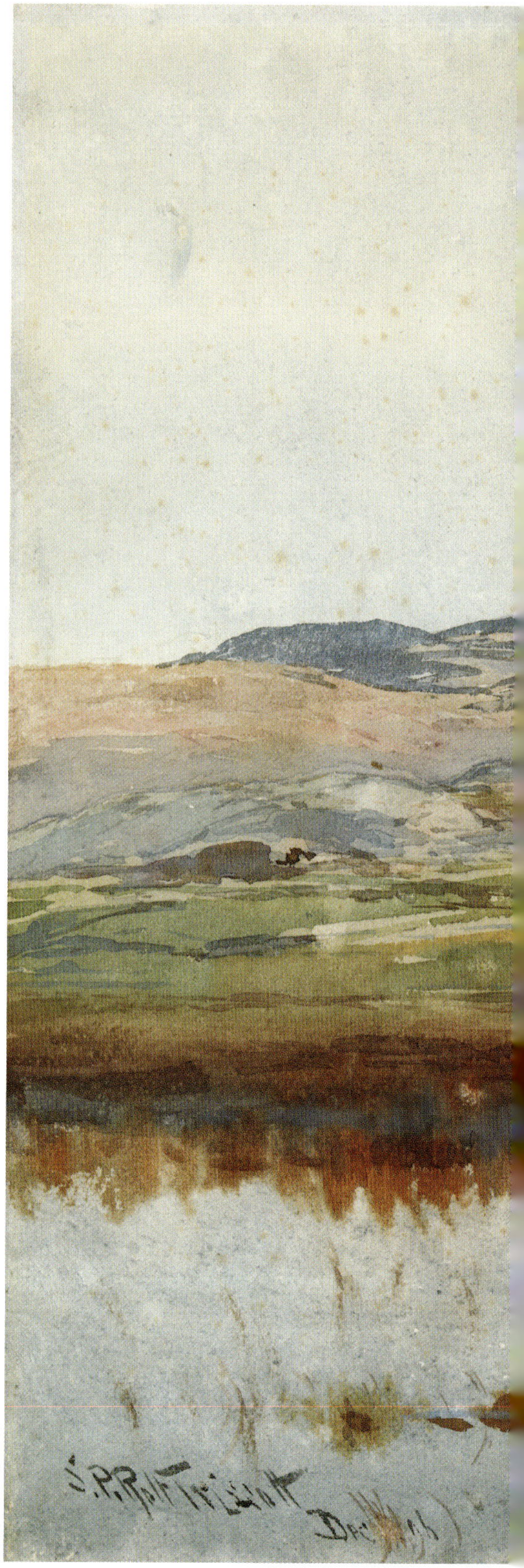

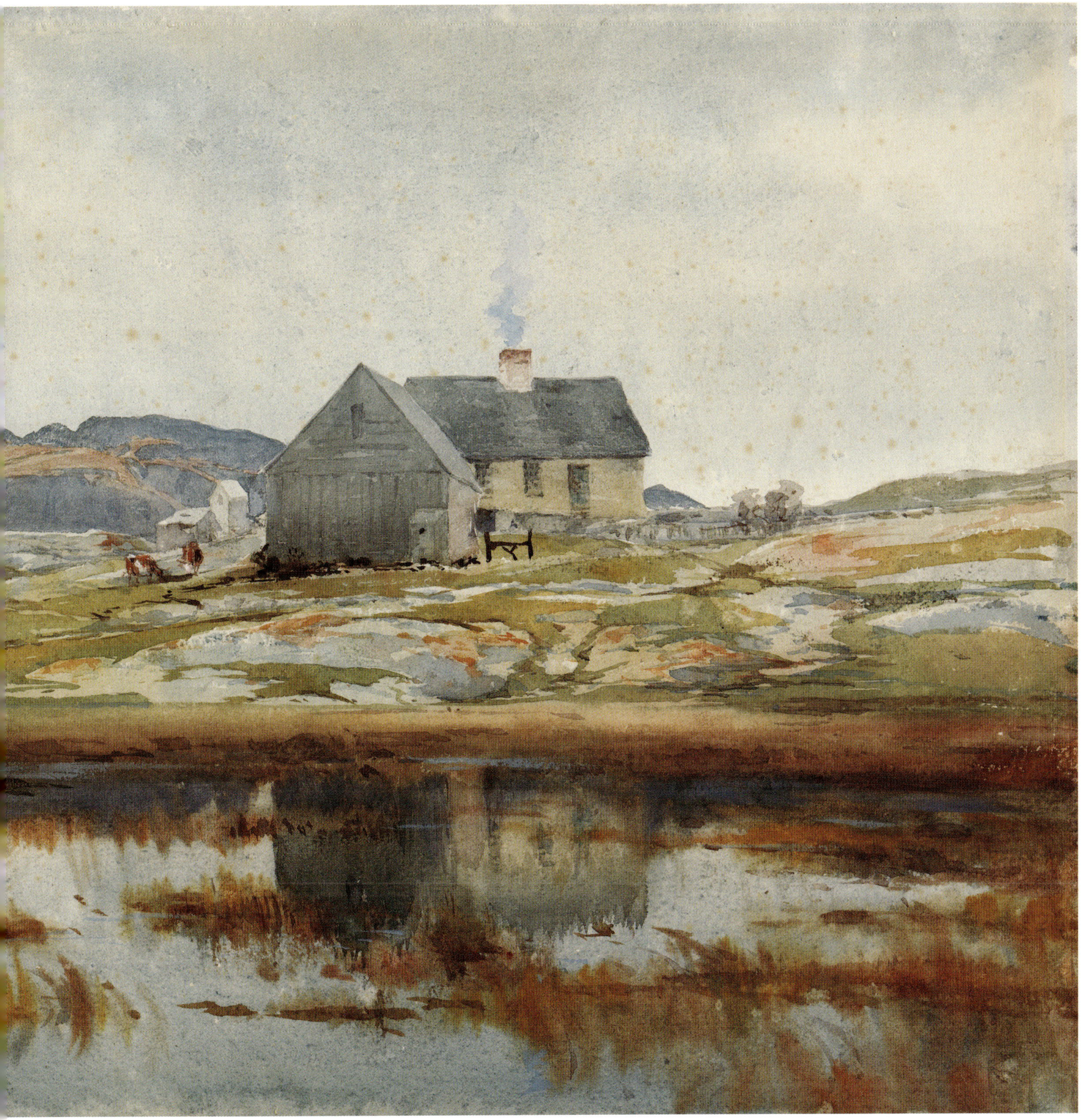

Samuel Peter Rolt Triscott (1846–1925),
The Pink House, Monhegan Village, 1896.
Watercolor on paper, 14½ x 21½ inches.
Portland Museum of Art, Maine. Gift of Sally W. Rand and Earle G. Shettleworth, Jr., 2002.49

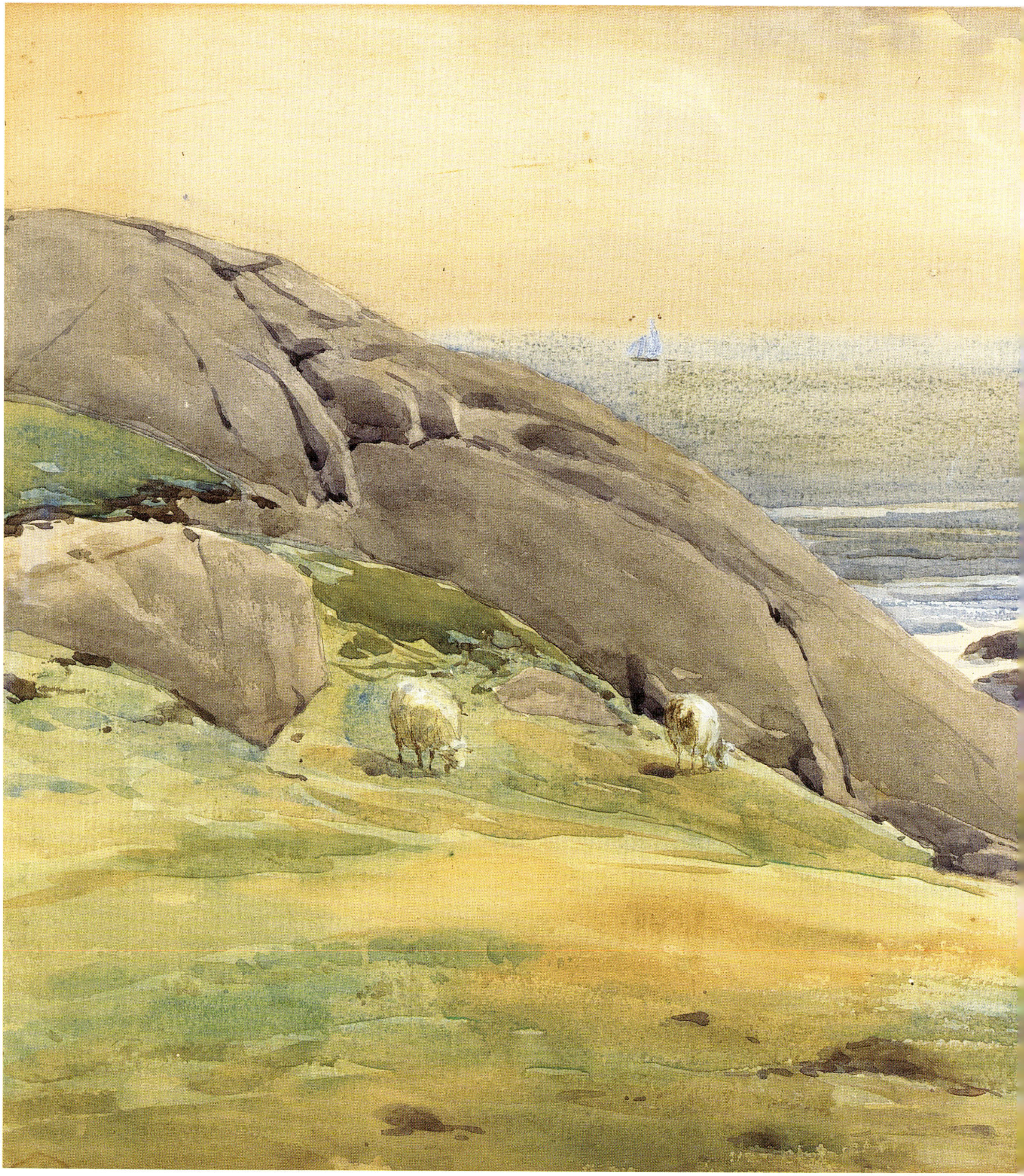

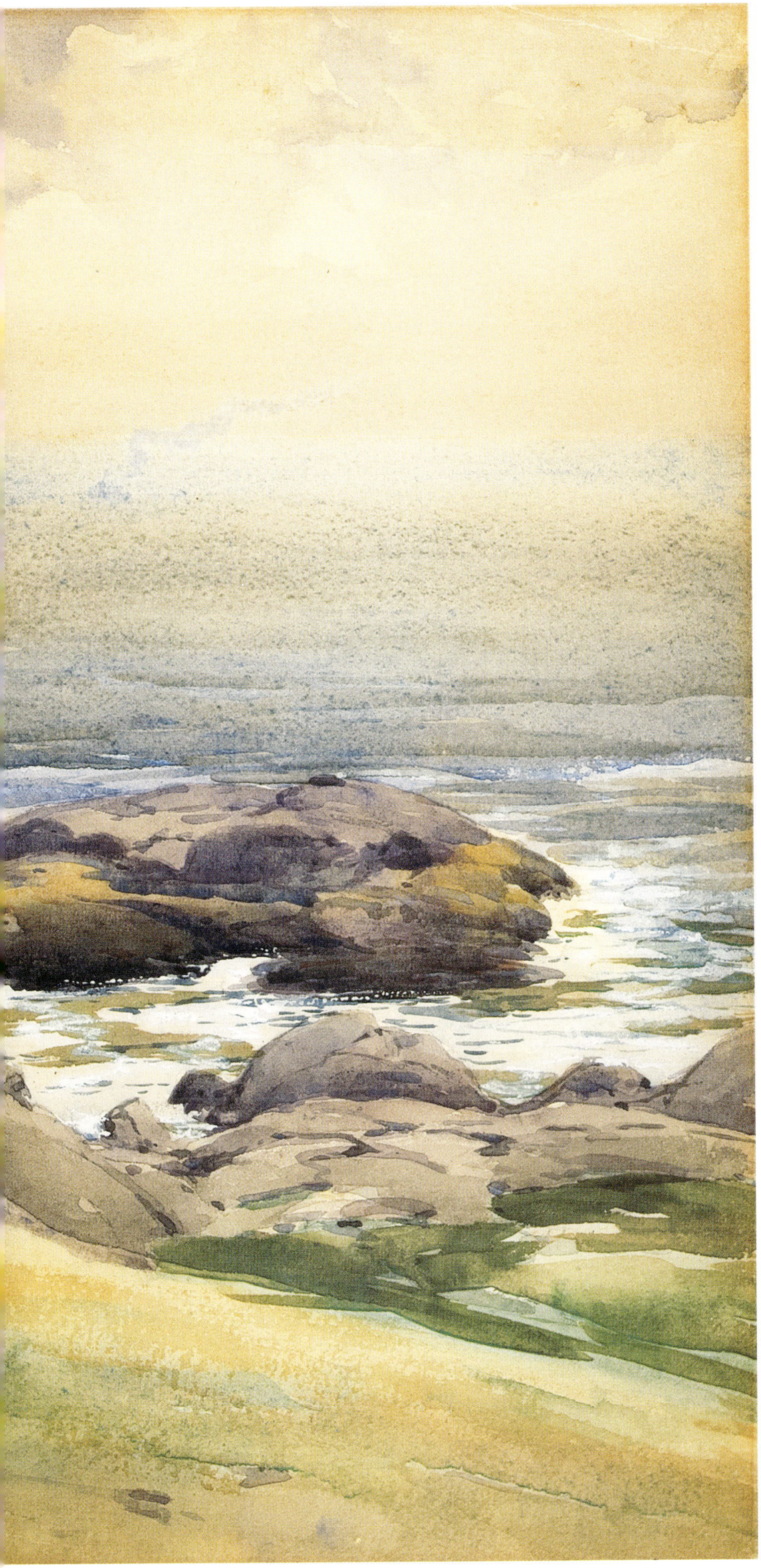

Samuel Peter Rolt Triscott (1846–1925), Untitled, ca. 1900. Watercolor on paper, 12⅝ x 19 inches. Private collection

Edward Robinson (1865–1929), Trees and headlands, Monhegan, ca. 1895. Gelatin silver print. Courtesy of the Maine Historic Preservation Commission

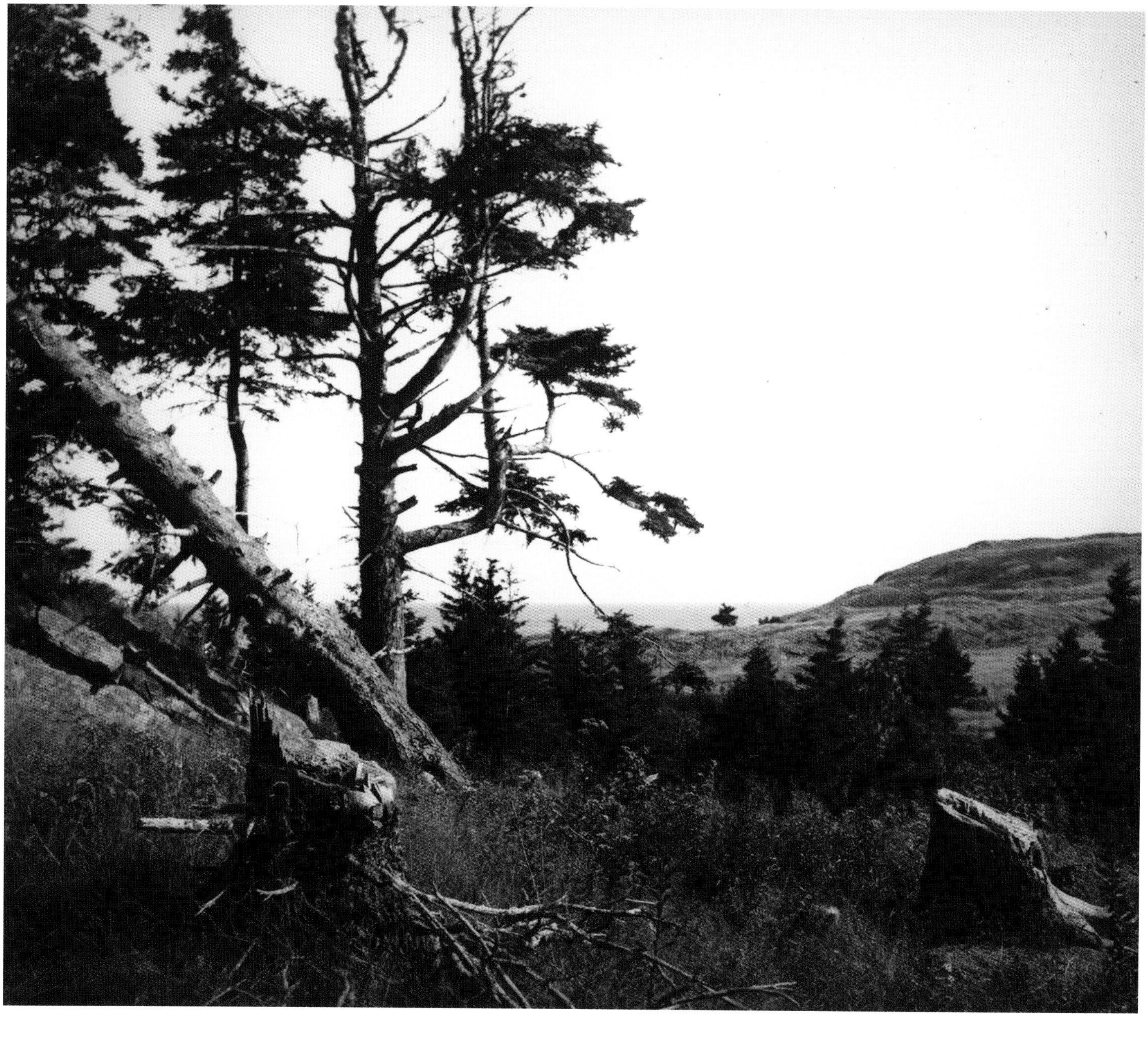

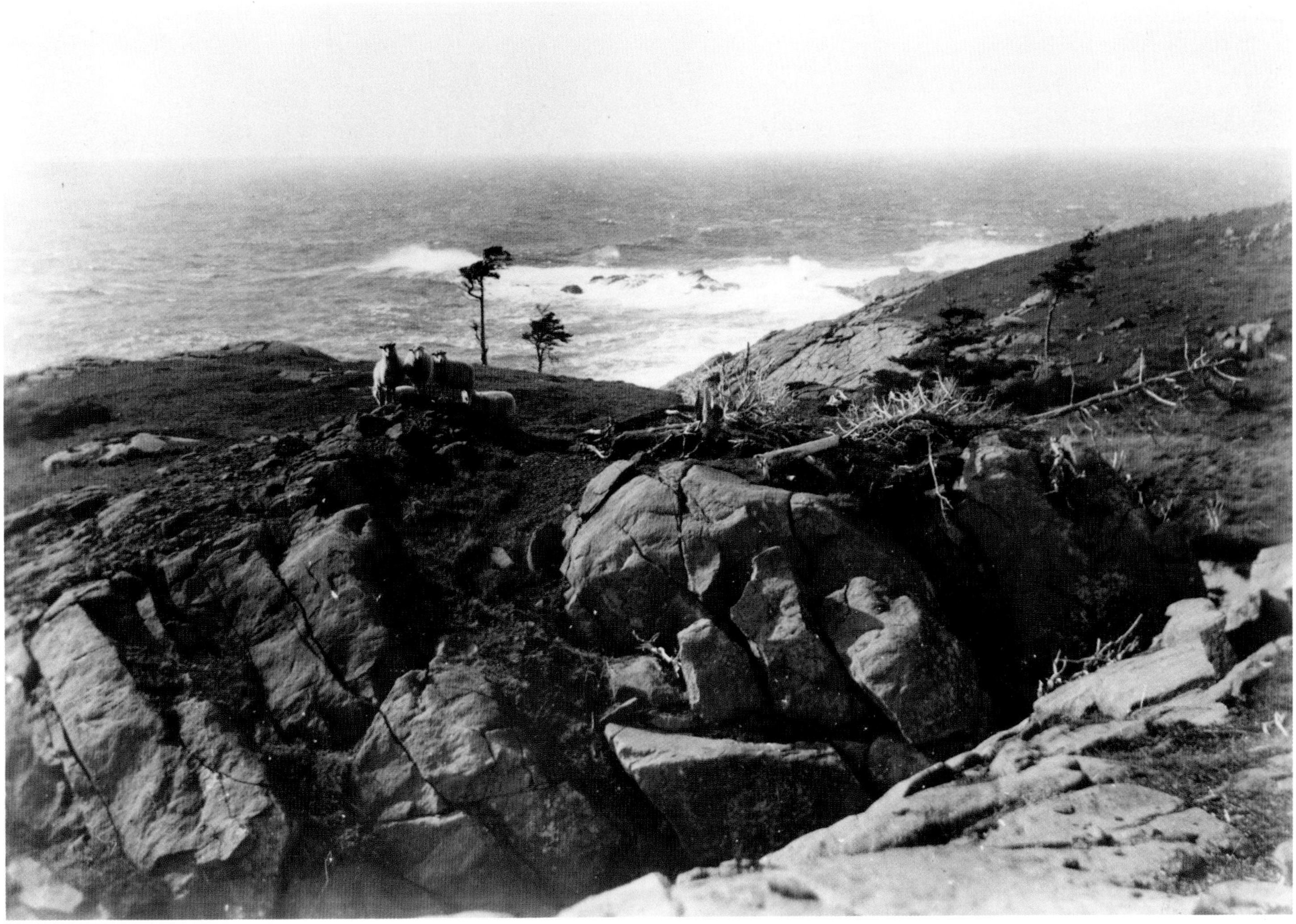

Samuel Peter Rolt Triscott (1846–1925), Sheep on the headlands, ca. 1895. Maine Historic Preservation Commission

by some islanders: "They look with distinct disapproval upon the intrusion of outsiders, especially those who buy land for speculative purposes. Quiet summer people they tolerate." Despite these tensions, the journalist concluded that "Monhegan's merits as a summer and health resort are becoming widely known. Artists, professional men, and other lovers of health, beauty, and quiet flock there in numbers that increase each year."[9]

The growing numbers on Monhegan led to increased attention to all aspects of island life. While maritime work was much commented upon and in general much celebrated, the island's sheep population became a source of statewide controversy. Since the introduction of sheep in the 1830s, their population had grown steadily. Their meat was an important staple in islanders' diets and their wool was sold or used to create clothes, blankets, and other necessities. As the *Globe* reporter noted, "Every self-respecting woman on the island has a spinning wheel of many generations' use on which she can spin good yarn."[10]

However, in the late nineteenth century, sheep farming suffered a steep decline. On Monhegan and across the region, the practice was largely abandoned. Multiple factors explain the closure of the era of free-roaming sheep: Migration westward across the continent and the creation of the Erie Canal opened fertile Ohio River valleys to agriculture and connected farmers to markets along the eastern seaboard. Thin, rocky, postglacial New England soil could not sustain competitive productivities. The Civil War had restricted the North's access to Southern cotton, driving up demand for local wool as a source of fiber. The vicissitudes of federal tariff policy swung in favor of free trade, flooding the American market with imported wool.

Raising sheep was likely always a supplemental source of income on Monhegan. As such, changes in the economics of sheep farming probably had less dramatic impact than was felt elsewhere. Yet, on the island and all along the Maine coast, the plight of abandoned island sheep and those receiving only minimal care contributed to the rise of an animal welfare movement. The Maine State Society for the Protection of Animals—founded in Portland in 1872 to protect the horses that pulled that city's streetcars and fire engines—took up the cause in the 1890s. Upon the receipt of complaints, representatives of the Society visited Monhegan and secured the commitment from sheep owners that they would erect a shelter and provide forage. Alas, Stanley Pullen, Society president, later asserted that the shelter was not placed where the sheep roamed and may have served no practical benefit. The Society turned to the courts in 1896, when further complaints and a follow-up visit suggested that the living conditions of Monhegan sheep had not improved. Owners of the sheep did not contest the finding of the Grand Jury of the Supreme Judicial Court for Lincoln County, which levied a fine and sought the sheep's removal. According to the Society's report, free-roaming sheep were gone from Monhegan before the start of 1897.[11]

While several residents owned oxen and a few dairy cows, and small, penned flocks of sheep were occasionally kept on Monhegan in the twentieth century, the era of sheep farming on the island had effectively closed by the late 1890s. The impact of this sudden change was transformative to Monhegan's economy and accelerated the burgeoning tourist industry. Ecologically, it ushered in a new chapter for the island in general and for its forests especially.

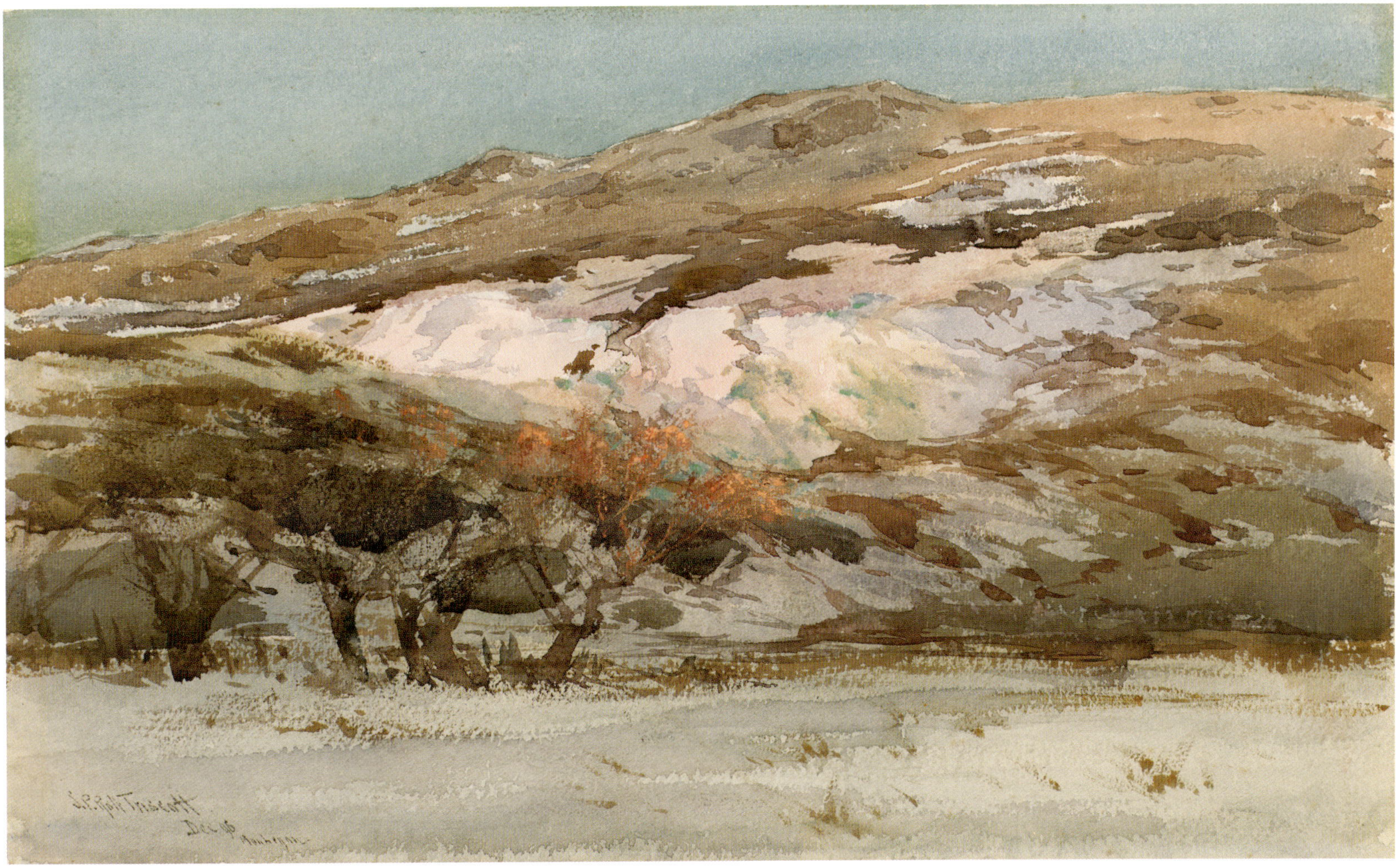

Samuel Peter Rolt Triscott (1846–1925), *Monhegan Winter*, 1896. Watercolor on paper, 10½ x 17⅜ inches. Bowdoin College Museum of Art, Brunswick, Maine. Gift of Stephen H. Israel, 2021.55.2

Monhegan Becomes a Destination

Earle G. Shettleworth, Jr., Maine State Historian

Between the end of the American Revolution and the beginning of the Civil War, Monhegan became a prosperous fishing and farming community of approximately one hundred individuals living amid the ocean off Midcoast Maine. During the 1850s, antiquarianism, art, and tourism converged to transform this remote island into a destination for visitors.

Monhegan's history of visitation by such early seventeenth-century English explorers as George Weymouth and John Smith and the presence of markings on adjacent Manana Island attracted the attention of Maine historians. In 1855, eight members of the Maine Historical Society visited the islands to inspect what was thought to be a Norse inscription. After one historian made a rubbing of the markings, the party feasted on a mackerel and cod dinner prepared by a local fisherman named Davis before returning to the mainland.

In 1856, history and art were joined in the person of Augustus C. Hamlin, a Bowdoin College graduate who practiced medicine in Bangor. During his visit to Monhegan, Hamlin made a cast of the Manana markings, which he sent to the Royal Nordic Society of Antiquaries in Copenhagen in hopes of having them deciphered. While the response of the Danish authorities is unknown, many nineteenth-century accounts of the island remarked on the Norse origin of the markings. However, most more recent writers describe them as geological formations. Hamlin also sketched a view of Monhegan from the water that appeared the next year as a wood engraving in a magazine, probably the first published image of the island.

In the spring of 1858, aspiring Portland artist Harrison Bird Brown set out to explore the Maine coast with fellow painter Aaron Draper Shattuck. The two young men sailed aboard a US Lighthouse Service vessel, which made a stop at Monhegan. There, Brown and Shattuck became among the first artists to sketch the island's rugged beauty. They would soon be followed by many others.

After the Civil War, Monhegan experienced a significant increase in visitation by tourists and artists. Enterprising steamboat companies offered day trips to the island, while residents provided meals and lodging to those who stayed longer. In 1877, Wilson L. Albee opened the first boardinghouse. After he died in 1878, his widow, Sarah, expanded the boardinghouse into a hotel, which she operated until her death in 1909. Such was the growing demand for summer accommodation that Edward Brackett opened the Monhegan House in 1891, followed by Frank Pierce, who opened the Island Inn in 1907.

During the 1870s, marine artists William E. Norton and Milton J. Burns painted on Monhegan. Norton depicted fishermen on Fish Beach in 1875, while Burns provided illustrations for an article titled "Fish and Men in the Maine Islands" that appeared in *Harper's New Monthly Magazine* in September 1880. In 1881, New York artist and illustrator George Wharton Edwards discovered Monhegan, which led to his summering on the island and, in 1890, to purchasing the first home intended for seasonal use. Edwards portrayed Monhegan life in prose and sketches in his 1897 book *P'Tit Matinic' and Other Monotones*.[12] A sketching trip to the island in 1892 by Boston watercolorist Samuel Peter Rolt Triscott resulted in his purchasing a house the following year. By 1902, Triscott was living and painting there year-round, becoming the first artist to reside permanently on the island. Like Edwards and Triscott, Boston artist Eric Hudson was captivated by his first visit to Monhegan in 1897 and returned the next year to build a summer home overlooking the harbor.

By the 1890s, Monhegan had achieved a widespread reputation as a rustic summer retreat. The *Pemaquid Messenger* reported on August 25, 1895: "It is a favorite resort for artists who flock to its comfortable quarters and can be seen on pleasant days sketching and painting. Monhegan is just now overflowing with summer visitors, some of whom have brought their cots with them and lodge in fish houses."[13]

Such popularity led to land speculation, which was common in late nineteenth-century coastal Maine summer communities from Kennebunkport to Eastport. George B. Kenniston of Boothbay Harbor was Monhegan's leading developer. In 1891, he purchased seventeen acres, resulting in two subdivisions, Prospect Hill and Harbor Lots. That year, Bainbridge Davis divided his property into forty-seven lots, which he called "Surfside." In 1895, Kenniston increased his holdings by purchasing thirty-two of Davis's lots. Neither of these entrepreneurs realized a quick profit, as cottage building on the island proved a gradual process.

As Monhegan entered the twentieth century, the island was firmly established as a summer destination. During the second half of the nineteenth century, Monhegan had evolved from a remote fishing village to a thriving seasonal community without sacrificing the essential character that was its primary asset. The stage was then set for Monhegan to become a major art colony, with early twentieth-century members including Robert Henri, George Bellows, Rockwell Kent, Randall Davey, and Frederick J. Waugh. As A. G. Pettengill wrote in an 1898 article for the *New England Magazine*: "Monhegan is full of interest and charm; and its power of attraction is increasing every year. . . . The artist turns hither for new and striking subjects, of which the village and shore are full, making the island the most paintable of any on the coast."[14]

Monhegan's rich artistic heritage has engaged me for more than forty years. I first learned about artists Samuel Peter Rolt Triscott and Eric Hudson through the photographs they took of the island in the 1890s. The survival of their glass plate negatives enabled me to coauthor books about Triscott and Hudson that illustrate their accomplishments as Monhegan photographers and artists of their time.[15] I continue to study the work of the many photographers who have been inspired by Monhegan from the 1850s to the present.

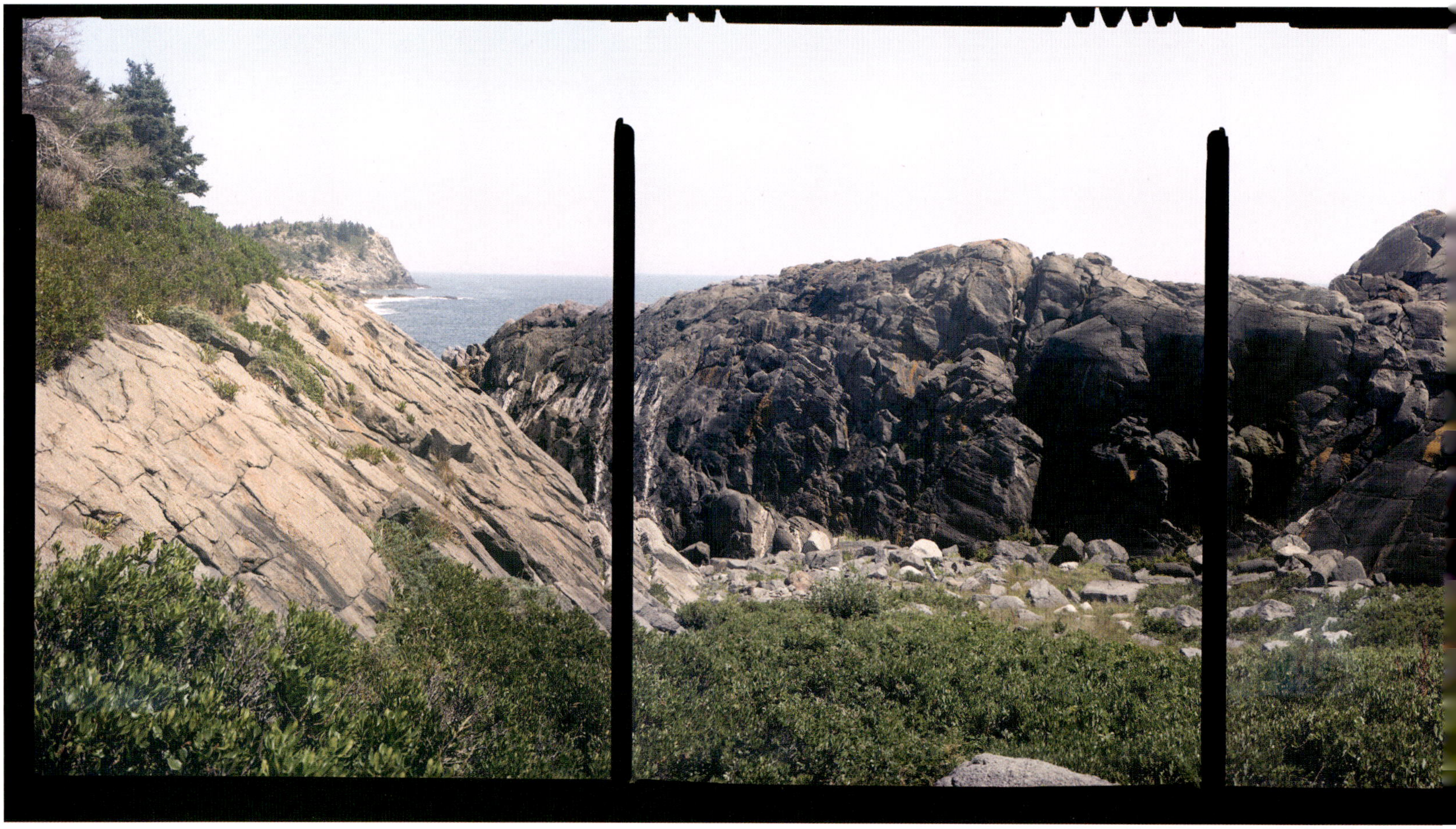

Accra Shepp (born 1962), *Gull Rock with View of Black Head*, 2022. Archival pigment ink print. Courtesy of the artist

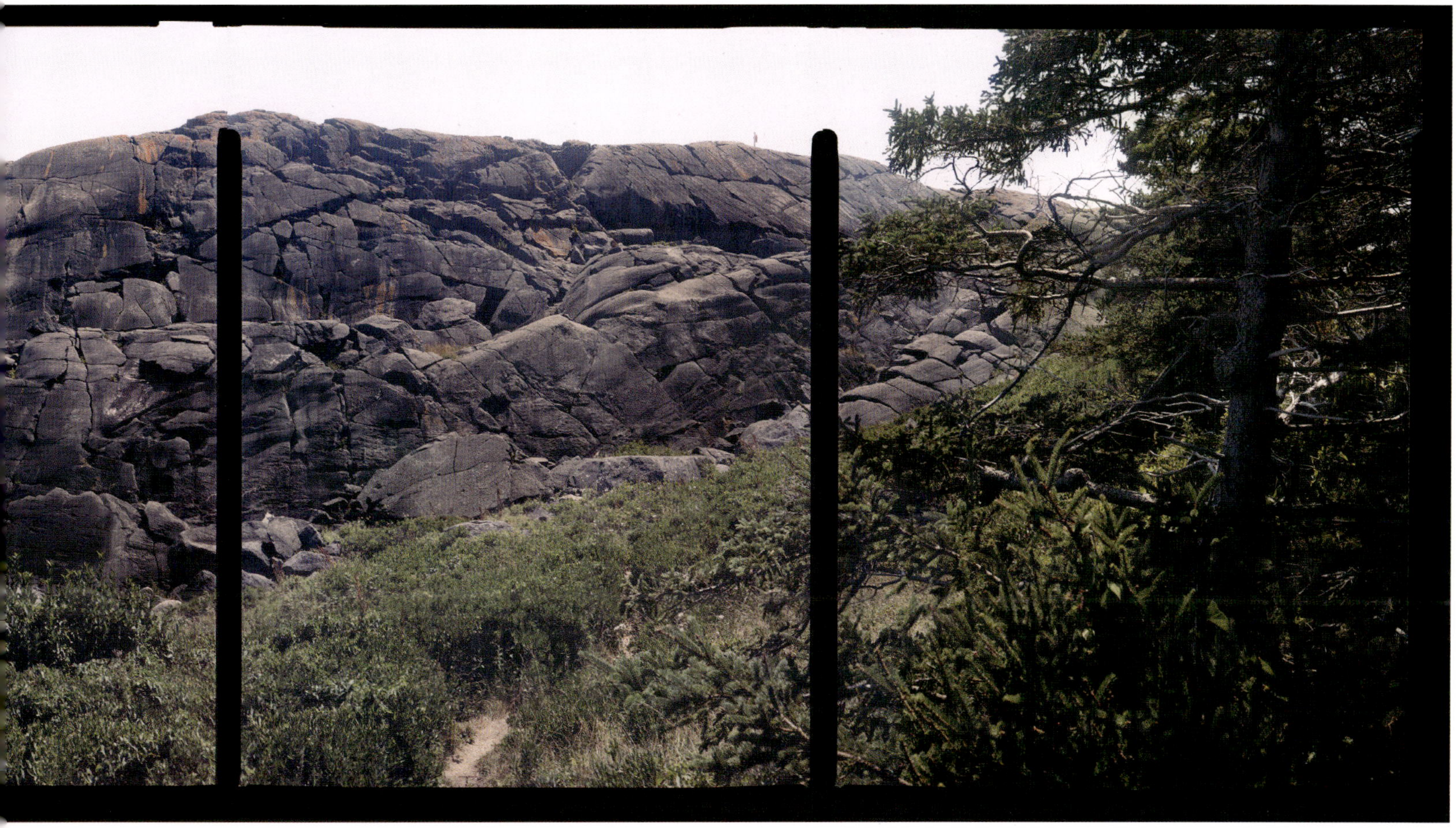

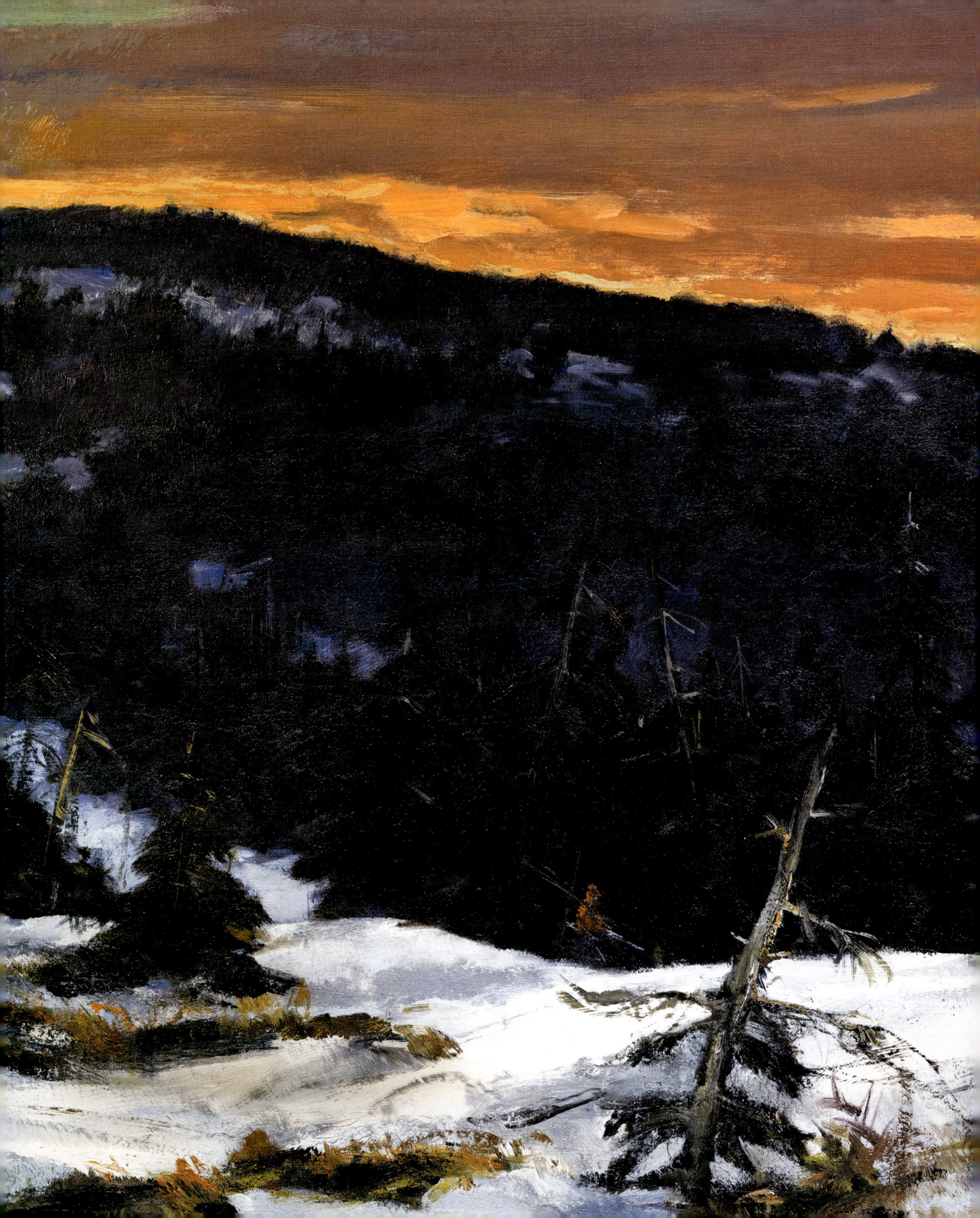

Chapter 4

Wilderness Preservation, Ted Edison, and the Monhegan Associates, 1929 to 1954

> At least as long ago as 1908 I started spending summers on Monhegan as a child, and I and other members of my family have fond memories of Monhegan as it was "in the old days." The beauty and freedom with which I was then surrounded probably had much to do with making me want to help in saving enough samples of wilderness on Monhegan and elsewhere to permit future generations to enjoy what I had known. —Ted Edison[1]

Following half a century of tremendous growth, in which Monhegan transformed from an island primarily inhabited by people descended from the Trefethren, Starling, and Horn families, who repopulated the island in the late 1700s, to a community of more than 120 people year-round, with a robust summer population and amenities for tourists, the 1930s were characterized by a sudden decline in development. Early in the decade, the effects of the Great Depression were felt, evident by a decrease in property sales and construction. During the years between 1900 and 1930, seventy-nine homes had been built; and between 1930 and 1940, only nine.[2] It was during this period that Ted Edison became a property owner on Monhegan.

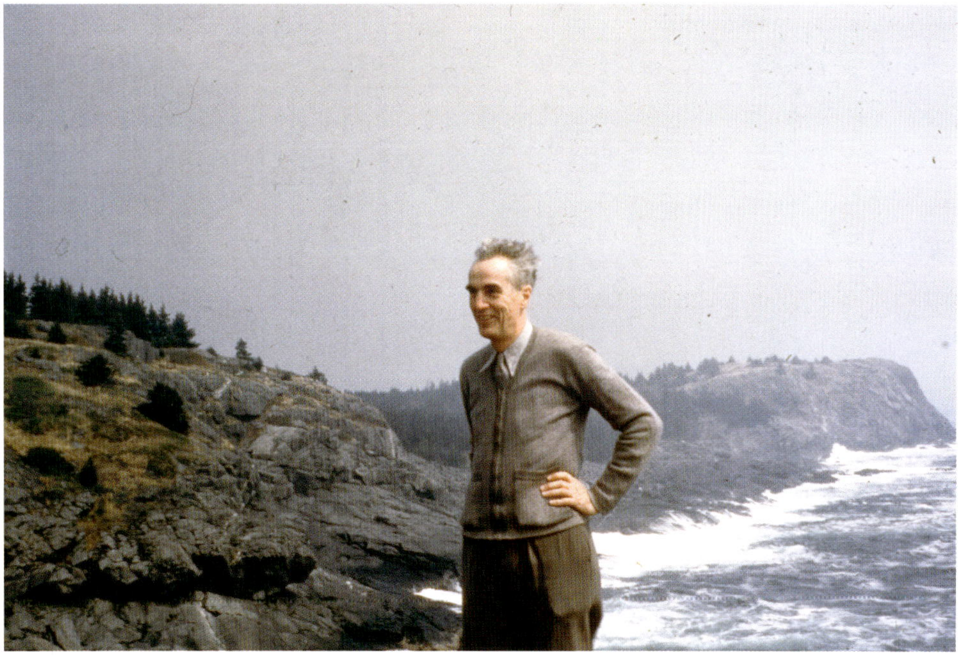

Unidentified photographer, Ted Edison on Monhegan, ca. 1950. Chromogenic print. Monhegan Museum of Art & History

The youngest son of celebrated inventor and entrepreneur Thomas Edison, Theodore "Ted" Miller Edison was ten years old when he first came to Monhegan in 1908 with his mother, Mina Miller Edison. Mina's sisters, Grace Miller and Mary Miller (later Nichols), often spent time on the island with their friend Grace Waymouth, who owned a small cottage named "Grace Note" near Lobster Cove. In 1911, Ted's aunt, Mary Miller, bought nearly nine acres of land on the southern part of Monhegan that included a portion of Gull Rock.

This visit was to be followed by many more. Regular letters and telegrams between family members document Ted Edison's frequent trips to the island, and after their 1925 marriage, his wife, Ann Osterhout Edison, also expressed her delight in their island adventures.[3] In 1929, Edison made his first purchase of land on Monhegan—nine acres located on the southern end of the island between the main road, Burnt Head, and Gull Rock. This property was adjacent to that owned by his aunt Mary Miller Nichols, which Edison inherited in 1946. Much of the land depicted (laterally reversed) in Stow Wengenroth's 1938 lithograph *Monhegan* was part of these properties. Edison correctly felt that this section containing Gull Rock at an elevation of seventy-five feet above sea level, pastureland, and remnant and encroaching second-growth spruce forest, "represents in miniature many of the features found elsewhere on the island."[4] Initially, this was the only portion he intended to preserve.[5] His second land acquisition occurred in 1938, when he purchased two lots north of Burnt Head from George Putnam. It was not until the early 1950s that Edison began acquiring land at a rapid rate.

Throughout the 1930s, the island population, both summer and year-round, remained stable. The 1930 census records indicate that the year-round population hovered at one hundred residents and thirty-five households. According to Monhegan Plantation annual reports, the school maintained a healthy attendance of about fifteen students. Fishing was the primary

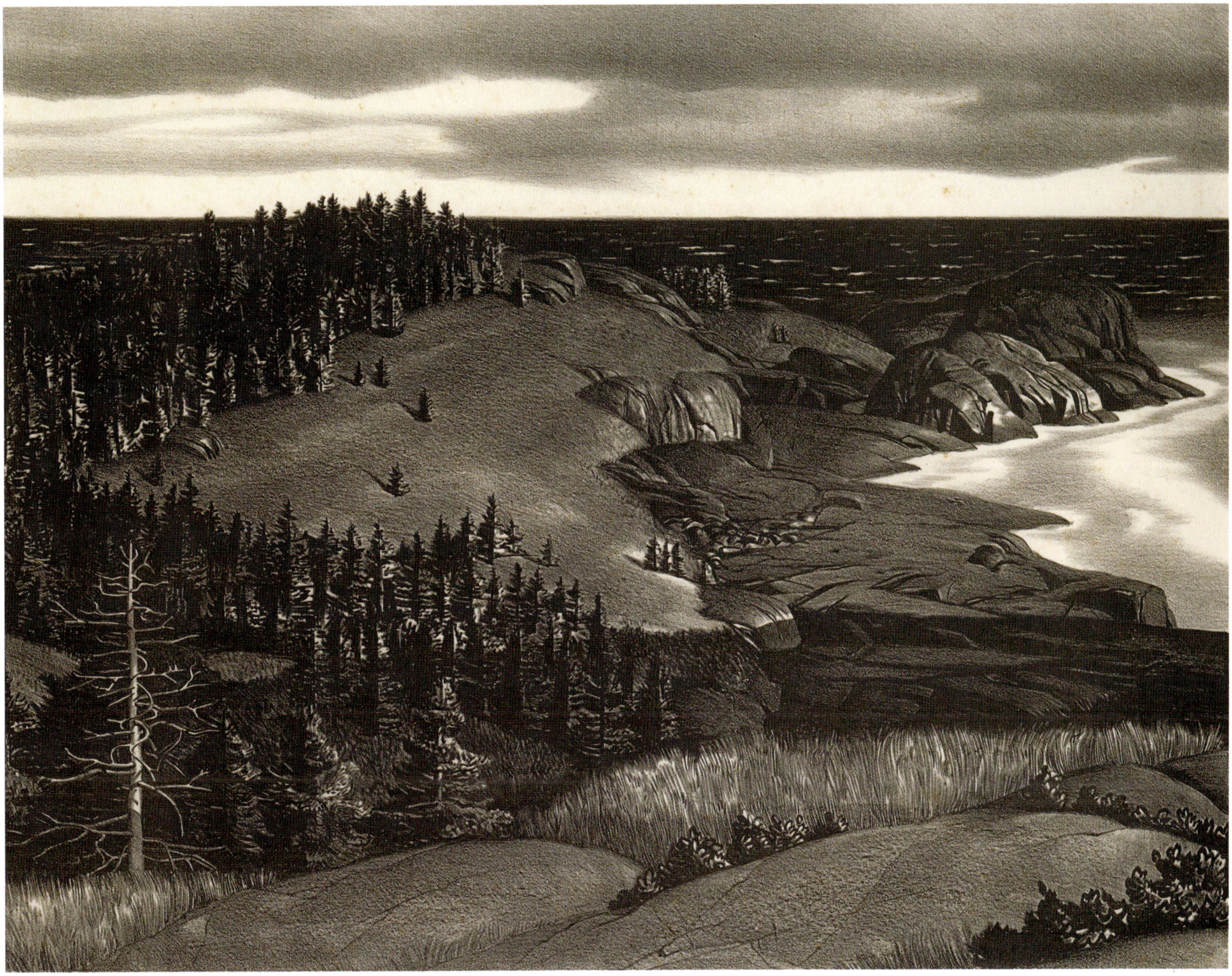

Stow Wengenroth (1906–1978),
Monhegan, 1938. Lithograph,
16 x 21⅛ inches. Bowdoin College
Museum of Art, Brunswick, Maine.
Gift of Charles Pendexter, 2009.16.768

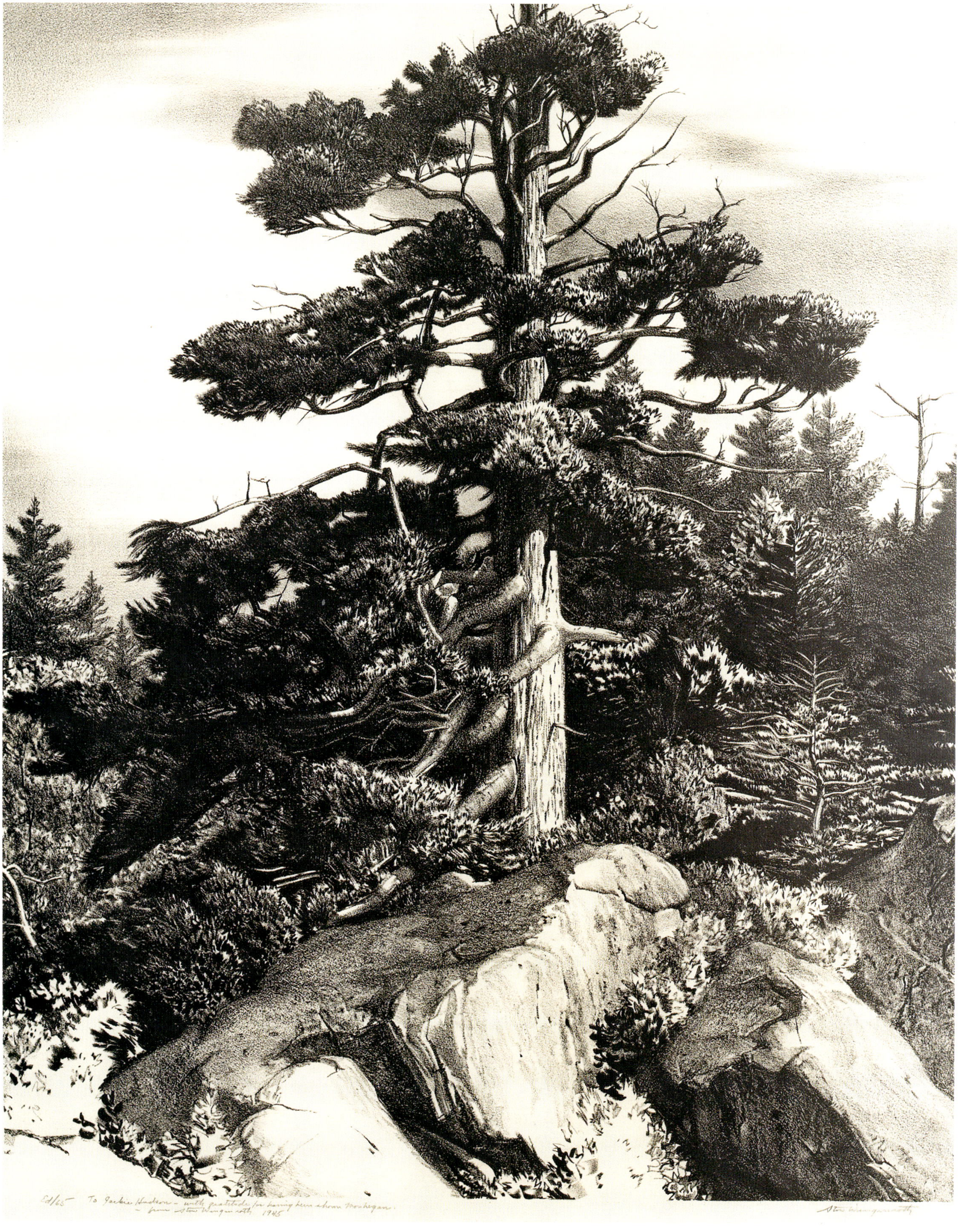
Ed/65 To Jackie Hudson – with gratitude for having been shown Monhegan.
– from Stow Wengenroth 1945
Stow Wengenroth

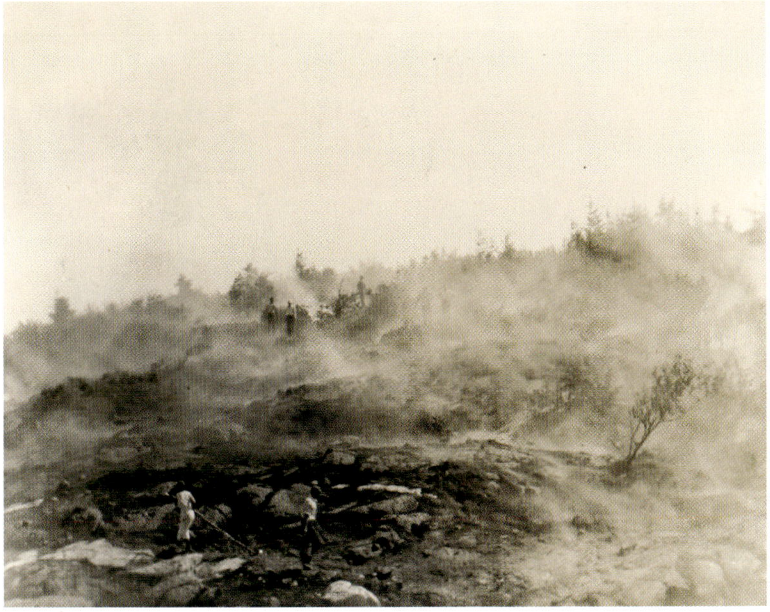

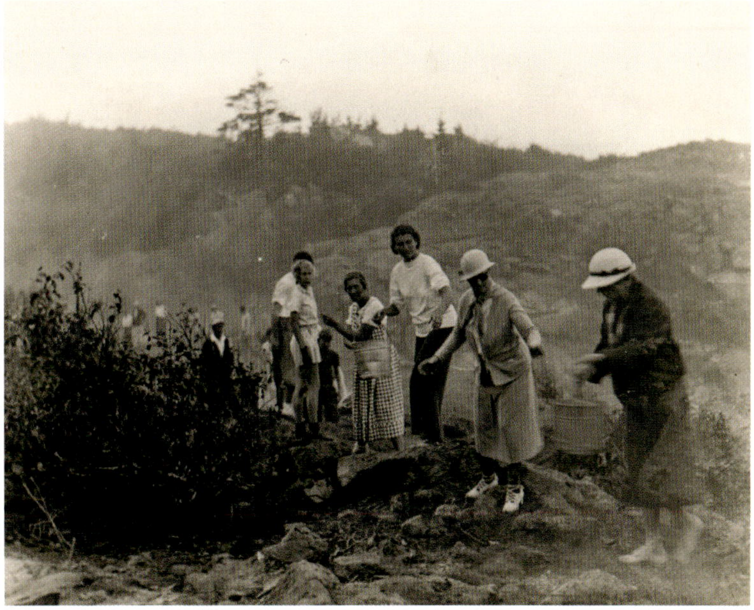

Above, left: Unidentified photographer, Black Head fire, 1934. Gelatin silver print. Monhegan Museum of Art & History

Above, right: Unidentified photographer, Black Head fire bucket brigade, 1934. Gelatin silver print. Monhegan Museum of Art & History

occupation, with carpentry and the fog and light signal stations also employing a significant number of island residents. Relations between the summer and year-round communities were mainly convivial, and a steady flow of letters and holiday cards passed between them. The islanders rallied around events to benefit the newly constructed library, which opened in 1930. These fundraisers included a masquerade ball, a homegrown circus, and a gymkhana in which islanders showcased their athletic skills. There were also dances in the Dance Hall; baseball, cribbage, and bridge games; and a variety of "tearooms" offered spaces for refreshments and socializing.

In August 1934, the entire island community was brought together by an event of a different sort when a fire broke out on Black Head. Widely believed to have been caused by an unextinguished cigarette, flames fanned by a strong southwesterly breeze are said to have reached twenty feet high. Assisted by the Coast Guard, two hundred people formed a bucket brigade, passing pails of seawater, hand to hand, hundreds of yards, from the shore to Black Head, while others used wet sacks, shovels, and brooms to fight the flames. The fire was extinguished before reaching the village, but approximately one-third of the island was left charred.[6]

This sobering occurrence was replicated in location and nearly every other detail fourteen years later, though on this occasion, Coast Guard cutters stood by to evacuate the island in the event that the village caught on fire.[7] These remarkably similar incidents underscored the importance of fire safety and led community members to raise funds for the purchase of firefighting equipment to combat future blazes that, if not contained, might engulf the entire island.

Historically, red spruce–dominated forests of the region experienced infrequent fire. Driven by the combination of accumulating fuel loads, dry conditions, and lightning strikes, the intervals between fires could be measured in centuries.[8] That two significant fires occurred on Monhegan within two decades highlights the heightened risk human activities present with regard to forest fire.

Opposite: Stow Wengenroth (1906–1978), *The Big Tree* or *The Landmark*, 1946. Lithograph, 17¼ x 14¼ inches. Monhegan Museum of Art & History. Gift of Jacqueline Hudson

In the years following the 1934 fire, events were organized to raise money for the purchase of a two-wheeled chemical fire engine. Island artist Jay Hall Connaway coordinated summer art exhibitions with fellow artists and photographers, including James Fitzgerald, Charles Ebert, and Warner Taylor; and the Pyle family held a bridge party and charged admission to support the fire fund. These funds were transferred to the local government, and in the following years, taxes were levied to purchase additional fire equipment.

Ongoing concern about fire danger was a prevalent theme in correspondence between Rockwell Kent and Monhegan Plantation assessor James McAlpin Pyle. The idea of a state park on Monhegan having come to Kent's attention, he showed his support for this initiative in a document titled "Suggestions for State Park Promotion," which he shared with Pyle in the summer of 1951. Kent wrote: "It should be not just the people of Monhegan and those who happen to know Monhegan but the people of the State of Maine who want the Island made a park. Of course, outstanding among the benefits of the project to the Monhegan people as a whole is the removal of that whole area as a fire hazard and the assumption of maintenance and fire protection by the State authorities. That alone should enlist the active support of every property holder on Monhegan."[9]

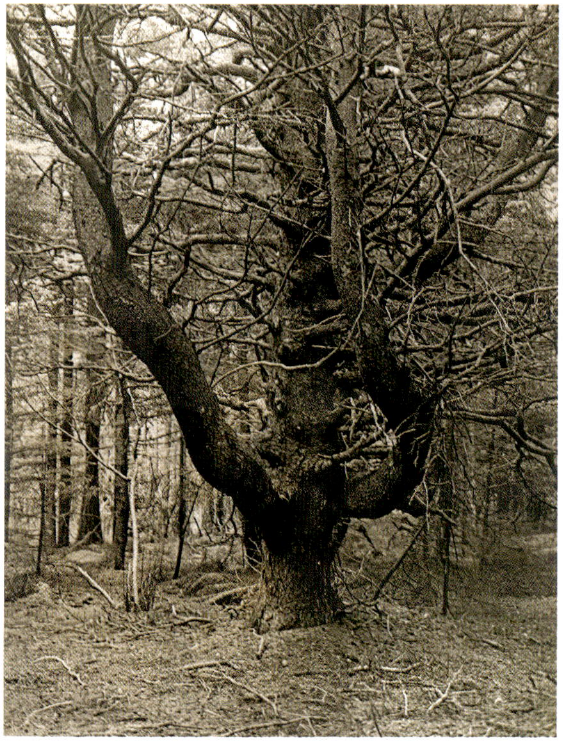

Above: Warner Taylor (1880–1958), Untitled, ca. 1950. Gelatin silver print, 14 x 11 inches. Monhegan Museum of Art & History. Gift of Lucia Taylor Miller

Artists continued to be attracted to Monhegan through the 1930s and 1940s, though the dominance of the American Impressionists and followers of Robert Henri gave way to a new generation of painters that included Jay Connaway, James Fitzgerald, Abraham J. Bogdanove, Alfred Fuller, and Andrew Winter, who were captivated by the rugged weather, stormy seas, and working life of the islanders. No doubt the artists of the Henri school inspired and perhaps even motivated those artists following in their wake.

How did these artists place their work in dialogue with the art of those who preceded them? This question is especially complicated when one considers the dynamic landscape serving as their subject matter. Ecologically, the island during the first decades of the twentieth century differed profoundly from that of the middle decades. While many painted what was in front of them, Jay Connaway, in *Seas at White Head, Monhegan* appears to have reached back to an era before his own. His treeless headland speaks directly to the headlands captured by Kent and Edward Hopper and others, even as a photograph of Connaway, perhaps by happenstance, clearly shows white spruce encroaching on the headland.

During this era, the summer art colony included several women from Philadelphia who became best known for their depictions of island life, village scenes, flower gardens, and the daily tasks of mending fishing nets and hanging laundry. Depictions of stormy seas and the struggles of humankind against the forces of nature—favored subjects of their male counterparts—drew less of their attention. Alice Kent Stoddard, Rockwell Kent's first cousin, initially came to Monhegan to visit her aunt Dorothy Kent in 1909. Though Kent sold her Lobster Cove home in 1923, Stoddard continued to paint the island and its people until her death in 1976. Celebrated for her portraits, she rendered generations of islanders, but she was also an accomplished genre painter. Often her friend Mary Townsend Mason worked alongside her. In the early 1920s, Stoddard had convinced Mason, a sister Philadelphian, to join her on Monhegan, and in 1925, Mason purchased what would be the first of several homes. She returned

Opposite: James Fitzgerald (1899–1971), *Sentinels I*, ca. 1960. Watercolor and Chinese ink with graphite underdrawing on paper, 30 x 22 inches. Private collection

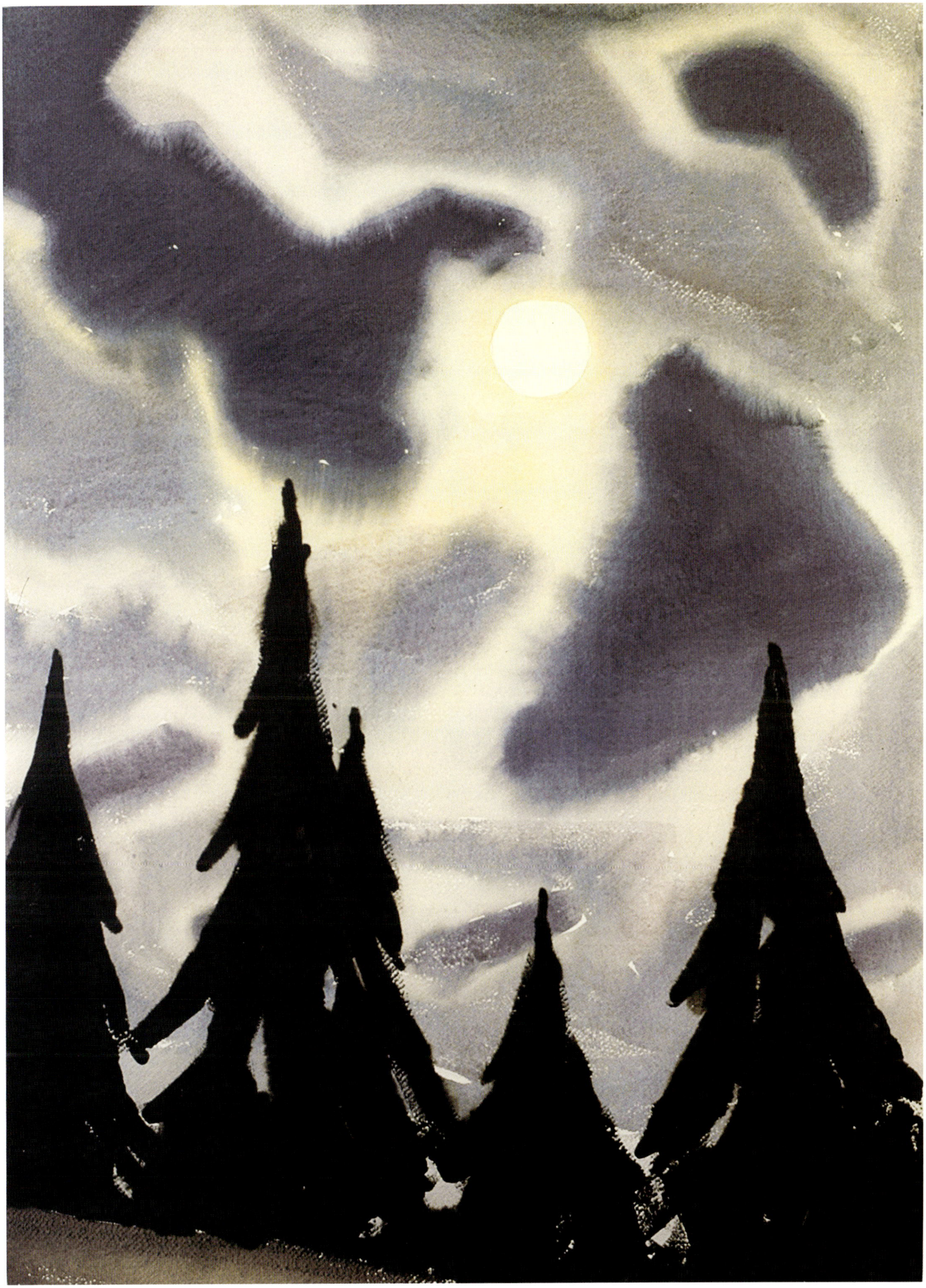

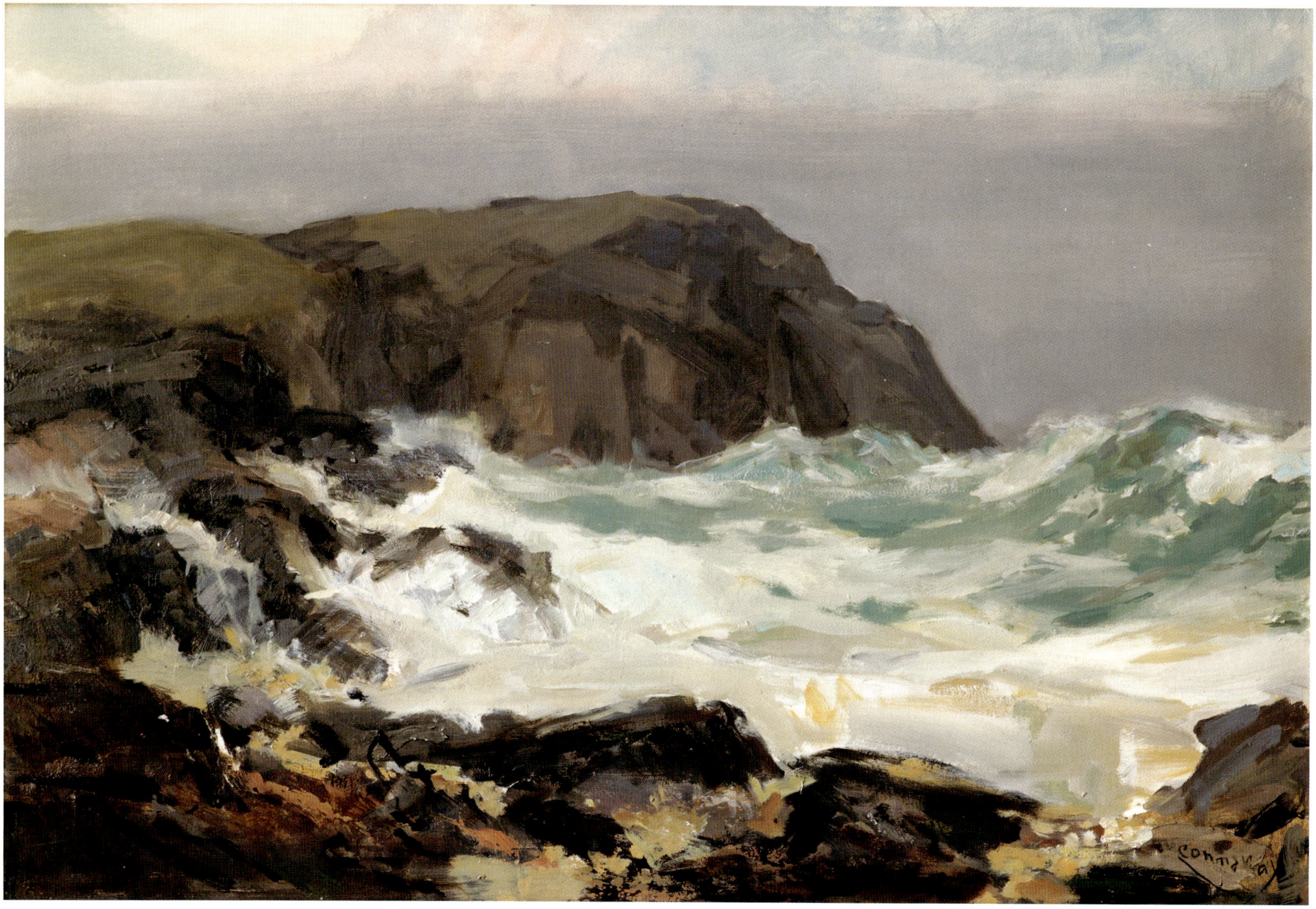

Jay Hall Connaway (1893–1970), *Seas at White Head, Monhegan*, ca. 1940. Oil on board, 20 x 36 inches. Collection of Stephen S. Fuller and Susan D. Bateson

Jay Hall Connaway (1893–1970),
Windblown Spruce, ca. 1940.
Oil on Masonite, 24 x 36 inches.
Monhegan Museum of Art &
History. Gift of Geraldine King Tam

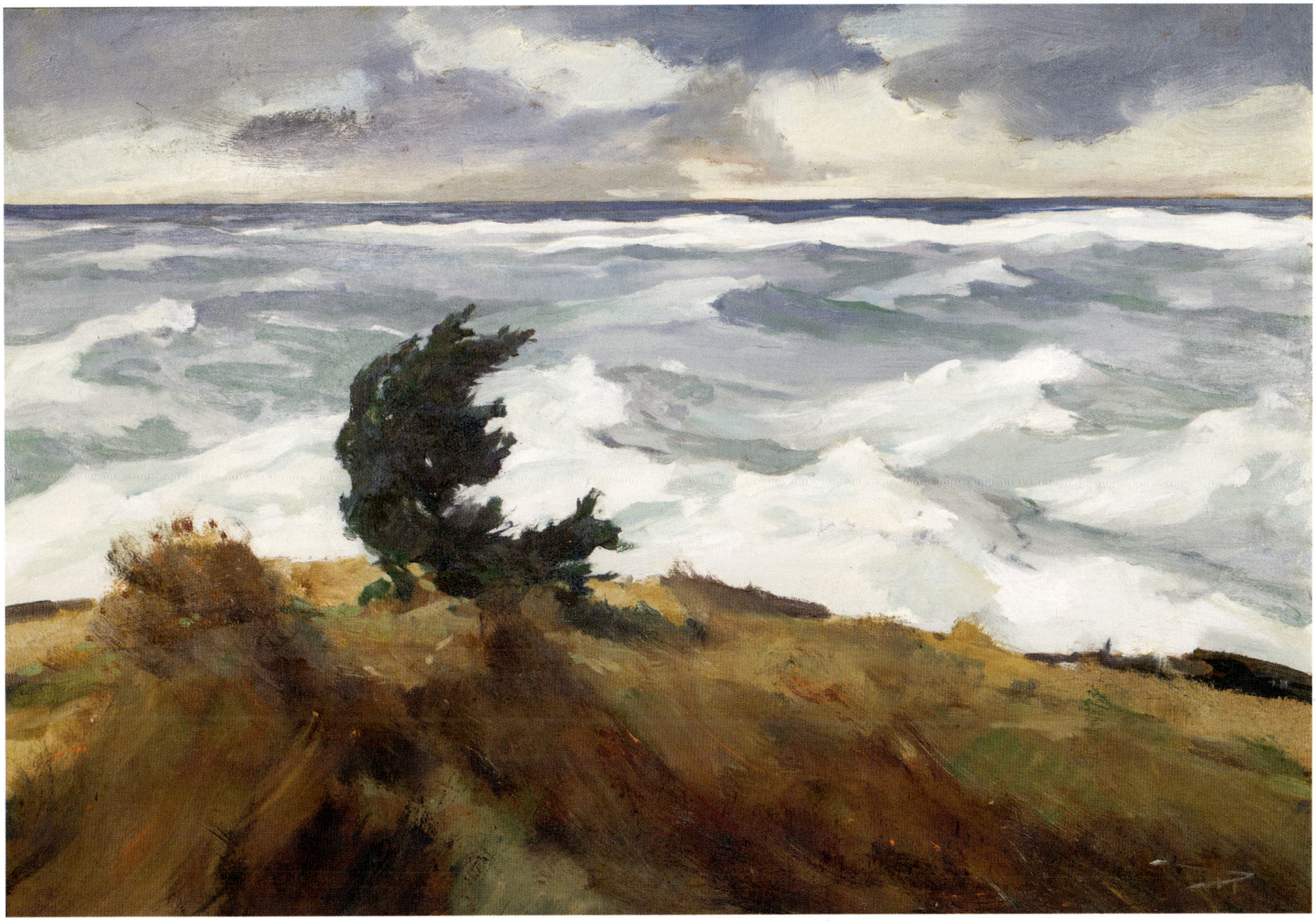

each summer for over forty years. Constance Cochrane and Isabel Branson Cartwright, two members of the Philadelphia Ten, an accomplished group of female artists who exhibited together between 1917 and 1945, maintained summer studios on the island beginning in the 1930s. Both Cartwright and Cochrane were known for their seascapes and paintings of vibrant island gardens, though Cartwright also completed portraits of island residents during her decades on Monhegan. Cochranes's *Glory of Fall, Monhegan* (see p. 121) illustrates the view of Manana from the southern end of the island, a vista that was increasingly obscured by the growth of spruce trees shortly after this work was completed. The lack of trees in the village area during the 1930s is confirmed by Mary Mason's painting *Sidney's Garden* (see p. 120).

Each of these artists owned a house, spent much time on the island, and was active in the community. Ultimately, Connaway, Fitzgerald, and Winter chose to make Monhegan their year-round home. This abundance of artists was captured by Phyllis Chadwick in her playful 1940 map, *Monhegan Island, Maine*, which depicts four men and women with their easels scattered across the island's eastern headlands (see p. 114). An amateur painter and descendant of the Trefethren family, Chadwick was raised on Monhegan among these artists and moved to the mainland in 1942.

By the late 1930s, even remote Monhegan was feeling the effects of increasing tensions in Europe prior to World War II. Ships built at the nearby Bath Iron Works were seen conducting their sea trials in the distance, and there were several submarine sightings near the island. Once the United States joined the war in 1941, all the island's young men who were eligible for service enlisted in the military and traveled overseas. New construction, which had already slowed in the 1930s, ceased entirely. Fewer people were taking holidays, and summer residents were hesitant to travel to their island homes. Some of the effects of the war were more conspicuous locally. The island mail boat was conscripted for military service, food and fuel were rationed, the signal from the lighthouse was dimmed, and Coast Guard troops patrolled the headlands at night for enemy vessels. Some island residents moved to the mainland to support the war effort or to earn a livelihood in building trades. Enrollment in the school dwindled to only four students, who received their lessons at their teacher's home due to a scarcity of fuel to heat the schoolhouse.

The end of the war marked the beginning of a period of revitalization for Monhegan. All of the men returned from war, most married, and soon the number of children on the island grew. School enrollment swelled to an average of ten students in the 1950s. Building trades resumed, and new artists arrived from New York, bringing with them a more abstract approach to artmaking. Many of these artists had been employed by the Works Progress Administration Federal Art Project or had studied under celebrated art teacher Hans Hofmann through the GI Bill. These artists, veterans, and their families formed the core of the community on Monhegan that flourished in the second half of the twentieth century.

From the mid-1930s until the early 1950s, due to other commitments on his time, Ted Edison did not make the journey to Monhegan. Upon his return in 1952, he quickly recognized that the postwar boom of tourism and construction could result in dramatic development. Having experienced rapid growth in his

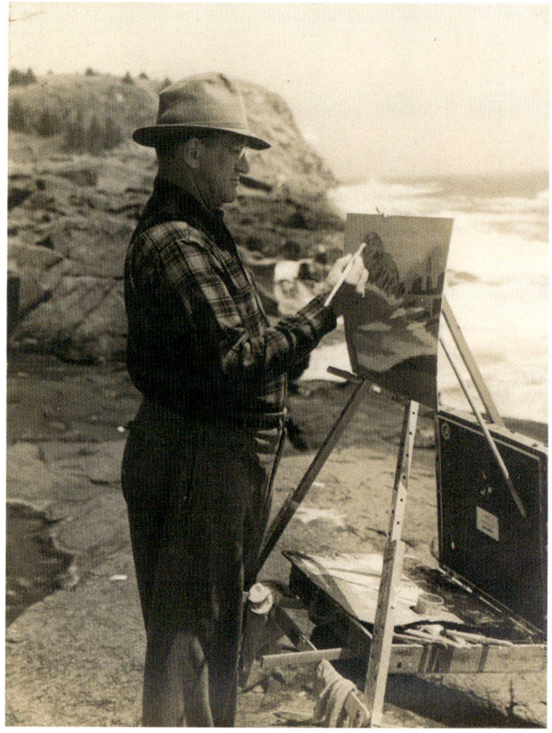

Unidentified photographer, Jay Connaway painting Gull Rock, 1940s. Gelatin silver print. Monhegan Museum of Art & History

home state of New Jersey, he treasured the relatively slow pace of change on the island. He cited the writings of Robert Marshall, one of the founders of the Wilderness Society, created in 1935 as an "organization of spirited people who will fight for the freedom and preservation of the wilderness," to express his feelings about preserving the natural environment.[10] As Marshall wrote: "The wilderness is also unique esthetically in that it stimulates not just the sense of sight, as does art, or the sense of sound, as does music, but all of the senses which man has. . . . The wilderness is all of these senses harmonized with immensity into a form of beauty which to many human beings is the most perfect experience of the earth."[11]

Edison's concerns about what might happen to the island if large tracts of land were to pass to off-island owners inspired him to begin buying property in order to preserve the Wildlands so that others could "enjoy what he had known." Many of these properties were part of George B. Kenniston's Prospect Hill development of 60-by-120-foot lots between Whitehead and Burnt Head. In some instances, the property transfer history was so complex that Edison was obliged to purchase the same lot multiple times from different owners to obtain a clear title. In the years between 1952 and 1959, Edison acquired all of the Prospect Hill lots through twenty-seven separate transactions. Despite owning such a significant portion of the island, Edison never pursued a home for himself, choosing instead to make these lands available to all, and going so far as to remove the one house that had been constructed on the headlands. Visible in maps drawn by Frederic Dorr Steele and Phyllis Chadwick as a black rectangle atop Burnt Head, the Budd Cottage, built in the early 1920s, was a grand summer home overlooking the sea. In 1956, Edison persuaded island artist Philip Shumaker, owner of the cliffside cottage, to sell his summer home and property. Edison then hired an island carpenter to tear it down. Shumaker relocated to the village, and the headlands were once again free of human-built constructions. Edison's action in this instance is an early example of conservation via "deconstruction," which can reconnect properties to create contiguous landscapes and is an approach commonly used in contemporary stewardship.

It was in the early 1950s that Edison began considering the idea of a land trust on Monhegan to preserve the land in perpetuity. From the outset, he was cognizant of the need to maintain a balance between preserving the Wildlands and sustaining the island community. He did not wish to stand in the way of carpenters pursuing their trade or of residents having land to build homes. He described this tension:

> Of course, Monhegan is no longer in strictly primeval form, but its woods and headland side offer a good approximation—and the fact that Monhegan is surrounded by the ocean offers some hope that it may be possible to insure [*sic*] the permanence of a place where one can go to find immensity and solitude. . . . Unfortunately, in nature-preservation work, there is an almost unavoidable conflict between the interests of the many people who have a deep yearning for a place where they can go, at least for short periods of time, to escape from the complexities and tensions of urban life, and the interests of the permanent residents of such a place, who may consider the lack of complexities an inconvenience.[12]

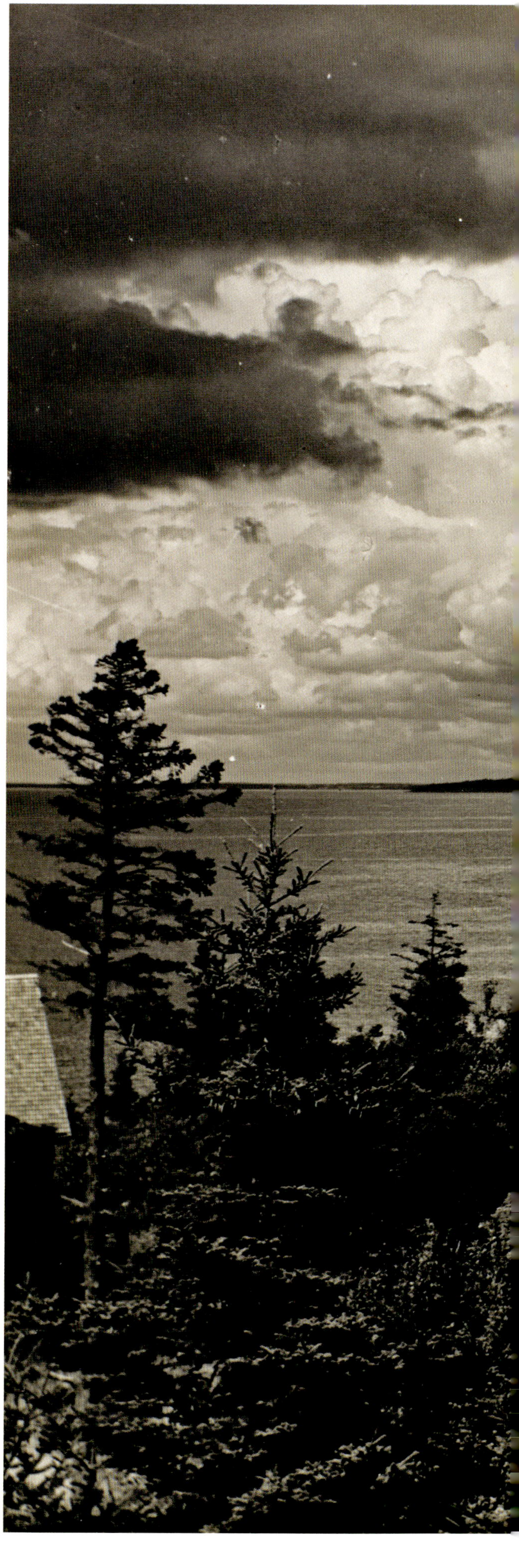

Warner Taylor (1880–1958), Untitled (Monhegan—view over treetops to the west), undated. Gelatin silver print, 11¾ x 14¾ inches. Portland Museum of Art, Maine. Gift of Earle G. Shettleworth, Jr., 2006.22.5

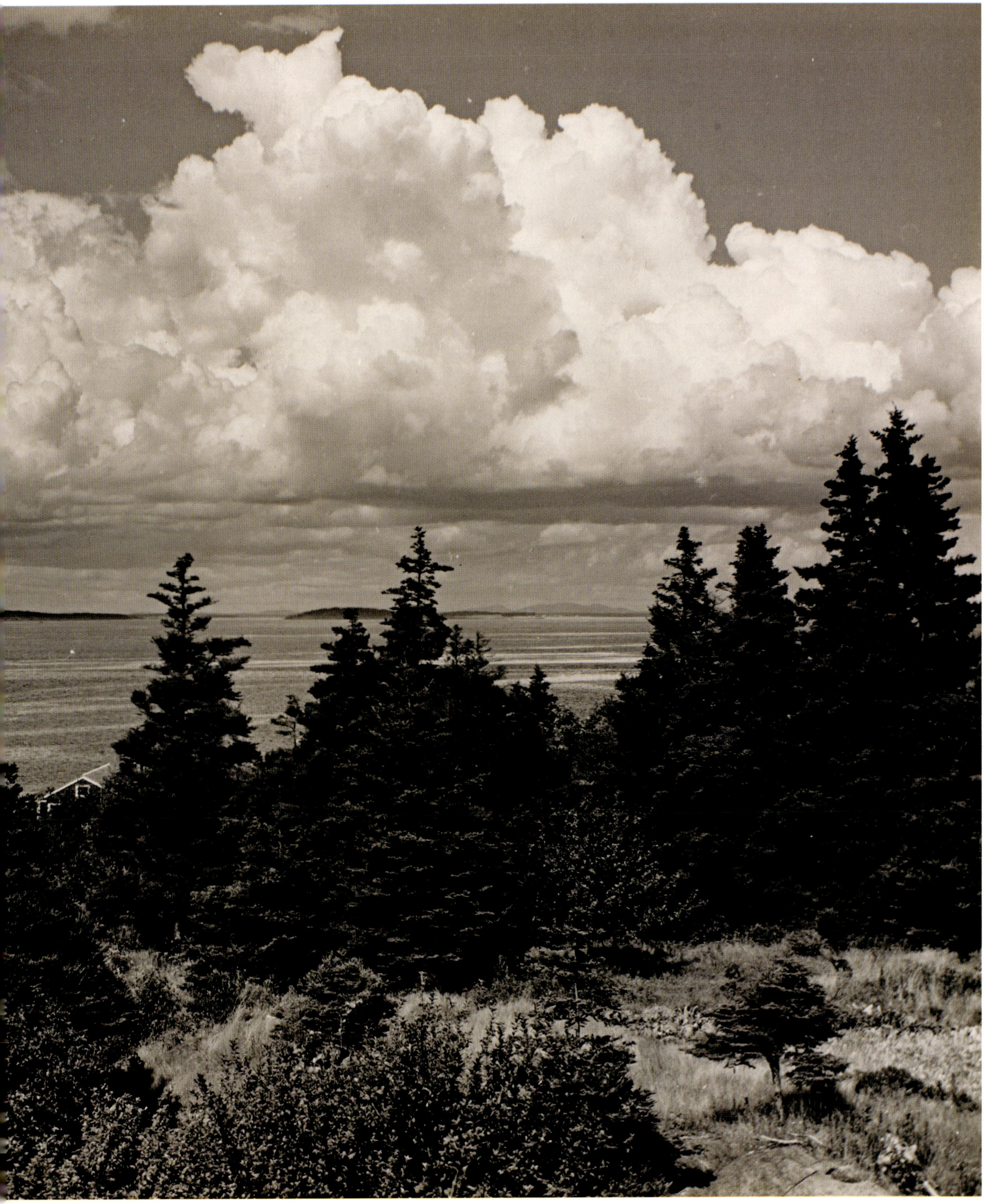

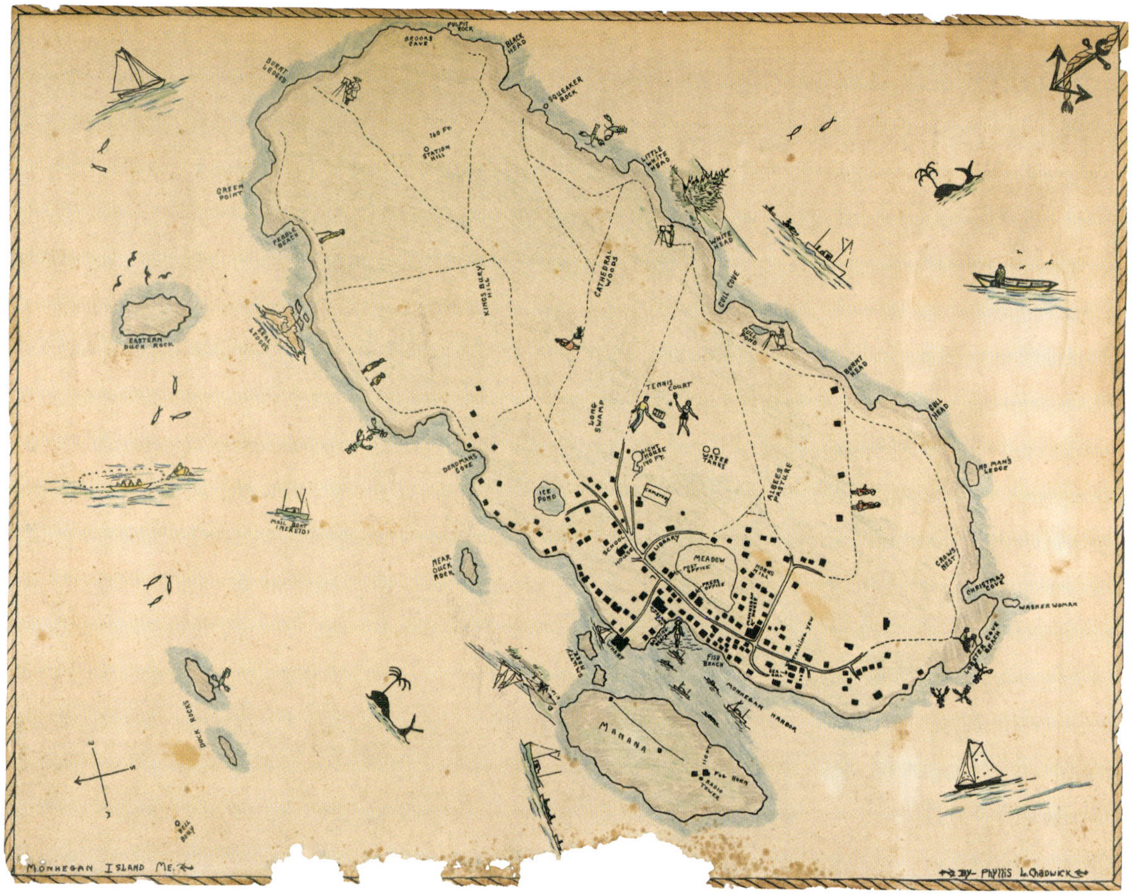

Left: Phyllis Chadwick (1918–1991), *Monhegan Island, Maine*, 1940. Osher Map Library, University of Southern Maine

Opposite: *Land of G. B. Kenniston. Prospect Hill. Monhegan, Me.*, 1908. Blueprint. Monhegan Museum of Art & History

Edison was aware that members of the community might view his property purchases with suspicion. Rumors abounded, fueling fears that outside influence would interfere with the interests of the islanders. To address these concerns, Edison knew that he needed to work in partnership with island residents. In the postwar island community, no individual commanded greater influence or respect than lifelong island resident Sherman M. Stanley, who was born in 1925 and had enlisted in the navy at age seventeen. Upon returning home after serving in the Pacific, he emerged as a leader in both the community and the fishing fleet despite his youth. When Edison revisited the island in 1952, Stanley had recently been elected first assessor, the highest office in the government of Monhegan Plantation and a post he would hold for twenty of the following twenty-five years. Recognizing that he would need a partner from within the island community to build support for his vision, Edison began cultivating a relationship.

Stanley later recalled his meetings with Edison in the early 1950s:

> And so he (Edison) came and chatted with me about his idea. And I guess that in that particular summer we did mostly chat about one thing and another because I wanted to find out for sure just how much of the island he had in mind. I had to take into consideration the people who lived here and did carpenter work and various jobs on the island because I knew

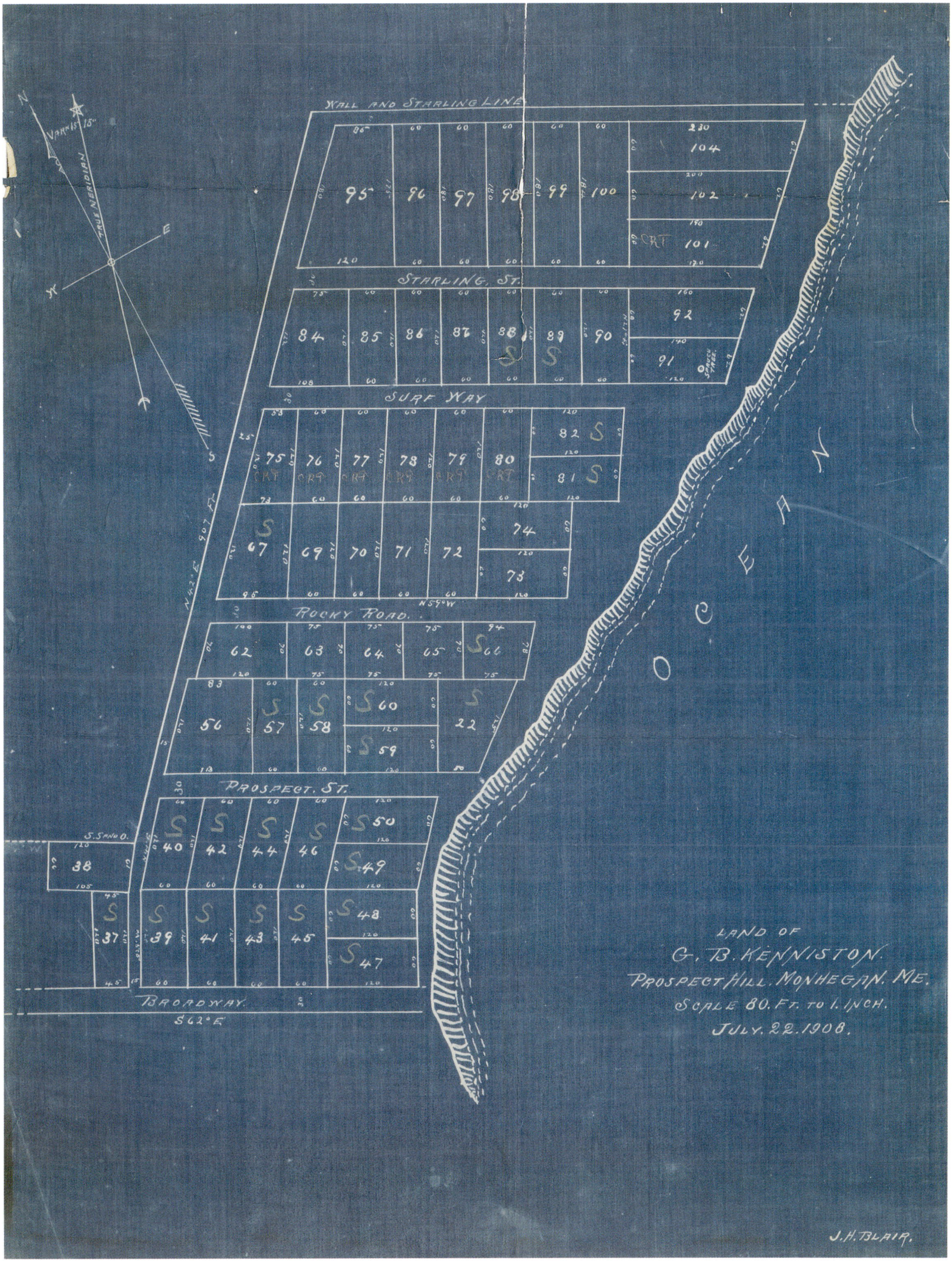

WALL AND STARLING LINE
STARLING ST.
SURF WAY
ROCKY ROAD
PROSPECT ST.
BROADWAY
S 62° E
N 42° E 907 FT.
N 59° W
TRUE MERIDIAN
VAR. 15° 15'
N
E
W
S
OCEAN
LAND OF
G. B. KENNISTON.
PROSPECT HILL. MONHEGAN. ME.
SCALE 80. FT. TO 1. INCH.
JULY. 22. 1908.
J. H. BLAIR.

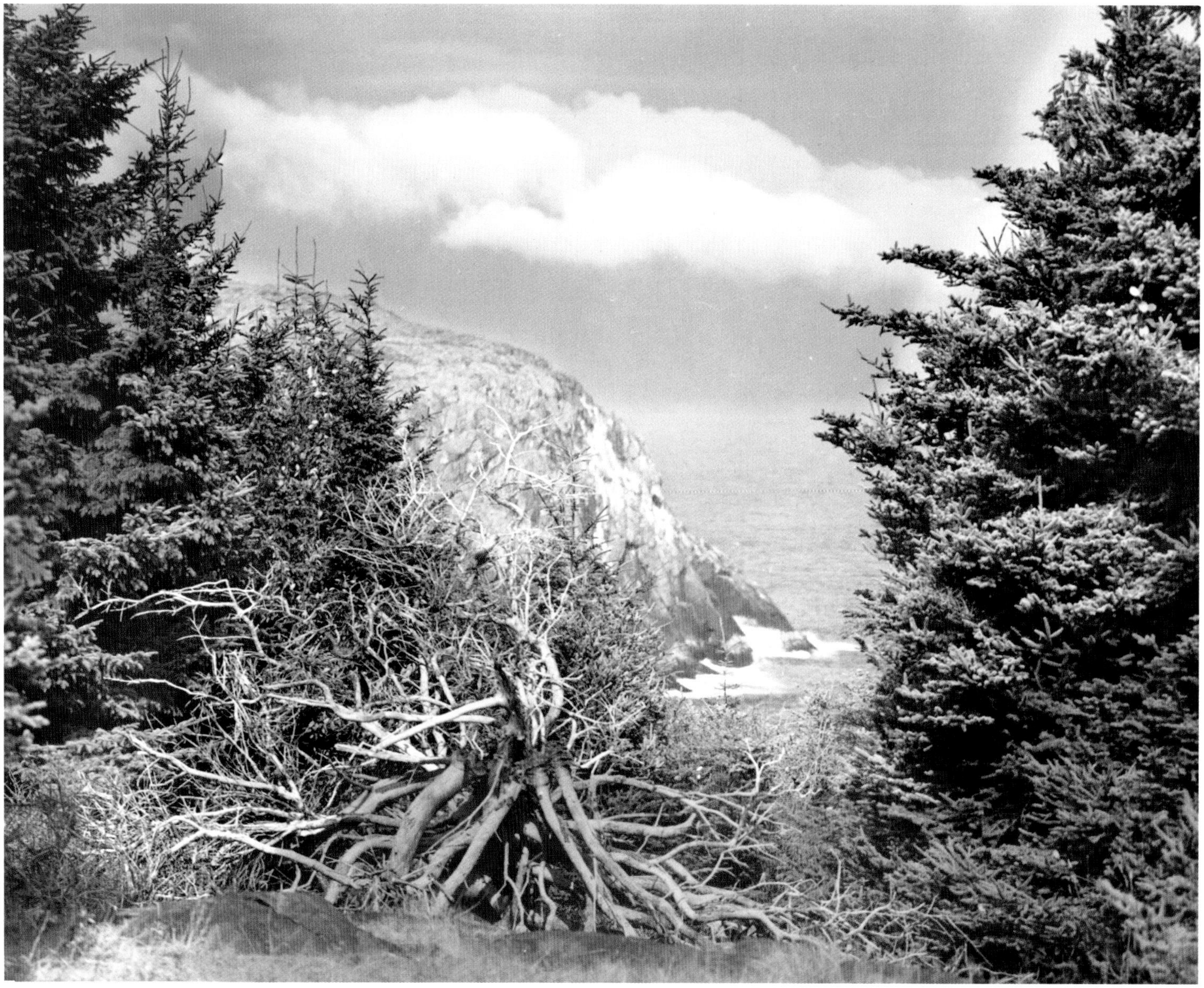

Warner Taylor (1880–1958),
Untitled—Whitehead from Burnt
Head, 1930s. Silver gelatin
print, 11 x 14 inches, Monhegan
Museum of Art & History.
Gift of Lucia Taylor Miller

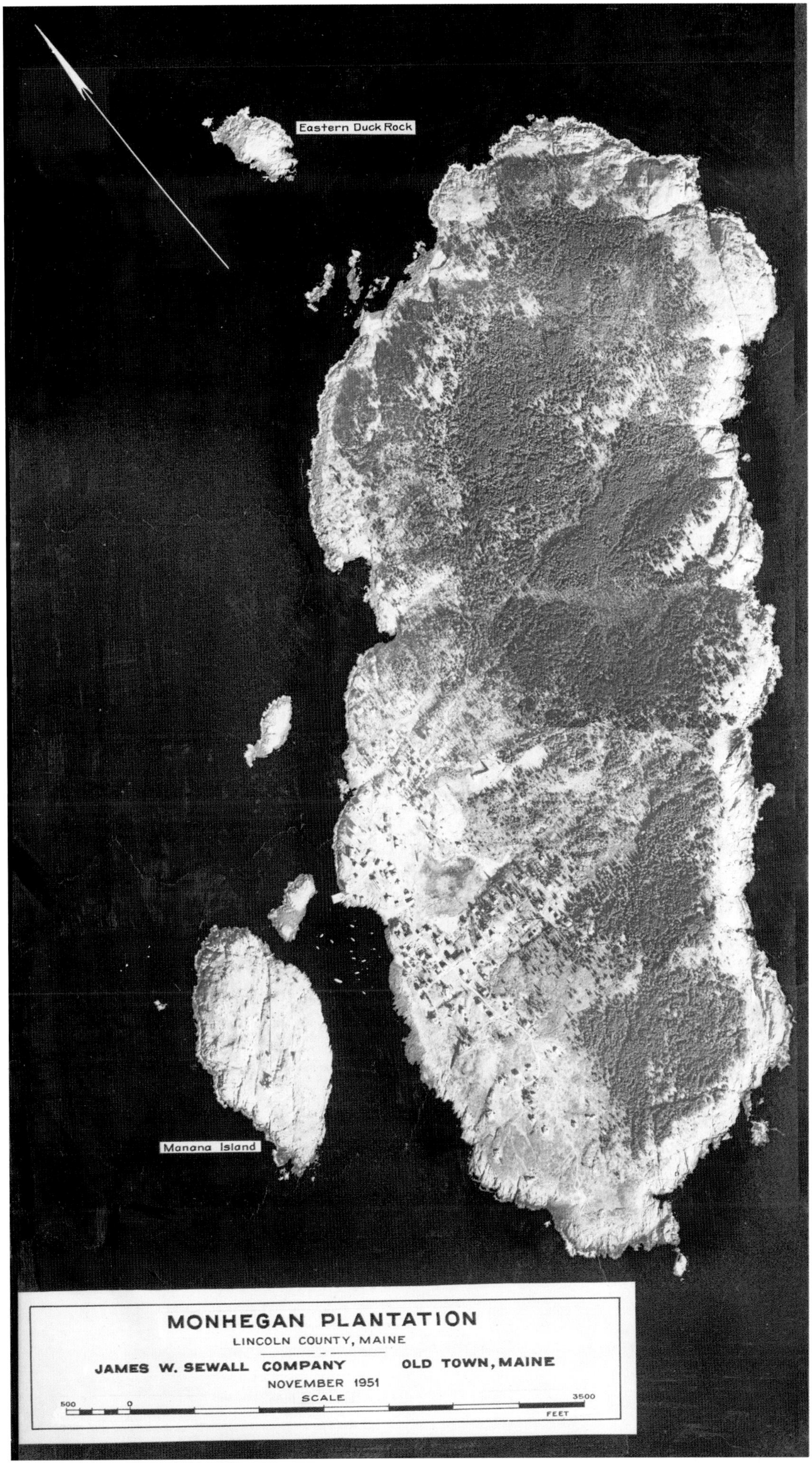

James W. Sewall Company, Aerial survey of Monhegan Island, November 21, 1951. Gelatin silver print. University of Maine at Orono

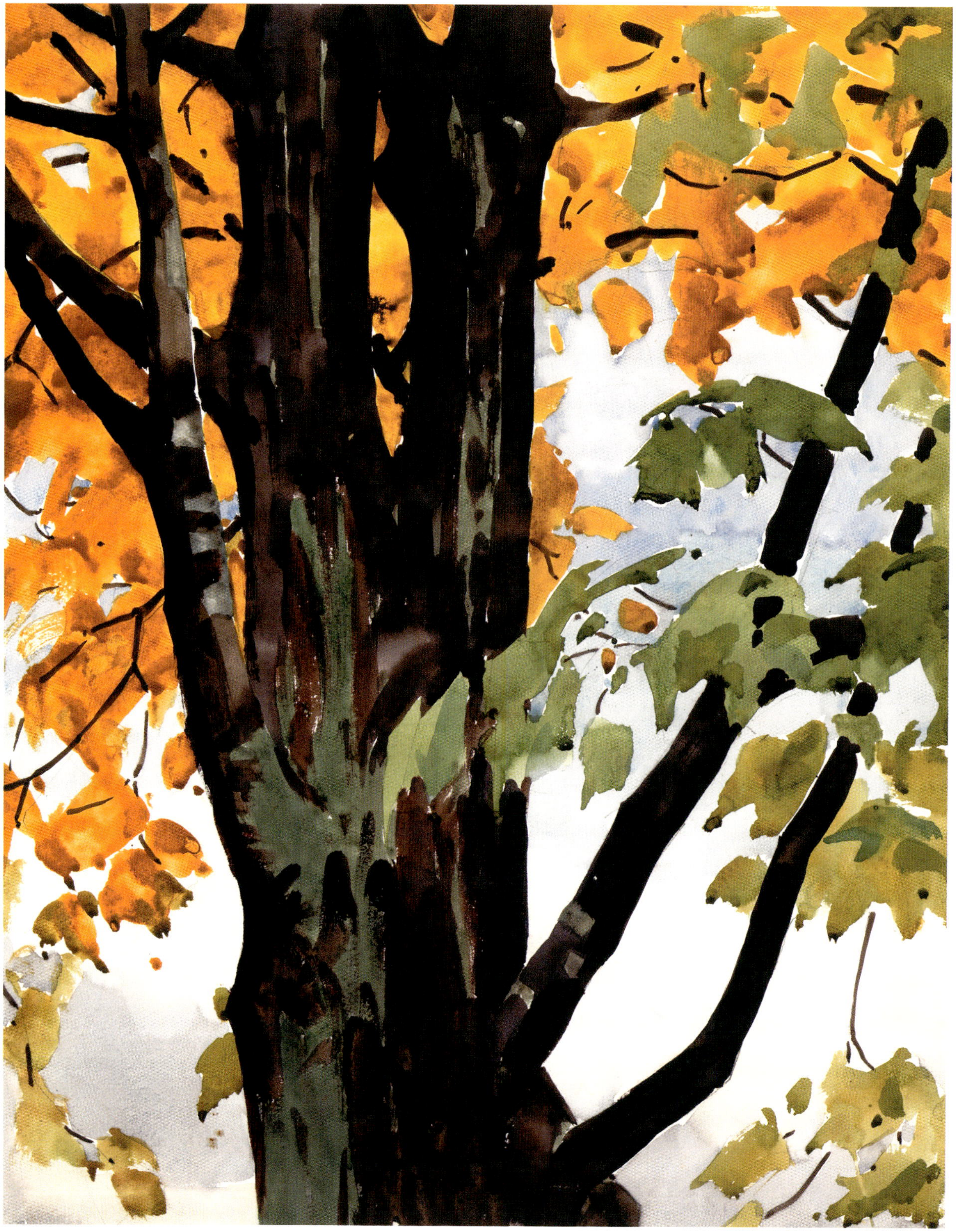

James Fitzgerald (1899–1971),
Autumn Maple, ca. 1955.
Watercolor on paper, 23 x
19 inches. Private collection

Andrew Winter (1892–1958), *Monhegan Twilight*, ca. 1943. Oil on canvas. 24 x 40 inches. Collection of the Farnsworth Art Museum, Rockland, Maine. Gift of Mr. William Goadby Lawrence, 1976.2030

> there would be quite a little bit of people raising their eyebrows, asking "Who's this man coming in, gonna get all this property? Develop it. And ruin the island." Naturally there was a lot on people's minds. So I wanted to be a go-between if I could, as long as I felt this man was sincere, which I believed he was.[13]

Initially, Stanley was Edison's primary contact within the year-round community, but as plans for a land trust began to take shape and Edison was able to spend more time on the island, he endeavored to secure the community's agreement and participation. Edison approached well-respected members of the community and enlisted seasonal and full-time residents alike, including artists, innkeepers, fishermen, rusticators, and elected officials. He explained his intentions, asked them to support his plan, and then invited them to be founding trustees and officers of a new organization, which came to be known as the "Monhegan Associates."

In 1954, the Associates incorporated "to preserve for posterity the natural wild beauty, biotic communities, and desirable natural, artificial, and historic features of the so-called 'wild-lands' portions of Monhegan Island, Maine, and its environs, as well as the simple, friendly way of life that has existed on Monhegan as a whole."[14]

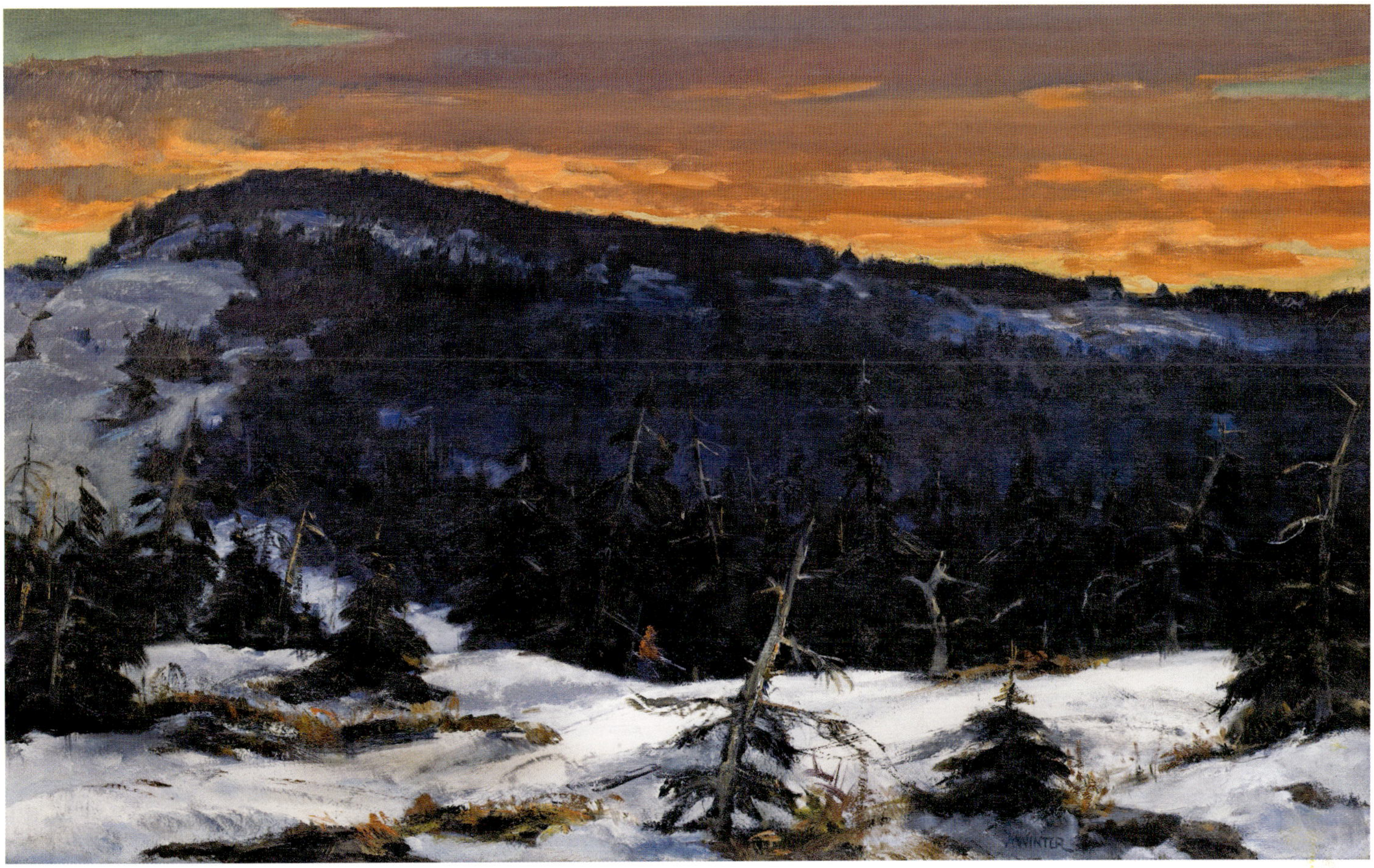

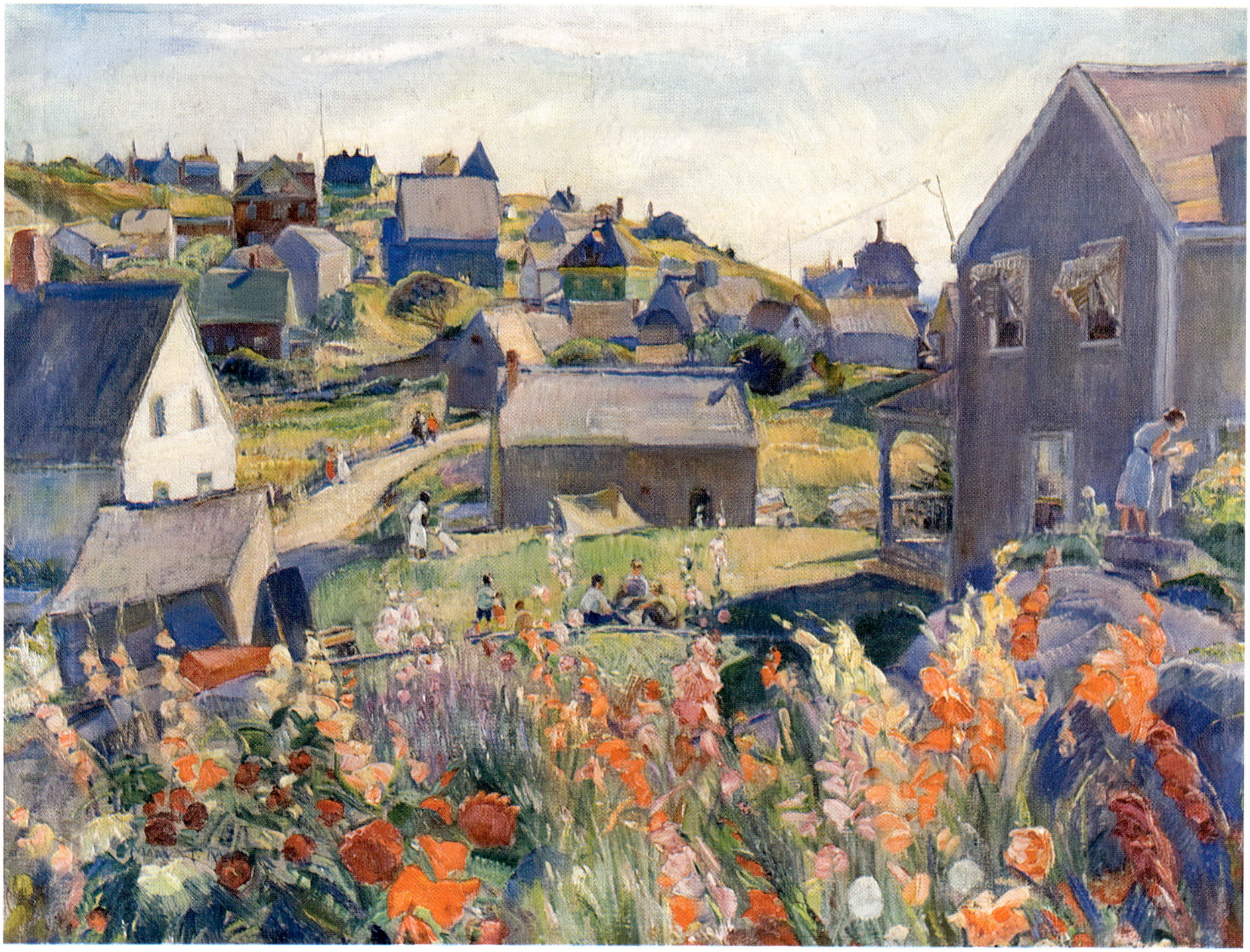

Mary Stuart Mason (1886–1964), *Sidney's Garden,* 1930s. Oil on canvas, 22 x 30 inches. Monhegan Museum of Art & History. Gift of Dickson and Hudson Families

Constance Cochrane (1888–1962), *Glory of Fall, Monhegan* or *Monhegan Garden in Bloom,* ca. 1930. Oil on canvas, 28 x 36 inches. Monhegan Museum of Art & History. Collection of Stephen S. Fuller and Susan D. Bateson

The twelve founding officers and trustees were Edison, Stanley, Marion H. Cundy, Virginia L. Davis, Ann O. Edison, Isabel N. Farrell, Earl S. Field, Leo J. Meissner, Mildred J. Meissner, Ruth S. Nunan, Frank C. Pierce, and Teco Slagboom. Illustrating Edison's success in gathering support from the community for this land trust, eight of these individuals were either living full-time on Monhegan or had done so in the recent past. The remaining four had long-standing relationships on the island. Edison stepped down as president of the Monhegan Associates in 1961, though he served as secretary until 1972. Stanley remained vice president of the organization for fifty years, retiring in 2005.

Despite having encouraged the concept of a state park on Monhegan only a few years prior, Rockwell Kent wrote to Ted Edison in May 1953 to express appreciation for the work Edison was doing:

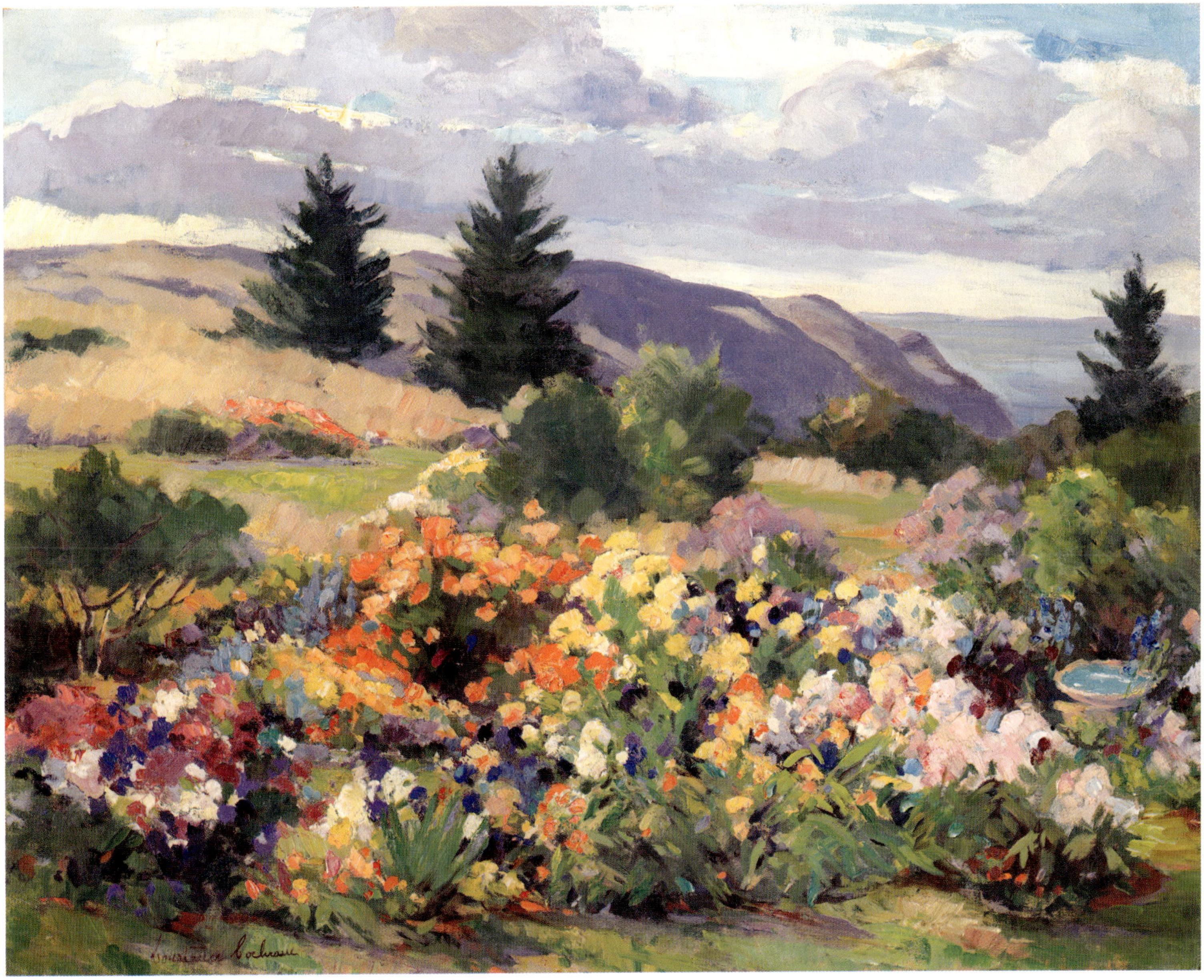

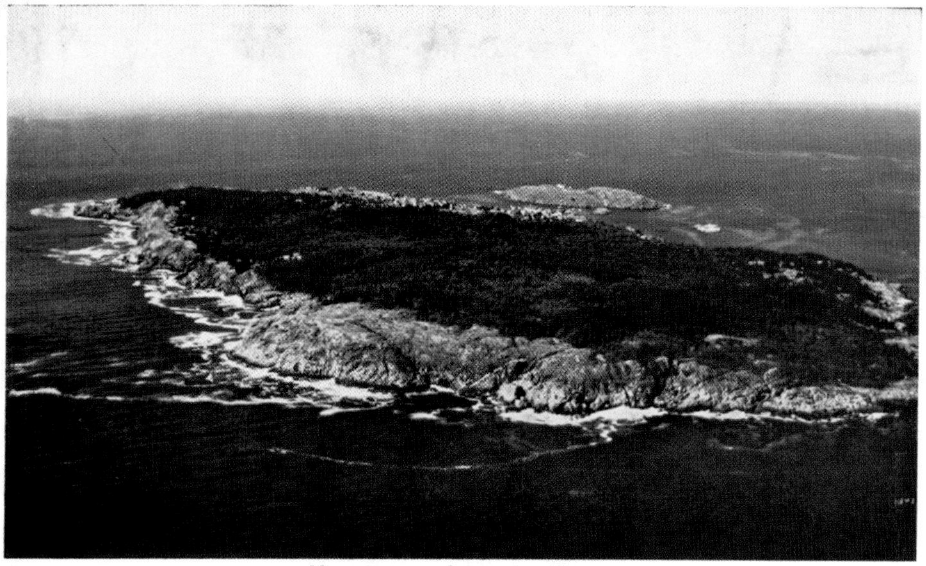

Published by Luther S. Phillips (1891–1960), *Monhegan Island, Aerial View,* undated. Monhegan Museum of Art & History

My dear Mr. Edison:

As one of the many people who, loving Monhegan Island, have been concerned about the continuous encroachments of cottagers on what is left of its natural scenery, I am prompted to tell you how deeply we appreciate what you are doing to preserve the island.

It is just forty-eight years ago that I first came here and, returning after a lapse of many years, I was shocked at the change that has come over the place. Considering how large a part of the island has been built upon, we can still be grateful for what is left, and very grateful to you who have acted to preserve it.

Faithfully yours,
Rockwell Kent[15]

The anxiety Kent expresses over the extent of development on Monhegan and his gratitude that Edison has acted to preserve "what is left" is a remarkable statement. Indeed, it clearly indicates shifting baseline expectations when one considers that fully three-quarters of Monhegan Island is preserved for nature. It is hard to imagine a contemporary figure regarding this fact as anything but a conservation triumph.

The significance of Ted Edison's role in preserving Monhegan's Wildlands cannot be overstated; however, he did not act alone. In fact, the first property owned by the Monhegan Associates was received in 1956 as a bequest of founding trustee Frank Pierce. The growth of the organization's landholdings throughout the seventy years since its inception has been supported by the island community through gifts and opportunities to purchase property at far less than market value.

Edison described his motivation for preserving natural areas in a later Monhegan Associates report:

> It is undoubtedly almost impossible for people living on Monhegan to realize how much a feeling of Monhegan's permanence can mean to a city dweller, because changes on Monhegan have been so slow, that permanence may be taken more or less for granted. In contrast, millions of people who live in suburban areas are now seeing the few remaining quiet woods and marshes disappear, and their very homes destroyed, to make way for housing developments, industry, super-highways, and other elements of what is termed "progress." . . . In my own case, things are changing so much at home, that I almost feel as if I had more anchors with the past here than there; and that is one reason why I am devoting so much time, effort, and money to this project. Another reason is that I am interested in many other nature preservation projects, and I have hopes that if this project works well, experience gained here can smooth the way for similar projects elsewhere.[16]

With a significant portion of the island's land protected from development, and strong community support, this unique partnership between seasonal and full-time residents crafted by Edison played a critical role in shaping the social and ecological future of the island.

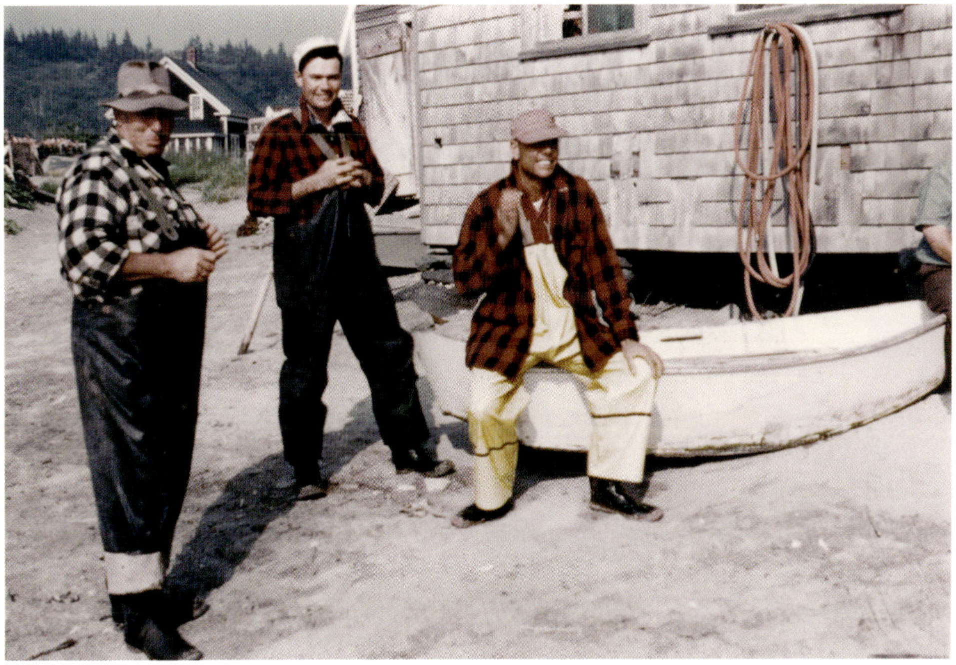

Dwight, Sherman, and Alfred Stanley on Monhegan, 1955. Chromogenic print. Monhegan Museum of Art & History

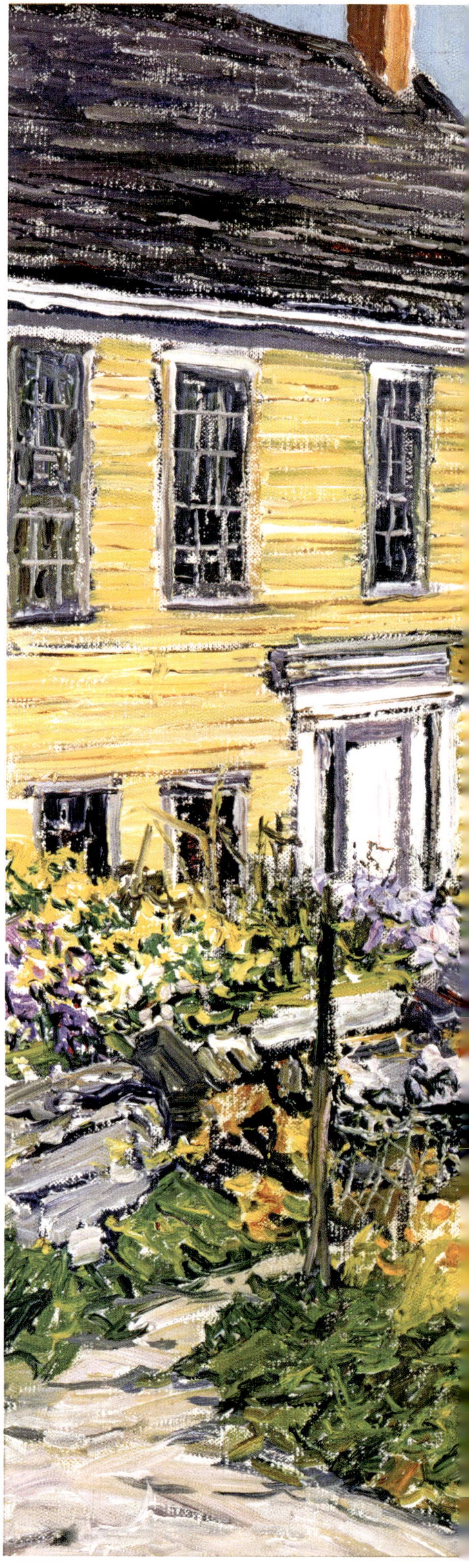

Edward Redfield (1869–1965), *The Toy Maker's Home*, 1929. Oil on canvas, 26 x 32 inches. Monhegan Museum of Art & History. Bequest of Elizabeth B. Noyce

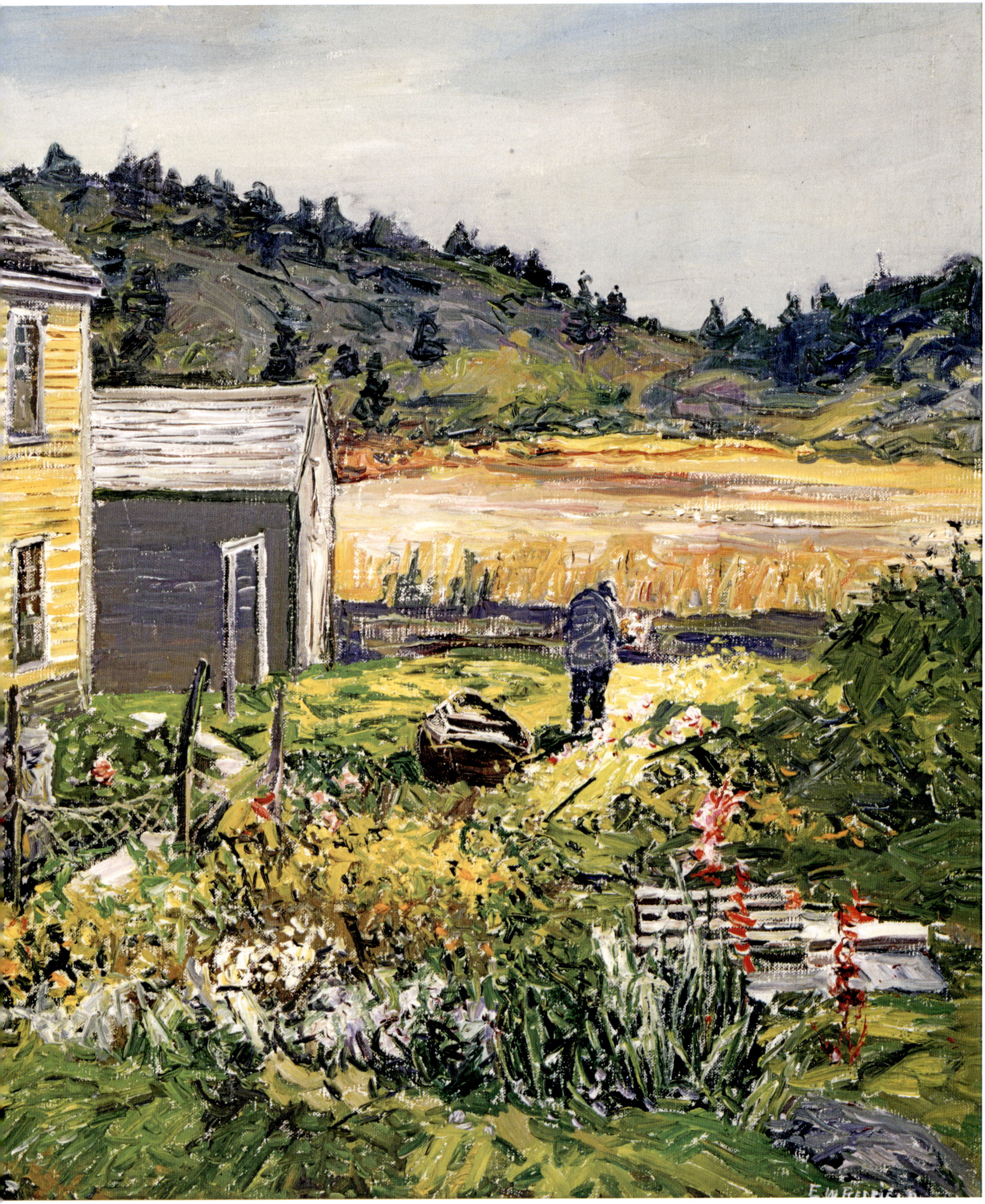

Small Island, Big Questions: The Monhegan Associates and the Entangled Histories of Conservation

Matthew Klingle, Associate Professor of History and Environmental Studies, Bowdoin College

Conservation has never been a preordained triumph. Its contradictory history entails sometimes bitter disputes over what nature is worth protecting and who will benefit. A thumbnail history of the Monhegan Associates, established in 1954 to preserve the island's "natural wild beauty" and the "simple friendly way of life," illuminates the faults of casting conservation as a morality play.

The history of the Monhegan Associates underscores that conservation can be a local affair often driven by monied citizens. Many of the nation's earliest and most iconic preserved places were the product of wealthy property owners. Five generations of Rockefellers gifted thousands of acres and millions of dollars to build parks from Wyoming to Maine. Theodore Miller Edison, or simply "Ted," the youngest son of Thomas Alva Edison, followed this model with a key difference. He blended public and private interests into a local land trust.

Edison was the prime mover behind the Monhegan Associates. Having spent childhood summers on the island, followed by a successful career as an inventor and businessman, he began acquiring properties beginning in 1929. Twenty-five years later, in the summer of 1954, Edison invited all island landowners to a meeting in which he announced that he was creating a trust with his parcels, which he would donate to the Monhegan Associates, Inc., with the aim of protecting the island's "wildlands in perpetuity."[17] Drawing from a long American tradition equating propriety and property, Edison created a pragmatic instrument to advance environmental permanence through public persuasion.[18]

Determining who was part of the "public" was not straightforward, however. Meeting minutes from the early years capture the frank conversations necessary on a tiny island to decide who would oversee the land trust. From the outset, early leadership wanted to give "voting control to true 'Monheganites'" who were full members while also thwarting "outside interests" who could exploit property-holding requirements.[19] But some islanders balked at property ownership stipulations in the Associates' bylaws, while others questioned if the organization "was trying to tie up too much land."[20]

The back-and-forth helped clarify membership eligibility. As Edison explained in 1959, "Qualification requirements were made initially tight" because it was easier to relax guidelines than to impose new ones.[21] Property ownership and associated restrictions were meant to promote lasting interest in retaining the island's character and prevent the Associates from becoming "a private social club."[22] Recent bylaws still require property ownership for full members or another connection that proves long-standing dedication to the island community.[23]

Locality has been a key feature of the Associates. The leadership was keen to avoid having the organization captured by national environmental groups or beholden to the federal government. Not unlike former Maine governor Percival P. Baxter, who purchased and then donated the lands encircling Mount Katahdin to form the eponymous state park, Edison wondered how best to balance competing interests. Baxter had asked similar questions; one answer was to create the Baxter State Park Authority in 1931, an independent entity that had its own financial resources. Edison followed a similar playbook. Representatives from both the Nature Conservancy and Wildlife Preserves, Inc., joined at the start, but Edison was still wary, as late as 1976, to avoid "any possible conflicts of interest." He looked askance at how national parks were "suffering from an invasion of too many people," with places such as Yosemite Valley facing problems that "one usually associates with city slums."[24] Without careful supervision, Edison intimated, Monhegan could face a similar fate.

Edison's worries over protecting Monhegan's isolation point to another complexity: defining nature is also about defining human values and behavior. Early conservationists from John Muir to William Temple Hornaday justified expelling Native peoples from national parks or banning subsistence hunting by poor immigrants or African Americans to safeguard vanishing wilderness and wildlife. Such regulatory weapons were aimed at controlling people and eliminating activities perceived as unworthy and undesirable.[25] Tensions between protecting nature and policing people persisted into the postwar era as conservation morphed into environmentalism. With the rise of outdoor recreation, new arguments flared over how to prevent loving places to ruin.[26]

Monhegan was no exception. Litter and vandalism were two key concerns. A 1961 report warned that more visitors were causing more litter, but the same report also distinguished "between garbage and trash," since the former was an inevitable part of living on an island. The report also warned that rare "wildflowers and plants" were being stolen by tourists and residents alike.[27] Yet seasonal "summer people," many of whom were Associates leaders, noted their "duty to help find answers" since they too were residents.[28]

For the Associates, keeping Monhegan "wild," a mission emblazoned on letterhead and on the website, is the goal.[29] It is an idealistic mission politically but a fraught mission historically. Wilderness, as historian William Cronon observes, is "a product of civilization" rather than something beyond its "contaminating taint." It is "a mirror" reflecting what we choose to see and believe. It is a troubled and troubling concept.[30]

Such ambiguities have defined American wilderness for over a century. In Maine, while Percival Baxter called for the park encircling Mount Katahdin to be kept "forever wild," reality proved more challenging. Nearby residents clamored to hunt, fish, and trap in woods and waters once open through common use, something that Baxter eventually allowed in certain sections. At the same time, selective logging in a designated thirty-thousand-acre Scientific Forest Management Area helped fund the park authority.[31] Forever wild was an elastic ambition.

The Monhegan Associates also faced their own troubles with wilderness. In 1970, Alfred Fuller summarized the dual goals of the trails committee he chaired as "to keep the trails in good walking condition and at the same time to preserve their beauty in its wild state."[32] Year after year, the annual minutes detailed efforts to remove downed trees, thin underbrush with chain saws, and repair roads for trail crews. By the 1980s, invasive Japanese barberry was choking out native flora, and the discovery of Lyme disease in deer ticks threatened human health. Fire was perhaps the greatest peril and the one that demanded the greatest effort. A 1995 presentation by the Maine Forest Service and Monhegan Fire Department warned Associates members that the island had a Class 3 fire rating, the highest at the time, with potential for "crowning fires . . . that jump from treetop to treetop." Only continuous vigilance to remove underbrush, maintain roads, and train firefighters could prevent disaster.[33]

The hard work of sustaining wilderness continues. As of 2023, the Monhegan Associates own outright about four hundred acres of the island's approximately five hundred fifty acres. Detailed policies address prohibiting herbicides

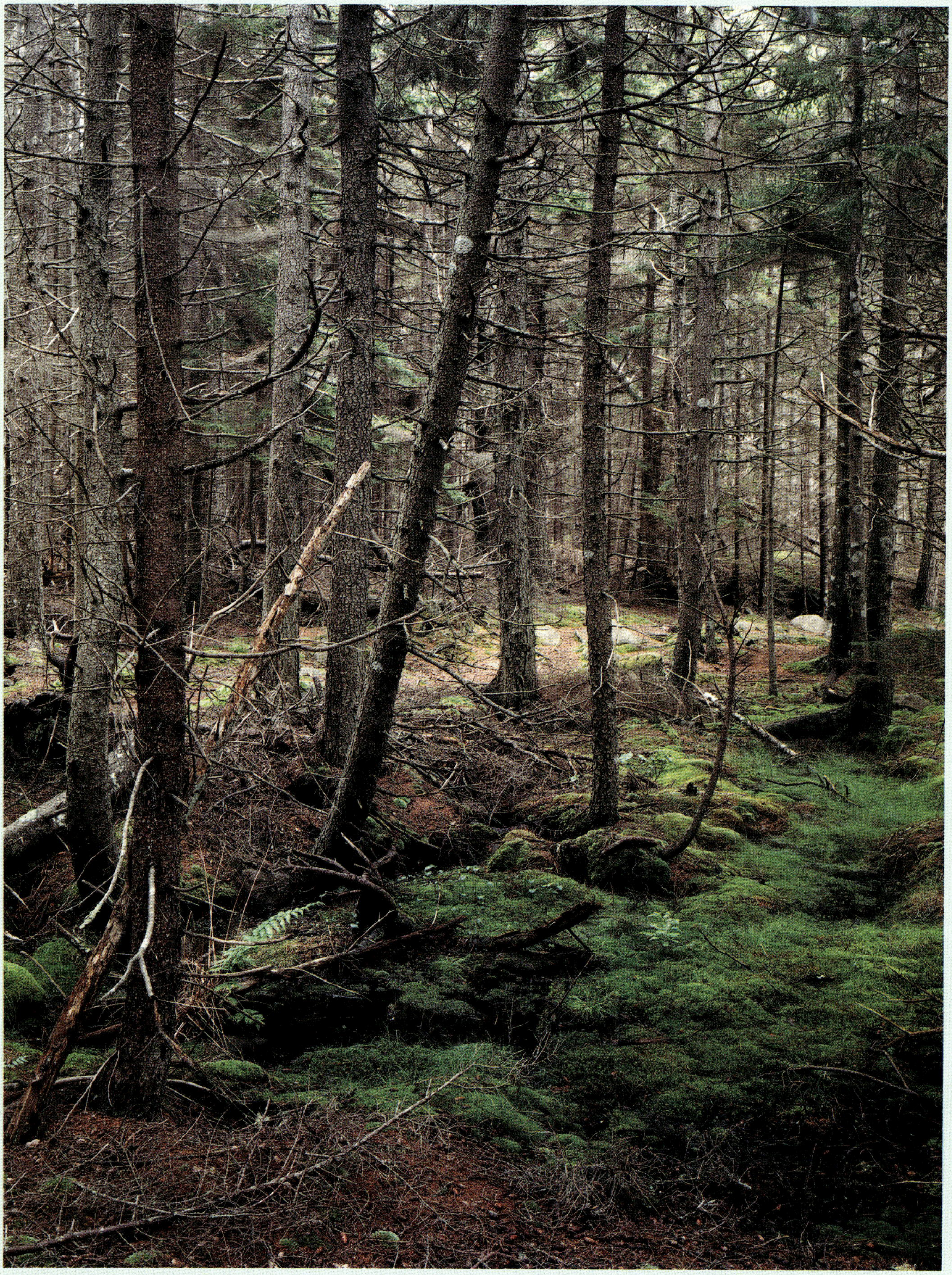

to combat invasive plants, curbing drone operations, mitigating poison ivy and stinging insects, keeping up trails and signage, and fire management. A stewardship plan adopted in 2004 declares that "natural processes are meant to prevail, and human manipulation of the forest is strictly limited."[34] Still, lofty rhetoric does not match lived reality. Richard Farrell, a former vice president, stated in 2018 that the Associates' founders "had no illusion that the island was a primeval wilderness." Preserving the Wildlands, he concluded, always called for "*some* human intervention."[35]

If history is any guide, there will be more toil and more trade-offs as two enormous questions loom. First, how will Monhegan continue to be a place where a wide range of people can live and enjoy its Wildlands? Like so many Maine coastal communities, year-round residents are dwindling as seasonal residents increase. The state has one of the highest percentages of secondary or vacation homes in the nation, while affordable housing on Monhegan has vanished.[36] Working waterfronts are also disappearing as affluent consumers crowd coastlines from the Pacific Northwest to New England, raising the specter of gentrification through recreation.[37]

Second, how will global climate change affect the Wildlands and life on Monhegan? The Gulf of Maine is one of the world's fastest warming bodies of water in the planetary ocean.[38] Lobster and groundfish are moving farther north and out into the Atlantic, imperiling communities dependent on ebbing fisheries. Warming has also changed the composition of Monhegan's forests and associated biota while elevating fire danger and the risk of drought. Protecting the Wildlands along with the island's simple way of life might be a chimerical goal. As Farrell wryly observed, in the face of constant flux, the Associates will need to ask what kind of wild they want to preserve: the way "the woods look *now* in 2018," the way they looked in the past, or "something in between."[39]

In such questions burn the sparks of an "ethic of place" that rejects the dualities of environmentalist thinking. Fueling this ethic requires valuing human and nonhuman alike in all their entanglements. Encouraging this ethic obliges ditching the politics of purity.[40]

The history of the Monhegan Associates suggests how to forge a more sensible kind of environmentalism. It is a laudable endeavor for a place that prides itself on independence and practicality. Small islands might have still more answers to very big questions.

Accra Shepp (born 1962), *Large Mossy Puddle Bog, Pebble Beach Trail* (detail), 2023. Archival pigment ink print. Courtesy of the artist

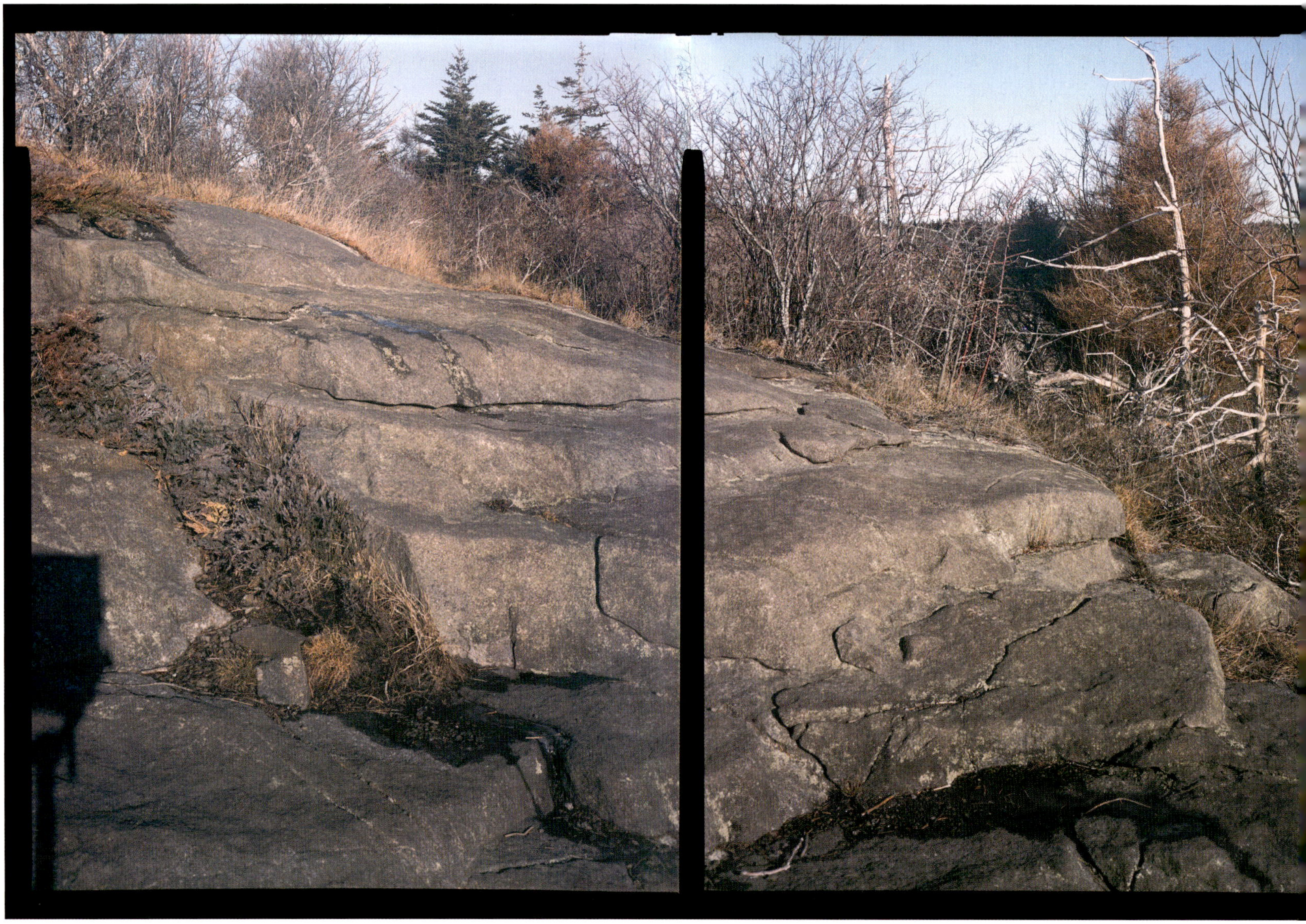

Accra Shepp (born 1962), *Whitehead from Burnt Head*, 2022. Archival pigment ink print. Courtesy of the artist

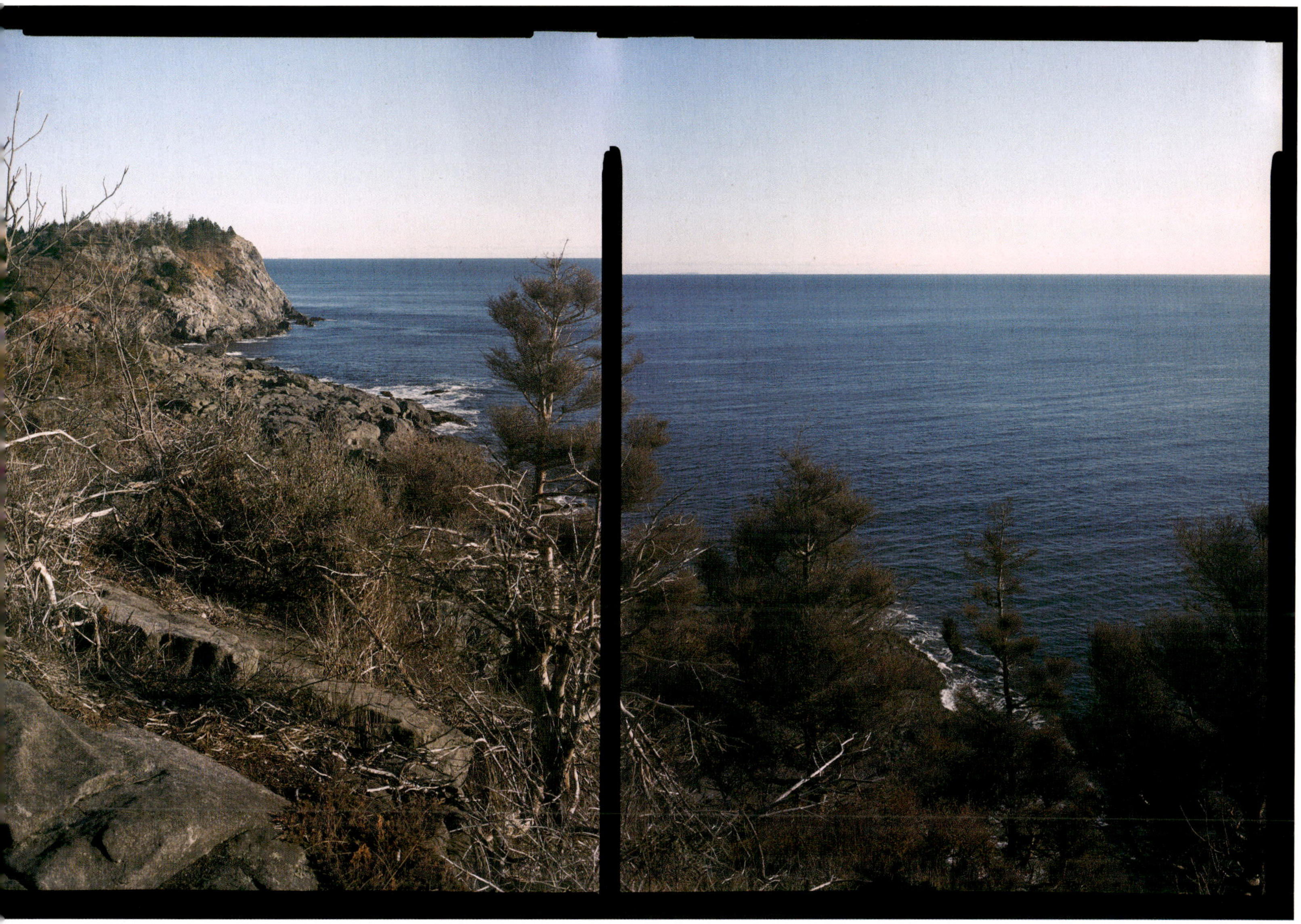

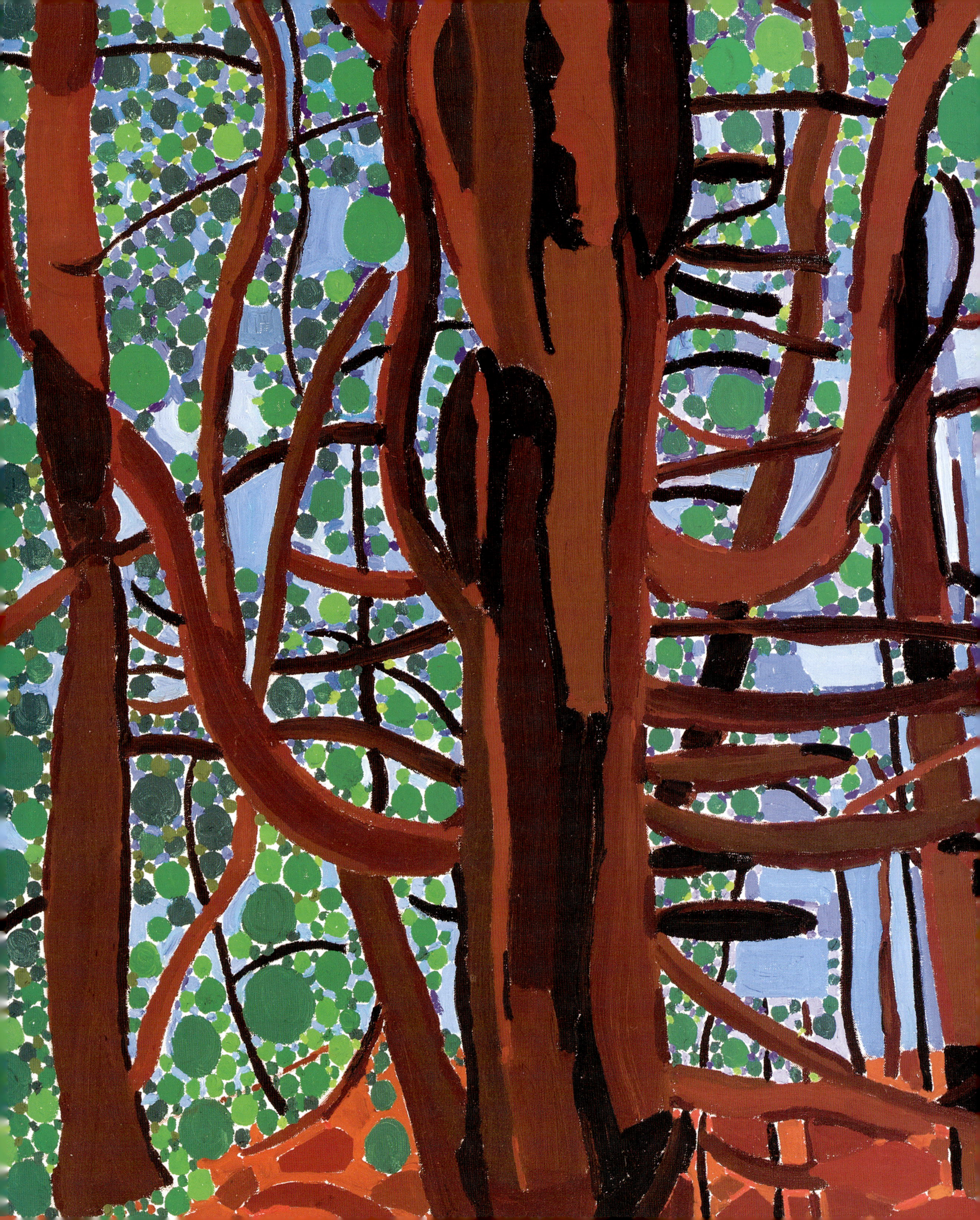

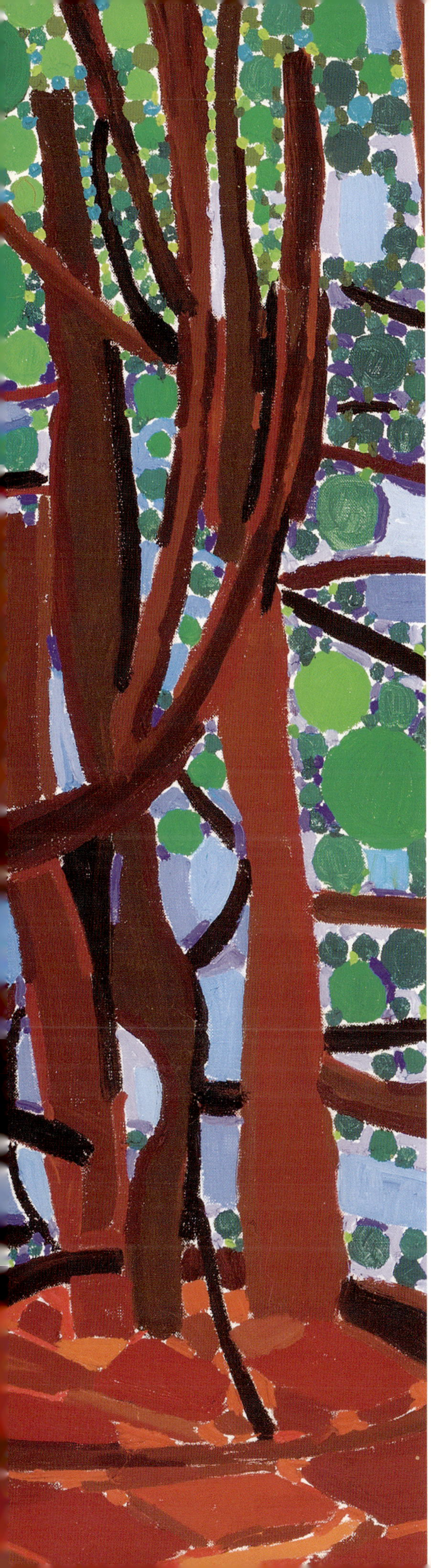

Chapter 5

The Era of Introduced Deer on Monhegan, 1954 to 1999

In the spring of 1954, the three assessors of Monhegan Plantation—Sherman M. Stanley, Teco Slagboom, and Marion H. Cundy[1]—made a request to the Maine Department of Inland Fisheries and Game (IF&G) for the release of a small number of white-tailed deer on the island "to amuse tourists and to give locals game to shoot."[2] IF&G (today IF&W) acted with breathtaking swiftness. Six deer roamed Monhegan within ten days of the department's receipt of the assessors' letter. Monhegan's request was well timed as IF&G was just concluding its annual trapping operation at its game management area on Swan Island, where the upper Kennebec River spills into Merrymeeting Bay.

No doubt, many tourists were amused, and many islanders profited from the availability of an on-island source of meat. However, the ecological impacts of deer and the disease risks associated with the ticks they host were far-reaching. Deer have occupied an outsize place in the history of the Monhegan Wildlands. They acted as ecosystem engineers, modifying the appearance of the forest understory, resetting (or stalling) successional trajectories, and facilitating invasion by unwelcome, introduced plants. Though they are now gone, the legacy of their presence is felt across the island to this day.[3]

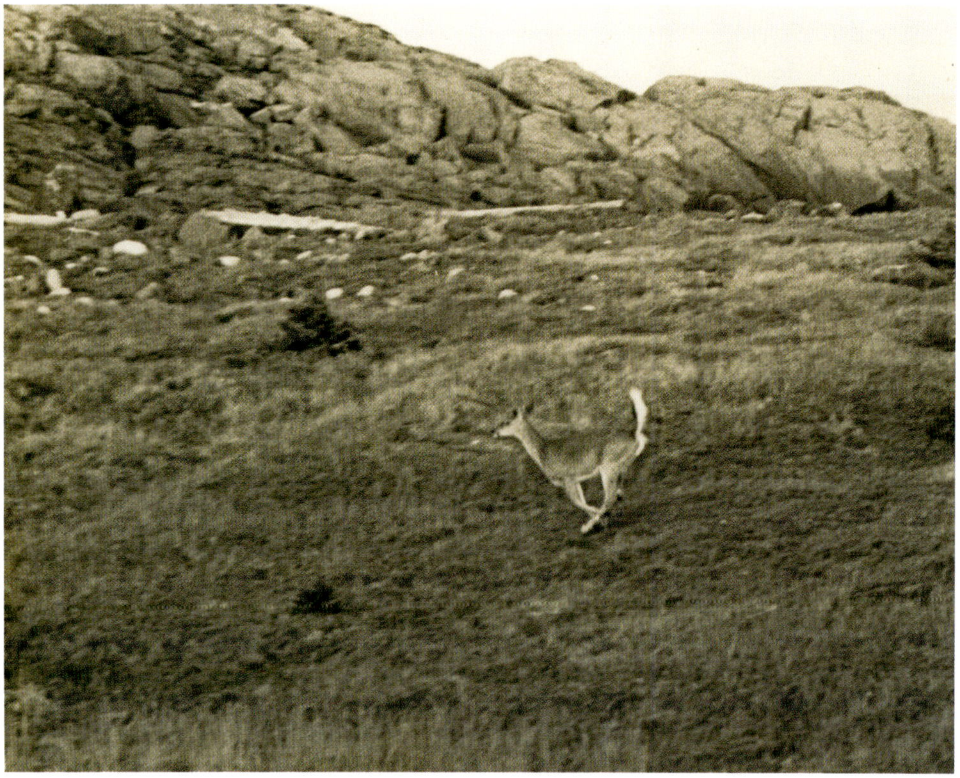

Henry Levy (1922–1996), Deer on Monhegan, undated. Monhegan Museum of Art & History. Gift of Susan Finkin

Admired for their grace and beauty, deer have enjoyed iconic status in American culture as denizens of our forests. It remains a particular delight to witness deer passing by, and yet they were not always found in the robust numbers many in the Northeast have grown accustomed to today. In fact, during the period of peak deforestation in the nineteenth century, naturalist Henry David Thoreau was inspired to make note in his journal of a deer sighting a day's travel away.[4] Deer numbers crept up over the decades of the twentieth century as abandoned farmland returned to forest and the earlier project of eradicating predatory gray wolves proved successful. Today, a density of ten deer per square kilometer (twenty-six per square mile) is common. At such densities, deer browsing sculpts plant communities, and favored plants can be browsed into local extirpation. This, in turn, facilitates the flourishing of plants they find unpalatable because of some combination of thorns, chemical defenses, toughness, poor digestibility, or low nutritional content.[5]

Deer garnered little attention in the years immediately after their release onto Monhegan. However, on-island deer did what deer do especially well: they reproduced. Their population boomed, and by the 1990s, one upper-end estimate of their density exceeded fifty deer per square kilometer (130 per square mile)—notably, severalfold higher than densities regarded as "high" on the mainland.[6] On September 4, 1969, just fifteen years after their introduction to the island, artist Geraldine King Tam wrote to Ted Edison to voice her concern:

> As a summer resident of Monhegan for more than twenty years, and as a student and illustrator of the wild flora of the Island, I wish to express my

> concern over the devastation done by deer herds in the wild lands owned by Monhegan Associates. In walks through the woods this year, I have observed that the destruction of rare flowering plants and the undergrowth that nourishes them has reached alarming proportions. Among the aesthetically desirable and important plants that have disappeared, or are fast disappearing are:
>
> Pink Lady's Slipper (*Cypripedium acaule*)
> Fringed Gentian (*Gentiana crinita*)
> One-flowered Pyrola (*Moneses uniflora*)
> Corn-lily (*Clintonia borealis*)
> Twisted Stalk (*Streptopus amplexifolius*)
> Shinleaf or Pyrola (*Pyrola elliptica*) . . . carpets of this fragrant and delicate flower used to grow near the end of the Gull Cove Trail, but this year I found not a single plant.[7]

A few years prior to Tam's letter to Edison, in 1966, Monhegan had been designated a National Natural Landmark by the National Park Service. This landmark status is bestowed upon sites that "contain outstanding biological and geological resources," and Monhegan was recognized for the "coastal and island flora . . . considered the only sizeable example in near-virgin condition in the northeastern United States. The site supports dense, almost pure stands of red spruce, over 400 species of wildflower, and a variety of bird species."[8]

As well as threatening the rare and abundant (mostly) native flora of the island, the presence of deer exacerbated the establishment of introduced, unwelcome plants in the Wildlands. Take Japanese barberry as an example: Japanese barberry was long favored as an ornamental—and still is by some—since it grows well in most temperate environments and forms an effective and attractive hedge, with thorns that keep creatures at bay and persistent red berries that draw the eye. The source of barberry now in the Wildlands is not known. Did it escape cultivation in the community, or did birds transport seeds from the mainland? Regardless, Japanese barberry flourished, its fingernail-sized leaves tucked neatly inside ranks of thorns, protected from browsing.

The management of unwelcome plants was among the early stewardship responsibilities that garnered much attention among the membership of Monhegan Associates, Inc. The status of a plant as unwelcome—or a "weed"—reflects the values of the human community in which it is found, and not simply any ecological role the plant may play. Indeed, even regarding any particular plant as "introduced" or "invasive" is complicated by the dynamic nature of the vegetation on an island that was bare rock only thirteen thousand years ago.

The Monhegan Associates first focused attention on "the poison ivy problem," as the Trails Committee expressed in 1959 in its contribution to the fifth annual report.[9] Poison ivy, albeit probably best thought of as native to Monhegan, cried out to membership as compromising the experience of the Wildlands and in need of control. Over the years, various measures have been implemented. Herbicides were sprayed into the 1990s, in keeping with the embrace of chemical solutions common elsewhere.[10]

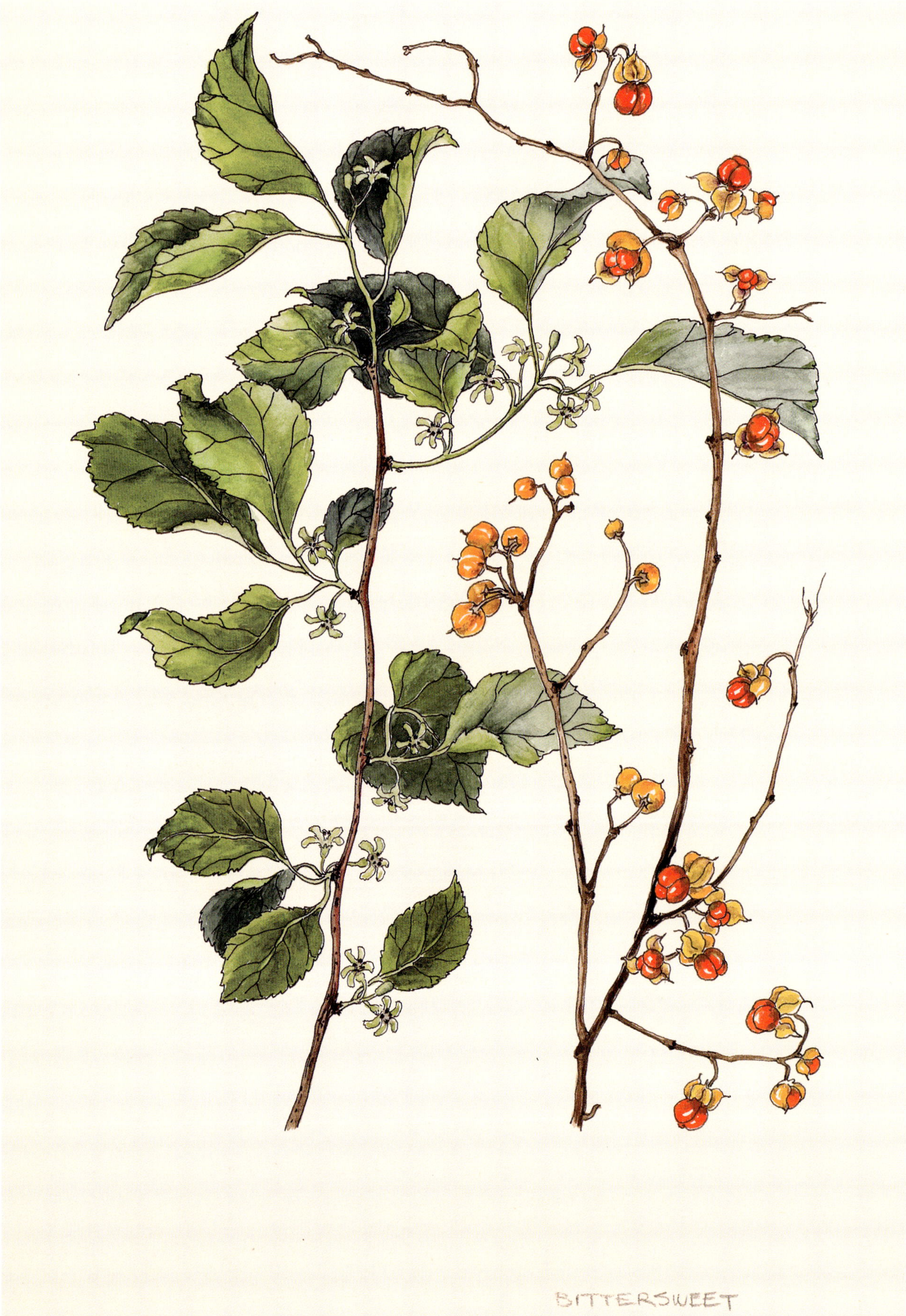
BITTERSWEET

Likewise, much energy and attention was dedicated to eradicating barberry, the growth of which was described as "rampant" in 1991 Ecology Committee contributions to the Monhegan Associates' annual meeting minutes, along with black swallow-wort, another recently arrived recalcitrant weed "which strangles anything in its path."[11] Soon after, pulling parties numbering more than twenty volunteers were assembled and fanned out into the Wildlands to "beat [them] back." Plants were sprayed with an organic herbicide and removed if possible. Where root systems resisted removal, crowns were cut and stumps brushed with the herbicide Roundup.[12]

Rampant construction of "fairy houses" in Cathedral Woods presented yet another concern. This practice of creating miniature domiciles made of natural materials—twigs, cones, moss, fern fronds, etc.—had a long-standing history to which many felt a sentimental attachment. To be sure, fairy houses all but defined Cathedral Woods for some visitors to Monhegan. Although the tradition of these whimsical constructions dictated that they be subtle and modest in size, some visitors succumbed to one-upmanship, building sprawling, outsize structures. At any size, fairy houses disturbed the forest. Moss harvested for their construction, for example, could have taken decades to achieve its size. The Monhegan Associates expressed concern over fairy houses as far back as the 1960s. Their growing prevalence was observed in the 1970s, and their expansion in size and appearance in settings beyond Cathedral Woods was noted in the Monhegan Associates' minutes in the 1990s.[13] Signage discouraging their construction, especially using living plant materials, appeared to curb sprawl and bring the tradition under a measure of restraint.

The risk of fire, and the memory of fires of the recent past, also occupied the Monhegan Associates throughout the second half of the twentieth century. A Fire Prevention Committee, established in 1957, was among the first committees formed. It grappled with many related issues, among them the trade-off between maintaining the character of the pedestrian trails versus widening them to allow greater access by firefighting vehicles and equipment. The threat presented by smokers elicited much discussion, although smoking was not explicitly prohibited until the 1970s. Blowdowns presented a particular conundrum. Their tangle of deadfall was an unambiguous fire risk. Clearing it from trails rendered easier access for firefighting, but was an intrusion on natural processes and one that encouraged hikers who, with their cigarettes, exacerbated fire risk.

The newly founded organization was deeply engaged in conversations about fire risk, poison ivy, and trail maintenance in 1957, when news arrived that the Monhegan Island Light Station was to be automated and, in time, its buildings likely sold at auction. Edison wrote immediately to the Coast Guard to express his interest in purchasing the property, and the concept of a museum on Monhegan first appeared in the minutes of the Monhegan Associates' annual meeting that year, on August 23, 1957: "Lighthouse.—The President said that he had heard that there was a possibility that the Lighthouse keeper's house would be auctioned off and thought that in such an event, Monhegan Associates, Inc. might be interested in buying it to preserve it as an Island feature—for example, by converting it into an Island Museum and headquarters for the corporation. This was merely mentioned as a possibility to consider, and no specific action at this time was recommended."[14]

Geraldine King Tam (1920–2016), *Bittersweet*, undated. Ink and watercolor on paper, 10⅝ x 7¼ inches. Monhegan Museum of Art & History. Gift of Cindy King

A 1959 survey of island residents resulted in an overwhelmingly positive response to the prospect of creating an island museum in the former Keeper's House, and in that same year, the Museum Committee first appeared in the Monhegan Associates' minutes alongside Trails, Fire Prevention, and numerous other committees. In 1962, Edison secured the purchase of the light station for the Monhegan Associates with an offer of five thousand dollars in a sealed-bid auction. As described in their 1954 Articles of Incorporation, the Monhegan Associates purposes included "To collect, collate, maintain, and preserve for posterity, records and archives respecting the flora, fauna, and human inhabitants and sojourners on said island, and to make the same publicly available for educational, literary, scientific, and historical research, study, and consultation."[15] A museum at the lighthouse would help realize those goals.

Despite the tremendous efforts of the Museum Committee, the Monhegan Museum was not open to the public until the summer of 1968. A fire in November 1963 destroyed several buildings in the center of the village, including the Monhegan Store, and so repairs to the Keeper's House were placed on hold while island carpenters worked to rebuild critical infrastructure. This delay allowed time for the Museum Committee to consult with other museums, plan exhibitions, and gather collections. Early displays, held in three rooms of the Keeper's House, gave prominence to the natural history and fishing traditions of the island, but the museum continued to grow to fill the entire structure and to mount a new art exhibition annually.

The new museum demanded an increasing portion of the Monhegan Associates' efforts each year. In 1983, when Ted Edison expressed his reluctance to gift the Monhegan Associates his original land acquisitions (the property on the southern end of the island including Gull Rock) due to his concern that if someone were to be injured at the museum that individual might acquire all of their holdings through a lawsuit, it was evident that the time had come for the Monhegan Museum and the Monhegan Associates to become independent organizations.

The Monhegan Historical & Cultural Museum Association was founded in 1984, and Edison donated his remaining island property to the Monhegan Associates later that year. Under the leadership of president and director Ed Deci, the small museum grew rapidly and expanded its focus to include highlighting the influence of Monhegan on generations of American artists. Enthusiasm abounded for the unique opportunity to view works of art in the environment in which they were created, to experience the vistas depicted, to walk the same trails, and even to sleep in the same lodgings as the artists; and the museum's art collection developed as a result of generous donations of paintings, sculptures, and drawings. By the mid-1990s, the collections had outgrown the Keeper's House. To alleviate crowding and create appropriate storage for the growing collection, the former Assistant Keeper's House and a shed that had been demolished in the 1920s were reconstructed to serve as a gallery, collections storage, and an archive. With the completion of this construction in 1998, the Monhegan Island Light Station appeared again as it did at the turn of the twentieth century.

During the middle decades of the twentieth century, the holdings of the Monhegan Associates increased rapidly to include much of the Wildlands

Geraldine King Tam (1920–2016). Top: *Pink Lady-Slipper, Moccasin Flower*, undated. Ink and watercolor on paper, 10⅞ x 8 inches. Bottom, left: *Devil's Paintbrush*, undated. Ink and watercolor on paper, 10½ x 7¼ inches. Bottom, right: *Black Swallow-wort*, undated. Ink and watercolor on paper, 10¾ x 7⅝ inches. Monhegan Museum of Art & History. Gift of Cindy King

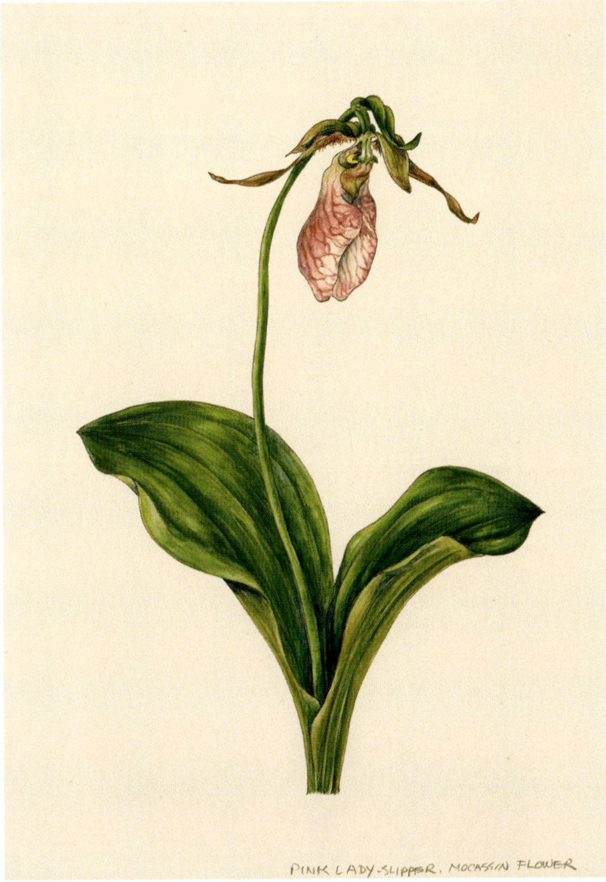

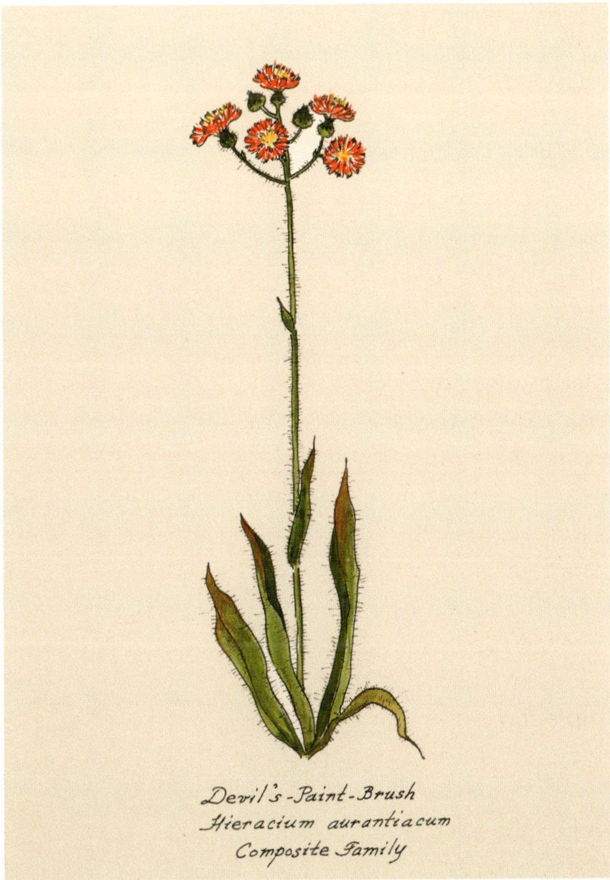

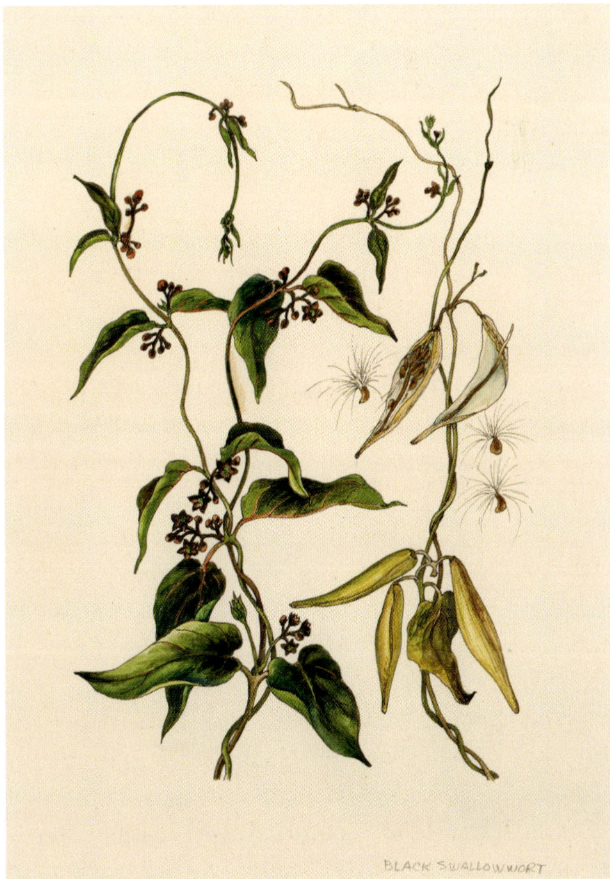

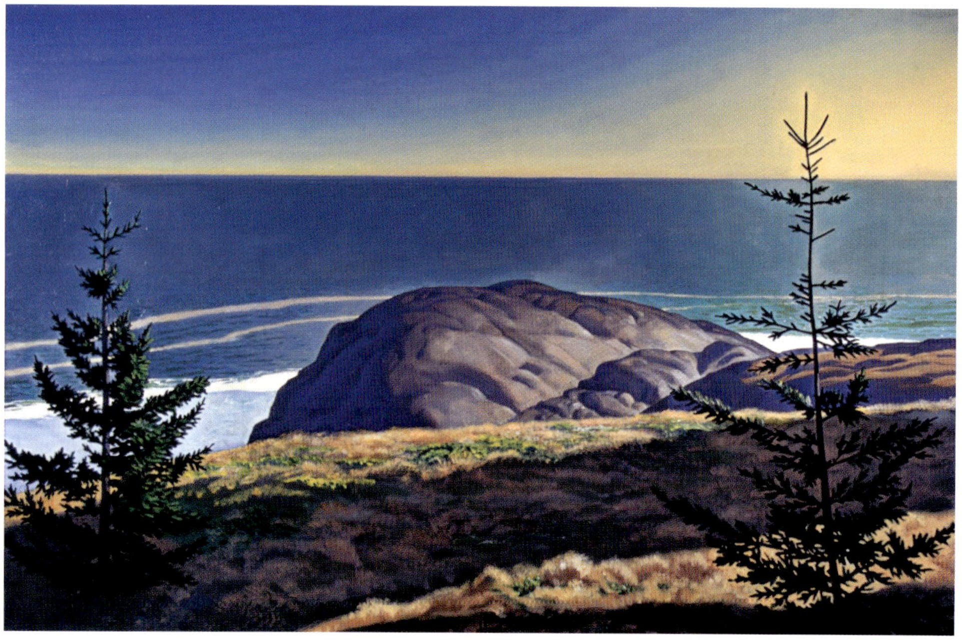

Rockwell Kent (1882–1971), *Young Spruces, Maine Coast*, 1955. Oil on canvas. The State Hermitage Museum, St. Petersburg, Russia

forest. White spruce carried on its steady march across what had once been sheep pasture. Some healthy young trees of modest height appeared alone among the grasses, as depicted in Rockwell Kent's *Young Spruces, Maine Coast*. Elsewhere on the island, white spruce reached densities that constituted a stand, as captured in photographs by Warner Taylor (see pp. 112–13) and in James Fitzgerald's *Sentinels I* (see p. 107). Regal though these white spruce stands were, trouble lay ahead for them. Deer largely left the recently established white spruce stands alone as the trees' tough, sharply pointed needles discouraged browsing. The threat faced by the trees was instead botanical—in the form of a parasitic plant called dwarf mistletoe.[16] The mistletoe's modified roots bore into shoots, allowing the plant to meet its needs for water and sustenance by tapping into its host tree's vascular system. After a several-year period of growth within its host, short mistletoe shoots erupt from host branches, flower, and set seed. These seeds are ballistically ejected under intense water pressure created in their fruits and can travel yards through the air. A sticky coating improves the chances that a seed will stick to any branch it strikes, which is a requirement for successful germination.

Although the shoots of the parasite are subtle and nondescript, mistletoe-infected trees can be spotted from a distance by their distorted branches, or so-called witches' brooms, evident in Accra Shepp's photographs (see pp. 130–31 and 164–65) and the subject of Barbara Petter Putnam's woodcuts (see pp. 176–79). To stave off branch shedding, which might otherwise rid a tree of infection, it appears that mistletoe releases hormones into its host that forestall branch death.[17] These same hormones promote branching—hence, the witches' brooms—and the delivery of the tree's resources to the site of mistletoe infection. In this way, the parasite hijacks the metabolism of its host to maintain the infection and claim a disproportionate share of the tree's resources. Over a period of twelve to twenty years, as the size and number of

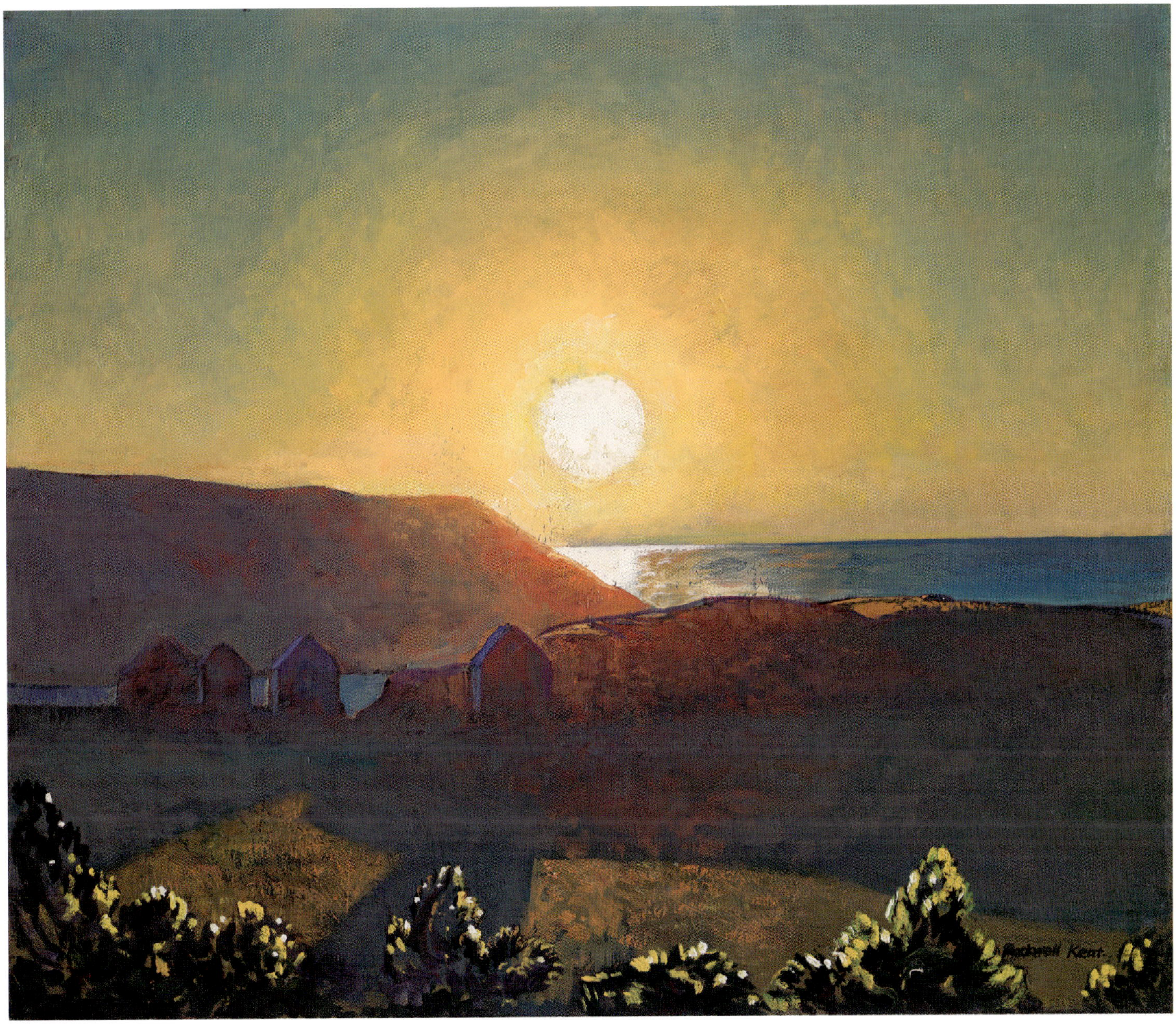

Rockwell Kent (1882–1971), *Sun, Manana, Monhegan*, 1907/ca. 1950. Oil on canvas, 20 x 24 inches. Bowdoin College Museum of Art, Brunswick, Maine. Museum purchase with funds donated anonymously, 1971.73. Rockwell Kent began this painting in 1907 and, upon returning to Monhegan in the 1950s after a long period away, added the sun-kissed spruce in the foreground. The proliferation of trees had grown to frame the view from his cottage in the years since his early tenure on the island.

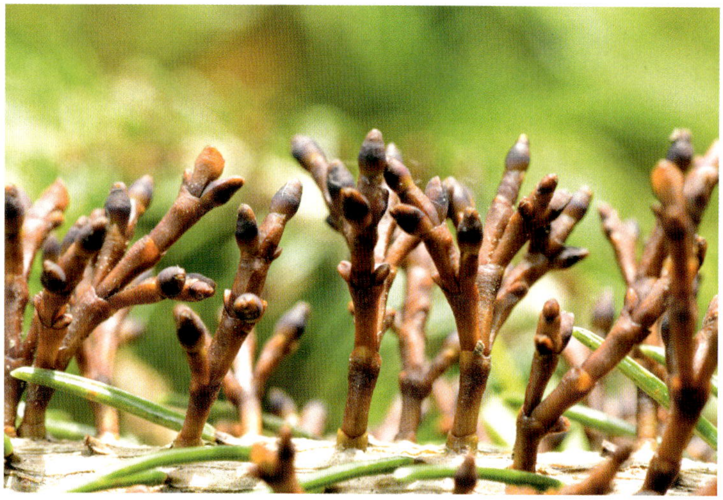

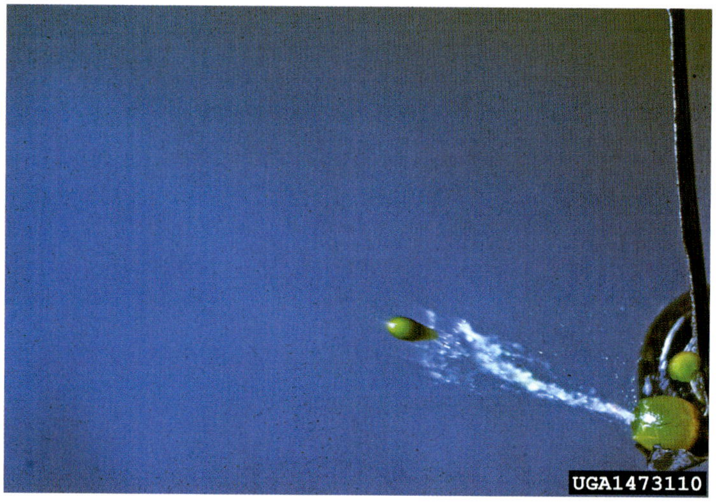

dwarf mistletoe infections grow, the resource pool of a host white spruce can be so thoroughly depleted that death ensues.[18] Killing one's host may seem an unwise strategy for a parasite, as it will die along with it; however, mistletoe will have been able to undertake years of seed set before host and parasite succumb.

Red spruce can also serve as a primary host for dwarf mistletoe; however, notably, red spruce kill off infected branches. Mistletoe rarely kills red spruce. Thus, two spruce species—red spruce and white spruce—living in close proximity exhibit entirely different responses to mistletoe infection. This distinction will be the focus of future research.

Eastern dwarf mistletoe is not an introduced threat to forest health; it is native to Monhegan Island. In fact, decades before the decline of white spruce attracted the attention of Wildlands visitors and the Monhegan Associates, dead, infected trees appeared at the center of George Bellows's *Ocean Headland, Black Head, Monhegan* (see p. 38) and Edward Hopper's *Monhegan Landscape* (see pp. 42–43). Mistletoe infection grew to be problematic as a consequence of nineteenth- and twentieth-century land-use practices. Whereas prior to the nineteenth century, white spruce might have been found along the shore and in occasional forest gaps, in the twentieth century, the trees formed dense stands over large areas, the result of the species's proclivity at establishing on abandoned pastureland. These dense stands represented a perfect breeding ground for widespread dwarf mistletoe infection. Vulnerable hosts were packed together in close proximity, within range of flying mistletoe seeds. Thus, the parasitic plant placed the secondary forest in a state of semi-arrest. Cycles of dwarf mistletoe infection shortened the lives of white spruce, their canopy never closing to the degree that might enable tree species of the Cathedral Woods, such as red spruce or balsam fir, to take root. A dense herd of deer browsed broad-leafed tree species and promoted an understory thicket rich with introduced plants.

In 1986, the impact of dwarf mistletoe on the health and appearance of the Wildlands prompted the Monhegan Associates to seek the input of pathologist Douglas Stark and Maine Forest Service manager Vladek "Kim" Kolman, who recommended "sanitizing" by removing dead and heavily infected trees and

Above, left: Aerial shoots of Eastern dwarf mistletoe projecting from a white spruce shoot.

Above, right: Limber pine dwarf mistletoe (*Arceuthobium cyanocarpum*) (A. Nels. ex Rydb.) seed being ballistically ejected from its fruit under water pressure

A white spruce displaying distorted, dwarf-mistletoe-infected branches, or so-called witches' brooms, 2016. Photograph by Gregório Ceccantini

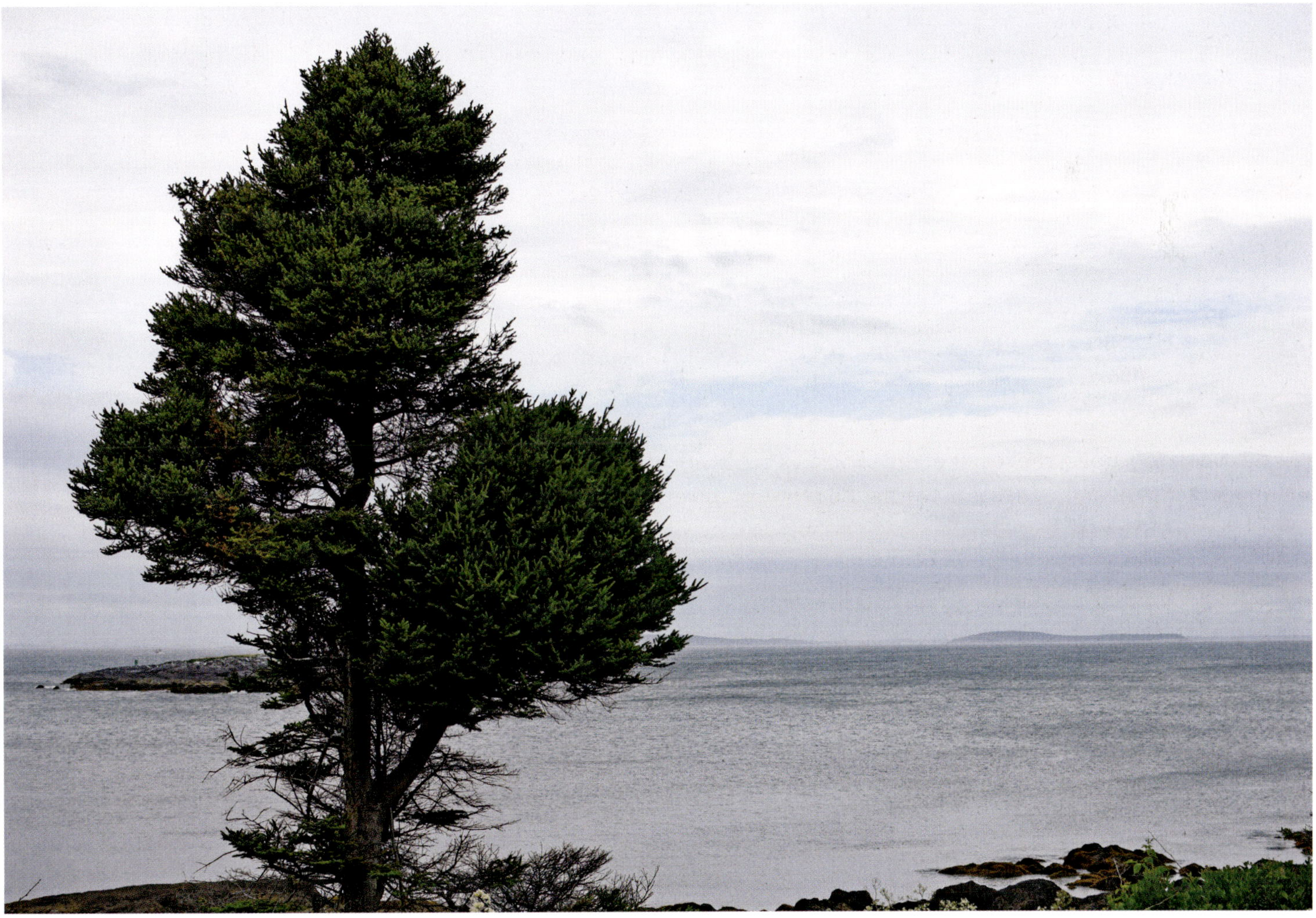

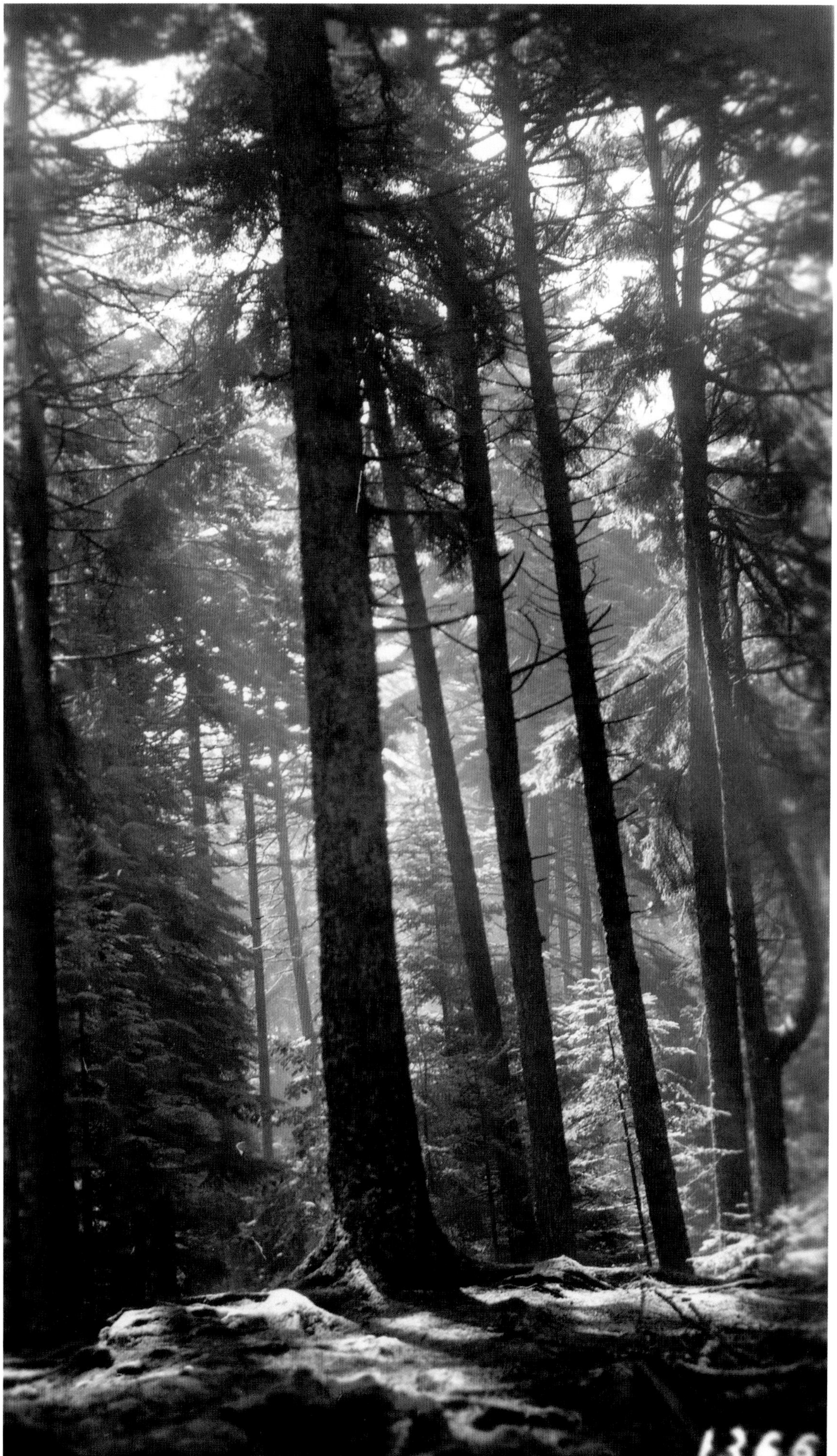

Lorimer Brackett (1904–1992), *Cathedral Woods, Monhegan, Maine,* undated. Postcard. Monhegan Museum of Art & History

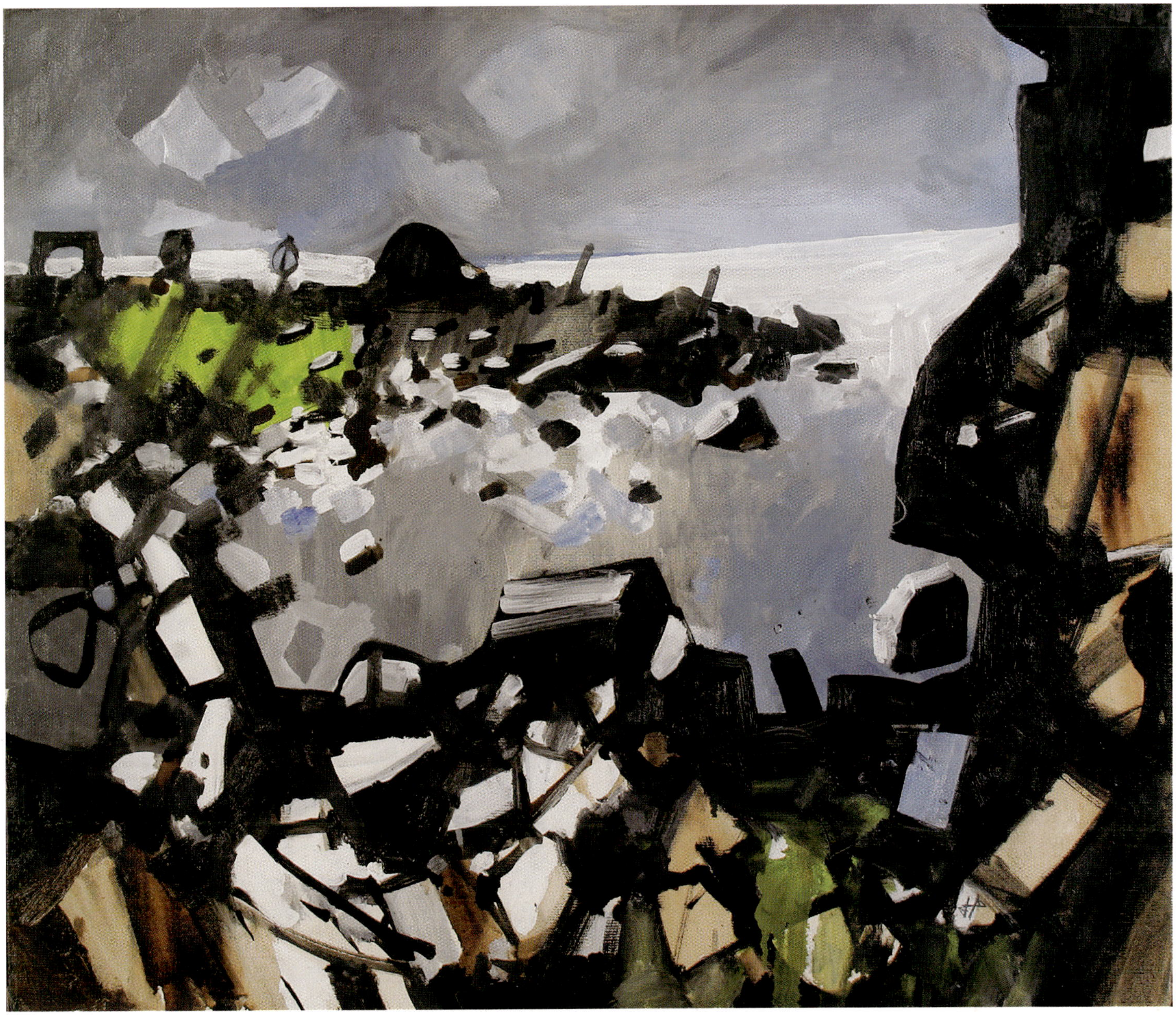

John Hultberg (1922–2005), *Monhegan #2, Lobster Cove from Afar,* 1961. Oil on canvas panel, 20 x 24 inches. Monhegan Museum of Art & History. Gift of the Elaine Wechsler Living Trust

lopping off infected branches of lightly infected trees. They further suggested replacing white spruce with jack pine and pitch pine, both of which are native to the Maine coast but do not serve as a primary host to mistletoe. On Monhegan, since tree removal had not been practiced on any scale since pasture was first formed in prior centuries and tree planting had never been undertaken in the Wildlands, these recommendations were not acted upon by the Monhegan Associates.

Into the postwar years, the forest continued to provide inspiration for the influx of artists from New York that continued throughout the twentieth century and brought cultural diversity and a modern aesthetic to the island's art community. Characterized by their tendency toward abstraction, this group was drawn by the landscape, community, and slower pace of life on Monhegan.

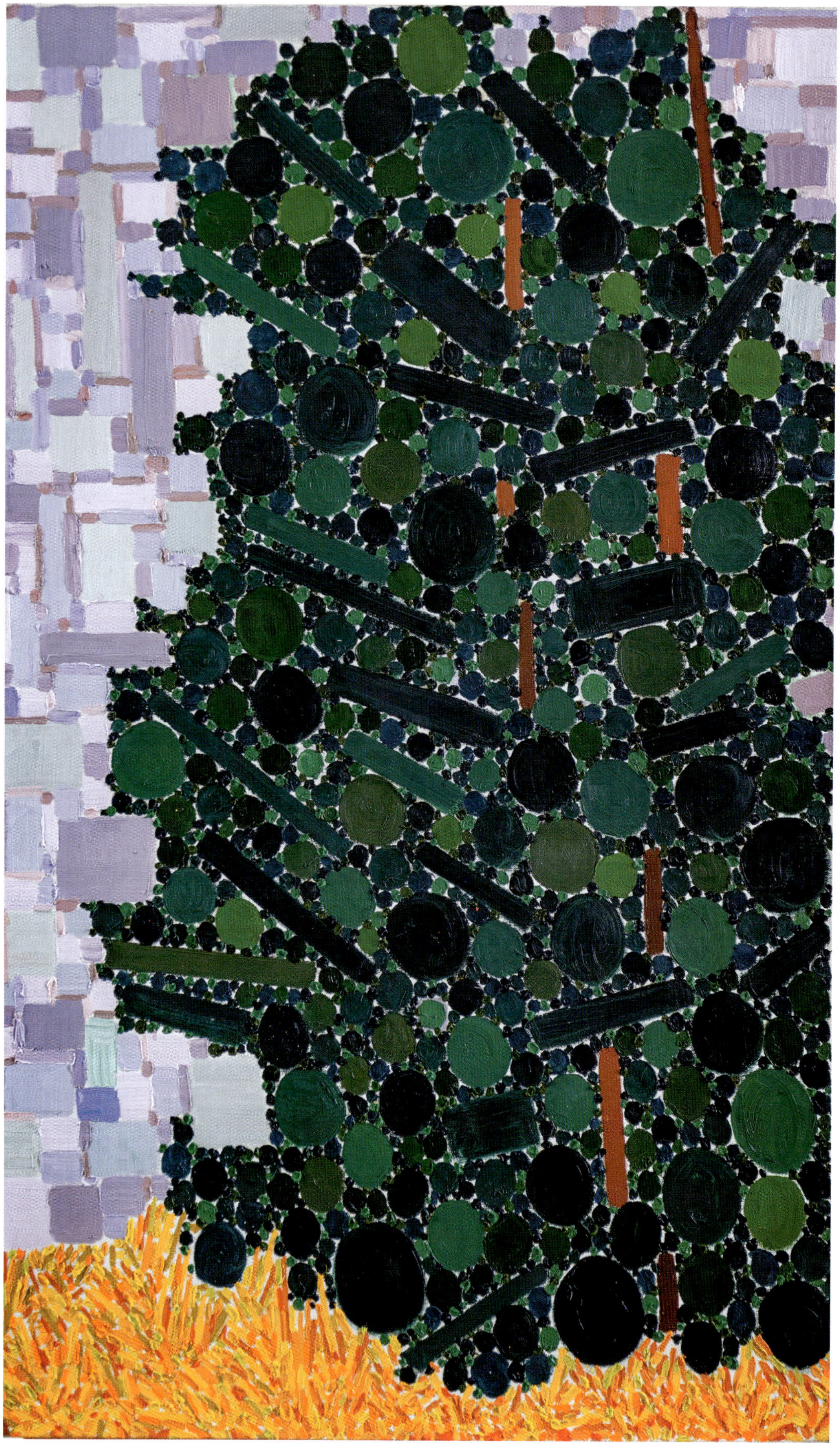

Left: Lynne Drexler (1928–1999), *Evergreen,* 1980. Oil on canvas, 39¾ x 23¾ inches. Bowdoin College Museum of Art, Brunswick, Maine. Museum purchase, Barbara Cooney Porter Fund, 2020.41

Opposite: Lynne Drexler (1928–1999), *Tree of Age*, 1981. Oil on canvas, 48 x 36 inches. Monhegan Museum of Art & History. Gift of Harry T. Bone and Bill and Barbara Manning

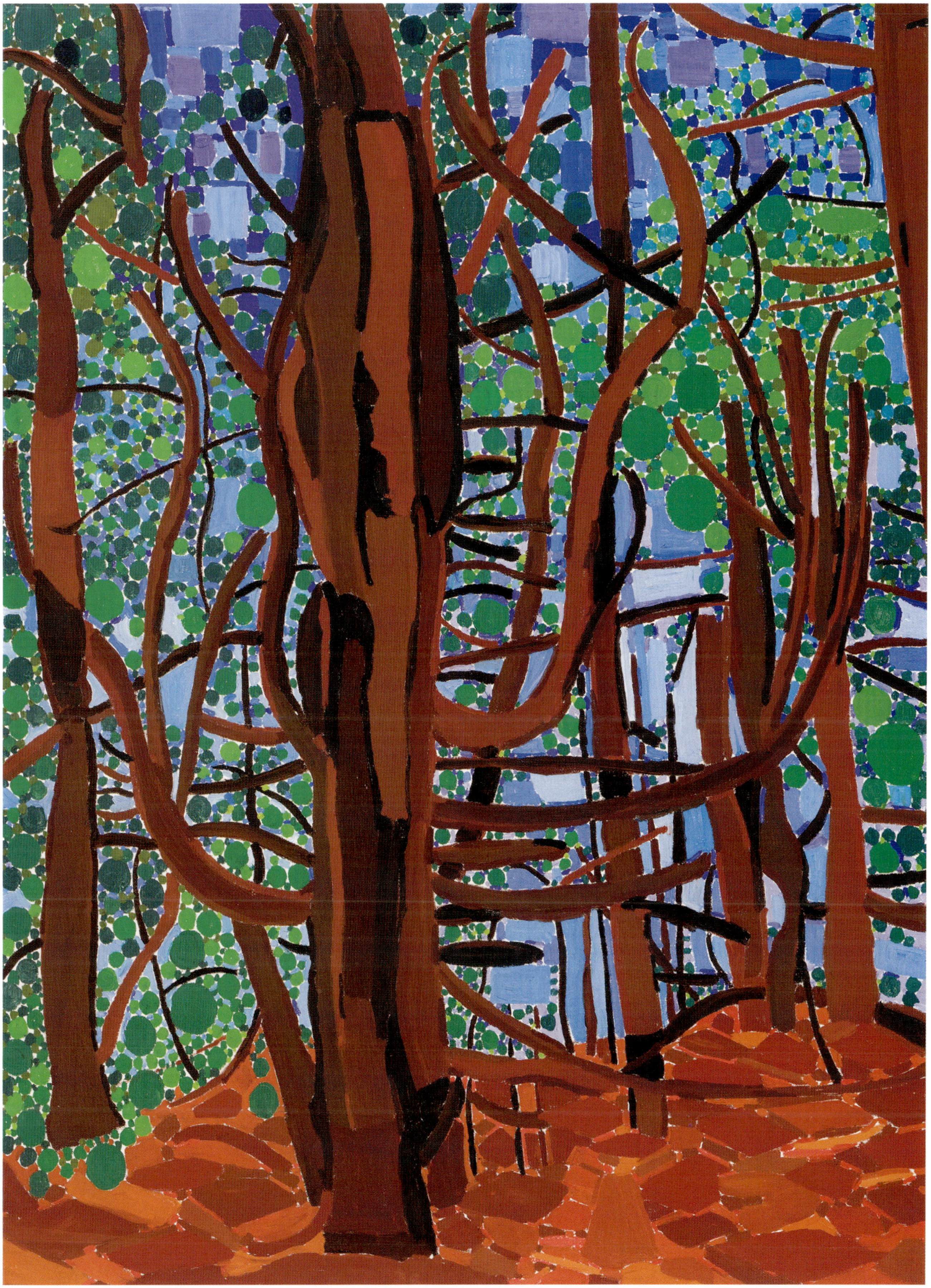

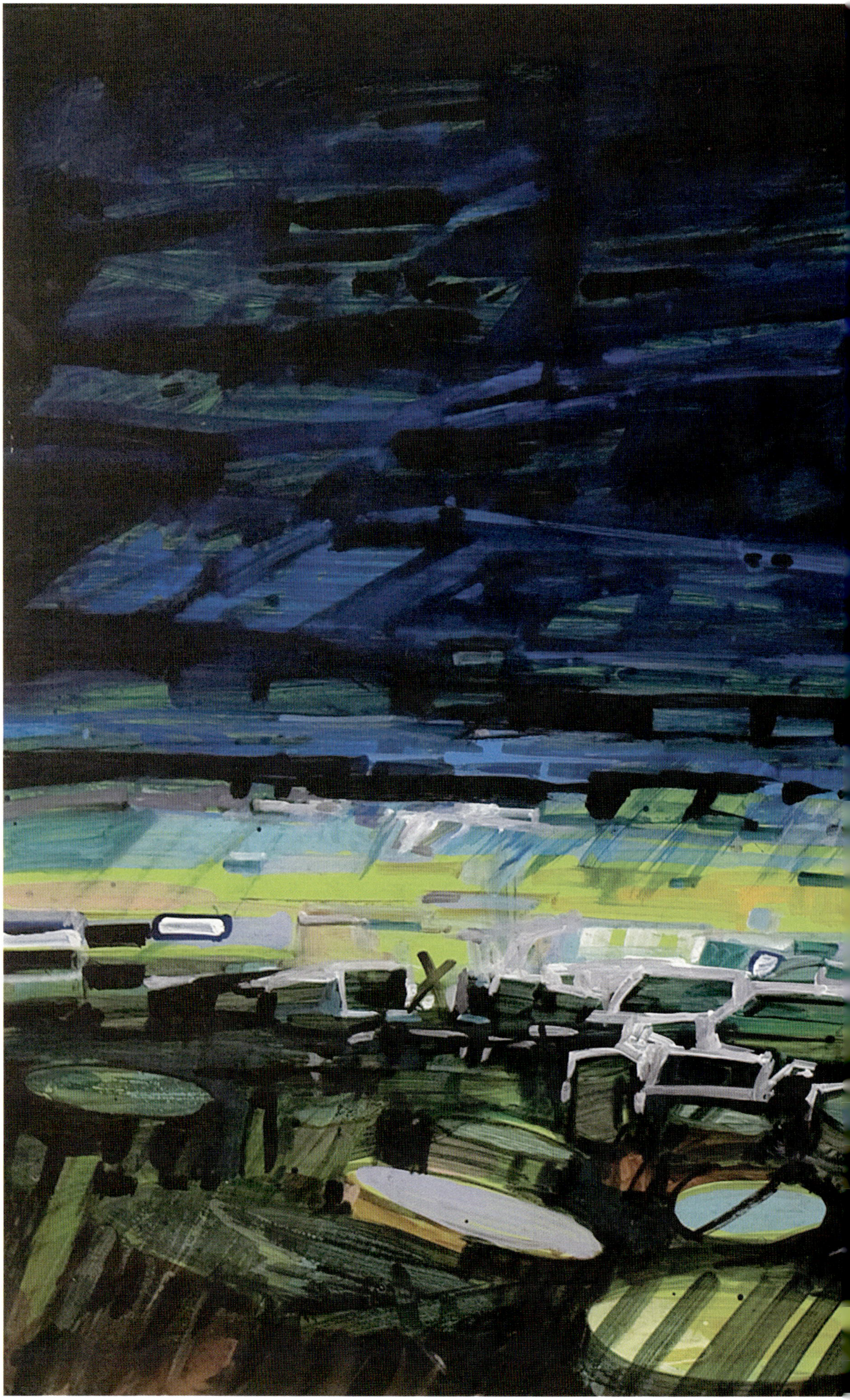

John Hultberg (1922–2005), *Forest Shrine (aka Felling the Forest)*, 1974. Acrylic on board, 28½ x 45½ inches. Monhegan Museum of Art & History. Gift of the Florsheim Foundation

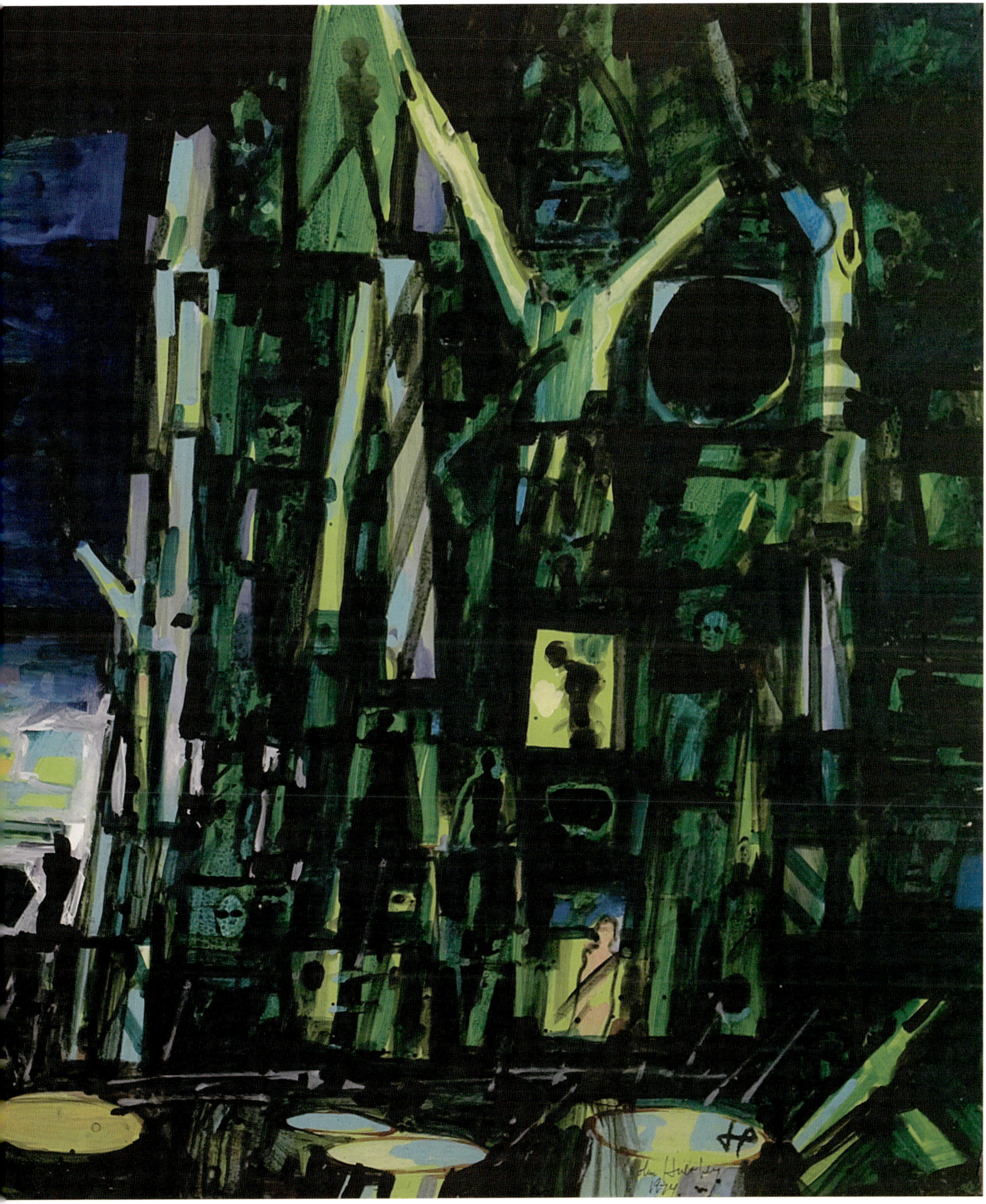

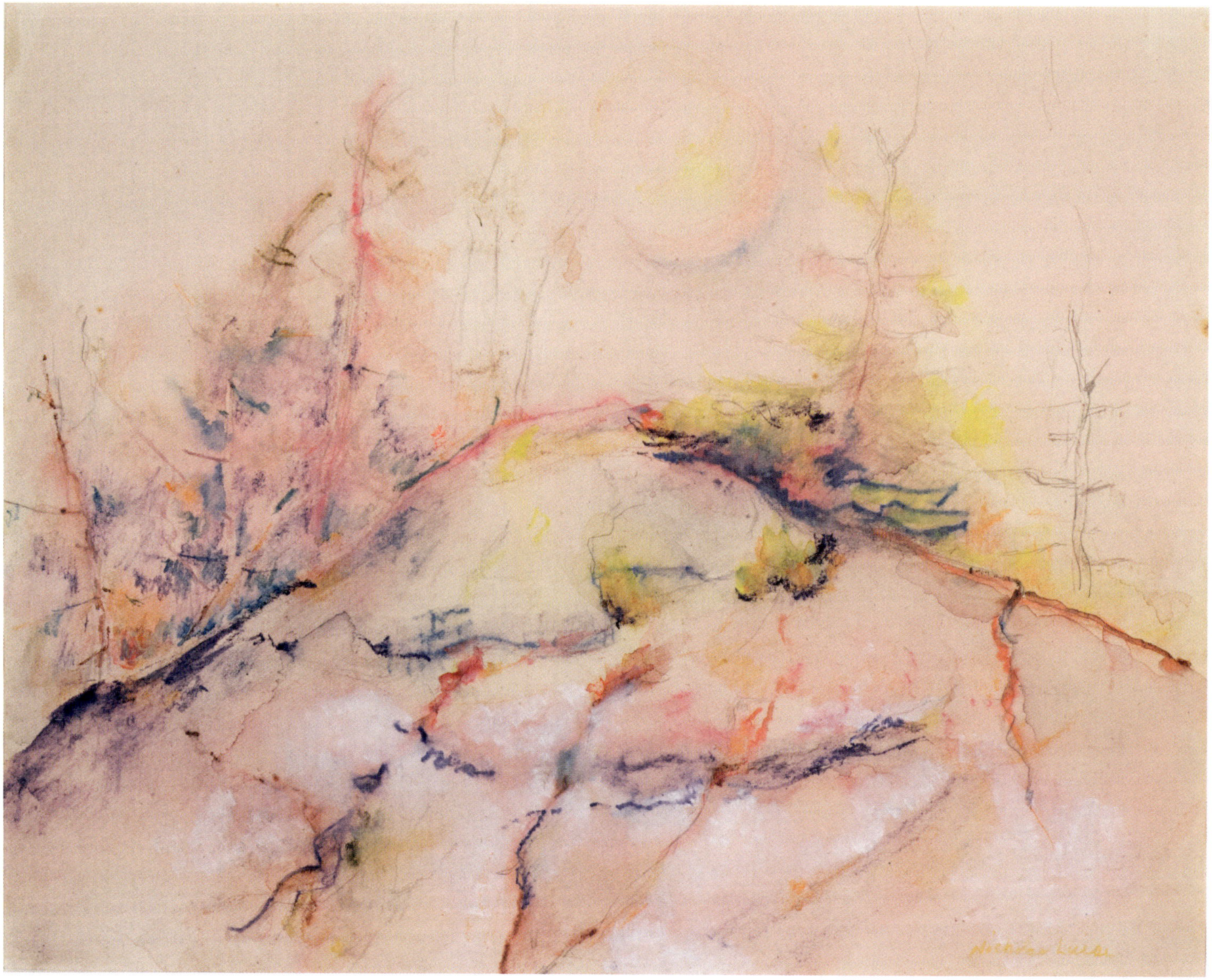

Artist John Hultberg served as chair of the Monhegan Associates' Trails Committee for five years beginning in 1982, though his fascination with the forest was evident as early as 1974, when he created his half-cathedral, half-wasteland homage to the island woods—*Forest Shrine (aka Felling the Forest)*. About the island's forests, he observed in 1985: "Over the years I have tried to paint the Monhegan forest. It seems too abstract a design and yet it stands up, it has a nice mood."[19] Hultberg's spouse and fellow painter Lynne Drexler was also captivated by Cathedral Woods, finding solace there when coping with the impending death of artist friend Alex Minewski in the late 1970s. Years later, in a 1999 interview, she recounted the experience: "I went out in the trees and saw what dignity they died in the forest with and felt a lot better about the whole thing."[20]

Works by Nicholas Luisi and Jean Liberté illustrate the steady progression of trees onto the island's once bare headlands, while abstractions created

Nicholas Luisi (1894–1977), *Rocks and Trees*, ca. 1960. Watercolor on paper, 11 x 14 inches. Monhegan Museum of Art & History. Gift of Richard D. Montross

Jean Liberté (1896–1965), *Cliffs and Trees*, 1950s. Gouache on paper, 15½ x 19¼ inches. Collection of Edward L. Deci

by other members of the New York group of artists such as Michael Loew, Reuben Tam, Joseph DeMartini, Remo Farruggio, Morris Shulman, and Murray Hantman reference the island's cliffs almost devoid of trees, instead focusing on the lines and blocks of color created by primeval rock formations. Not all artists during the postwar period fully embraced abstraction. Teco Slagboom, one of the Monhegan Associates' founding trustees and a long-term island resident was known for his mystical landscapes that, rendered in soft pastel, incorporated light filtering through the trees of the island forests. His close friend and neighbor Ruth Boynton said of her own work: "The wild intricate tangle of foliage and woods, and the wonderful pattern of rocks and cliffs intrigue me most. Although the result is realistic, I approach the painting as an abstract, emphasizing varying color and design."[21]

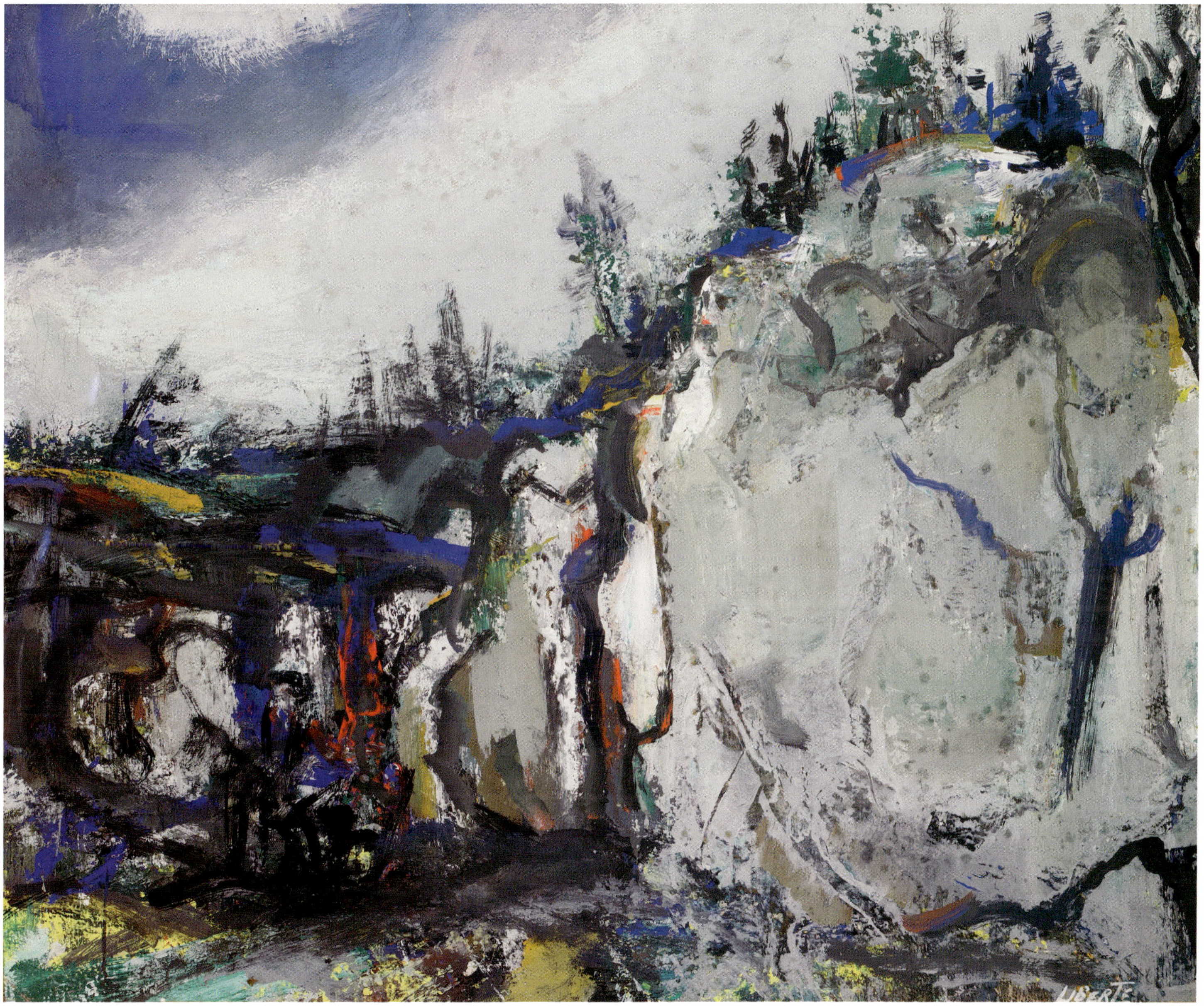

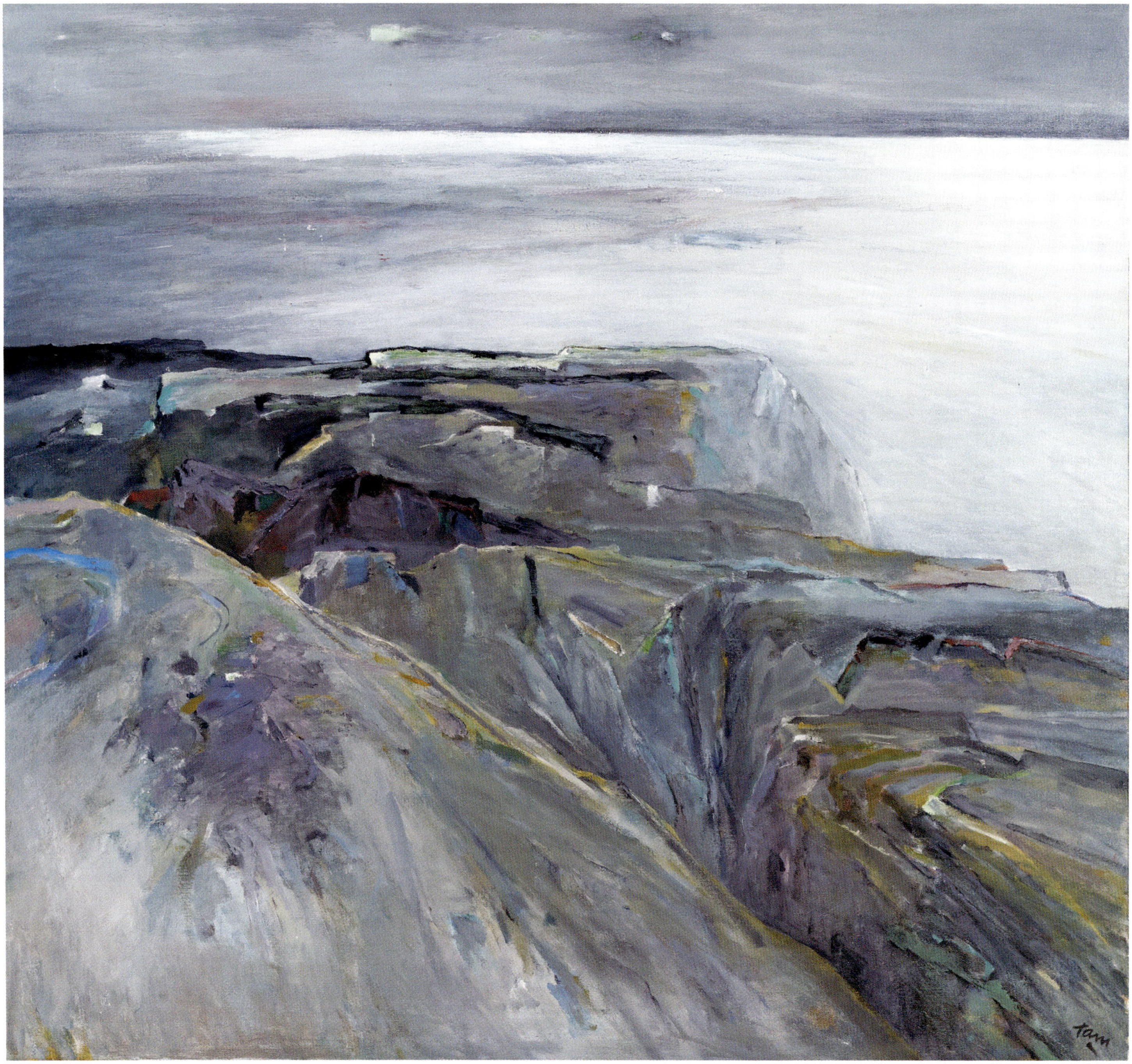

Reuben Tam (1916–1991), *North Rock Fall*, 1979. Oil on canvas, 38½ x 42½ inches. Monhegan Museum of Art & History. Bequest of Elizabeth B. Noyce

Reuben Tam (1916–1991), *Coastline Spruce*, undated. Brush, pen, and black ink on paper, 15 x $17\frac{11}{16}$ inches. Bowdoin College Museum of Art, Brunswick, Maine. Museum purchase, Elizabeth B. G. Hamlin Fund, 1970.52

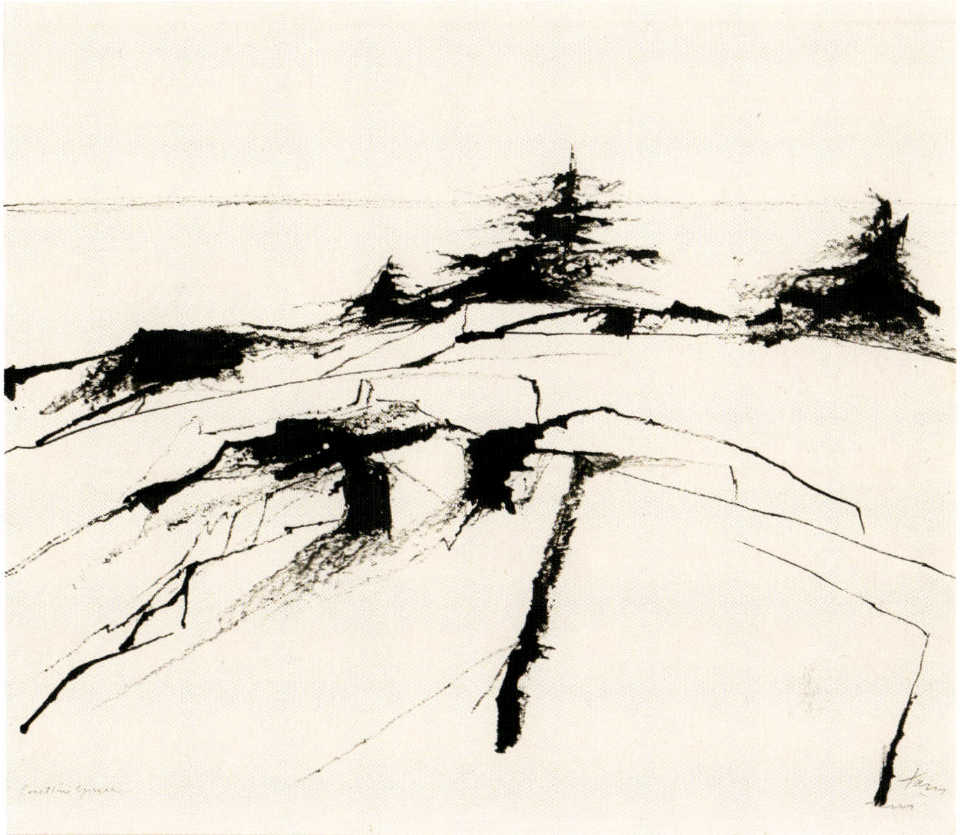

Tourism likewise flourished throughout the second half of the twentieth century. Though more people found Monhegan to be an affordable and attractive destination, the number of available beds on the island remained relatively stable. In response to demand, by the late twentieth century, additional daily boats from several ports on the mainland throughout the summer allowed for a substantial increase in day-trippers. Amenities and attractions came to include the Monhegan Museum, gift shops, an art gallery, and more dining options. The call for lodging and real estate boomed, as did the price of a visit to Monhegan.

Amid this vibrancy, as the twentieth century drew to a close, island visitors and the Monhegan community confronted a threat arising from the Wildlands and its deer herd: Lyme disease, which is caused by a tick-borne bacterium. Symptoms can include a bull's-eye rash at the site of the tick bite, flu-like illness, fatigue, and joint pain. The nature, and very existence, of persistent Lyme disease symptoms remains incompletely described and engenders passionate advocacy. Even if the boundaries of the condition we call Lyme disease are not fully known, it is a profound and dreaded public health crisis in the region. Numbers of black-legged ticks (also known as "deer ticks"), the Lyme vector, have exploded across the northeastern United States, as forest regrowth creates more favorable tick habitat—ticks require the humidity afforded by foliage—and warming weakens the winter kill that might otherwise have stemmed their northward advance.[22]

The first case of Lyme disease in Maine was documented in the 1980s, and the first Monhegan Islander received a Lyme diagnosis in 1989. By then, Monhegan had attracted the interest of Lyme disease researchers drawn by its engaged and informed community, its isolation and tractable size, and the unusual assemblage of mammals inhabiting the island. On Monhegan and other unbridged islands, these scientists launched an ongoing research program that deepens knowledge of Lyme disease ecology and guides Lyme control practices. As they got this work off the ground, leaders founded the Maine Lyme Disease Research Laboratory at the Maine Medical Center Research Institute (today the Vector-Borne Disease Laboratory at the MaineHealth Institute for Research).[23]

Researchers were at first intrigued by the presence of black-legged ticks on Monhegan, seemingly despite the lack of small mammal hosts. Ticks pass through several life stages, each requiring a blood meal: Eggs hatch into larvae, which feed on small mammals and birds. Larvae molt into nymphs, which feed on mammals of various sizes. Finally, nymphs molt into adults, which seek their blood meal from large mammals, principally white-tailed deer. Adults reproduce, producing eggs and completing the life cycle. The maintenance of a black-legged tick population therefore requires the presence of both small mammals and deer. Tick populations collapse in the absence of either. Humans and their pets insinuate themselves into the tick life cycle, to their detriment, as sources of blood meals for nymphal and adult ticks.

At the time of first intensive study, community members attested that the island was free of the small mammals known to be fed upon by larval and nymphal black-legged ticks, including mice, chipmunks, voles, and red squirrels. Their absence was confirmed by intensive but unsuccessful trapping campaigns. (This is no longer the case; mice have since found Monhegan.) Still, it was clear that Monhegan was home to a thriving black-legged tick population. How was this possible? Attention turned to Norway rats, longtime residents of the island that had escaped from visiting ships centuries earlier. Traps suitable for Norway rats were deployed. Rats were trapped in short order and shown to be heavily infested with black-legged ticks—in fact, the Lyme bacterium was found in a majority of the ticks pulled off of rats. Thus, the mystery was solved. Research on Monhegan added Norway rats to the list of small-mammal black-legged tick hosts and showed the world that they can serve as a reservoir for the Lyme bacterium. Anxiety over the risk of contracting Lyme disease grew through the ensuing period. As research progressed, tick "drags," a procedure to census tick populations by inspecting a cloth pulled across tick habitat, yielded twice as many ticks as they once had.[24] (It is worth noting here that Japanese barberry is known as especially good deer tick habitat.) Also worrying, the proportion of ticks carrying the Lyme bacterium rose from just less than 25 to 40 percent in the span of only two years. In 1991, the Monhegan Associates voted to deliver an article to the town to petition the state to remove the Monhegan deer herd, citing the loss to browsing of almost five dozen wildflower species and the growing risk of Lyme disease. The town declined by a more than two-thirds majority.

With removal of the deer herd off the table, researchers and islanders turned their attention to alternative ways of limiting Lyme disease risk.

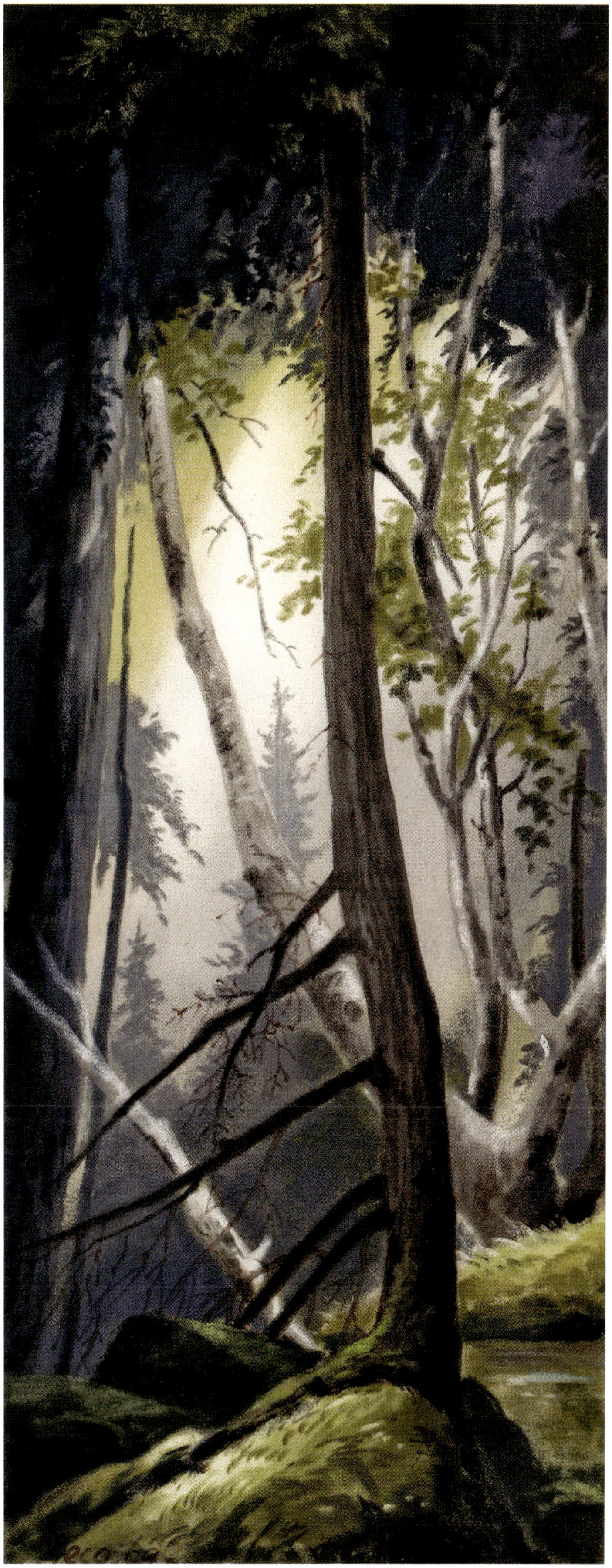

Teco Slagboom (1914–1988), Untitled, 1969. Pastel on paper, 14¼ x 5½ inches. Monhegan Museum of Art & History. Gift of Miriam Von Steinen

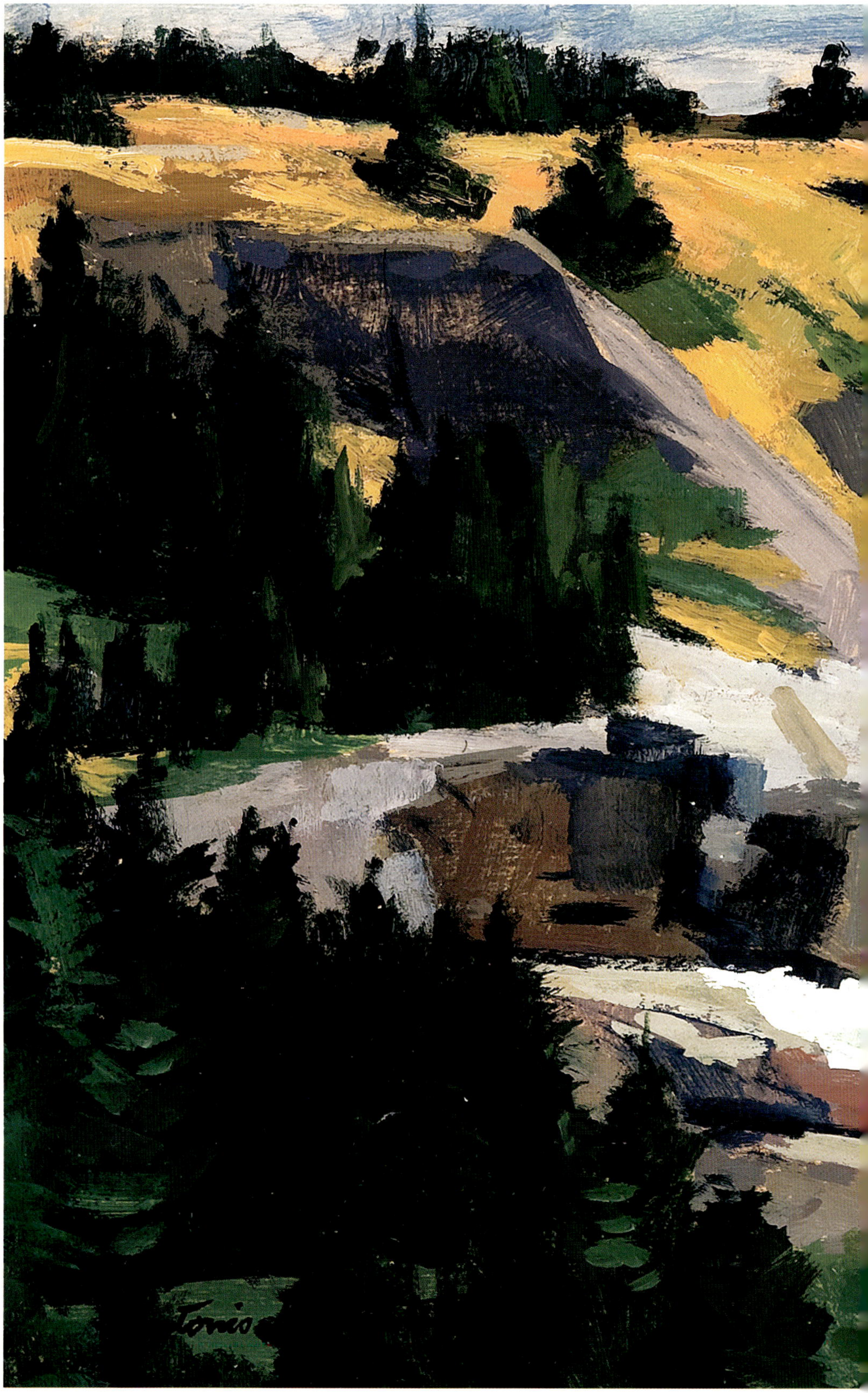

Antonio Pietro Martino (1902–1988), *White Head—Monhegan Island, Maine*, ca. 1960. Oil on board, 15 x 21 inches. Courtesy of Woodmere Art Museum, Philadelphia. Gift of John Egan, 1982

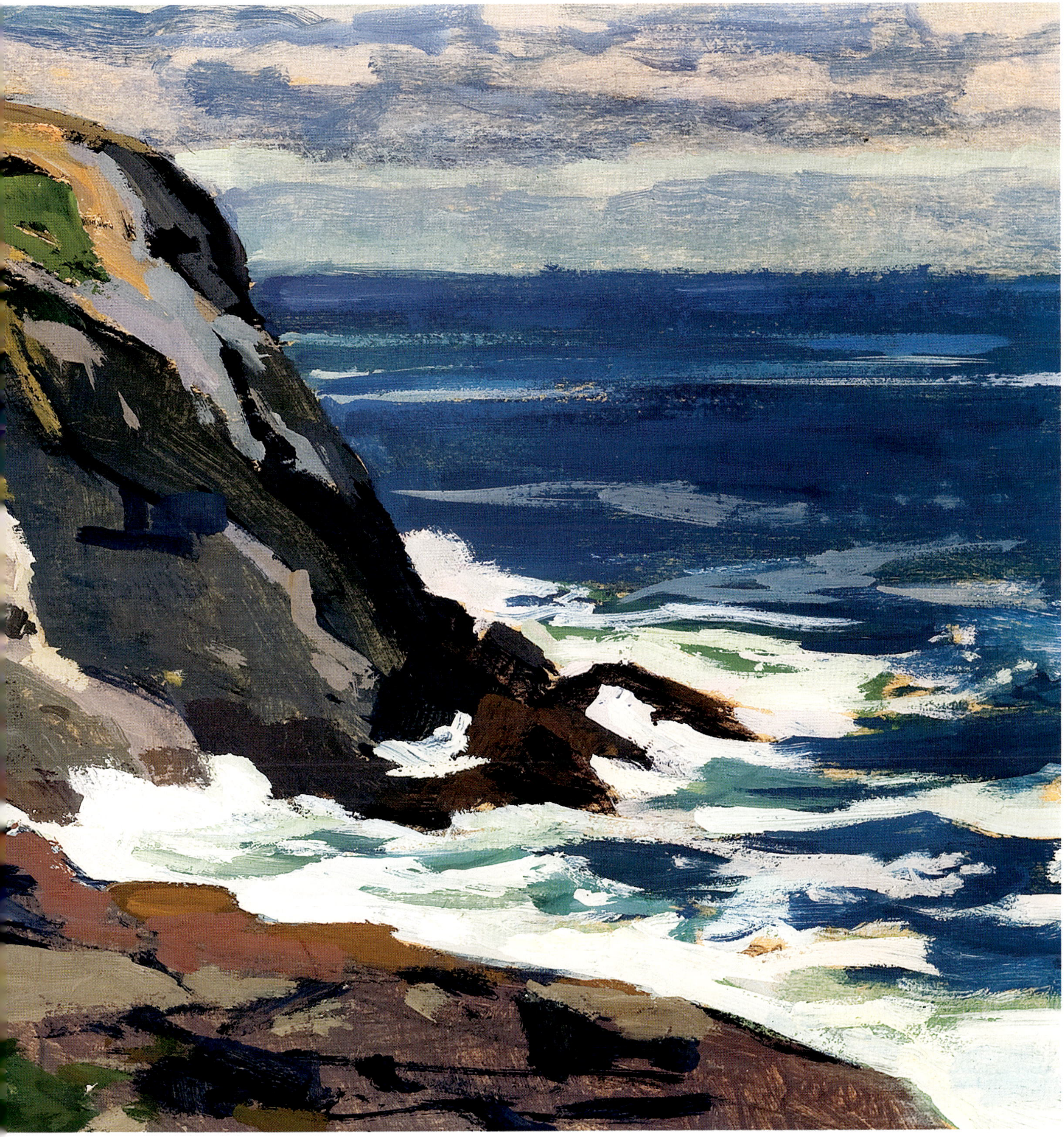

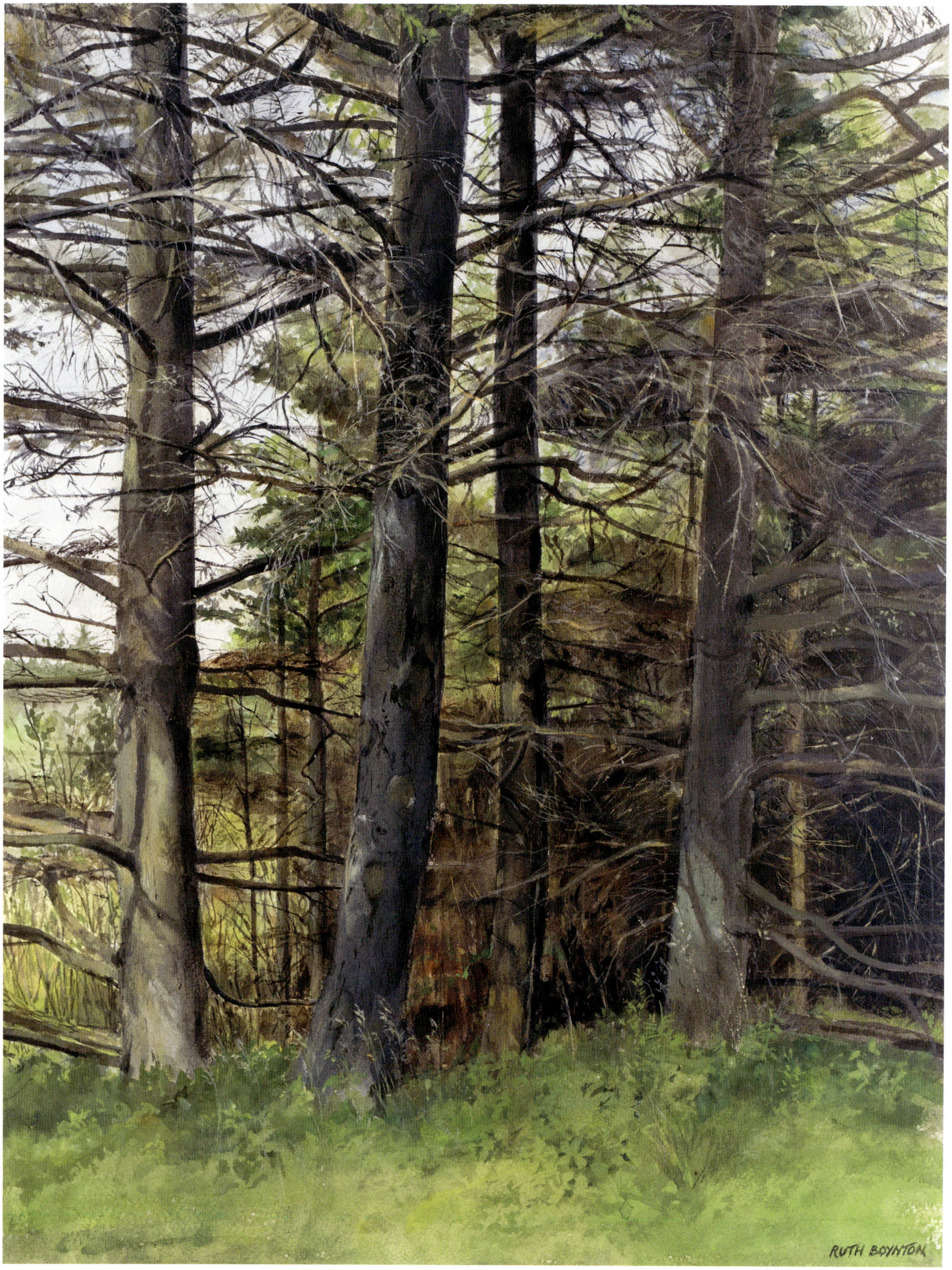
RUTH BOYNTON

They considered different strategies, including controlling the rat population and rendering rats or deer inhospitable to black-legged ticks. All were attempted, though none succeeded. A strategy not mentioned above might have involved spraying pesticide to knock down the tick population. That was never seriously considered, however, since the island's central water supply, the Meadow, is fed by runoff, and due to fears that pesticides could harm the lobster fishery, a principal source of income for year-round islanders.

Rendering rats inhospitable to deer ticks was attempted by the clever design of a tubular device that the rodents would enter in search of bait and in which they would be coated with permethrin, a powerful insecticide that would rid them of ticks. Alas, the maritime climate and biota of the island led these devices to be infested with slugs, and the rats showed little interest in them. Controlling rat numbers was no more effective. Although rodenticide could be placed in a manner that prevented sampling by curious, free-roaming pet dogs, the same could not be said of the rats who had consumed it. Twine, the Boehmer family's Jack Russell terrier, whose ancestry could be traced back to Jamie Wyeth's canine companions, required urgent veterinary care after dispatching a rat near a bait station. That episode precipitated the end of baiting.

Could a solution be found by ridding deer of black-legged ticks? Such an approach had shown some success in Texas, where lone star ticks infest white-tailed deer. This strategy involved dosing deer with ivermectin, an antiparasitic drug shown to also repel—even kill—ticks. For over a year, corn mixed with ivermectin was offered to the deer of Monhegan in troughs maintained in the community and feeding stations throughout the Wildlands, from which treated corn was spread at first once, and ultimately twice daily. This dedicated effort hinted at success, but ultimately failed. Deer that achieved desired blood ivermectin levels harbored fewer ticks. Those ticks were smaller and laid fewer eggs. Their eggs exhibited poor hatching success. This promise met with the reality that too few deer reached threshold blood ivermectin levels. Tick flagging showed no impact on tick numbers. Fourteen tons of ivermectin-laced corn hand-hauled to feeders and troughs could not put a dent in the tick population. The dominance hierarchies of deer herds did not help matters. Population-wide treatment with ivermectin was evidently thwarted by larger bucks, who drove off other deer, keeping the feast of treated corn all to themselves.

Although much was learned from years of invested effort, the risk of Lyme disease on Monhegan persisted. Between its first documented occurrence in 1989 and 1996, more than twenty-five year-round residents contracted confirmed or suspected cases of Lyme disease. A survey of nearly five hundred island visitors added eighteen additional cases. And, worryingly, there was evidence of another tick-borne illness, anaplasmosis, on the island. Attention focused again on control of the deer population.

Eventually, reduction of the deer herd was performed the old-fashioned way, by marksmen. In this case, Anthony DeNicola, who holds a doctorate in wildlife ecology, led the effort. White Buffalo Inc., DeNicola's natural-resource management and conservation organization, shot fifty-two deer over five April nights in 1996 (requiring only fifty-three shots). This left an estimated twenty-five deer remaining on the island. Culled deer were grossly underweight and showed other signs of chronic malnutrition, presumably the result

Ruth Boynton (1915–2003), *The Woods*, undated. Watercolor on paper, 14⅞ x 11⅝ inches. Collection of Edward L. Deci

A Natural Laboratory

In the 1990s, Monhegan was the site of important scientific studies of Lyme disease. For disease ecologists, islands like Monhegan serve as an important scientific opportunity: a tractable, closed system with minimal outside influence, unlike ecosystems on the mainland.

Lyme Disease Ecology

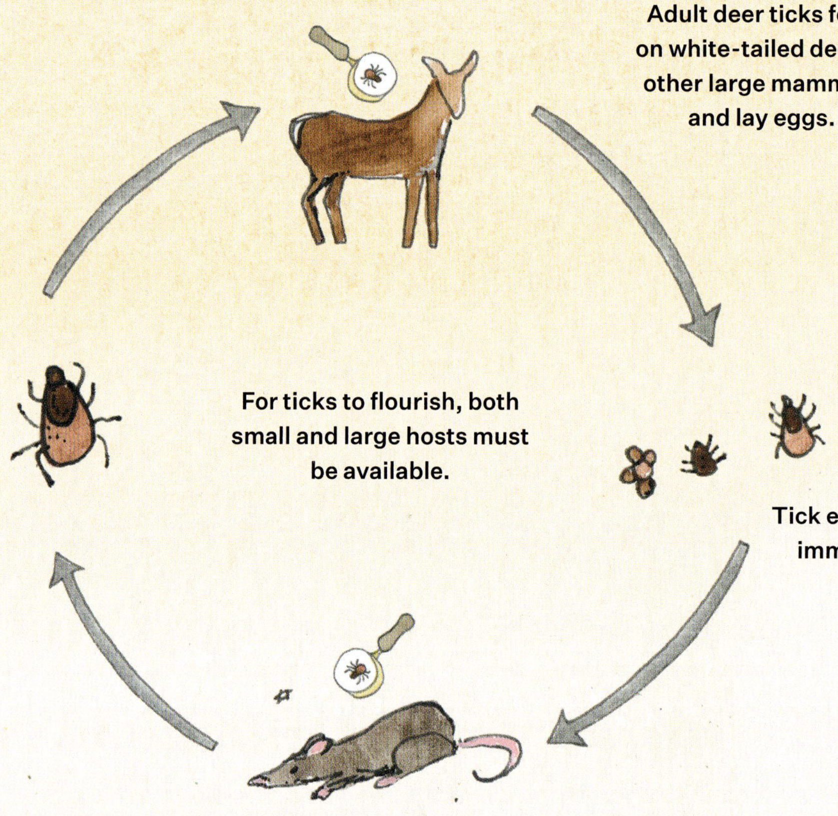

Adult deer ticks feed on white-tailed deer or other large mammals and lay eggs.

Tick eggs hatch into immature ticks.

Immature deer ticks feed on a mammal infected with Lyme bacteria.

Now infected with Lyme, the immature ticks grow into adults.

For ticks to flourish, both small and large hosts must be available.

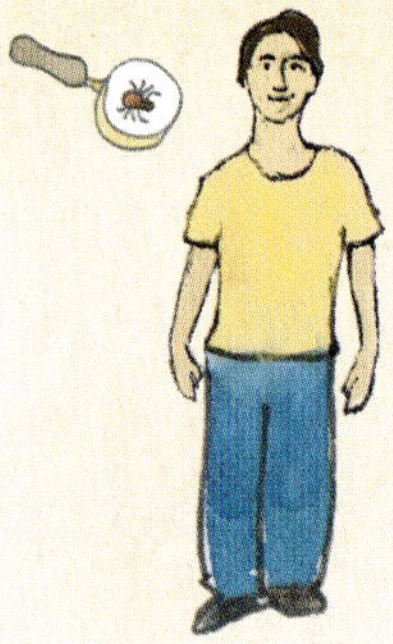

Human Consequences
When a tick with Lyme feeds on a human, it can infect them with the bacteria.

Interrupting this cycle reduces the risk of Lyme disease.

1989
Monhegan has its first case of Lyme. Many more cases follow.

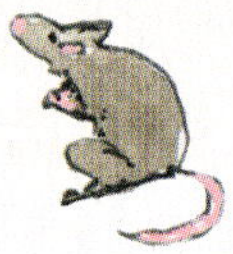

1990
The Vector-Borne Disease Laboratory discovers that rats, not mice, hosted ticks on the island.

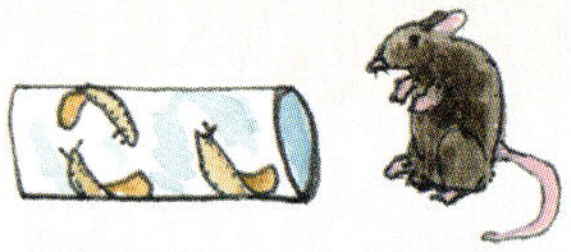

1992
Experimental tubes designed to dust rats with a tick repellent fail when they are overrun by slugs.

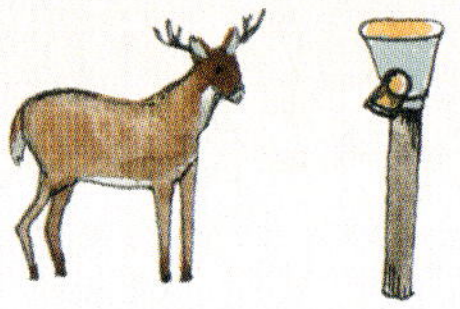

1995
Feed laced with ivermectin, which kills ticks, fails when dominant bucks monopolize feeding stations.

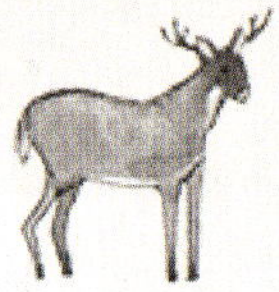

1997
The deer herd is culled with striking results. Adult tick numbers fall twenty-five fold, greatly reducing the risk of contracting Lyme on Monhegan.

James Wyeth (born 1946), *Islander*, 1975. Oil on canvas, 34 x 44⅜ inches. Collection of the Farnsworth Art Museum, Rockland, Maine. Bequest of Betsy James Wyeth Trust, 2021.1.9

of intense competition for diminishing forage in a dense population. One forecast suggested that remaining deer could rebuild the population to previous numbers in five years. Controlling the size of the deer herd would require a considerable, never-ending commitment of resources and effort. Decisions over further action were wrenching for the Monhegan community. Some felt that whatever problem they may have experienced had been addressed by the first cull. Others pushed for elimination of the deer herd altogether. The vote at a special town meeting on March 24, 1998, ultimately settled the matter: thirty-one were in favor of removal, twenty-three opposed. Within a month, White Buffalo Inc. proceeded with removal. Remaining deer were more skittish and fewer in number, drawing out the final cull. The last deer was taken on Monhegan in March 1999.

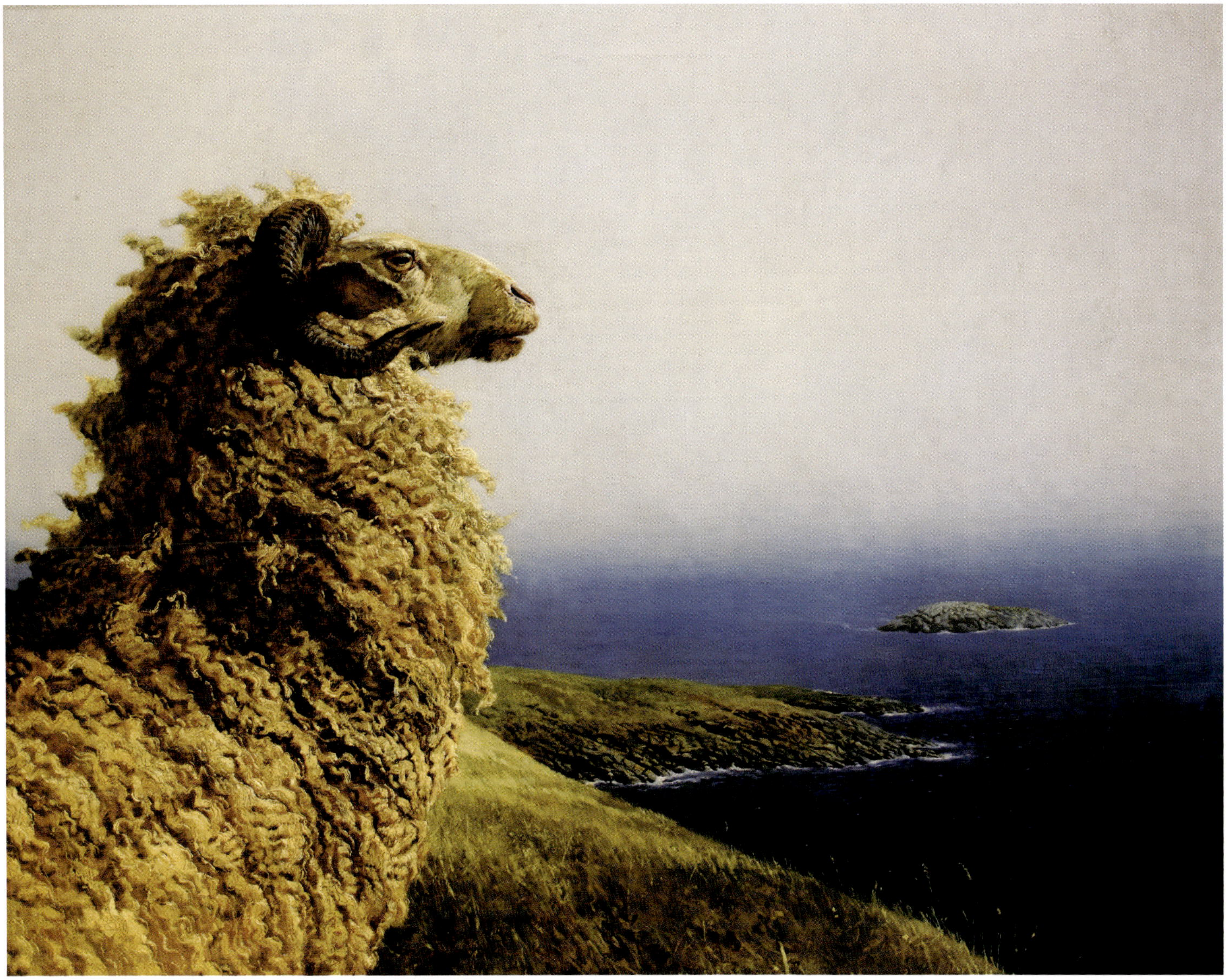

The Rise and Fall of Deer Ticks on Monhegan Island

Robert P. Smith, Physician; Co-Founder of the Vector-Borne Disease Laboratory, MaineHealth Institute for Research

In 1987, Martha Yandle, longtime Monhegan resident, found ticks for the first time on her cat Tanya. She sent them to Mark Wilson, a researcher at Harvard, for identification. A month or so later, at a scientific meeting in New York City, Mark told me about the deer ticks he had received from Monhegan. Deer ticks were largely unknown at the time outside of a few southern New England and New York coastal communities. I had just moved to Maine to work as a physician specializing in infectious diseases. "This is particularly interesting, you know," Mark said, "because it's claimed Monhegan Island has no mice, so the ticks there probably won't carry Lyme disease." In other areas of the Northeast, white-footed mice, which were ubiquitous, appeared to be the main source of the Lyme disease bacterium.

Mark was heading off to Africa to study Rift Valley fever. "OK if I go ahead and check this out?" I asked. "All yours," he replied. That chance encounter led to a series of questions about the arrival and colonization of Monhegan by deer ticks, which led in turn to over a decade of research involving deer, rats, birds, deer ticks, and Lyme disease there.

Two months after the New York meeting, I was huddled in an island bed-and-breakfast during a November gale, second-guessing the decision to "check things out." The *Laura B* mail boat's daily run was on hold due to the storm, and I was stuck. My tick flag, a square piece of white flannel tacked to the end of a broomstick, stood torn and soaked against the wall—and my tick collection vials were empty.

But Monhegan has a way of drawing the occasional visitor back. Subsequent trips would be more productive—and better planned! So much so that years later, one islander quipped, "You folks always seem to bring the good weather with you."

The next fall we arrived as a team. Peter Rand and Eleanor Lacombe, veteran medical researchers at Maine Medical Center, and I had begun a project aimed at finding out why and how the deer tick was spreading. We were joined on this trip by Harvard entomologist Andrew Spielman, an international authority on tick-borne disease, and his graduate student Sam Telford. We lugged a witch's bundle of white tick flags, several hundred live rodent traps, syringes for obtaining animal blood samples, a centrifuge, and a lot of peanut butter (for the live traps) up to Tribler Cottage, where we were met by the owners, Martha Yandle and Richard Farrell. They had already laid the groundwork for our visit, informing islanders not to be alarmed by strangers wielding white flags as we crisscrossed the island, waving them like semaphores, and placed metal boxes under bushes and trees around the village and in the Wildlands.

After two days on the island, we retrieved hundreds of traps—all empty. Tick flagging was also a bust. Yet Tanya came through with more ticks, and we retrieved another good sample as ticks dropped from a fresh deer hide hung over a basin of water. The first batch tested was negative for Lyme bacteria. Case closed? But then a second sample was tested, and 20 percent of the ticks were positive for *Borrelia burgdorferi*, the agent of Lyme disease. If there were no mice, could rats be the source? Rats had not been shown to harbor the Lyme disease bacterium. Less likely sources of infection included the few muskrats in the Meadow, or migratory and resident birds, or possibly a small number of pet dogs and cats. Only after getting a grant for a biology graduate student to spend the summer on the island did we conclusively demonstrate the novel finding that the rats were the key source of Lyme disease there.[25]

Martha Yandle arranged the first of what would become a series of meetings at the schoolhouse so that we could present our findings. Now that we had a handle on the ecology of Lyme disease on Monhegan, the next question was to consider ways to intervene. If the interventions were carefully studied within the confines of this island, we hoped it might lead to similar approaches applicable on the mainland. But any intervention hinged on the preferences of the town. Most agreed with our proposal to start with a focus on the rats.

We also sought permission to hold a blood-drawing clinic to assess baseline exposure to Lyme disease. The clinic was organized in the Monhegan Store with owner Jack Bell's blessing. We brought out two skilled phlebotomists from Maine Medical Center and set up our system with the blood centrifuge and cooler positioned on the meat counter. Fifty-five of seventy or so residents, including a few children, lined up on a sunny October afternoon outside the store. It turned out that only one had a positive test, a helpful finding. This individual developed a swollen joint in the interim, a cardinal symptom of Lyme arthritis.

Over subsequent years, we made many "expeditions" to the island to assess effects of our improvised efforts to get at the ticks. We flagged the vegetation, livetrapped rats, examined mist-netted birds, hung more deer hides, and tested the ticks we found. We obtained more blood samples from willing residents and from their sometimes less-than-willing family dogs and cats. All along, we worked in tandem with island residents, who contributed to citizen science by mapping rat tracks in the snow, sending us ticks found on different animal hosts, hiring on to assist with fieldwork, and offering a range of ideas for how to best customize our research there. But despite everyone's best efforts over nearly a decade, the ticks remained.

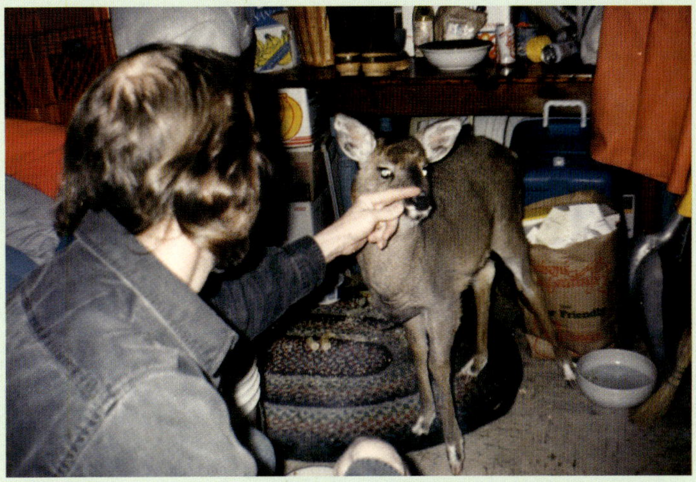

Kathie Krause Iannicelli, Harry and Honey, undated. Monhegan Museum of Art & History. Gift of Kathie Krause Iannicelli

The eventual vote to hire a wildlife expert and his team to remove the island's deer was wrenching for the island community, especially for those who had come to see the deer as a compelling aspect of the natural environment. Many islanders and visitors, including my own children, had an acquaintance with a doe dubbed "Honey," who hung out in town and accepted apples from passersby. But at the vote, even the resident who had befriended the deer agreed with the decision. We continued our monitoring of ticks and tick-borne diseases on Monhegan during and after the removal of all deer. Two years after the last deer was taken, deer tick populations crashed on the island, and never came back. As one island resident recently put it, "Those were tense years on the island, but the decisions made have been for the overall good."

Our research-learning curve was a long one, but the Monhegan studies contributed to a general understanding of the ecology of deer ticks and Lyme disease, including the role of migratory birds in tick dispersal, the capacity for different rodent hosts to maintain the Lyme disease bacterium in nature, and the critical role deer play in the tick's life cycle. Though our attempts to devise effective interventions short of removal of the deer failed, new approaches to deer tick control have benefited from the Monhegan experience. Also, we learned lessons beyond the science, most particularly how community engagement can help us find paths forward despite differences. To those of us fortunate enough to have been involved, the island experience underscored how connected we all are with nature and, ultimately, with each other.

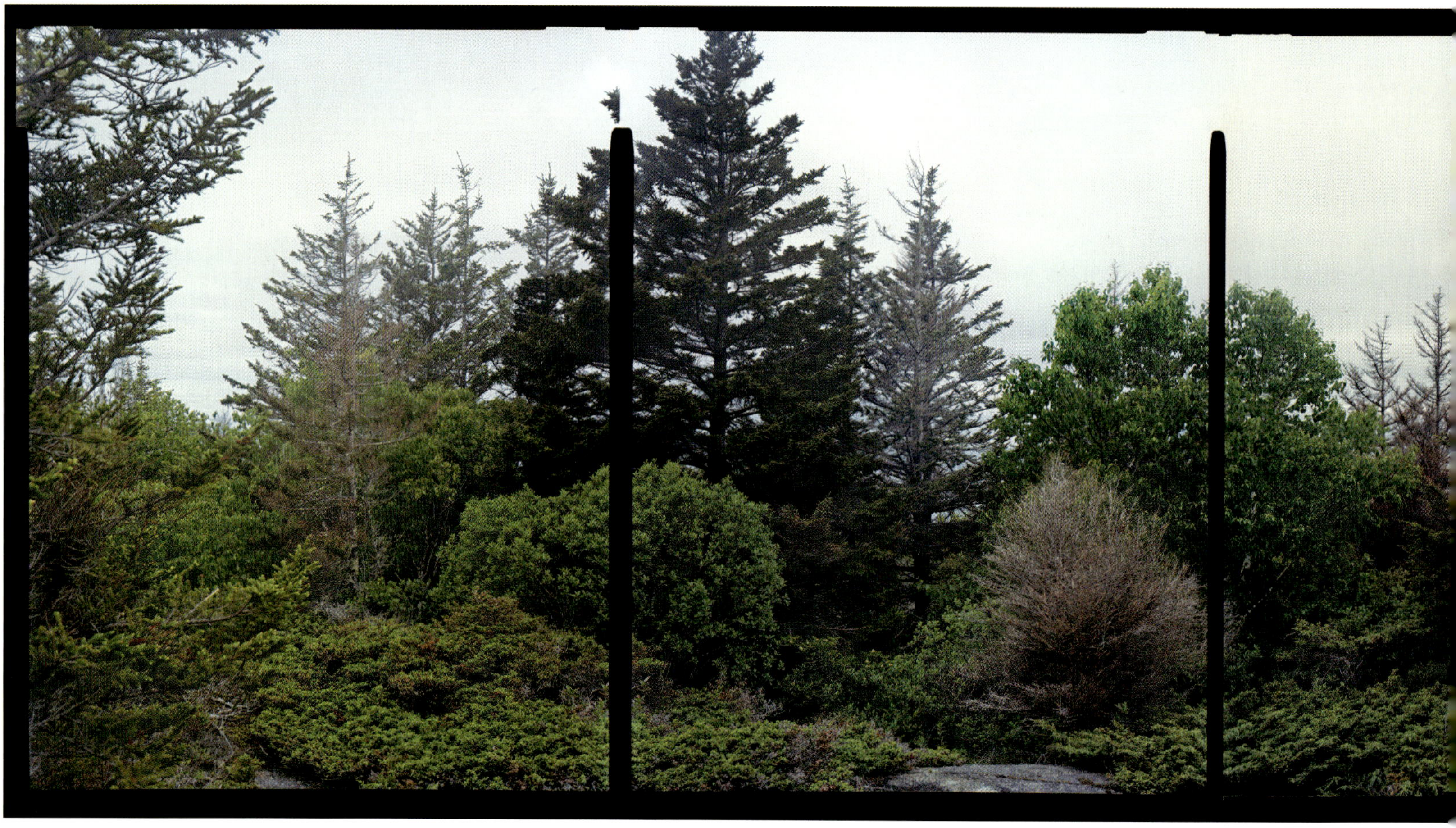

Accra Shepp (born 1962), *Barry's Trees*, 2023. Archival pigment ink print. Courtesy of the artist

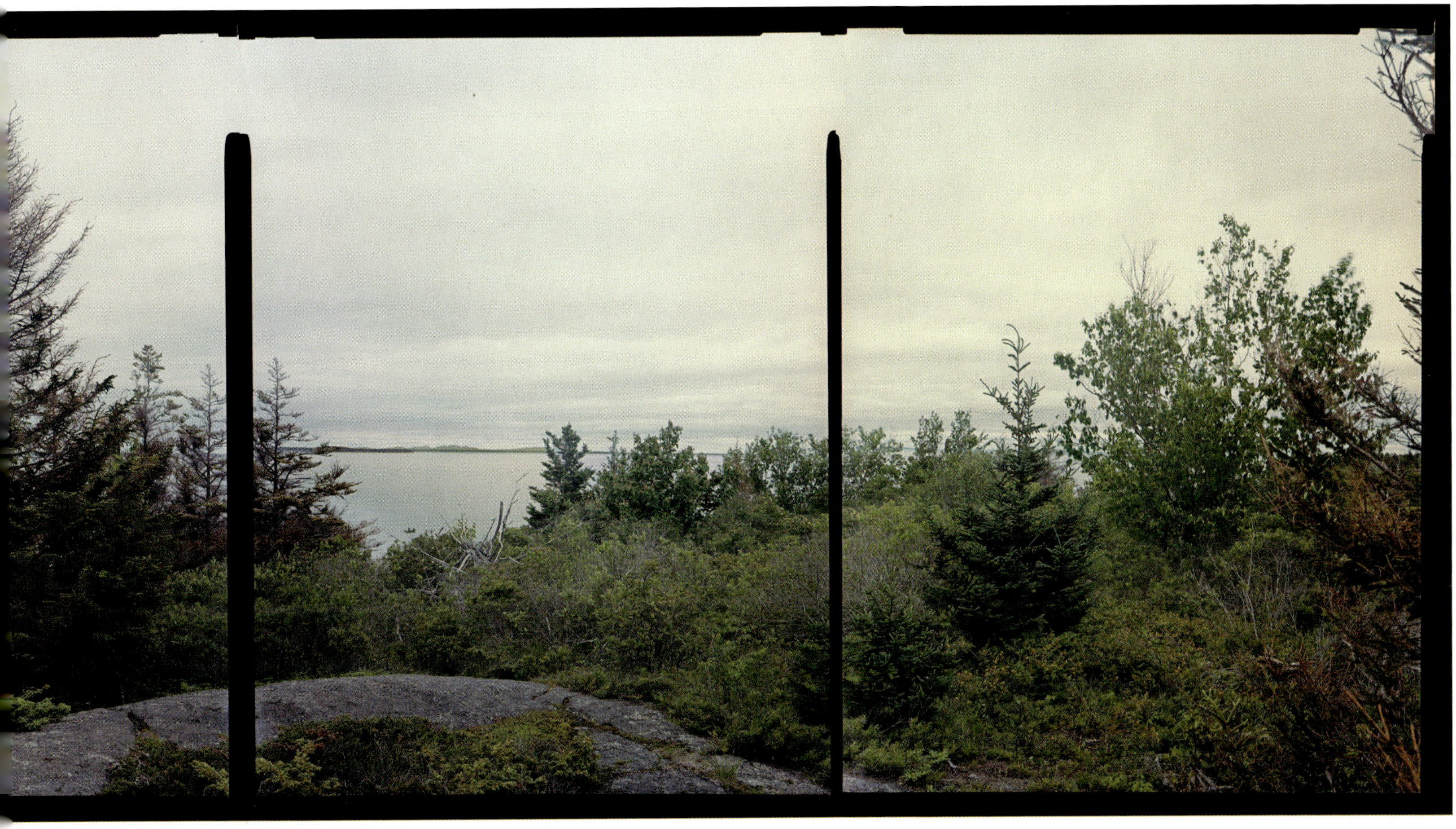

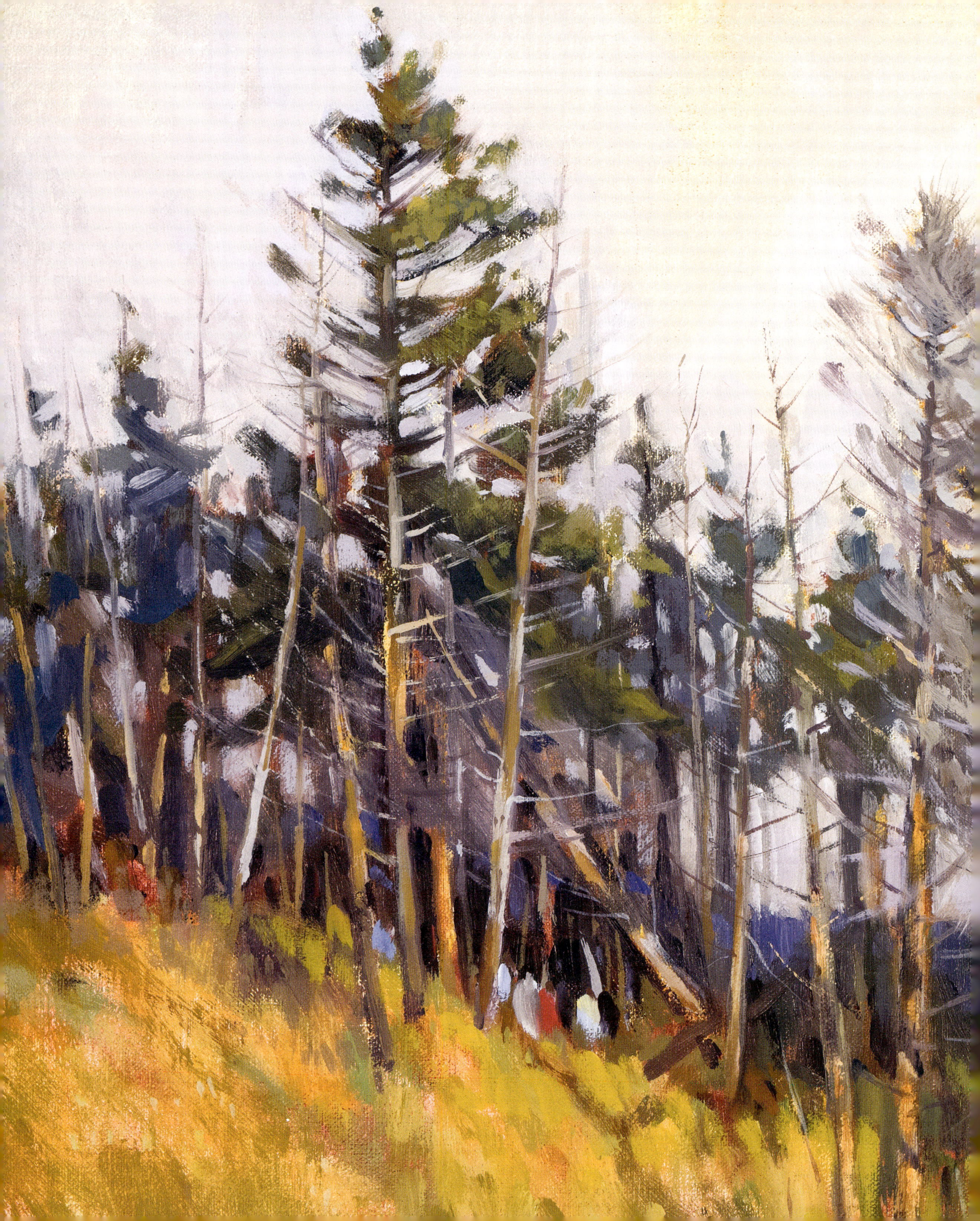

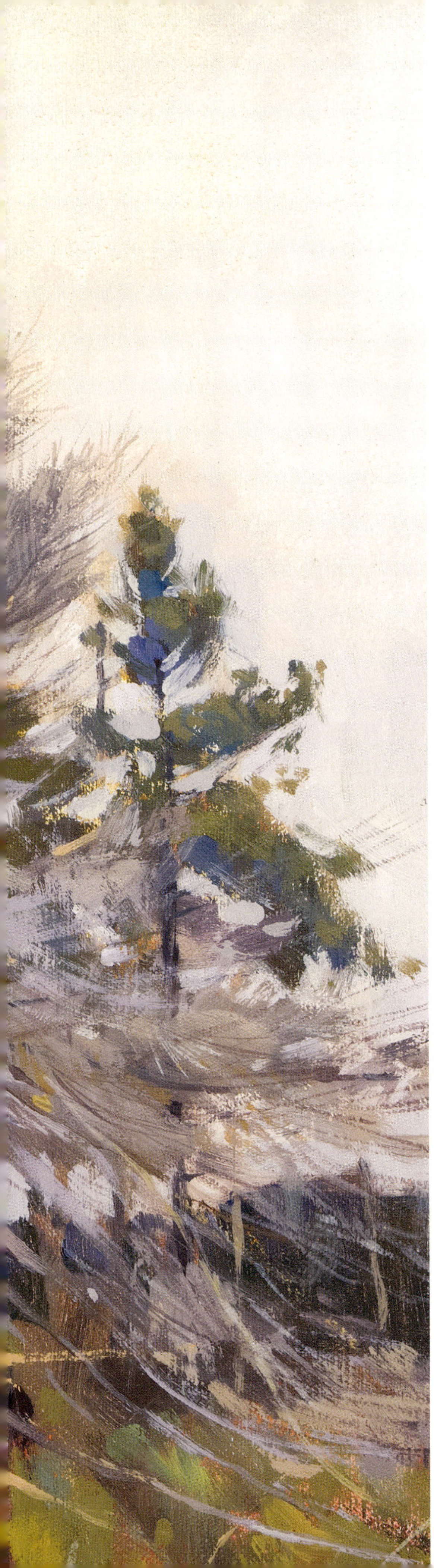

Chapter 6

The Recent Past and the Future of Monhegan, 2000 Onward

Monhegan's anxiety over Lyme disease was not immediately alleviated by the removal of the deer herd. In fact, subsequent tick drags turned up severalfold higher adult tick numbers than they had prior,[1] likely because the loss of their large primary mammalian host sent ticks questing for their blood meal. It would take only a few years without deer for the tick population to collapse, however, which profoundly reduced the risk of contracting Lyme disease on Monhegan Island. Although birds still import ticks, some of which may be infected, these are doomed to fail to complete their life cycle.

Lyme disease, now largely controlled, was not the only threat that the community was facing as the twentieth century neared its end. A lack of affordable year-round housing and worries about the continued exclusive use of the traditional lobstering grounds around the island were also troubling.

In keeping with the spirit of stewardship and conservation that inspired the Monhegan Associates, island fishers had participated for nearly a century in a lobstering season confined to the winter months. In the 1970s, two decades before the State of Maine adopted such measures,

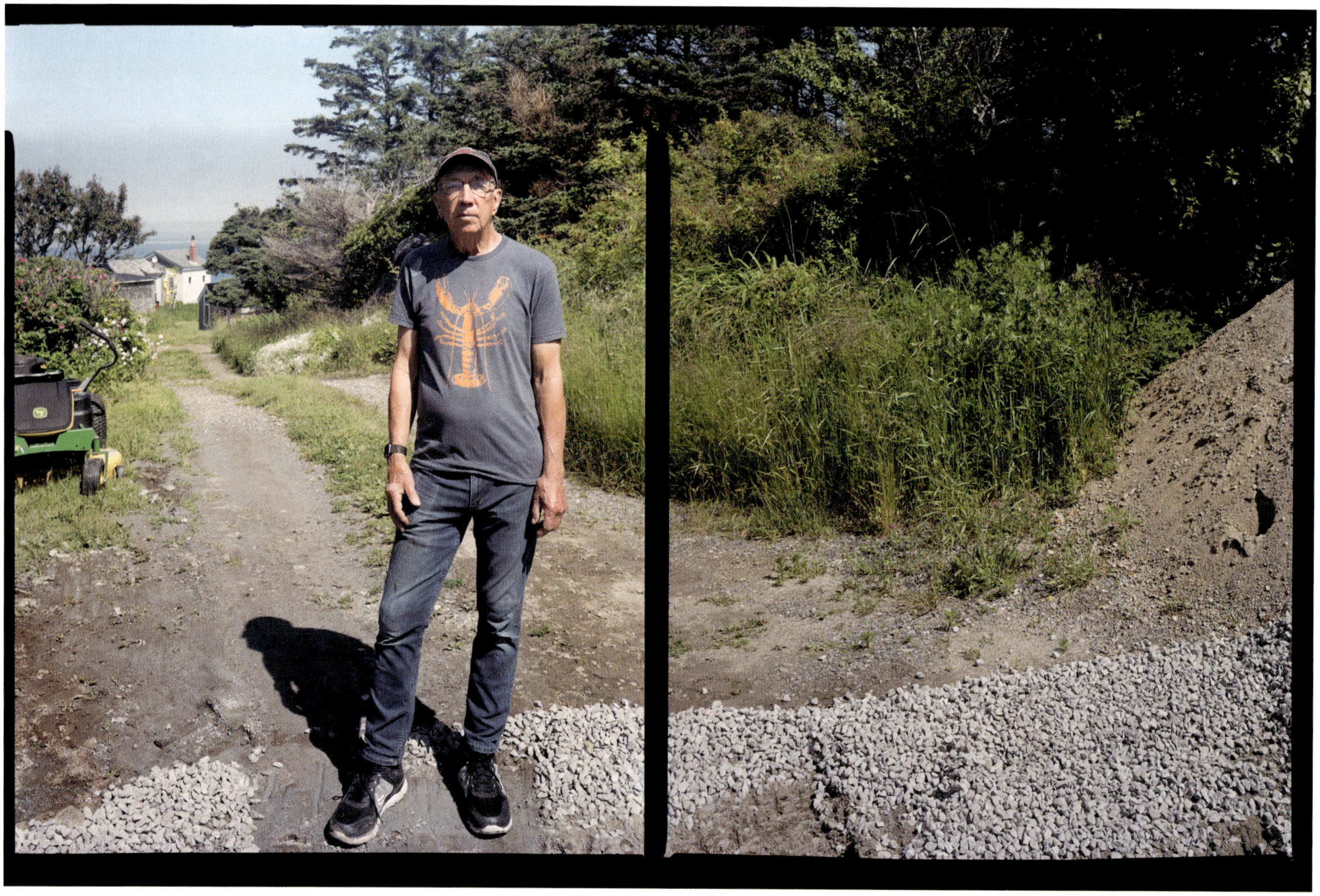

Accra Shepp (born 1962), *Doug Boynton* (detail), 2023. Archival pigment ink print. Courtesy of the artist

the islanders had instituted a limit of six hundred lobster traps for each license holder. The abbreviated season and reduced trap numbers in the zone around Monhegan remain the most restrictive conservation measures in the state. Indeed, along the rest of the coast of Maine, lobstering is a year-round endeavor.

During the fall of 1997, a loophole in state legislation permitted five fishermen from a nearby peninsula to be granted permission by the Maine Department of Marine Resources (DMR) to set their lobster traps in the waters surrounding Monhegan, an area that had traditionally been fished solely by island residents. Mainland fishers setting traps in these waters jeopardized the island's carefully stewarded resource, or as generational lobsterman Shermie Stanley stated, "If ten more people come into your cranberry bog, there's not going to be that many cranberries for you."[2]

Lobster grounds are fiercely guarded, and there is unwritten understanding of who may set their traps in any given area based on legacy, family, and friendships. To be sure, an unwelcome foray into new territory could result in costly losses of traps and gear. Monhegan, however, has mostly operated outside of this system. To fish the surrounding waters, one must live on the island, and in most cases, have completed an apprenticeship. The most desirable grounds are apportioned on a first-come, first-served basis. The small island fleet is not equipped to defend its traditional territory from an influx of mainland boats. Simply put, if there were to be a trap war, Monhegan would lose, and in the 1990s, most of the island's residents either earned a portion of their income from fishing or were partners or dependent children of members of the fleet. The loss of lobstering as a livelihood for those on Monhegan would be devastating.

The island came together to address this issue. Spearheaded by lobsterman Doug Boynton, Monhegan's "Save Our Season" (SOS) movement was born, and a fight that could not be won on the water was taken to the legislature. With an outpouring of support from both the summer and year-round communities, the members of the lobstering fleet reached out to the DMR, elected representatives, research scientists, and anyone in the State of Maine who might be able to exert influence. The entire fleet put lobbying before lobstering during its most lucrative time of year and set up camp in Augusta to plead its case. On February 27, 1998, the Monhegan Island Conservation Area was signed into law by Governor Angus King, who described the legislation as "really nothing new. It's a recognition by the Legislature and the governor of something that's been the law for nearly 100 years. . . . What we are doing today is establishing a limited zone for Monhegan lobstermen. We are also striking a blow for the preservation of a rural culture."[3]

Beyond the risk to the health of residents and visitors posed by Lyme disease, and the threat to the fishery, Monhegan was also struggling with housing, a less visible but equally critical issue. The limited number of houses and buildable lots contributed to astronomical prices for even a modest home. Finding a place to live had been a challenge for decades, with newcomers often "roughing it"—living in partially insulated homes without running water in the winter months and working for a hotel that provided staff housing in the summer—until they were able to secure a rental, and in time, even purchase a home. By the beginning of the twenty-first century, it had become unlikely, if not impossible, to become a homeowner on the income available to an island resident.

Community sustainability issues are not unique to Monhegan. If you research Maine island populations, it will not be long before you come across an oft-cited statistic. At the turn of the twentieth century, three hundred of Maine's three thousand–plus coastal islands hosted thriving year-round populations; today there are just fourteen. The original source of these numbers is not certain, but the premise is clear and alarming. Maine's island populations are in danger. The reasons that many islands ceased to host a year-round population are, no doubt, as varied as the islands themselves, but one thing is clear: living on an island is challenging. The populations that have succeeded are tenacious, resilient, and creative.

While the troubles are not unique, the housing solution that Monhegan enacted is. Doug Boynton, inspired by Ted Edison and the Monhegan Associates, began inviting people to his home for dinner, to talk about the housing crisis and to discuss his ideas for addressing it. In 2002, the Monhegan Island Sustainable Community Association (MISCA) was incorporated. A typical approach taken by affordable housing organizations is to build new homes. MISCA's approach is to purchase existing homes and sell the buildings to

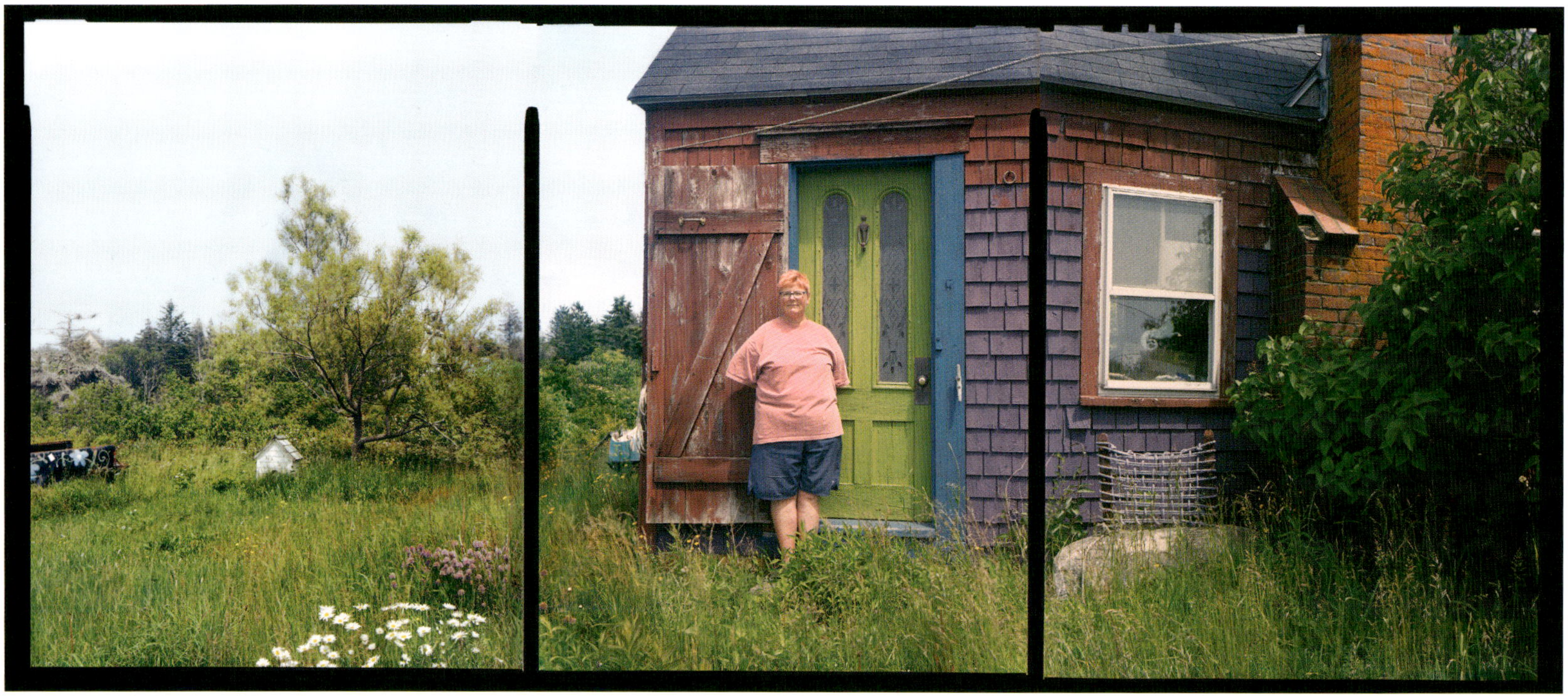

year-round residents at affordable rates while retaining ownership of the land. As founding president, Boynton thought that MISCA might buy six to ten houses in the next ten to fifteen years.[4]

Accra Shepp (born 1962), *Donna Cundy* (detail), 2023. Archival pigment ink print. Courtesy of the artist

MISCA's first purchase was the former Monhegan Store building in 2002. This structure in the center of town was a significant undertaking for the fledgling organization. Within its walls reside the post office, a laundromat, two year-round apartments, a retail space, and the town office. Since 2002, six additional homes and two buildable lots have been added to the MISCA fold, and over 20 percent of the island's approximately five dozen year-round residents live in homes purchased or rented from the organization.

In recent years, tourism has surpassed lobstering as the island's largest industry. The influx of visitors has placed significant strain on the island's limited infrastructure and caused concerns about overstressing the trails. A 2005 study confirmed what any islander could tell you: "Any significant growth in visitors, which by definition means a higher proportion of day visitors, will, over time, have strong negative impacts on the island's aggregate tourist revenues."[5]

The study showed that the most significant tourist revenue was generated by overnight visitors staying for a week or less, and that higher numbers of day-trippers resulted in overnight guests forming a less favorable impression of the island. At maximum capacity (that is, every tourist bed filled), Monhegan can host 350 additional people per night, and the ferry capacity is just over 700 people per day. Despite visitation during the time of the study being well below maximum, several overnight visitors noted that the island felt crowded. The study concluded that unrestrained day-trip visitation from more ferries or cruise ships would have a negative impact on tourist revenue and the "natural and mostly unspoiled characteristics of the island."[6]

Into the twenty-first century, the Monhegan Associates has maintained a steady internal dialogue about visitation and human impact on the Wildlands. They have continued to acquire land outside of the development zone, clarify property ownership and boundaries through land surveys, increase educational outreach, establish written policies regarding Wildlands stewardship and use, and work to refine their holdings by divesting themselves of properties within the village that do not further their mission. Land stewardship and the management of plants of concern are topics that have warranted much discussion. Formal policies of the Monhegan Associates capture their ever firmer embrace of minimalist land management, of allowing natural processes to prevail.[7] For example, herbicide use is now prohibited, as is the use of drones. However, stewardship, even—or especially—with a minimalist orientation, is never free from complexities. Take, for example, the installation of bridges or the placement of stepping stones, generally across wet areas on trails. The Associates have deemed these interventions permissible only in instances where careful study indicates that they would be less intrusive than the damage hikers might otherwise cause by trampling vegetation and widening the trail to avoid wet feet. Their policy on bees and other stinging insects likewise exemplifies their management approach. Instead of eliminating a hornet's nest along a Wildlands trail, the Monhegan Associates assessed the risk and elected to alert hikers with temporary signage. The risk a fire could pose to the village community garners attention, as it has been decades since fire reduced fuel loads. One possible outcome may be to allow abutting property owners to create a firebreak in the Wildlands of reduced fallen deadwood and other flammable materials by removing brush and deadfall on Monhegan Associates land that is adjacent to homes. These examples represent stewardship in action, management that is dynamic and responsive while hewing to a guiding philosophy.

Rising housing costs have taken a toll on the artist community. While the island continues to draw artists, fewer are able to spend the entire summer season there. The Monhegan Artists' Residency was created in the late 1980s in response, and through what is a juried program, each summer, a small number of rising artists are awarded a space on Monhegan for several weeks to spend time developing their work. Past residents include Marguerite Robichaux (1990), Michael Branca (2003), and Steve Budington (2022), all of whom, perhaps inadvertently, have documented forest succession in their work. Other contemporary artists attend workshops, a tradition going back to the summer art school established by Rockwell Kent and Julius Golz in 1910.

At the turn of the twenty-first century, the unofficial dean of the Monhegan Art Colony was Don Stone. Following in the footsteps of Jay Hall Connaway, Stone purchased Connaway's old home, the Fred Staples Cottage on Horn's Hill, in 1980. Like Connaway, Stone spent time living year-round on the island, taught workshops in the summer months, and was inspired by the fishing community and dramatic weather. A vibrant creative environment flourished around Stone, known for his charisma and wicked sense of humor. He enjoyed teaching and speaking about the work of earlier island artists. In the spirit of Robert Henri, his teaching made a mark as meaningful as his own work. Many artists painting on Monhegan today or leading their own workshops were

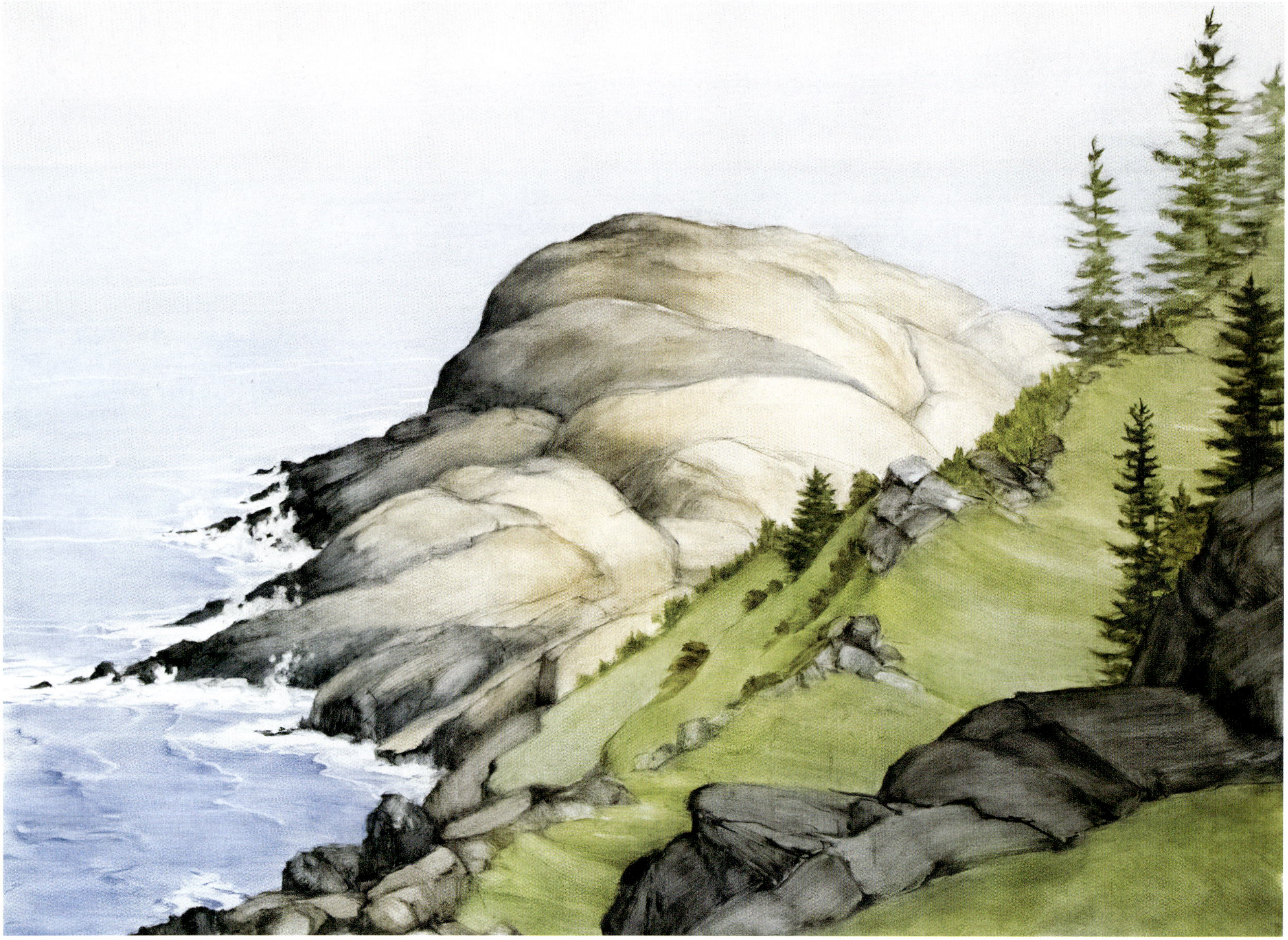

Above: Marguerite Robichaux (born 1950), *Gull Rock,* undated. Oil on linen, 40 x 56 inches. Monhegan Museum of Art & History. Gift of Betty and Ed Weisberger

Opposite: Don Stone (1929–2015), *Burnt Head Trail,* ca. 2000. Oil on canvas, 20 x 16 inches. Don Stone Trust

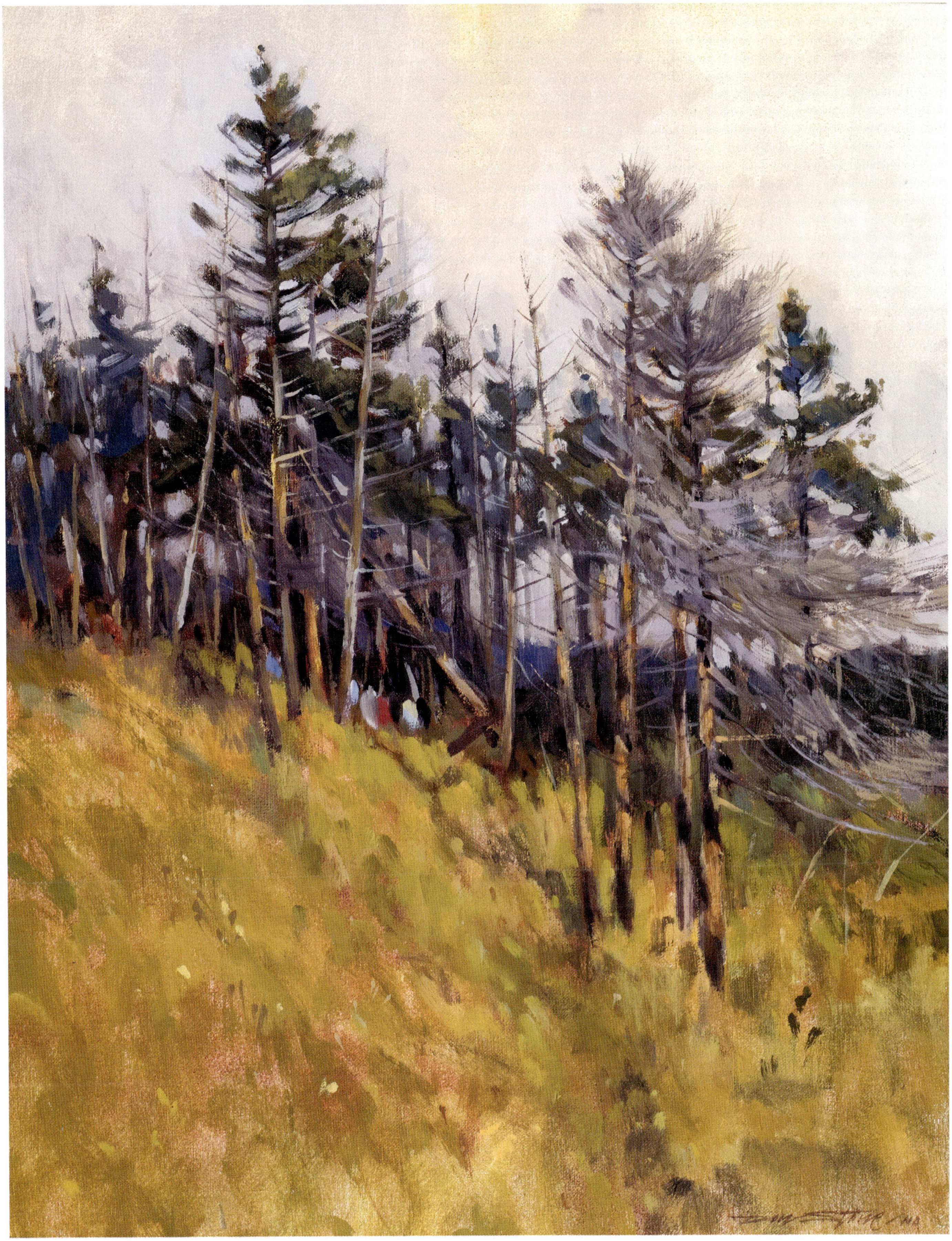

students, friends, and mentees of Stone, and his legacy continues in the dedication to plein air painting that he nurtured.

Unlike the "Stone School" of painters, the Women Artists of Monhegan Island (WAMI), established in 1991 under the direction of Elena Jahn and Frances Kornbluth, sprang from the post–World War II New York modernism that thrived on Monhegan throughout the second half of the twentieth century. Jahn and Kornbluth created this invitation-only organization of professional artists in response to the marginalization of women artists, both on and off Monhegan. Their intent was to garner recognition and exhibitions as a group that they might not realize as individuals. Since then, they have exhibited their work widely. While some female artists—most notably, Lynne Drexler—objected to grouping artists by gender and did not choose to join WAMI, for many others, the group was a welcome source of fellowship and critique.

The tradition of artists opening their studios to visitors became more formalized in the early 1960s, when artists began printing an annual map of studios with receiving hours. Initially, the Monhegan Artist Studio List included mostly men, and the few women represented often shared a studio with their husbands. This balance tipped in the 1980s, with the number of women listed surpassing men. Today the list is dominated by female artists. While many factors have contributed to the rising prominence of women artists, WAMI certainly played an important role in that transformation on Monhegan.

The dynamic social and ecological landscape of the island at the end of the twentieth century was profoundly impacted by the removal of the deer herd. This event set in motion dramatic ecological succession in the Wildlands, and more discreet transformations in the village. Kitchen gardens and elaborate flower beds, prized by residents and artists in the early twentieth century, have made a resurgence, and paintings and photographs can be dated by the presence of certain flowers, such as tulips, which were a favorite snack for the deer and so previously absent. In the forest, long-suppressed broad-leafed deciduous trees and shrubs now compete for space and have established themselves in the forest canopy. Pasture that Rockwell Kent and early artists trod, which went on to hold first vigorous and then declining second-growth white spruce stands, now harbors maturing specimens of paper birch, red maple, mountain ash, and quaking and bigtooth aspen, to name only a few of the more conspicuous and charismatic returnees. Michael Branca illustrates this ecological dynamic in *Blackhead Trail*, in which deadfall in the foreground obscures a mistletoe-infected white spruce flanked by lush broad-leafed trees. Chest-high shrubs complement these trees across the second-growth forest. All native to the region, these trees and shrubs form a forest perhaps unlike any that preceded it on Monhegan, in keeping with the unpredictable nature of a "let it be" Wildland stewardship ethos.

The ancient Cathedral Woods appear touched by the removal of deer as well. Walk through the deep forest today and, in places, balsam fir saplings grow from the trail in all directions. Once browsed heavily, balsam fir will, in time, again take its place in the canopy currently dominated by red spruce, restoring the "spruce-fir" character that has inspired some to describe it as boreal and James Rosier, a 1605 visitor on Weymouth's ship *Archangel*, to list "Firre" first among praiseworthy island trees.[8]

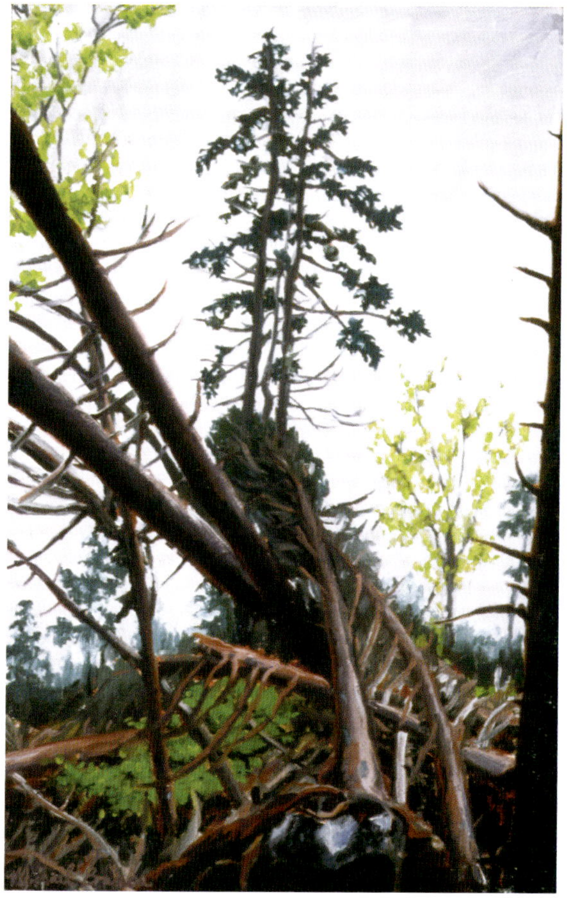

Above: Michael Branca (born 1974), *Blackhead Trail*, 2003. Oil on canvas, 17 x 11 inches. Photo courtesy of the artist

Opposite: Elena Jahn (1938–2014), *Bridge to the Woods,* 2008. Watercolor on paper, 9⅜ x 6⅜ inches. Monhegan Museum of Art & History. Gift of the Estate of Elena Jahn

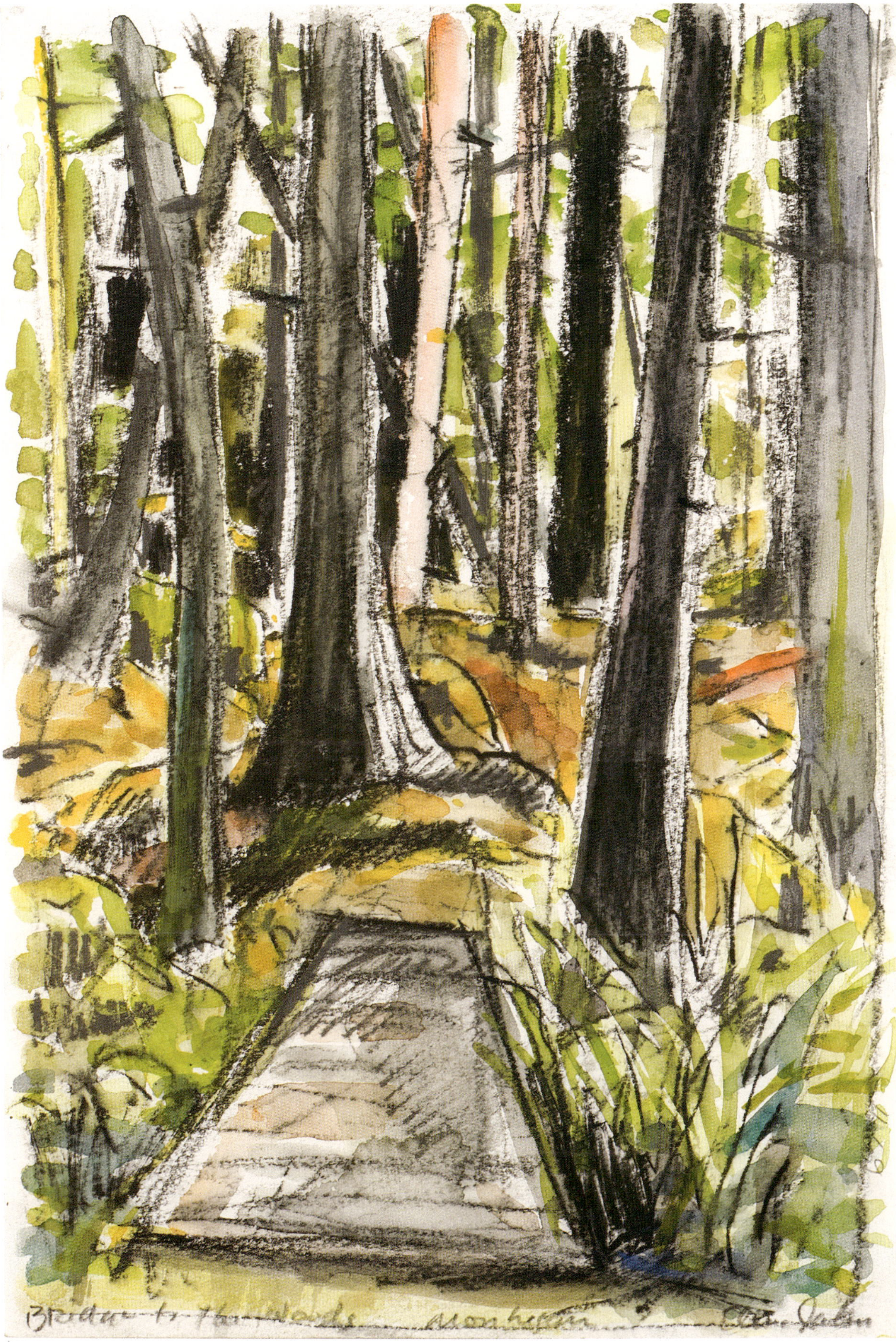

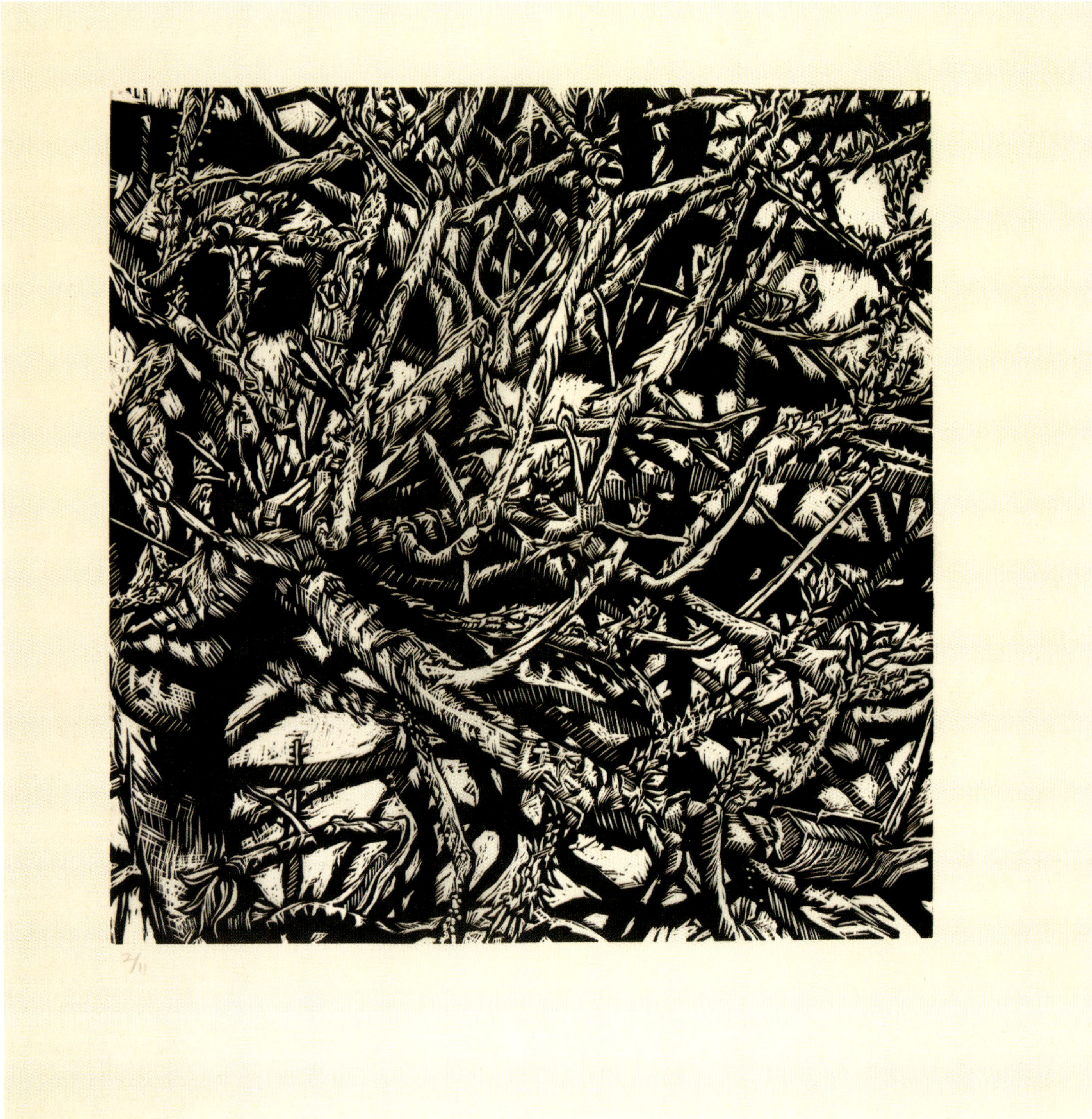

Barbara Petter Putnam (born 1954), *Monhegan-5*, 2023. Woodcut, 14 x 14 inches. Bowdoin College Museum of Art, Brunswick, Maine. Museum purchase, Anne Dorsey Loth Art Acquisition Fund (2023.45.1)

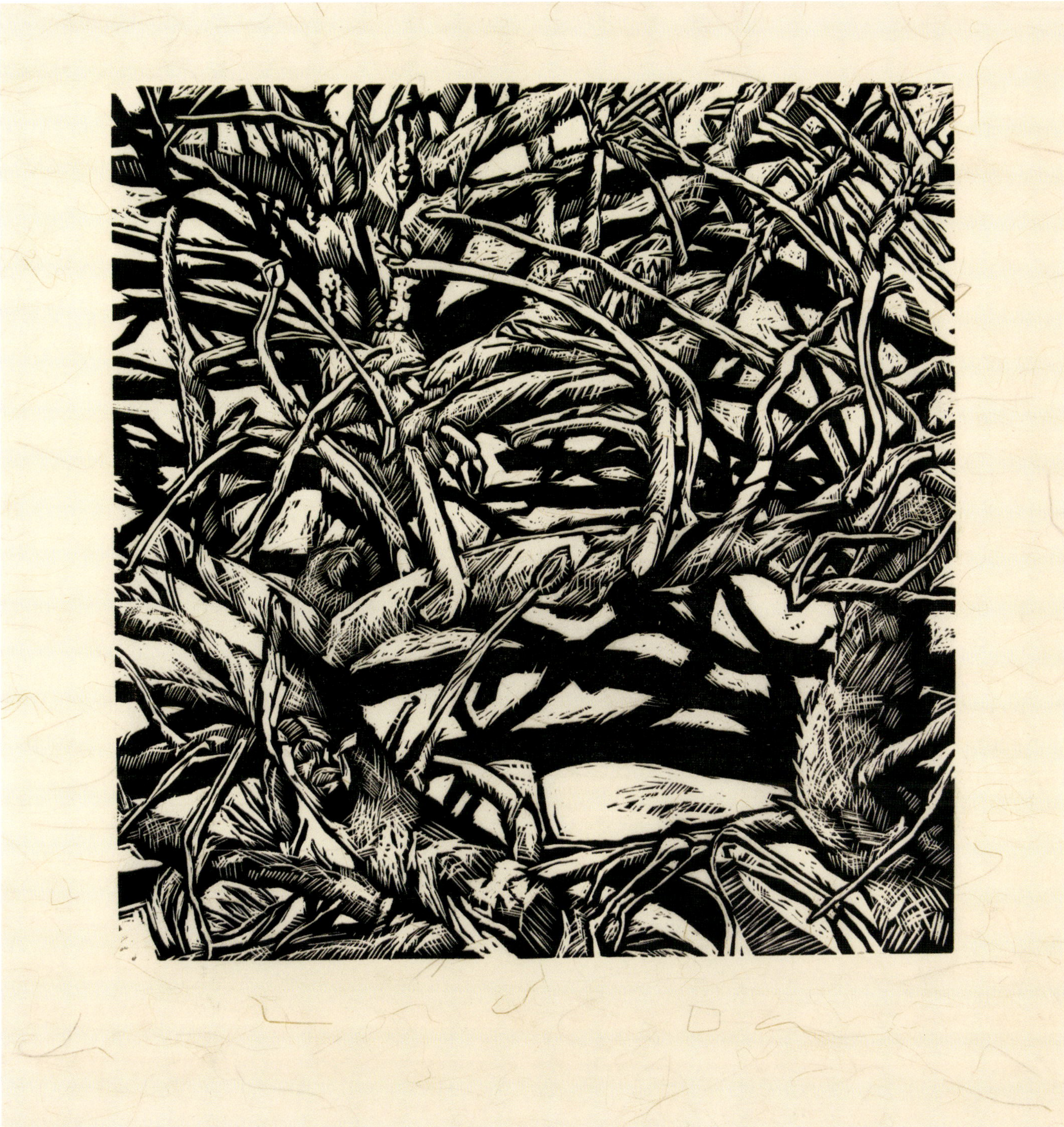

Barbara Petter Putnam (born 1954), *Monhegan-6*, 2023. Woodcut, 14 x 14 inches. Bowdoin College Museum of Art, Brunswick, Maine. Museum purchase, Anne Dorsey Loth Art Acquisition Fund (2023.45.2)

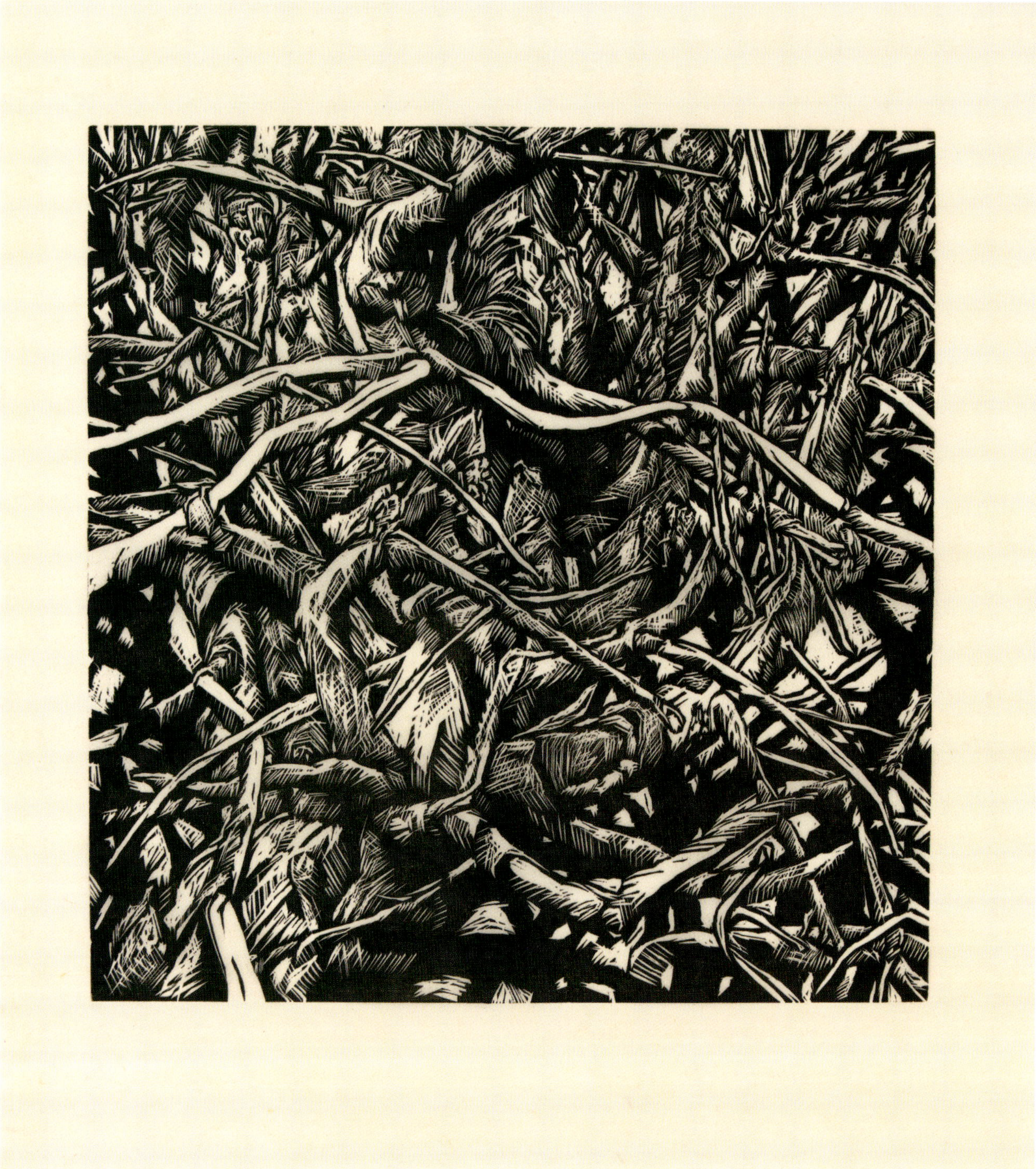

Barbara Petter Putnam (born 1954), *Monhegan-10,* 2023. Woodcut, 14 x 14 inches. Bowdoin College Museum of Art, Brunswick, Maine. Museum purchase, Anne Dorsey Loth Art Acquisition Fund (2023.45.4)

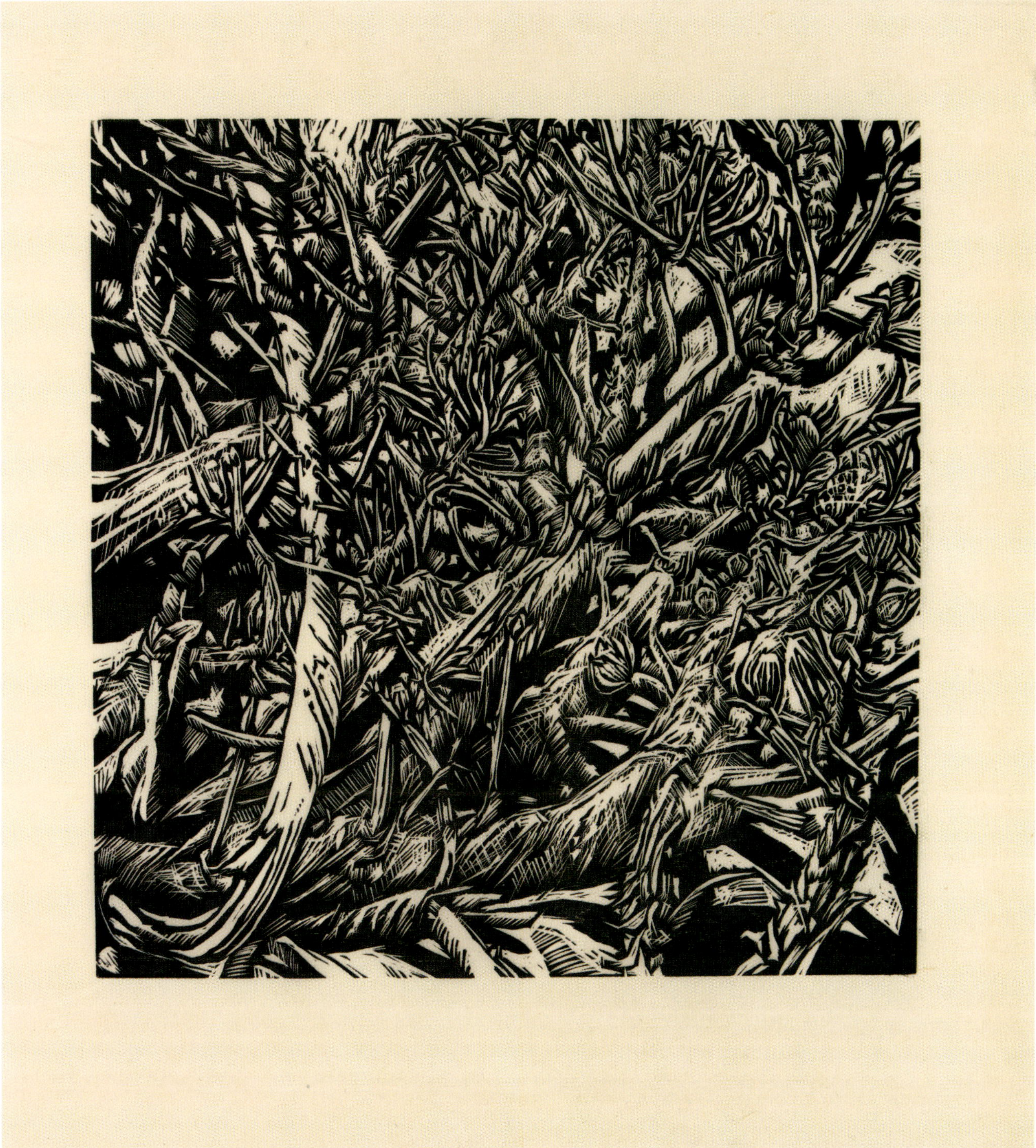

Barbara Petter Putnam (born 1954), *Monhegan-8b,* 2023. Woodcut, 14 x 14 inches. Bowdoin College Museum of Art, Brunswick, Maine. Museum purchase, Anne Dorsey Loth Art Acquisition Fund (2023.45.3)

Forest Succession Written in Rings

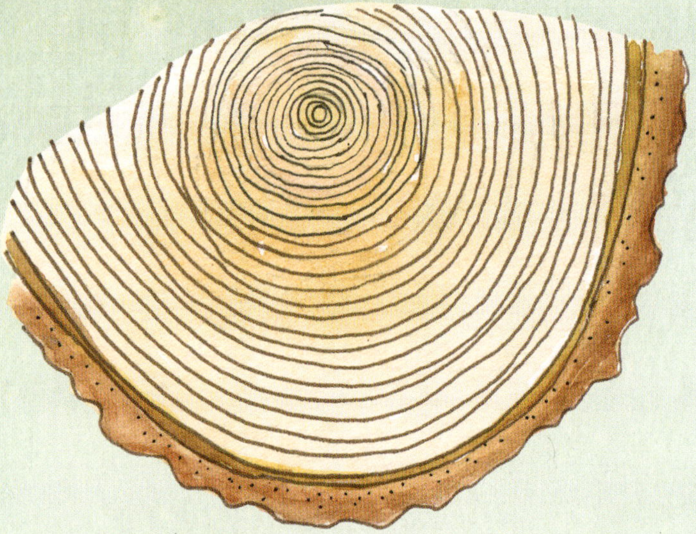

Trees share their age by laying down annual rings of wood.

Autumn wood is darker and denser than spring wood, marking the boundary between each year's growth.

Counting rings is something that children can do, and with a little assistance, the students of Monhegan Island School did just that.

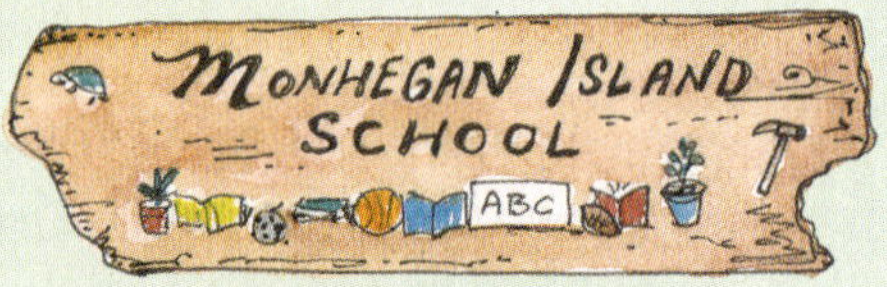

Students extracted cores from trees in secondary forest and counted rings. Maples and birches they examined had an average of twenty-one rings. This agrees with the students' hypothesis that broad-leafed trees appeared only after deer had been removed and browsing ceased.

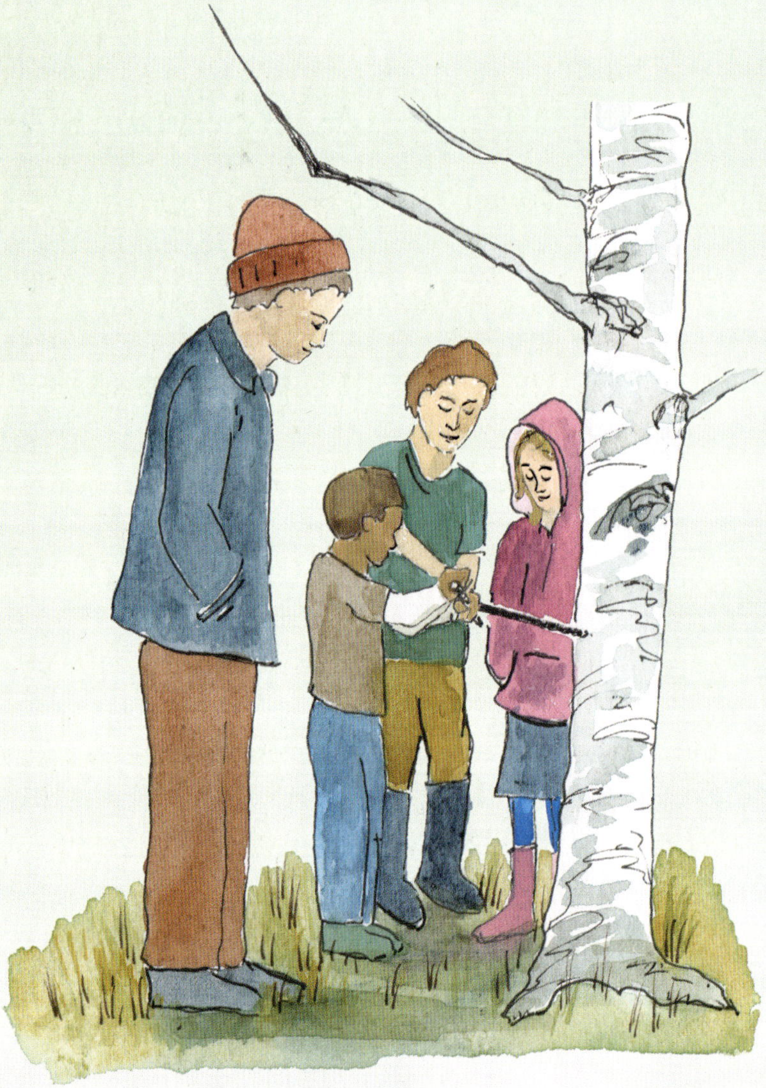

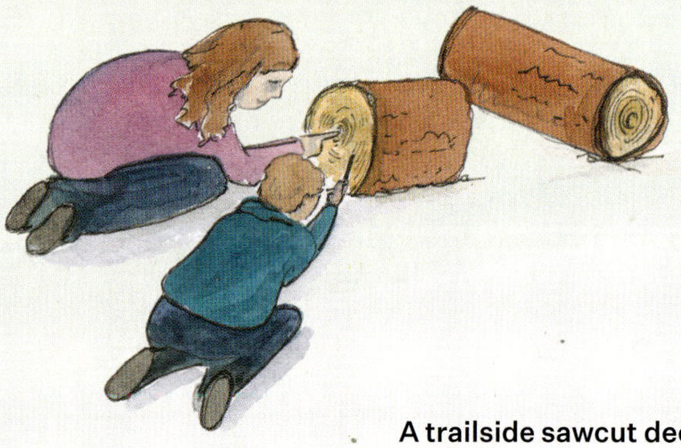

A trailside sawcut deep in the Cathedral Woods and the core on the opposite page reveal that some red spruce trees in the old-growth island interior are more than 120 years old.

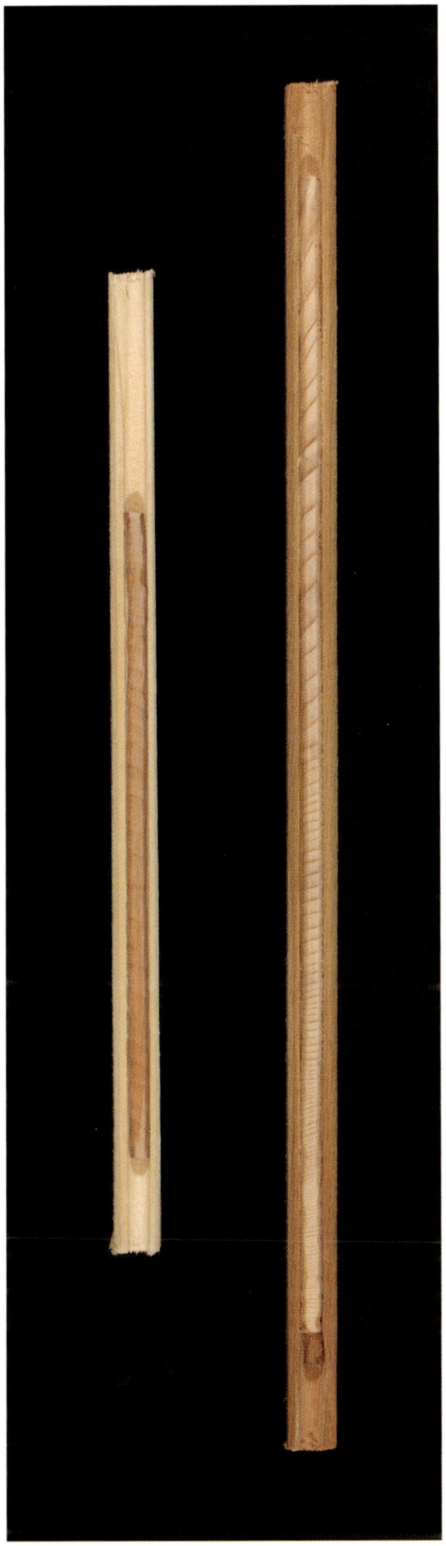

Woody tree cores of a paper birch (left) growing in secondary forest after deer removal and a red spruce (right) in the Cathedral Woods. Cores collected in 2022 by members of the Monhegan School community, Nora Chioffi, Dana Rollins, and Brownell Thomson.

Japanese barberry, the scourge of the late twentieth century, is not defeated, but it is in evident retreat. Although it's likely that the active forms of management practiced in previous decades—pulling and poisoning—had a meaningful impact on barberry prevalence, native vegetation is proving capable of containing this invader when it is not also contending with intense deer browsing. A principle of conservation biology is playing out on Monhegan Island: healthy ecosystems resist invasion. The removal of introduced deer has enabled the Monhegan Wildlands to keep itself from being overrun by introduced barberry.

Monhegan's continued focus for over a century on the sustainability, conservation, and preservation of the Wildlands, waters, and community has allowed it to maintain a unique appeal for residents and rusticators. The role that was filled a century ago by the "tearooms" as spaces for community gathering is now held by coffee shops and a seasonal craft brewery. Bridge games and baseball have given way to jamborees, concerts, and fundraising auctions. Yet the island still attracts birdwatchers, artists, and families looking for a slower pace and a place to regroup. The artist community endures and, in fact, thrives year-round. Local actions to preserve this unique piece of the world, however, are not sufficient to address global issues. Concerns for the future center on climate change and include fire danger, threats to the freshwater supply, sea-level rise, and the viability of the lobster fishery, and yet the qualities of tenacity, resilience, and creativity endure.

When given the opportunity, New England forests, and landscapes elsewhere, exhibit a remarkable ability to renew and sustain themselves. This is perhaps nowhere better demonstrated than on Monhegan. Its Wildlands embody what is possible when a community commits its resources to preservation and values wilderness. The prevailing stewardship ethos of the Monhegan Associates to allow natural processes to unfold with minimal human intervention brings with it a need to reconcile oneself to change. As described in preceding chapters and celebrated through the artwork depicting the Wildlands across the ages, change marks this place. Although history in large measure shapes present-day and future ecology, *wildness* is a prospective aspiration. It is about how land—and water—will be cared for, whatever its history of human disturbance might be. "Let it be" stewardship, although perhaps demanding less action, nevertheless calls for discipline. Stewardship of the Monhegan Wildlands will remain a communal effort, as it has always been. May communities everywhere and of every size find inspiration in the Monhegan Wildlands, their history, artistic portrayal, and ecological richness.

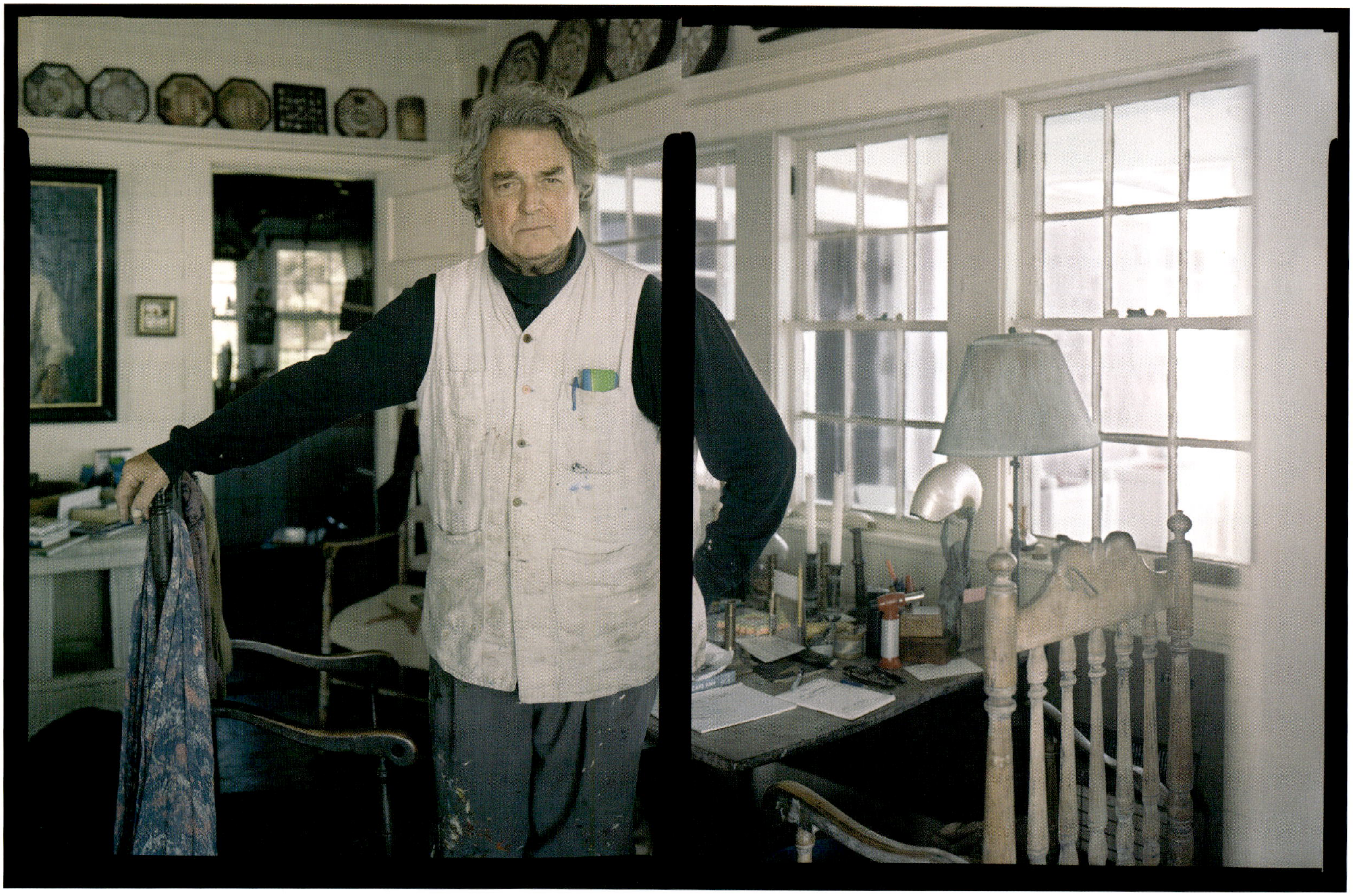

Accra Shepp (born 1962),
Jamie Wyeth (detail), 2023.
Archival pigment ink print.
Courtesy of the artist

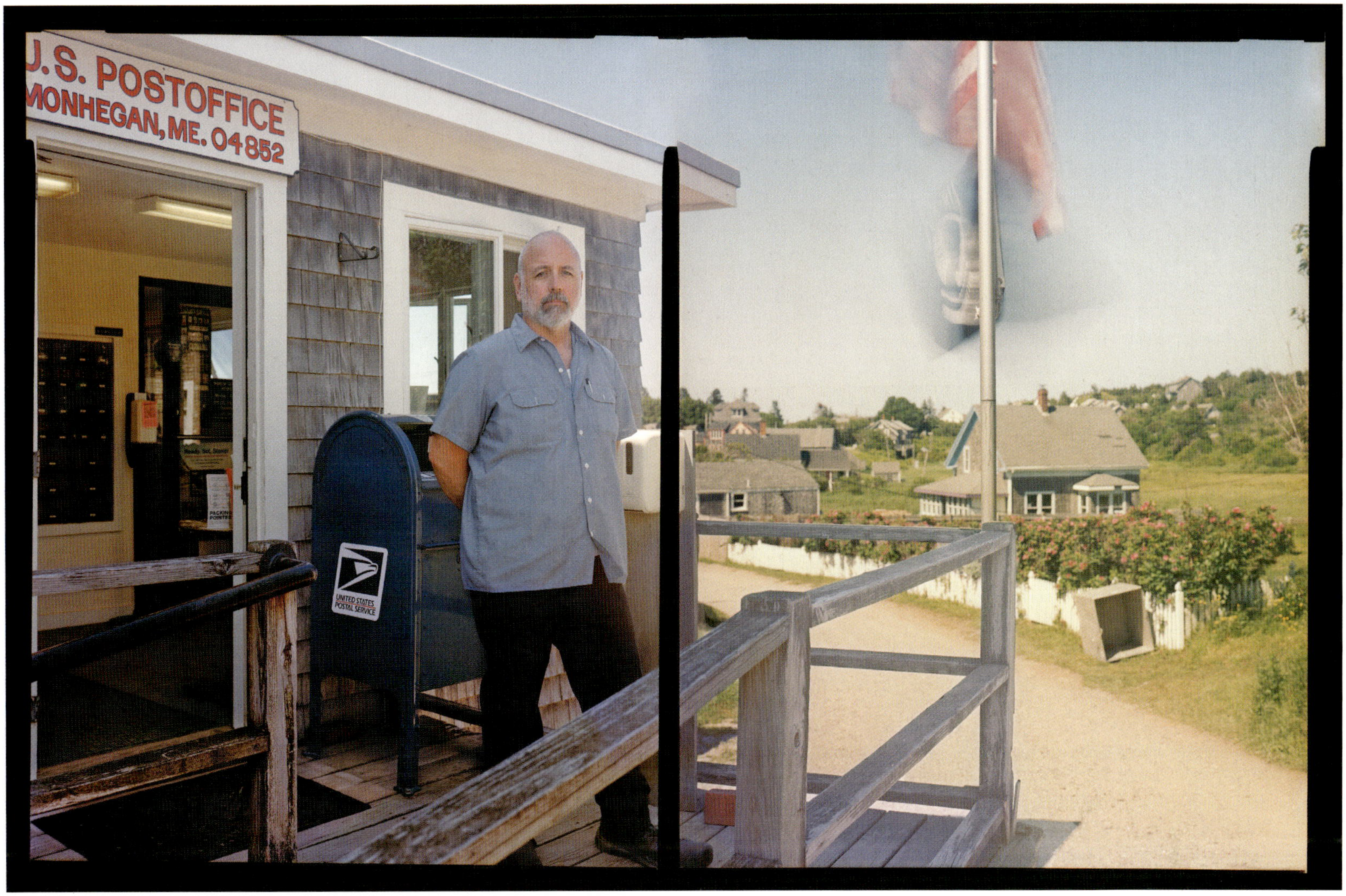

Accra Shepp (born 1962),
Jim, postmaster, 2023.
Archival pigment ink print.
Courtesy of the artist

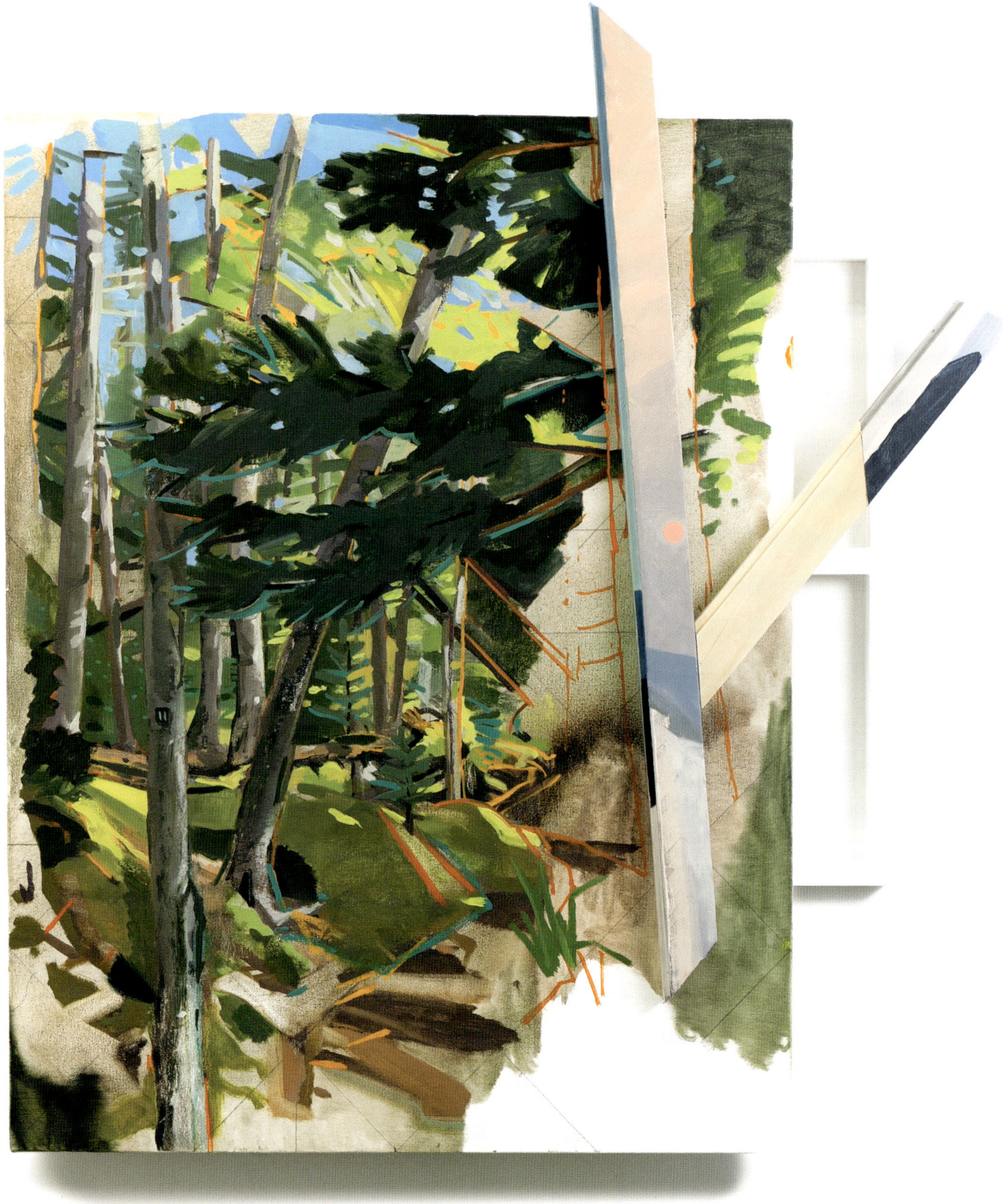

Steve Budington (born 1978), *forest, frame, window, trail blaze (trail 11 Monhegan Island, ME)*, 2022. Oil on canvas over wood panel (in 2 parts) and partial frame, 33 x 26 inches. Collection of the artist

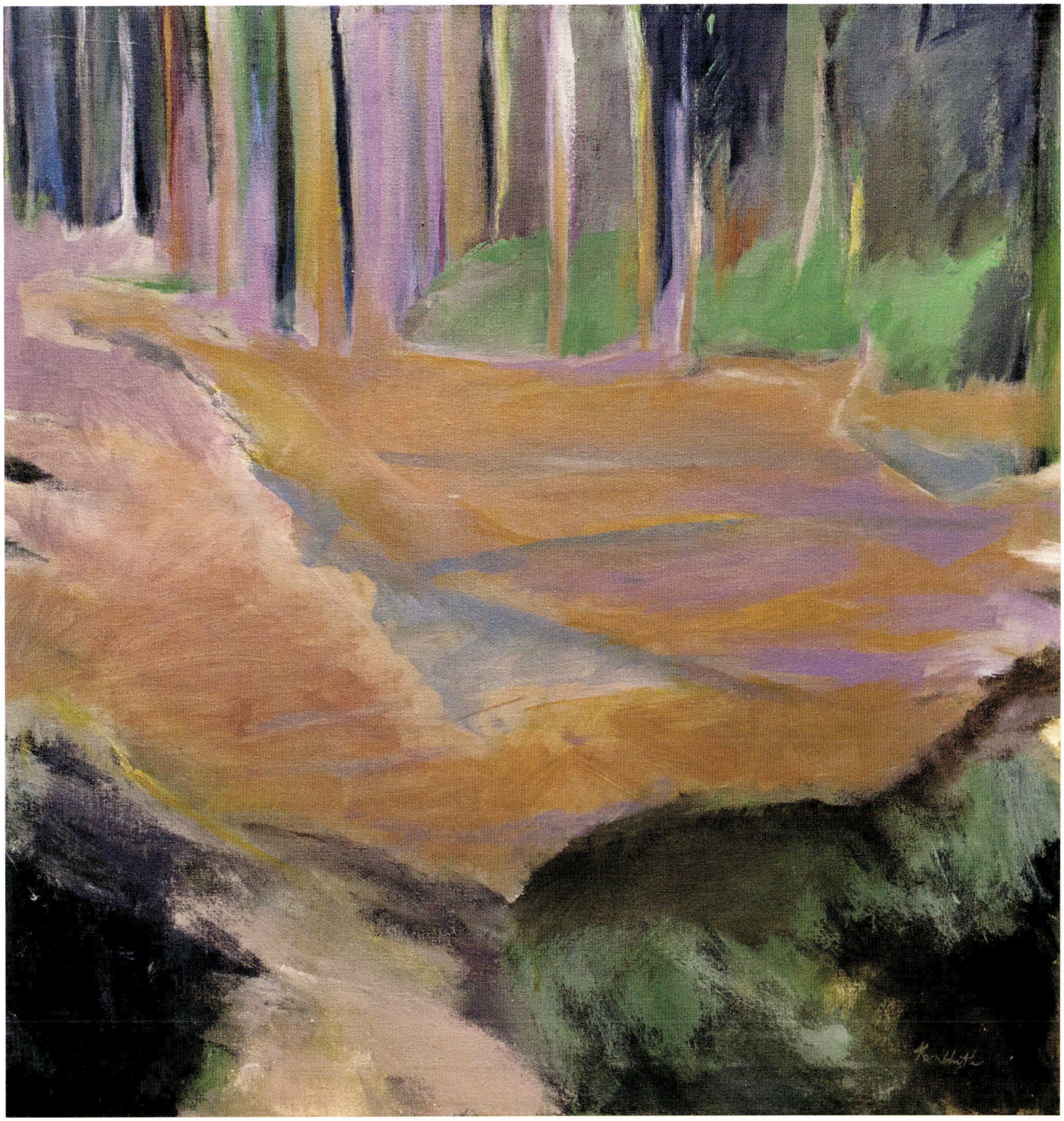

Frances Kornbluth (1920–2014), *Forest Path*, 1989. Acrylic on canvas, 32½ x 32½ inches. Collection of Colin Brooks

Lessons from Monhegan

Tish Miller, Monhegan summer resident

I love Monhegan. Approaching the island wharf on the ferry feels like coming home. As a child, I didn't spend much time on the island, perhaps a day or two each year. Those visits gave me and my siblings the impression that we were rugged adventurers, hiking through the forests, traipsing and scrambling across the headlands. While we were trusted to be careful, we were also reminded of the dangers, that the "island library was named after two children who'd been swept out to sea."

In the early years we used kerosene lamps to read and the fireplace for heat. There was no electricity, and there was only one phone for public use. My mother gave us instructions on the "Monhegan way." Use what you have close by, conserve water, recycle, compost, and give flowers to those leaving the island so they will return.

Three simple lessons, among many, shaped our family's values even when we were off-island: respect the community and the Wildlands, spend time in nature, and be careful with resources. We sought to pass these lessons down to the next generation.

Over time, our family spent parts of most summers there. Monhegan was great for children. They could walk by themselves to the Carina, the island store, to buy penny candy. We took hikes on the trails, played by the Ice Pond, read books, and enjoyed card games. Life moved more slowly.

Our family had the good fortune of having my grandfather, the photographer Warner Taylor, build a cottage on Monhegan in the 1920s. While I was too young to know him, he left the family with a love of the beauty of the island and a respect for the Wildlands. He was a quiet man. He observed the waves and birds and the people who lived there. His photographs could not have happened without the Wildlands, and in return, the Wildlands received the gift of being seen.

Growing up around his photographs validated that what I noticed daily mattered: the warm light, the way the fog turns into mist, the glow from the lighthouse moving through the night, the seagulls jumbled in the air. It was all worthy of being noticed, of being present for. He helped

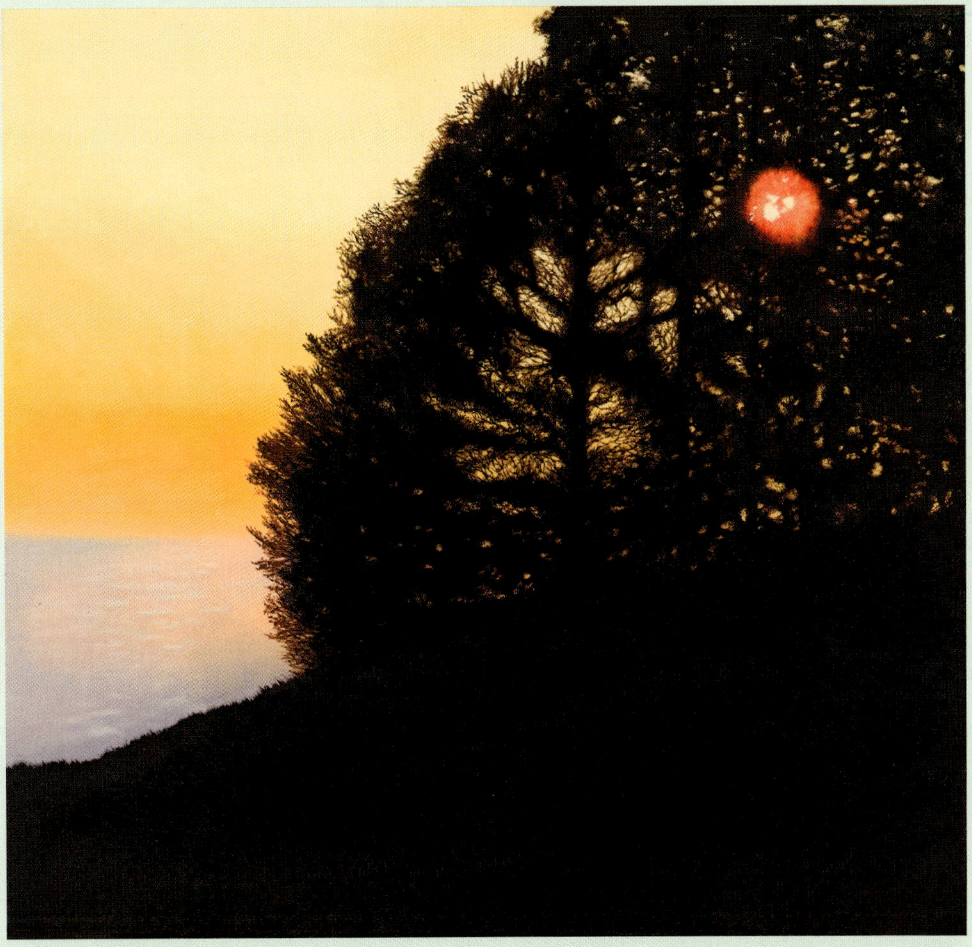

Sylvia Alberts (1928–2015), *Sunset Tree*, 1997. Oil on canvas, 26 x 28 inches. Private collection

make what is often invisible visible. My mother was an artist too, as are my siblings and I. Our children have also become artists. Each has their own practice and favorite subjects. I believe being around my grandfather's art at the cottage, visiting artists' studios, and seeing how supportive and welcoming the community is to art makers helped support our pursuits.

Leaning toward the comfort of solitude, I especially appreciate the quiet of the forest. Its ability to absorb much of the errant noise and emotion helps me feel regulated and calm. I love the moss underneath the trees and the sound of the ocean as you walk closer to the headlands. Their ability to hold the silence over the winter and then absorb the influx of day visitors during the summer is reassuring.

While the overall experience of the land has remained constant, because of visiting year after year, I notice the peculiarities of each specific year. In times of heavy rain, the forest floor is covered with mushrooms. In 2022, we experienced a drought and the near disappearance of water in the Ice Pond. I can notice the changing climate. I remember how, decades ago, the trail to Pebble Beach was enclosed by trees, a shaded tunnel of green sloping down to the shore. Then many of the trees died, and now the path is open to the sky with berry bushes on both sides.

These changes are one of the reasons I am involved with the Monhegan Associates and its Ecology Committee. What you love, you want to care for. The Monhegan Associates is dedicated to preserving the Wildlands for all. Knowing that a landscape from the past cannot be recreated, we are engaged in an ongoing conversation for the future—a future that is based on the strong shared values and mutual respect of the entire Monhegan community for the Wildlands.

It's a joy working with folks who share the same love. Having access to the land is important for personal contemplation. It is that direct, personal experience of being surrounded and embraced by the Wildlands that, if you give it time, changes you. I hope it will continue to help others develop empathy for the environment and the desire to care for it.

Shaping Lives: Monhegan's Secret Power

Doug Boynton, Monhegan resident

How is it that a winter community of sixty has recently produced so many exceptional people who may lack formal training but excel in their chosen fields—including a museum director, a lobsterman who runs the island's electrical system, self-taught contractors who keep the island running, an excellent coffee roaster, and a brewer who's established an island landmark? It's a small miracle.

Monhegan has a special power over people. Perhaps it is the stark beauty and remoteness. Maybe it is the step back in time. Good artists capture it. Residents feel it in their souls. Winter concentrates this feeling. We live close to the natural world. Despite its air of timelessness, Monhegan is a dynamic, evolving community. The original Native American inhabitants would not recognize what the island has become, nor would an islander from 1900. Unfortunately, one change is the shrinking of the year-round population. Among the reasons are the change in the lobster season, the scarcity of fish, the difficulty of daily living, and, most importantly, the lack of housing.

Everyone wants to know: "What is it like in the winter?" The easy answer is that it snows, town water is turned off, and the boat comes two days a week—weather permitting. It is isolated, but not lonely. Days of the week don't matter; wind and weather do. We are a collection of hermits, most of whom like to get together. We are survivalists out of necessity. If the boat didn't come for a week, it would be an inconvenience, not a disaster. It is hard work, but we are lucky to be close to nature. We earn our peaceful winters by having survived the summer. (I am mostly joking.)

Most people experience the island from the land. I was lucky enough to lobster for fifty winters and am passionate about keeping some version of the fishing community alive. We lobster in an exclusive conservation zone. It is another world, with more named places than there are on the island. The twelve square miles of Monhegan-controlled ocean dwarfs the island. Being part of the lobster fleet is exhilarating, challenging, and hard work. At the start of the season, you put on blinders and enter another world, in constant battle with storms, cold, and elusive lobsters. But what an office.

Artists generally paint the ocean and boats from the land. However, there are a few, including Jamie Wyeth, James "Fitz" Fitzgerald, and Andrew Winter who have spent time on the ocean, and it seems to have helped them capture its elusive feel.

When I was fifteen, Fitz had me row him around in his dory while he silently contemplated the scene with arms crossed. At night I dropped him off on Smutty Nose. He dipped cattails in kerosene, placed them alight on the side of the dory, and shoved me off. I pretended to haul nets in full gear. I was impressed we didn't burn the dory, but not by the sketches. To me, he went from strange to crazy. Years later I saw the finished oil painting and realized how important it was for him to seek authenticity. Now I love the sketch he gave me.

You can't know the ocean without putting in time. Preserving our maritime heritage is why I am passionate about keeping some version of Monhegan as a fishing community alive. Though most residents are not involved in fishing, for me it is unimaginable to have a winter community without fishing. For starters, having boats with competent captains is essential for the island's safety.

My efforts to help shape Monhegan came from two main goals: strengthening conservation and ensuring the survival of a vibrant winter community. There is a tension between these two goals, as most communities survive by growing and, for this, you need land. When Ted Edison started the Monhegan Associates, he built support by making an informal promise not to buy land on the west side to leave room for growth. When state-mandated zoning arrived in the mid-1970s, the only area for development became the existing village. We used this as a green light for the Monhegan Associates to acquire all the land outside the village.

In the early 1970s, Ted Edison learned of my interest in helping this organization acquire land, and so he invited me to spend a weekend in East Orange, New Jersey, reviewing the early land deeds and old maps. The five-block walk to the old Edison Labs was slow because Ted insisted on picking up every piece of litter on the way. Once in the lab, it was hard to concentrate on the files because of all the old experiments and machinery that he was eager to demonstrate. Eventually, I was given an education on the founding and purpose of the Monhegan Associates. I was surprised to learn how much land was essentially donated by community members. He felt the organization would not be viable without community buy-in. The first Earth Day had occurred four years earlier, but this was the first time I understood a coherent environmental vision.

Unlike his father, Ted was a humble man. It was a wonderful weekend except for the last evening. After dinner with a group of his friends, the entertainment was a competitive game of "brain teasers." It's not a game you want to play with the Edisons.

Putting so much land in conservation created an obligation to make year-round housing available. From the 1960s through the mid-1990s, island families, including the Stanleys, Odoms, and Partridges, sold property at a discount to winter residents. But rising prices, scarcity, and the fact these houses could be resold outside the winter community made a new solution essential. I came up with the idea of forming an affordable housing nonprofit, the Monhegan Island Sustainable Community Association (MISCA). Financed by the whole community, houses would remain year-round and affordable in perpetuity.

When I brought up the idea after a town meeting, almost nobody left. Clearly there was a lot of support. Many people pitched in, and we were able to buy our first building that year. Within a few years, eight residences, three businesses, and three community spaces were created. The pace was exhausting. My wife, Alice, worked particularly hard and, finally, after two years said, "If you come up with any other good ideas, keep them to yourself." I have faith that the power of Monhegan will help others find solutions to sustaining the community well into the future.

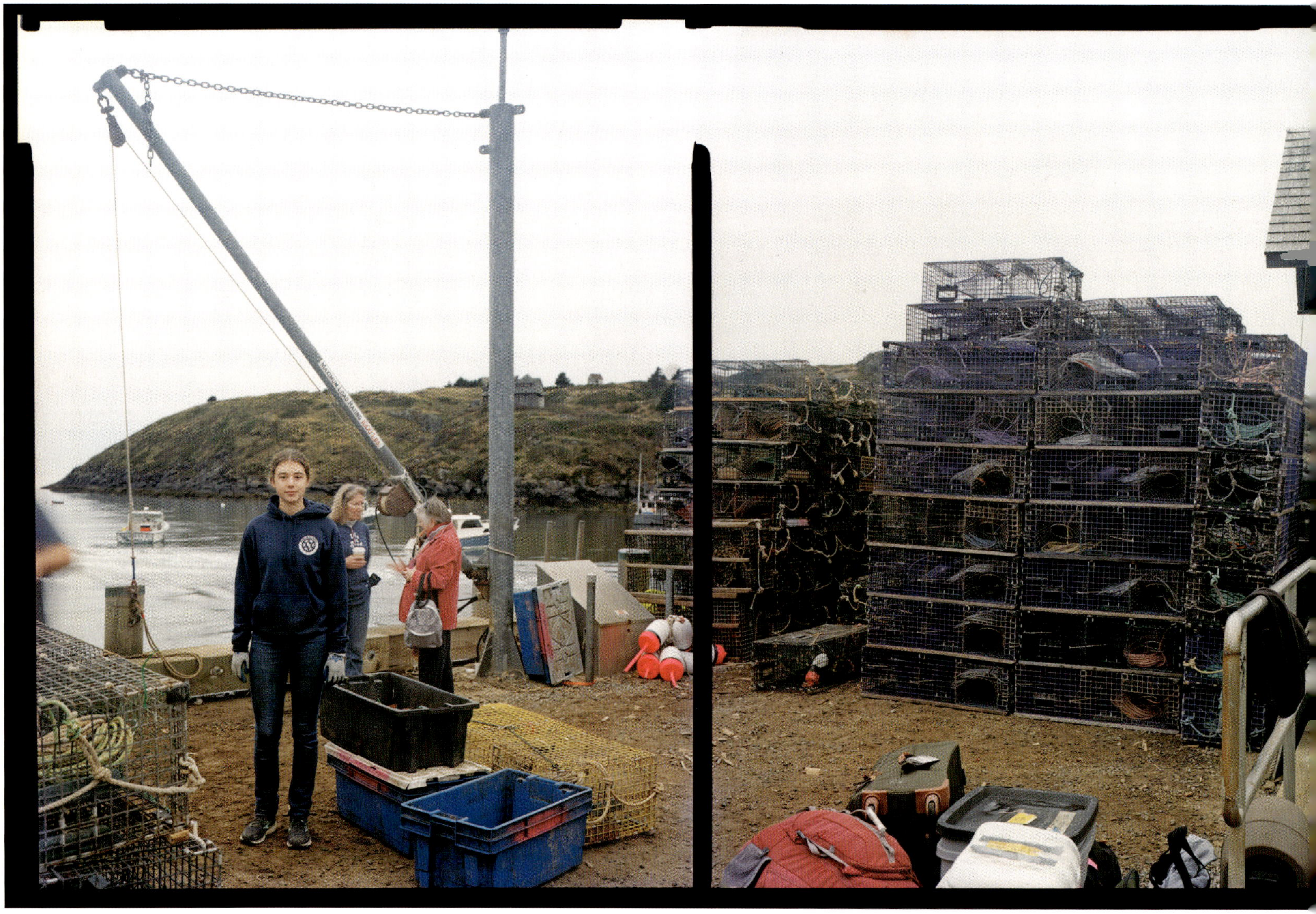

Accra Shepp (born 1962), *Trap Day with Margaret*, 2022. Archival pigment ink print. Courtesy of the artist

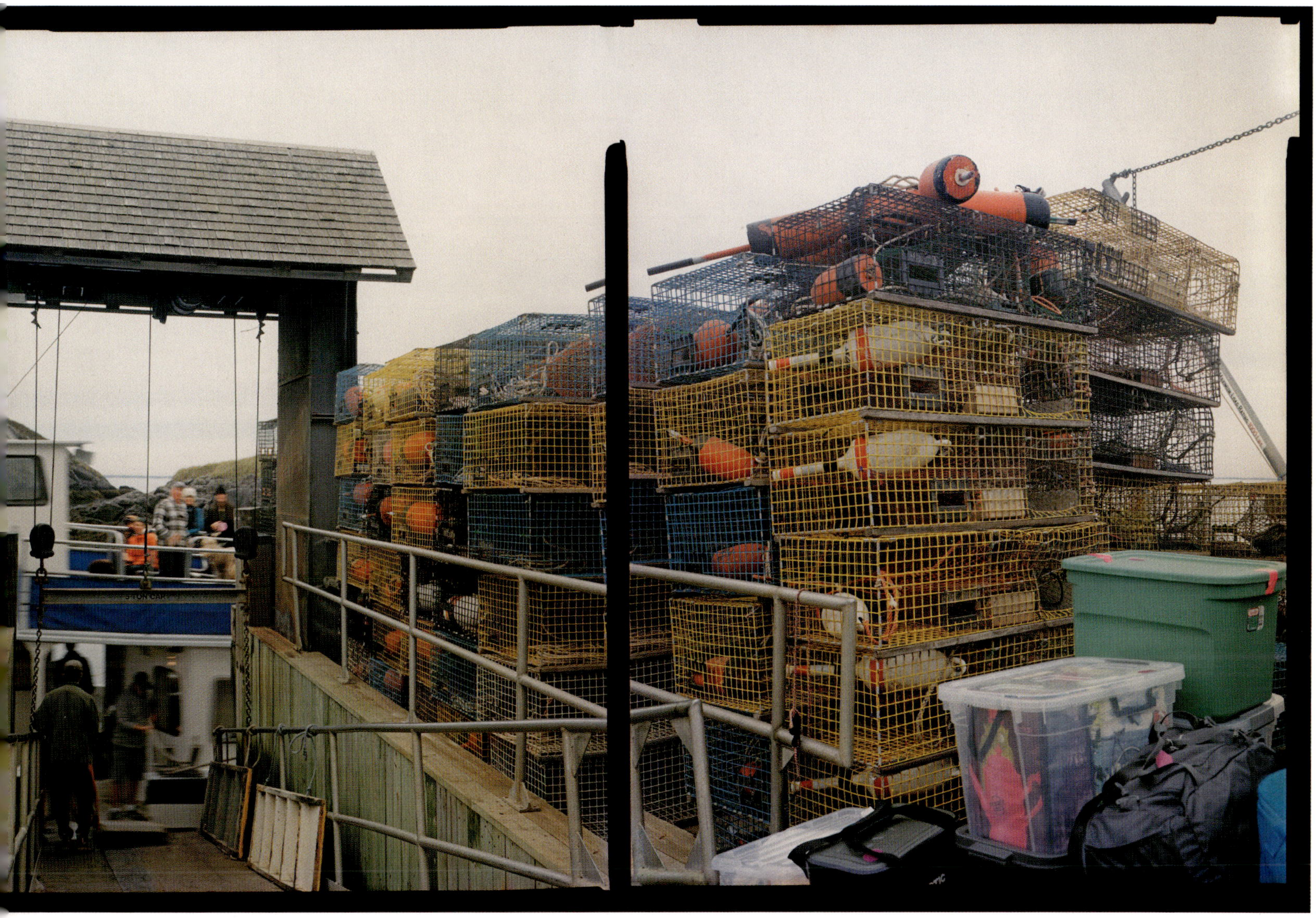

Afterword

Photographing Monhegan

Accra Shepp, School of Visual Arts, New York

The boreal forest is burning in Canada. In June 2023, smoke engulfed New York City as well as much of the United States. The skies above my house were an apocalyptic orange, and the air was foul and acrid. That was the week before I was scheduled to photograph the southernmost part of the coastal boreal forest on Monhegan Island. Today as I write, more than fifty thousand square miles in Canada have already burned—an area that is larger than the country of Greece. And the fires continue to burn. According to satellite data compiled by FireFringe, there are currently several thousand fires burning in the province of Quebec alone.

When I began this project, I knew I would learn a great deal. I also knew that climate change would inform much of that knowledge. I could not know when I started that the issues I sought to make visible through photography on Monhegan would also be in dialogue with what was happening across the United States and beyond.

I was born on an island, in a city of islands, and I still live on one of those islands today. My previous photographic work examining the archipelago that is New York City was what brought about the invitation to go to Monhegan and explore its environment and people. I had never heard of Monhegan and that lack of knowledge was, I feel, crucial while photographing the island. Without any memories of or emotional connection to the place, I was free to move about it without preconceived ideas and to see it in the present.

There appear to be two ways to experience Monhegan. There is the island as forest and the island as coastal environment. My introduction to the island drew my attention first to the forestlands—their history and ecology. An island, though, is defined by its perimeter, its separation from the rest of the world. One might say it is liminal.

Accra Shepp on Monhegan Island, January 2023. Photograph by Barry Logan

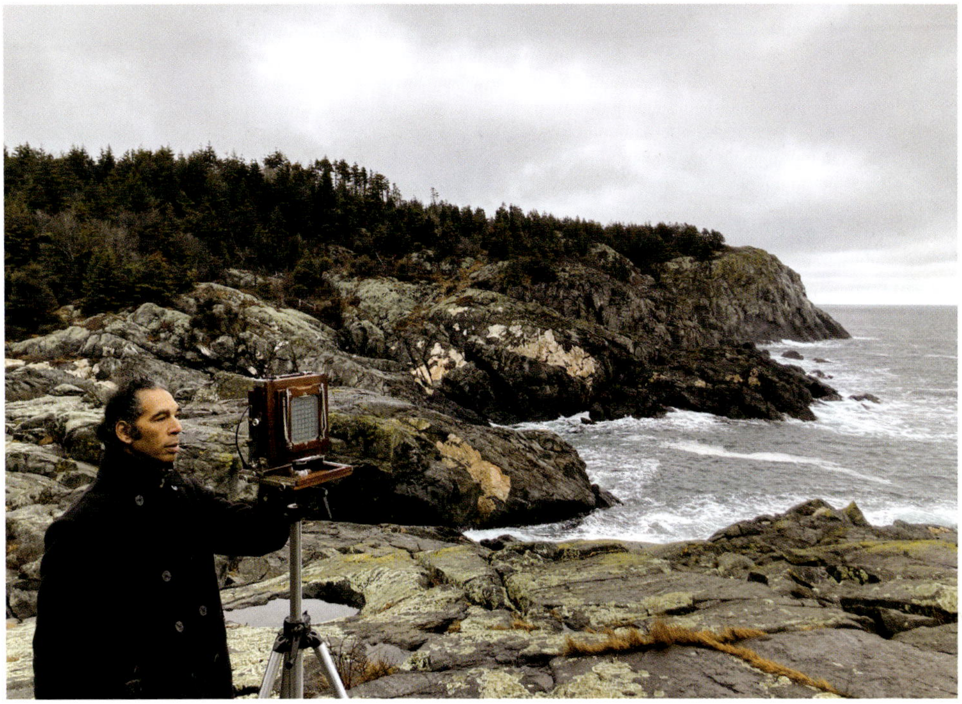

The village, its homes, full-time and seasonal residents, orient toward the shoreline and the ocean beyond. People look to the water for lobster and across it for the tourists who come from the mainland. I had imagined that visitors to Monhegan were interested in both the coast and the forest, but over the course of my work on the island, I saw that they were mostly focused on getting to rocky high points like Black Head or Whitehead. They wanted to take in the view, to experience what they may have seen in celebrated paintings by the likes of George Bellows, Rockwell Kent, and Jamie Wyeth.

Occasionally, I would observe visitors hiking toward one of these sites, and they would openly wonder what I could possibly be photographing in the middle of the forest so far from "anything of interest." The only reason to stop midway along the trail was to watch birds. Their confusion was probably twofold as I was using a view camera—which sits on a tripod with an accordion bellows and requires that I drape a dark cloth over my head to focus it. Able to gather more information than a digital camera, it is a very intentional tool and signals to onlookers that whatever I may be concentrating on, it is far from a casual encounter.

When I first arrived in the forest, I was surprised by how narrow the trees are, despite the fact that they may be as much as two centuries old. I had imagined behemoths, but island life is different. The soil has been built up slowly over millennia and is relatively shallow, thinly blanketing the bedrock of the island. As the soil is not deep, the trees' roots cannot go down very far but instead must go out, grasping at the earth, grasping at each other, making an anchor to grow tall. I was fascinated by their thick gnarly tangles. They are extraordinary. The winds that blow during winter storms are ferocious. Trees often topple. Yet because each tree is bound by its neighbors' roots in addition to its own, if a tree does fall, it generally snaps a few feet above the ground. The precious soil remains undisturbed, with little erosion. It seems as if the entire forest is working together to keep itself upright. The only time I saw a fallen tree with upturned roots was at the edge of a clearing, where the roots were not sufficiently protected by adjacent trees. This too was often a dramatic sight, with an enormous circle of roots—still holding the thin soil—propped up at a ninety-degree angle. Dead trees are important too since they ultimately add to the soil as they decay.

This led me to consider how we think we know trees, those green lollipops we used to draw as children. As adults we are used to seeing larger versions of these lollipops spaced at even intervals in our neighborhoods and parks. The full-time residents of Monhegan depend on one another, keeping the water running, keeping the lights on, being there for each other with conversation, and sharing meals during the long winter months. Like the trees, they exist in a collective and cooperative state.

I made images over the course of a year on Monhegan, including in the winter. I was taken with the light that filtered through the high canopy of the forest, with how it played off the lichens and the abundant moss. At times it felt like something remembered from a fairy tale. On the coast, low tide was my favorite moment, when a hidden submarine landscape suddenly revealed itself as an extension of the island.

My conversation with the island's residents, however, was not driven by the landscape—at least not the one that exists today—but rather by the landscape to come in the future. Though Monhegan is famous for lobstering, there were other fish that used to swim in its waters. Overfishing, abetted by industrial-scale techniques, depleted the waters of the cod and other fish that once were abundant. That left the lobster as the last fish standing (if you will). But the lobster fishery is also in jeopardy. In a few years, in ten or perhaps twenty, it is expected that the water will have become too hot for even the lobsters because of the warming climate. Monhegan's fishermen and the rest of the community are looking into alternatives that go as far as aquaculture. Instead of remaining hunters, they would become farmers, with the clear intent of maintaining their connection to the sea.

The changing climate has also upset long-standing weather patterns. When I began this project, the island was experiencing a severe drought. I noted that many of the crossings built using planks of wood over marshy areas in the trails were entirely unnecessary. The ground beneath was dry and hard. The following year, at the same point in the calendar, the weather remained unseasonably cool and wet. The marshes overflowed and water was everywhere. Both extremes pose challenges for the island. The hot, dry weather increases the risk of fire and stresses Monhegan's power supply, which must keep refrigerators running in the heat and pump extra water. On the other hand, the cool, damp weather delays the onset of spring, compressing an already short growing season for the forest and wildlife.

As much as I enjoyed witnessing the beauty of the land and the coast, I felt a responsibility to see it clearly. As change comes to the island in the years ahead, these images will be part of the record of this moment in time.

Acknowledgments

This project has involved many individuals and organizations. We appreciate greatly their thoughtful and generous contributions. Foremost, we thank the Monhegan Associates for their careful, forward-looking stewardship of the island's Wildlands. Of primary importance to this project are the many voices and perspectives represented in this volume, including Doug Boynton, David Foster, Molly Holmberg Brown, Matthew Klingle, William Livingston, Tish Miller, John Bear Mitchell, Barbara Putnam, Accra Shepp, Earle G. Shettleworth, Jr., and Robert Smith. Their words and images have added much to this project. We also express our gratitude to others with whom we worked during the book's development, including Libby Bischof, Alice Boynton, Glenn Burdick, Connie Y. Chiang, Lucas Chioffi, Edward L. Deci, Clare Durst, Susan Elias, Fred Faller, Ed Faison, Cipperly Good, Hannah Mellor, Laurel Mitchell, Kaitlyn O'Donnell, Pamela Rollinger, Arthur Spiess, Paul Smitherman, Joseph "Jay" Taylor, Matt Weber, Matthew Wheeler, and Susan Winchell-Sweeney. Great thanks to the students of the Monhegan School—Nora Chioffi, Dana Rollins, and Brownell Thomson—for their enthusiasm, curiosity, and excellent work counting tree rings. We relied heavily on the superb ecological research of Jaret Reblin at Bowdoin College and Rick Dyer at the University of Maine at Orono. Our thanks to Mollie Sandock and David Foster for incisive input on early drafts. We thank Jane Gillette for her helpful exploration of the minutes of Monhegan Associates, Inc. Three Bowdoin College students provided invaluable assistance. Our thanks to Silas Brown '24 and Brandon Lozano-Garay '24 for assembling and reviewing literature and for archival research. Mer Feero '23 contributed in myriad ways on island and off, by sharpening our understanding of Lyme disease ecology, supporting the creation of a modern map through floristic observations of the Wildlands, and the acquisition of images.

This book is one result of a special partnership between the Bowdoin College Museum of Art and the Monhegan Museum of Art & History. We have thoroughly enjoyed the opportunity to work together. We are also grateful to many museums and private collectors who have allowed us to reproduce artworks in this book. Additionally, many have lent works to the two related exhibitions. These contributors include Susan Bateson and Stephen Fuller, Glenn and Carol Burdick, Edward L. Deci, the Farnsworth Art Museum, the Fogler Library at the University of Maine, the Herbert F. Johnson Museum of Art at Cornell University, the State Hermitage Museum, the Library of Congress, the Maine Historic Preservation Commission, the Maine State Archives, the Maine State Museum, the National Archives, the Smithsonian's National Portrait Gallery, the Naval History and Heritage Command, the New Britain Museum of American Art, the Osher Map Library at the University of Southern Maine, the Penobscot Marine Museum, the Portland Museum of Art, Fiona True, the University of Maine at Orono, the Woodmere Art Museum, and Jamie Wyeth.

We recognize that such ambitious projects require many kinds of support. Our thanks to the Wyeth Foundation for American Art for their generous financial contributions as well as the Elizabeth B. G. Hamlin Fund at the Bowdoin College Museum of Art. In addition, we want to acknowledge the outstanding museum professionals involved in this project, including at the Monhegan Museum of Art & History, Rebecca FitzPatrick and Emily Grey, and at the Bowdoin College Museum of Art, Suzanne Bergeron, Cassandra Braun, Theresa Choi, Anne Collins Goodyear, Jo Hluska, Sean Kramer, Laura Latman, Sabrina Lin, Amy Morin, Steve Perkins, Rachel Rodrigues, Jose Ribas, and Amanda Skinner. At Rizzoli, we thank Margaret Chace for her confidence in this project and for her input. We further thank Susan Homer, the catalogue's editor, and Anjali Pala, its designer, for vital contributions and with whom it was a pleasure to collaborate, and Charles Miers (publisher), Kelli Rae Patton (proofreader) and Alyn Evans (production manager). We also thank Sarah Rafson, founder and creative director of Point Line Projects, and Laurel Mitchell, rights and reproductions specialist, for their assistance in assembling the publication-quality reproductions and permissions for this catalogue's many images.

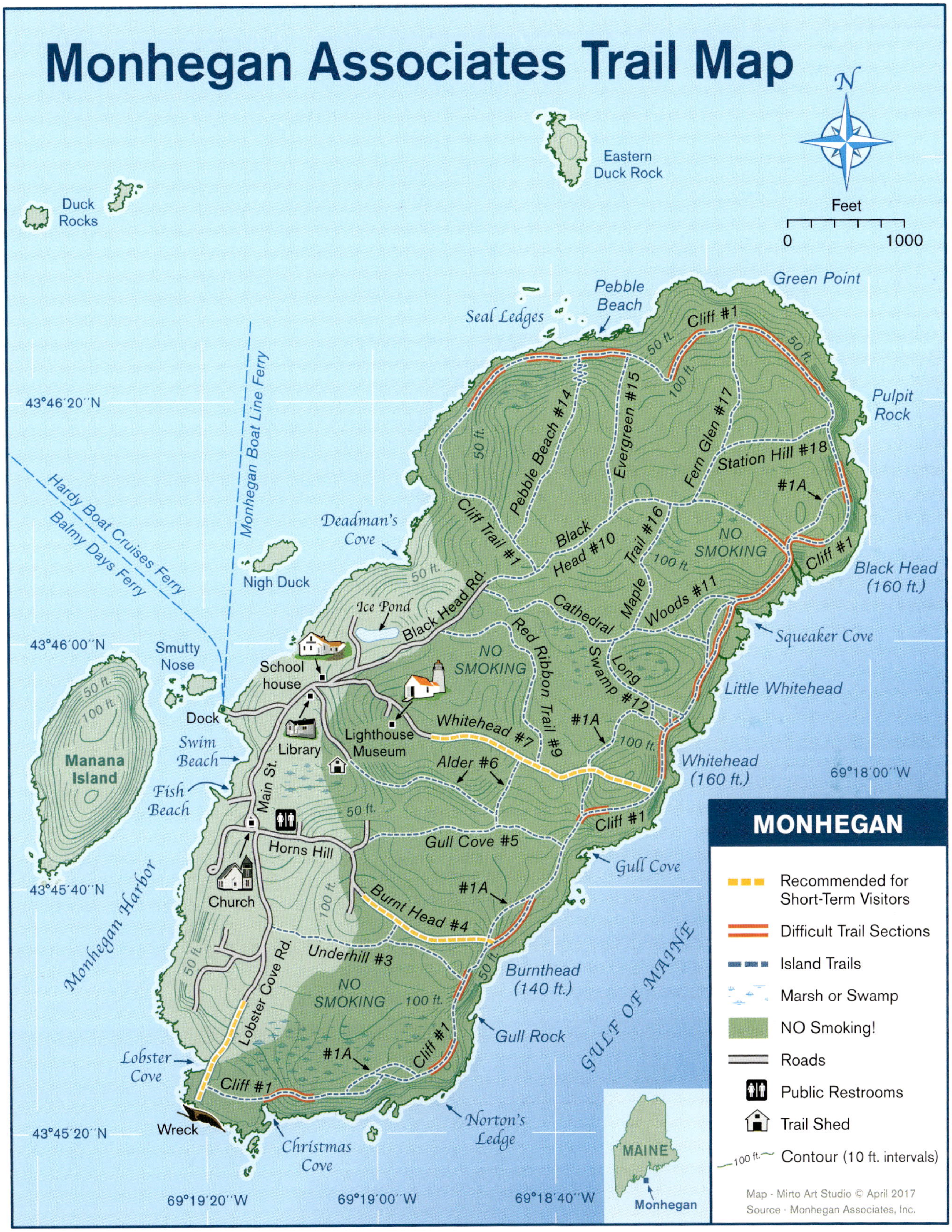

Monhegan Associates Trail Map.
Courtesy of Monhegan Associates, Inc.

About the Authors

Barry A. Logan is the Samuel S. Butcher Professor in the Natural Sciences in the Biology Department at Bowdoin College, where he teaches at all levels of the curriculum, with a focus on plant function, form, and distribution. After earning his BA at Cornell University, Logan's graduate school mentors, instructors, and fellow students at the University of Colorado Boulder (PhD) awakened his wonder about the natural world and nurtured his explorations. The author of numerous scientific articles and reviews, Logan is thrilled that the Monhegan Wildlands are the subject of his first book-length collaboration. Interest in the interactions between parasitic dwarf mistletoe and host spruce prompted his first visit to Monhegan more than twenty years ago and inspire his and his students' on-island research to this day.

Jennifer Pye is director and chief curator of the Monhegan Museum of Art & History. A year-round resident of Monhegan Island, she has been involved with the Monhegan Museum and immersed in the history and culture of the island since 2000. With a focus on community sustainability and engagement, she has overseen the development of broad-reaching virtual and in-person programs. Her ongoing aspiration to improve the preservation environment for museum collections in a challenging island climate has led to the facilitation of projects that embrace innovative passive and mechanical approaches to meeting the preservation needs of the museum's holdings while remaining sensitive to Monhegan's fragile island environment.

Frank H. Goodyear III is co-director of the Bowdoin College Museum of Art. A graduate of Princeton University (AB) and the University of Texas at Austin (MA, PhD), Goodyear specializes in the history of photography and American art history. He is the author of eleven books and exhibition catalogues, including *American Cool* (with Joel Dinerstein, 2014), *Winslow Homer and the Camera: Photography and the Art of Painting* (with Dana Byrd, 2018), *At First Light: Two Centuries of Artists in Maine* (with Anne Collins Goodyear and Michael K. Komanecky, 2020), *Marcia Resnick: As It Is or Could Be* (with Lisa Hostetler and Casey Riley, 2022), and *In Light of Rome: Early Photography in the Capital of the Art World, 1842–1871* (with John F. McGuigan Jr., 2023). His most recent publication, *Gordon Parks: Herklas Brown and Maine, 1944* (2024), investigates a little-known photographic series that the legendary photographer created at the height of World War II. Goodyear was previously a curator of photographs at the Smithsonian's National Portrait Gallery.

Molly Holmberg Brown is an artist and mapmaker who integrates cartographic design with painting and printmaking to create custom maps and geographic expressions about place. She discovered cartography while a student at Middlebury College and went on to earn a PhD in geography from the University of Colorado Boulder. She received both a Thomas J. Watson Fellowship and a National Science Foundation Research Fellowship to explore the value of mapmaking for communities and individuals. Through MollyMaps, her work has grown to include commissions, workshops, murals, and school mapping projects throughout New England. Brown is a part of the fourth generation of the Barker family, who together own two cottages in Deadman's Cove. She lives with her family in Cape Elizabeth, Maine.

Doug Boynton was born in Bethel, Maine, in 1948, and grew up in Saigon. He made Monhegan his home in the United States in 1956. After graduating from Trinity College, he planned to spend time on the mainland but got waylaid by a "temporary" job lobstering, a passion he pursued for fifty years. Boynton was part of a group of new winter residents who, by 1980, had swelled the population to a high of more than one hundred people. Boynton's town jobs have included constable, fire chief, road commissioner, and chair of Monhegan Associates' Land Committee. With his wife, artist Alice Boynton, he was instrumental in forming the Monhegan Island Sustainable Community Association and in helping pass legislation to protect Monhegan's lobster conservation zone.

David R. Foster is an ecologist and director emeritus of the Harvard Forest, Harvard University's four thousand–acre ecological laboratory. His research focuses on interpreting landscape dynamics from climate change, human use, and other factors and applying these results to conservation. In 2005, David and colleagues developed *Wildlands and Woodlands—A Vision for the New England Landscape*, an ambitious initiative for forest and farmland conservation integrated with community development. David is editor of *Forests in Time: The Environmental Consequences of 1000 Years of Change in New England* (with John D. Aber, 2004) and *Hemlock: A Forest Giant on the Edge* (2014), and he is author of *A Meeting of Land and Sea: Nature and the Future of Martha's Vineyard* (2017).

Matthew Klingle is associate professor of History and Environmental Studies at Bowdoin College. He is author of the award-winning book *Emerald City: An Environmental History of Seattle* (2007) as well as numerous articles, reviews, and general audience essays. His forthcoming book *Sweet Blood: Diabetes and the Changing Nature of Modern Health* is an interdisciplinary history of how today's health crisis stems from changing relations with nature over the past 150 years. Klingle earned his BA from the University of California, Berkeley, and his PhD from the University of Washington. He lives with his family in Brunswick, Maine.

William H. Livingston has been on the forest resource faculty at the University of Maine since 1985. His teaching and research are focused on forest health and have involved studies on eastern white pine, balsam fir, American beech, black ash, and the forests of Monhegan. He is currently director of the School of Forest Resources, where he has helped lead innovations in the education of students in the university's nationally recognized forestry programs. Dr. Livingston's efforts have improved the understanding of forest health, and they continue to keep students engaged with hands-on learning and to involve the forest resource community of the state with student education and work experience. By working together with students and external partners, Dr. Livingston's goal is to ensure the sustainability of the state's forests.

Tish Miller is a member of the Miller family, who together, own a cottage that's been in their family for five generations. Currently she is co-vice president of the Monhegan Associates and co-chair of the Ecology Committee. Before retiring, Miller was program director of MIT Professional Education's Advanced Study Program, founder of a nonprofit art gallery, and an art teacher. Most of the year she lives in Arlington, Massachusetts, with her husband, Jack Matson. Like many of her relatives, Miller is an artist.

John Bear Mitchell grew up on Indian Island in the middle of the Penobscot River—the headquarters of the Penobscot Nation. He is a citizen of the Penobscot tribe and has many relatives in the Passamaquoddy tribe of Sipayik. He serves as coordinator of the Native American Waiver and

Educational Program, outreach and student development coordinator of the Wabanaki Center, and lecturer of Wabanaki Studies at the University of Maine. He has served on numerous museum and educational boards throughout the state with missions based on Maine's Wabanaki people, and he is a well-known Penobscot storyteller.

Barbara Putnam makes prints and quilts that join beauty with urgency for environmental responsibility and education. Her content spans fragile botanical and intertidal information to "still lifes" of plastic waste at the local transfer station. Putnam is collaborating with research scientists in Italy, Spain, and Bowdoin College on projects making scientific data collection accessible through art. Her work is held in many public collections, including the Art Institute of Chicago, Denver Art Museum, Cleveland Museum of Art, New Orleans Museum of Art, Harvard Art Museums, Yale University Art Gallery, and Bowdoin College Museum of Art, among others.

Accra Shepp is a New York–based artist and writer focused on our relationship to place and the environment. His images have been exhibited worldwide and are in the collections of the Museum of Modern Art, the Art Institute of Chicago, and the Victoria and Albert Museum, among many other institutions. His writing has appeared in the *New York Times* and the *New York Review of Books*. He is the recipient of a Fulbright Fellowship; has participated in residencies at MacDowell, Civitella, and Light Work; and is a 2023–24 Jean Strouse Fellow at the Cullman Center for Scholars and Writers at the New York Public Library. Shepp teaches at the School of Visual Arts in New York.

Earle G. Shettleworth, Jr., was born and raised in Portland, Maine. He attended Deering High School, Colby College, and Boston University and has received honorary degrees from Bowdoin College and the Maine College of Art. He became architectural historian for the Maine Historic Preservation Commission in 1973 and the organization's director in 1976, a position from which he retired in 2015. Shettleworth has lectured and written extensively on Maine history and architecture and has served as Maine State Historian since 2004.

Robert P. Smith is an infectious disease physician and cofounder of the Vector-Borne Disease Laboratory at MaineHealth Institute for Research, where his team studies the ecology and clinical aspects of newly recognized and emerging diseases. He has authored or co-authored numerous research and review articles on infectious diseases and is a professor of medicine at Tufts University School of Medicine. Smith still visits Monhegan regularly, but now only with binoculars in hand to seek out spring and fall bird migrants. He thanks the Monhegan Island community for their support throughout the research project, and his fellow team members at the Vector-Borne Disease Laboratory.

Notes

Foreword

1. Certificate of Organization of Monhegan Associates, Inc., State of Maine, Article 2(a), dated September 8, 1954, Monhegan Associates, Inc., Archives (hereafter MAI Archives)
2. David Foster et al., *Wildlands of New England: Past Present, and Future* (Redding, CT: Wildlands, Woodlands, Farmlands & Communities, 2023), https://wildlandsandwoodlands.org/resources/wildlands-in-new-england/.
3. Bernadette Dimientieff [*sic*], "A Gwich'in Perspective," in Wilderness and Traditional Indigenous Beliefs: Conflicting or Intersecting Perspectives on the Human-Nature Relationship?" ed. Corey Himrod, Alaska Wilderness League website, December 17, 2021, https://alaskawild.org/blog/wilderness-and-traditional-indigenous-beliefs/.
4. Henry David Thoreau, journal entry dated May 17, 1854. *The Journal of Henry D. Thoreau*, vols. 1–7, *(1837–October, 1955),* ed. Bradford Torrey and Francis H. Allen (New York: Dover Publications, 1962), 735.
5. Henry David Thoreau, "Walking," *Atlantic Monthly* 9, no. 56 (June 1862): 665.
6. Richard Farrell, comments recorded in the minutes of the sixty-second annual meeting of members of Monhegan Associates, Inc., August 19, 2016, MAI Archives.

Chapter 1

1. Rockwell Kent, *It's Me O Lord: The Autobiography of Rockwell Kent* (New York: Dodd, Mead, 1955), 118, 119.
2. Charles B. McLane, *Islands of the Mid-Maine Coast*, vol. 3, *Muscongus Bay and Monhegan Island* (Gardiner, ME: Tilbury House, 1992).
3. Kent, *It's Me O Lord*, 77.
4. Kent, *It's Me O Lord*, 116.
5. William Butler Yeats, "Mr. Synge and His Plays," in *The Well of the Saints. By J. M. Synge, with an Introduction by W. B. Yeats. Being Volume Four of Plays for An Irish Theatre* (London: A. H. Bullen, 1905), vi.
6. A. G. Pettengill, "Monhegan, Historical and Picturesque," *New England Magazine*, n.s., 19, no. 1 (September 1898): 66.
7. In 1914, Monhegan held a major art exhibition as part of its tercentenary celebration. Charles Ebert, George Bellows, and Frederick J. Waugh were the jurors, and the show was held in Bert Poole's studio. Participants included Woodhull Adams, George Bellows, Homer Boss, Robert William Broderick, Randall Davey, Charles Ebert, Mary Roberts Ebert, George Clowes Everett, Robert F. Gagen, Agnes Harrison Lincoln, James P. Haney, Eric Hudson, Wilson Irvine, Dorothy Kent, Helen Mosley, Bert Poole, Karl Schmidt, Serverio Serveni, Anna L. Stacey, Alice Kent Stoddard, Alice Swett, Samuel Peter Rolt Triscott, F. Coulton Waugh, and Frederick J. Waugh.
8. See Hans Nienstaedt and John C. Zasada, "*Picea glauca* (Moench) Voss: White Spruce; Pinaceae; Pine Family," in *Silvics of North America*, vol. 1, *Conifers*, Agriculture Handbook 654 (Washington, DC: Forest Service, United States Department of Agriculture, December 1990), 204–26.

Chapter 2

1. Jonathan C. Lothrop, Darrin L. Lowery, Arthur E. Spiess, and Christopher J. Ellis, "Early Human Settlement of Northeastern North America," *PaleoAmerica* 2, no. 3 (2016): 192–251.
2. Lisa Gay Bostwick, "An Environmental Framework for Cultural Change in Maine: Pollen Influx and Percentage Diagrams from Monhegan Island" (master's thesis, University of Maine, Orono, 1978), 68.
3. Bryan Shuman, Paige Newby, Yongsong Huang, and Thompson Webb III, "Evidence for the Close Climatic Control of New England Vegetation History," *Ecology* 85, no. 5 (May 2004): 1297–310.
4. Mirjami Tolonen, "Pollen Evidence of Vegetational Change following Early European Settlement of Monhegan Island, Maine, Northeastern USA," *Boreas* 12, no. 3 (September 1983): 201–15.

5. Bruce Bourque, *The Swordfish Hunters: The History and Ecology of an Ancient American Sea People* (Boston: Bunker Hill Publishing, 2012).
6. Ida Sedgwick Proper, *Monhegan, The Cradle of New England* (Portland, ME: Southworth Press, 1930), 24.
7. Henry S. Burrage, ed., *Rosier's Relation of Waymouth's* [*sic*] *Voyage to the Coast of Maine, 1605, with an Introduction and Notes* (Portland, ME: Stephen Berry for the Gorges Society, 1887), 94–95.
8. John Smith, "A Description of New England" (1616), *Zea E-Books in American Studies* 3, https://digitalcommons.unl.edu/zeaamericanstudies/3.

Chapter 3

1. William D. Williamson, *The History of the State of Maine; from Its First Discovery, A.D. 1602, to the Separation, A.D. 1820, Inclusive* (Hallowell, ME: Glazier, Masters, 1832), 1:61.
2. Williamson, *The History of the State of Maine*, 1:61.
3. Aaron Draper Shattuck to Marian Colman, June 13, 1858. Collection of Katherine and Eugene Emigh. Quoted in Edward Deci, "One Hundred Sixty Years of Monhegan Island Art," in *The Monhegan Museum: Celebrating Fifty Years, 1968–2018*, exh. cat. (Monhegan: Monhegan Museum of Art and History, 2018), 77.
4. William Henry Bishop, "Fish and Men in the Maine Islands. II," *Harper's New Monthly Magazine* 61, no. 364 (September 1880): 500.
5. Charles B. McLane, *Islands of the Mid-Maine Coast*, vol. 3, *Muscongus Bay and Monhegan Island* (Gardiner, ME: Tilbury House, 1992), 250.
6. Bishop, "Fish and Men in the Maine Islands. II," 500–501.
7. Samuel Adams Drake, *Nooks and Corners of the New England Coast* (New York: Harper, 1875), 102, 104.
8. For more on Triscott, see Richard H. Malone and Earle G. Shettleworth, Jr., *Rediscovering S. P. Rolt Triscott: Monhegan Artist and Photographer* (Gardiner, ME: Tilbury House, 2002).
9. "Isle of Cousins," *Boston Daily Globe*, February 25, 1894, 9.
10. "Isle of Cousins," 9.
11. Maine State Society for the Protection of Animals, *The Case of the Island Sheep* (Portland, ME: George D. Loring, 1907), 5.
12. George Wharton Edwards, *P'tit Matinic' and Other Monotones* (New York: Century Co., 1897).
13. "From Historic Monhegan," *Pemaquid Messenger*, August 29, 1895. Reprinted from the *Courier Gazette* [Rockland, Maine], August 27, 1895, 1.
14. A. G. Pettengill, "Monhegan, Historical and Picturesque," *New England Magazine*, n.s., 19, no. 1 (September 1898): 81.
15. See Earle G. Shettleworth, Jr., and W. H. Bunting, *An Eye for the Coast: The Maritime and Monhegan Island Photographs of Eric Hudson* (Gardiner, ME: Tilbury House, 1998); and Malone and Shettleworth, *Rediscovering S. P. Rolt Triscott*.

Chapter 4

1. Theodore Miller Edison, "Notes on the Background and Early History of Monhegan Associates, Inc.," May 30, 1976, MAI Archives.
2. Ruth Grant Faller, *Monhegan: Her Houses and Her People, 1780–2000* (Melrose, MA: Mainstay Publications, 2001).
3. The Thomas A. Edison Papers Digital Edition, Rutgers School of Arts and Sciences, Rutgers, The State University of New Jersey, New Brunswick, NJ, https://edisondigital.rutgers.edu.
4. Edison, "Notes on the Background and Early History of Monhegan Associates, Inc."
5. Edison, "Notes on the Background and Early History of Monhegan Associates, Inc."
6. "Brush Fire Threatens Rich Homes," clipping from unknown newspaper, August 23, 1934, Monhegan Museum of Art & History Archives (hereafter MMAH Archives).
7. "Maine Island Folk Prepare to Flee Fire," *Herald-News* [Passaic, NJ], September 7, 1948, 14.
8. Ross W. Wein and Janice M. Moore, "Fire History and Recent Fire Rotation Periods in the Nova Scotia Acadian Forest, *Canadian Journal of Forest Research* 9, no. 2 (June 1979): 166–78, https://doi.org/10.1139/x79-031.
9. Rockwell Kent, "Suggestions for State Park Promotion," 1951, Rockwell Kent papers, ca. 1840–1993, bulk 1935–1961, Reels 5153–5249, 5256, 5740–5741, Archives of American Art, Smithsonian Institution (hereafter RKP).
10. "Our History," Wilderness Society website, https://www.wilderness.org/about-us/our-team/our-history.
11. Robert Marshall, *Living Wilderness* 19, no. 49 (Summer 1954).
12. Theodore Miller Edison, "Report of the President," minutes of a special meeting of members of Monhegan Associates, Inc., August 17, 1957, MAI Archives.
13. Ted Bernard and Jora M. Young, *The Ecology of Hope: Communities Collaborate for Sustainability* (Gabriola Island, BC: New Catalyst Books, 1997), 51.
14. Certificate of Organization of Monhegan Associates, Inc., State of Maine, Article 2(a), dated September 8, 1954, MAI Archives.
15. Rockwell Kent to Theodore Miller Edison, May 1953, RKP.
16. Edison, "Report of the President."
17. Edison, "Notes on the Background and Early History of Monhegan Associates, Inc."
18. Legal scholar and theorist Carol M. Rose has written extensively on the role of property and social behavior. See Rose, *Property and Persuasion: Essays on History, Theory, and Rhetoric of Ownership* (Boulder: Westview Press, 1994).
19. "Notes to 'Foreword'" for proposed membership invitation, minutes of the fourth annual meeting of members of Monhegan Associates, Inc., August 22, 1958, MAI Archives.
20. "Report of the Announcement Committee," minutes of the fourth annual meeting of members of Monhegan Associates, Inc.
21. "Notice of Proposal to Amend the By-Laws of Monhegan Associates, Inc., at the Annual Meeting," copy in the minutes of the fifth annual meeting of members of Monhegan Associates, Inc., August 28, 1959, MAI Archives.
22. "Notification of Membership Transfer," minutes of the fifth annual meeting of members of Monhegan Associates, Inc., MAI Archives.
23. By-Laws and Certificate of Organization of Monhegan Associates, Inc., Organized September 8, 1954 (amended August 15, 2008), 2, https://monheganassociates.org/wp-content/uploads/2016/10/bylaws2008-complete.pdf. The most recent bylaws require that full members own at least one-eighth acre of land on or within four miles of Monhegan or have a fractional interest in a larger amount of real estate. Other pathways to full voting membership may include service as a former trustee or officer, having a relationship to a qualifying person through direct family ties by marriage or immediate descendance, or donating land to the Associates for direct protection or a conservation easement.

24. Edison, "Notes on the Background and Early History of Monhegan Associates, Inc."
25. For more on this still widely unacknowledged history, see Mark David Spence, *Dispossessing the Wilderness: Indian Removal and the Making of the National Parks* (New York: Oxford University Press, 1999); Louis S. Warren, *The Hunter's Game: Poachers and Conservationists in Twentieth-Century America* (New Haven, CT: Yale University Press, 1999); Karl Jacoby, *Crimes Against Nature: Squatters, Poachers, Thieves, and the Hidden History of American Conservation* (Berkeley: University of California Press, 2001); Miles A. Powell, *Vanishing America: Species Extinction, Racial Peril, and the Origins of Conservation* (Cambridge, MA: Harvard University Press, 2016); and Dorceta E. Taylor, *The Rise of the Conservation Movement: Power, Privilege, and Environmental Protection* (Durham, NC: Duke University Press, 2016).
26. For an early reassessment of environmentalism, see Robert Gottlieb, *Forcing the Spring: The Transformation of the American Environmental Movement*, rev. ed. (Washington, DC: Island Press, 2005). For two recent works, see Carl A. Zimring, *Clean and White: A History of Environmental Racism in the United States* (New York: New York University Press, 2015); and Ellen Griffith Spears, *Rethinking the American Environmental Movement Post-1945* (New York: Routledge, 2019). Maine was often a bellwether in environmental politics; see Richard W. Judd and Christopher S. Beach, *Natural States: The Environmental Imagination in Maine, Oregon, and the Nation* (Washington, DC: Resources for the Future, 2003).
27. "Report of the Public Relations Committee" and "Proposal Concerning Preservation of Natural Resources," minutes of the seventh annual meeting of members of Monhegan Associates, Inc., August 25, 1961, MAI Archives.
28. Eugene K. Twining, comments recorded in the minutes of the sixteenth annual meeting of members of Monhegan Associates, Inc.," August 28, 1970, MAI Archives.
29. The website footer reads: "Dedicated to Preserving the Natural Wild Beauty, Biotic Communities, and Desirable Natural, Artificial, and Historic Features of Portions of Monhegan, as well as the Simple Friendly Way of Life that has Existed on the Island as a Whole." See Theodore M. Edison, "Subject: Proposed By-law Changes," August 1, 1956, minutes of the second annual meeting of members of Monhegan Associates, Inc., August 24, 1958, MAI Archives. The website footer banner today reads: "Monhegan's wildlands: inspiring generations in a timeless, unspoiled sanctuary," Monhegan Associates, Inc., website, https://monheganassociates.org/.
30. William J. Cronon's famed essay has been reprinted numerous times. See Cronon, "The Trouble with Wilderness," *New York Times Sunday Magazine*, August 13, 1995, 42–43; and Cronon, "The Trouble with Wilderness; or, Getting Back to the Wrong Nature," in *Uncommon Ground: Rethinking the Human Place in Nature*, ed. William Cronon (New York: W. W. Norton, 1995): 69–90.
31. For a brief history of Baxter State Park, see Matthew Klingle, "A Magnificent Obsession," *Bowdoin Magazine* 90 (Winter 2019): 36–43. Most of the evidence and analysis from this article come from Luke Joseph McKay, "'No Man's Garden': The Changing Nature of the Wilderness Idea in Maine" (honors thesis, Bowdoin College, 2007); copy at George J. Mitchell Department of Special Collections and Archives, Bowdoin College Library, Brunswick, ME.
32. "Trails Committee," minutes of the sixteenth annual meeting of members of Monhegan Associates, Inc., August 28, 1970, MAI Archives.
33. "Ecology Committee Report" and "Trails Committee Report," minutes of the forty-first annual meeting of members of Monhegan Associates, Inc., August 18, 1995, MAI Archives.
34. *Monhegan Forest: Stewardship Management Plan; Monhegan Plantation, Lincoln County, Maine*, prepared by Mark Miller, LPF #851, Conservation Forestry, January 2005, https://monheganassociates.org/wp-content/uploads/2016/10/monheganplan.pdf. See also the proposed "2016 Steward Management Plan, DRAFT 8-13-16," https://monheganassociates.org/wp-content/uploads/2019/07/Stewardship-Plan-Draft-8-13-2016.docx-1.pdf.
35. Richard Farrell, "Vice-President's Report," minutes of the sixty-fourth annual meeting of members of Monhegan Association, Inc., August 17, 2018, MAI Archives (emphasis in the original).
36. David Marino, Jr., "Maine has the highest share of vacant homes in the country," *Bangor Daily News* (May 9, 2022), https://www.bangordailynews.com/2022/05/09/business/maine-home-vacancy-rate-joam40zk0w/. This article includes data from the 2020 American Community Survey Data, United States Census Bureau, https://www.census.gov/programs-surveys/acs/data.html.
37. Matthew W. Klingle, "The Nature of Desire: Consumption in Environmental History," in *The Oxford Handbook of Environmental History*, ed. Andrew C. Isenberg (New York: Oxford University Press, 2014), 467–51; Joseph E. Taylor III, *Persistent Callings: Seasons of Work and Identity on the Oregon Coast* (Corvallis: Oregon State University Press, 2019); Monique Coombs, *The State of Maine's Working Waterfront* (Brunswick, ME: Maine Coast Fishermen's Association, March 2020), https://repository.library.noaa.gov/view/noaa/38651; and Merritt T. Casey, *The Critical Nature of Maine's Working Waterfronts and Access to the Shore* (Rockland, ME: Island Institute, August 2021), https://www.islandinstitute.org/wp-content/uploads/2021/11/WWF-Report_web.pdf. On efforts to secure affordable housing on Monhegan, see Evan Houk, "As Year-Round Island Populations Disappear, Monhegan Organization Works to Preserve Culture," *Lincoln County News*, September 10, 2019, https://lcnme.com/currentnews/as-year-round-island-populations-disappear-monhegan-organization-works-to-preserve-culture/. According to Jennifer Pye, director of the Monhegan Museum of Art & History, year-round residents have "not been able to purchase an island home without the help of MISCA [Monhegan Island Sustainable Community Association] for over 20 years." MISCA is one organization referred to in the 2019 article from the *Lincoln County News*. Jennifer Pye, email message to author, August 28, 2023. For one case study of an extreme example of affluent domination, focused on Teton County, Wyoming, see Justin Farrell, *Billionaire Wilderness: The Ultra-Wealthy and the Remaking of the American West* (Princeton, NJ: Princeton University Press, 2020).
38. Nina M. Whitney et al., "Rapid 20th Century Warming Reverses 900-Year Cooling in the Gulf of Maine," *Communications Earth & Environment* 3, no. 179 (2022). https://doi.org/10.1038/s43247-022-00504-8.
39. Richard Farrell, "Vice-President's Report" (emphasis in the original).

40. For an "ethic of place," see Matthew Klingle, *Emerald City: An Environmental History of Seattle* (New Haven, CT: Yale University Press, 2007), xi–xii, 1–11, 265–80; for purity, see Richard White, "The Problem with Purity," Tanner Lectures on Human Values, Delivered at the University of California, Davis, May 10, 1999, http://www.tannerlectures.utah.edu/.

Chapter 5

1. In the Monhegan Associates articles of incorporation, Marion Cundy signed her name "Marion H. Cundy" (maiden name Humphrey), but as a Monhegan Plantation assessor, she is listed as "Marion L. Cundy" (middle name Louise).
2. Jason Wolfe, "Decision Over Deer Herd Comes Hard," *Maine Sunday Telegram*, April 12, 1998.
3. T. P. Rooney, "Deer Impacts on Forest Ecosystems: A North American Perspective," *Forestry* 74, no. 3 (May 2001): 201–8, https://doi.org/10.1093/forestry/74.3.201.
4. Henry David Thoreau, journal entry dated September 13, 1860. *The Journal of Henry D. Thoreau*, vols. 8-14, *(November, 1855–1861)*, ed. Bradford Torrey and Francis H. Allen (New York: Dover Publications, 1962), 1686.
5. Steeve D. Côté et al., "Ecological Impacts of Deer Overabundance," *Annual Review of Ecology, Evolution, and Systematics* 35 (December 2004): 113–47, https://doi.org/10.1146/annurev.ecolsys.35.021103.105725.
6. Peter W. Rand, *Of Ticks and Islands: Memoirs from the Lyme and Vector-Borne Disease Laboratory of the Maine Medical Center Research Institute* (Maine Science Stories, 2017).
7. Geraldine King Tam to Theodore M. Edison, September 4, 1969, Monhegan Associates, Inc., MAI Archives.
8. "National Natural Landmarks: Monhegan Island," National Parks Service website, https://www.nps.gov/subjects/nnlandmarks/site.htm?Site=MOIS-ME.
9. "Trails Committee Report," minutes of the fifth annual meeting of members of Monhegan Associates, Inc., August 28, 1959, MAI Archives.
10. The use of herbicide spray is noted in the minutes of the annual meetings of members of Monhegan Associates, Inc., held in August 1960, 1968, 1970, 1976, 1977, 1991, and 1997. MAI Archives.
11. Helga Houmere, chair of the Ecology Committee, comments recorded in the minutes of the fortieth annual meeting of members of Monhegan Associates, Inc., August 19, 1994, MAI Archives.
12. Houmere, comments recorded in the minutes of the forty-first annual meeting of members of Monhegan Associates, Inc., August 18, 1995, MAI Archives.
13. Concern regarding fairy houses is recorded in the minutes of the ninth annual meeting of members of Monhegan Associates, Inc., August 23, 1963. The minutes of the nineteenth annual meeting of members of Monhegan Associates, Inc., August 17, 1973, record that fairy houses were again being built in Cathedral Woods. MAI Archives.
14. Minutes of the third annual meeting of members of Monhegan Associates, Inc., August 17, 1957, MAI Archives.
15. Certificate of Organization of Monhegan Associates, Inc., State of Maine, Article 2(b), dated September 8, 1954, MAI Archives.
16. Frank G. Hawksworth and Delbert Weins, *Dwarf Mistletoes: Biology, Pathology, and Systematics*, Agricultural Handbook 709 (Washington, DC: US Department of Agriculture, Forest Service, 1996).
17. Barry A. Logan et al., "Impact of Eastern Dwarf Mistletoe (*Arceuthobium pusillum*) on Host White Spruce (*Picea glauca*) Development, Growth and Performance across Multiple Scales," *Physiologia Plantarum* 147, no. 4 (April 2013): 502–13, https://doi.org/10.1111/j.1399-3054.2012.01681.x.
18. Johnathon A. de Villier, Jaret S. Reblin, and Barry A. Logan, "Needle Properties of Host White Spruce (*Picea glauca* [Moench] Voss) Experiencing Eastern Dwarf Mistletoe (*Arceuthobium pusillum* Peck) Infections of Differing Severity," *Botany* 95, no. 3 (December 2016): 295–305, https://doi.org/10.1139/cjb-2016-0254.
19. *John Hultberg, Painter of the In-Between: Selected Paintings, 1953–1984: An Exhibition*, exh. cat. (Clinton, NY: F. L. Emerson Gallery, Hamilton College, 1985).
20. Lynne Drexler, interview by Tralice Bracy and Beth Van Houten, September 1998, MMAH Archives.
21. Ruth Boynton, artist's statement, *Women Artists of Monhegan Island* (WAMI) exhibition, Island Inn, Monhegan, 1997. MMAH Archives.
22. Peter W. Rand et al., "Passive Surveillance in Maine, an Area Emergent for Tick-Borne Diseases," *Journal of Medical Entomology* 44, no. 6 (November 2007): 1118–29; and John J. Halperin, ed., *Lyme Disease: An Evidence-Based Approach* (Oxfordshire, UK: CABI, 2018), 259–70.
23. Rand, *Of Ticks and Islands*.
24. Peter W. Rand et al., "Attempt to Control Ticks (Acari: Ixodidae) on Deer on an Isolated Island Using Ivermectin-Treated Corn," *Journal of Medical Entomology* 37, no. 1 (January 1, 2000): 126–33, https://doi.org/10.1603/0022-2585-37.1.126.
25. Robert P. Smith et al., "Norway Rats as Reservoir Hosts for Lyme Disease Spirochetes on Monhegan Island, Maine," *Journal of Infectious Diseases* 168, no. 3 (September 1993) 687–91.

Chapter 6

1. Peter W. Rand et al., "Abundance of *Ixodes scapularis* (Acari: Ixodidae) after the Complete Removal of Deer from an Isolated Offshore Island, Endemic for Lyme Disease," *Journal of Medical Entomology* 41, no. 4 (July 2004): 779–84.
2. Colin Woodard, *The Lobster Coast: Rebels, Rusticators, and the Struggle for a Forgotten Frontier* (New York: Viking Penguin, 2004), 13.
3. W. Griffin, "King Signs Monhegan Law," *Bangor Daily News*, February 28, 1998.
4. Doug Boynton, "Monhegan Island Sustainable Community Association (MISCA)," *New Monhegan Press* 14, no. 5 (August 2002): 3.
5. FutureMetrics, *Report on the Characteristics and Habits of Visitors to Monhegan Island: A Simulation Forecast of Visitor Behavior and Island Revenues* (Bethel, ME: FutureMetrics, 2005), https://monheganassociates.org/scientific-research.
6. FutureMetrics, *Report on the Characteristics and Habits of Visitors to Monhegan Island*.
7. "Land Use and Other Policies," Monhegan Associates, Inc., website, https://monheganassociates.org/land-use-policies/.
8. "This Iland is woody, grouen with Firre, Birch, Oke and Beech, as farre as we saw along the shore." Henry S. Burrage, ed., *Rosier's Relation of Waymouth's* [sic] *Voyage to the Coast of Maine, 1605, with an Introduction and Notes* (Portland, ME: Stephen Berry for the Gorges society, 1887), 95.

For Further Reading

Bourque, Bruce J. *The Swordfish Hunters: The History and Ecology of an Ancient American Sea People*. Piermont, NH: Bunker Hill, 2012.

Brooks, Lisa. *Our Beloved Kin: A New History of King Philip's War*. New Haven, CT: Yale University Press, 2018.

Bunting, W. H., and Earle G. Shettleworth, Jr., *An Eye for the Coast: The Maritime and Monhegan Photographs of Eric Hudson*. Gardiner, ME: Tilbury House, 1998.

Burns, Russell M., and Barbara H. Honkala. *Silvics of North America*. 2 vols. Agriculture Handbook 654. Washington, DC: Forest Service, United States Department of Agriculture, December 1990.

Burrage, Henry, ed. *Rosier's Relation of Waymouth's Voyage to the Coast of Maine, 1605*. Portland, ME: Gorges Society, 1887.

Côté, Steeve D., Thomas P. Rooney, Jean-Pierre Tremblay, Christian Dussault, and Donald M. Waller. "Ecological Impacts of Deer Overabundance." *Annual Review of Ecology, Evolution, and Systematics* 35 (2004): 113–47.

Curtis, Jane, Will Curtis, and Frank Lieberman. *Monhegan: The Artists' Island*. Camden, ME: Down East Books, 1995.

Faller, Ruth Grant. *Monhegan: Her Houses and Her People, 1780–2000*. Melrose, MA: Mainstay Publications, 2001.

Foster, David R. *A Meeting of Land and Sea: Nature and the Future of Martha's Vineyard*. New Haven, CT: Yale University Press, 2017.

Foster, David, Emily E. Johnson, Brian R. Hall, Jonathan Leibowitz, Elizabeth H. Thompson, Brian Donahue, Edward K. Faison, Jamie Sayen, David Publicover, Nancy Sferra, Lloyd C. Irland, Jonathan R. Thompson, Robert Perschel, David A. Orwig, William S. Keeton, Malcolm L. Hunter Jr., Susan A. Masino, and Lillian Howell. *Wildlands in New England: Past, Present, and Future*. Harvard Forest Paper 34. Harvard University, 2023.

Foster, David R., and Glenn Motzkin. "Ecology and Conservation in the Cultural Landscape of New England: Lessons from Nature's History." *Northeastern Naturalist* 5, no. 2 (1998): 111–26.

Gross, Kenneth Paul Kiel. "Monhegan: A Prescription for Resilience." Capstone, University of Southern Maine, Muskie School of Public Service, 2016. https://digitalcommons.usm.maine.edu/muskie_capstones/120/.

Hawksworth, F. G., and Delbert Wiens. *Dwarf Mistletoes: Biology, Pathology, and Systematics*. Agriculture Handbook 709. Washington, DC: Forest Service, United States Department of Agriculture, March 1996.

Jenney, Charles Francis. *The Fortunate Island of Monhegan: A Historical Monograph*. Worcester, MA: Davis Press, 1922.

Kent, Rockwell. *It's Me O Lord: The Autobiography of Rockwell Kent*. New York: Dodd, Mead, 1955.

Little, Carl, and Arnold Skolnick. *The Art of Monhegan Island*. Camden, ME: Down East Books, 2004.

Lothrup, Jonathan C., Darrin L. Lowery, Arthur E. Spiess, and Christopher J. Ellis. "Early Human Settlement of Northeastern North America." *PaleoAmerica* 2, no. 3 (2016): 192–251.

Malone, Richard H., and Earle G. Shettleworth, Jr., *Rediscovering S. P. Rolt Triscott: Monhegan Artist and Photographer*. Gardiner, ME: Tilbury House, 2002.

McLane, Charles B. *Islands of the Mid-Maine Coast, vol. 3, Muscongus Bay and Monhegan Island.* Gardiner, ME: Tilbury House, 1992.

Motzkin, Glenn, David Foster, Arthur Allen, Jonathan Harrod, and Richard Boone. "Controlling Site to Evaluate History: Vegetation Patterns of a New England Sand Plain." *Ecological Monographs* 66, no. 3 (August 1996): 345–65.

Nicoll, Jessica F. *The Allure of the Maine Coast: Robert Henri and His Circle, 1903–1918.* Portland, ME: Portland Museum of Art, 1995. Exhibition catalogue.

Proper, Ida Sedgwick. *Monhegan: The Cradle of New England*. Portland, ME: Southworth Press, 1930.

Rand, Peter W. *Of Ticks and Islands: Memoirs from the Lyme and Vector-Borne Disease Laboratory of the Maine Medical Center Research Institute.* Maine Science Stories, 2017.

Rich, Louise Dickinson. *The Coast of Maine: An Informal History and Guide*. 3rd edition. New York: Thomas Y. Crowell, 1970.

Rooney, T. P. "Deer Impacts on Forest Ecosystems: A North American Perspective." *Forestry* 74, no. 3 (2001): 201–8.

Shuman, Bryan, Paige Newby, Yongsong Huang, and Thompson Webb III. "Evidence for the Close Climatic Control of New England Vegetation History." *Ecology* 85, no. 5 (May 2004): 1297–310.

Stahl, Robert, ed. *The Monhegan Museum: Celebrating Fifty Years*. Monhegan, ME: Monhegan Museum of Art & History, 2018.

Stone, Brandee L., Yvonne Tourand, and Catherine A. Brissette. "Brave New Worlds: The Expanding Universe of Lyme Disease." *Vector-Borne and Zoonotic Diseases* 17, no. 9 (September 2017): 619–29.

Woodard, Colin. *The Lobster Coast: Rebels, Rusticators, and the Struggle for a Forgotten Frontier*. New York: Viking Penguin, 2004.

Credits

Jacket front
Edward Hopper © 2024 Heirs of Josephine N. Hopper / Licensed by Artists Rights Society (ARS), NY.

p. 14
Photograph © The State Hermitage Museum / Photo: Andrey Terebenin. Image is used from www.hermitagemuseum.org, courtesy of the State Hermitage Museum, St. Petersburg, Russia.

p. 30
Photo: Alan Lavallee

pp. 34–35
Photo: Dave Clough

p. 38
Photo: Alan Lavallee

p. 39
Photo: Kristian Whipple

pp. 40–41
Edward Hopper © 2024 Heirs of Josephine N. Hopper / Licensed by Artists Rights Society (ARS), NY.

pp. 42–43
Image courtesy of the Johnson Museum. Edward Hopper © 2024 Heirs of Josephine N. Hopper / Licensed by Artists Rights Society (ARS), NY

p. 58
Illustrations by Molly Holmberg Brown with inset pollen illustrations by Barbara Petter Putnam. Design concept by Mer Feero.

p. 119
Photo: Dave Clough

p. 40
Photograph © The State Hermitage Museum / Photo: Andrey Terebenin. Image is used from www.hermitagemuseum.org, courtesy of the State Hermitage Museum, St. Petersburg, Russia.

p. 142
(Left) Photo: Gregório Ceccantini. (Right) Distributed under the terms of Attribution 3.0 United States (CC BY 3.0 US) license. Photo: Thomas E. Hinds, USDA Forest Service, Bugwood.org

p. 159
Illustrations by Molly Holmberg Brown. Design concept by Mer Feero.

p. 180
Illustrations by Molly Holmberg Brown. Design concept by Mer Feero.

p. 181
Photo: Luc Demers

This book is published on the occasion of the exhibition *Art, Ecology, and the Resilience of a Maine Island: The Monhegan Wildlands*, organized by Bowdoin College Museum of Art, Brunswick, Maine, and Monhegan Museum of Art & History, Maine

Exhibition itinerary:

Bowdoin College Museum of Art,
Brunswick, Maine
December 12, 2024–June 1, 2025

Monhegan Museum of Art & History, Maine
July 1–September 30, 2025

Major support for this exhibition was provided by the Elizabeth B. G. Hamlin Fund at the Bowdoin College Museum of Art and by Harpswell Capital Advisors, LLC.

This catalogue was supported by a generous grant from the Wyeth Foundation for American Art.

First published in the United States of America in 2024 by

Rizzoli Electa
A division of Rizzoli International Publications, Inc.
300 Park Avenue South
New York, NY 10010
www.rizzoliusa.com

in association with

Bowdoin College Museum of Art
9400 College Station
Brunswick, Maine 04011
www.bowdoin.edu/art-museum

and

Monhegan Museum of Art & History
1 Light House Hill Road
Monhegan, Maine 04852
www.monheganmuseum.org

Charles Miers, Publisher
Margaret Rennolds Chace, Associate Publisher
Susan Homer, Editor
Alyn Evans, Production Manager

Design: Anjali Pala

Jacket front: Edward Hopper, *Monhegan Landscape* (detail): see pp. 42–43
Jacket back: Accra Shepp, *Large Mossy Puddle Bog, Pebble Beach Trail* (detail): see pp. 128–29
Endpapers, front and back: Stow Wengenroth, *Monhegan* (detail): see p. 103
pp. 2–3: Randall Davey, *Headland and Sea* (detail): see p. 39
pp. 18–19: Rockwell Kent, *Monhegan Headlands* (detail): see pp. 36–37
pp. 54–55: Samuel Peter Rolt Triscott, *In the Woods, Monhegan* (detail): see pp. 26–27
pp. 72–73: Mary King Longfellow, Untitled (detail): see p. 25
pp. 100–101: Andrew Winter, *Monhegan Twilight* (detail): see p. 119
pp. 132–33: Lynne Drexler, *Tree of Age* (detail): see pp. 146–47
pp. 166–67: Don Stone, *Burnt Head Trail* (detail): see pp. 172–73

Printed in China

MIX
Paper | Supporting responsible forestry
FSC™ C005748

2024 2025 2026 2027 / 10 9 8 7 6 5 4 3 2 1

ISBN: 978-0-8478-3672-7

Library of Congress Control Number: 2024934486

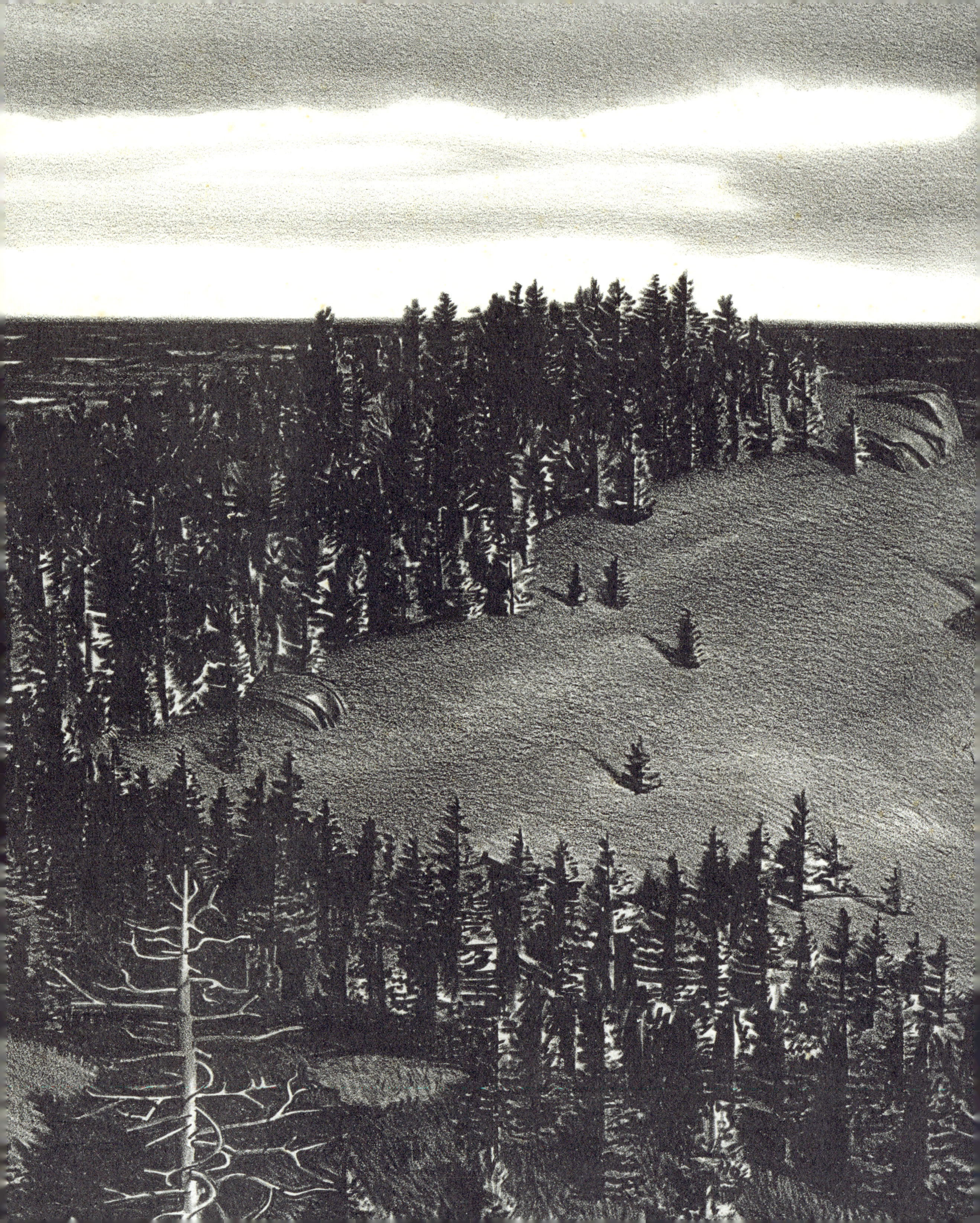